SPARKS OF
GENIUS

Books by Robert Root-Bernstein

Discovering: Inventing and Solving Problems at the Frontiers of Scientific Knowledge

Rethinking AIDS: The Tragic Cost of Premature Consensus

By Michèle Root-Bernstein

Boulevard Theater and Revolution in Eighteenth-Century Paris

By Robert and Michèle Root-Bernstein

Honey, Mud, Maggots and Other Medical Marvels

Sparks of Genius

ROBERT AND MICHÈLE
ROOT-BERNSTEIN

SPARKS OF GENIUS

The Thirteen Thinking Tools
of the World's
Most Creative People

A MARINER BOOK

HOUGHTON MIFFLIN COMPANY

BOSTON · NEW YORK

First Mariner Books edition 2001

For information about permission to reproduce selections from
this book, write to Permissions, Houghton Mifflin Company,
215 Park Avenue South, New York, New York 10003.

Visit our Web site: www.houghtonmifflinbooks.com

Library of Congress Cataloging-in-Publication Data

Root-Bernstein, Robert Scott.
Sparks of genius : the thirteen thinking tools of the world's
most creative people / Robert and Michèle Root-Bernstein.
p. cm.
Includes bibliographical references and index.
ISBN 0-395-90771-3
ISBN 0-618-12745-3 (pbk.)
1. Creative thinking. I. Root-Bernstein, Michèle. II. Title.
BF408 R66 2000
153.3'5 — dc21 99-048005

Printed in the United States of America

Book design by Victoria Hartman

QUM 10 9 8 7 6 5 4 3 2

ACKNOWLEDGMENTS

OVER THE LAST TWENTY YEARS many people have encouraged, influenced, and supported our exploration of the imagination and its tools for thinking. We thank all of them, and particularly Robert Gray, the late Raffi Amram, Tom Rodriguez, Diane Newman, and Steve Fraser. During the more recent writing of this book, we have been greatly helped by many persons staffing museums, libraries, associations, and publishing houses, especially Janet Hicks of the Artists Rights Society in New York. Many individuals have been generous with their materials, among them Bill Cambry, Patrick Dillon, Gerd Fischer, Nat Friedman, Steve Heidemann, Benoir Mandelbrojt, Ron Meyer, Desmond Morris, Claes Oldenburg, Roger Penrose, Vernon Reynolds, Helen Samuels, Doris Schattschneider, Todd Siler, and Ken Snelson. Among the many colleagues with whom we have discussed tools for thinking, the arts in education, and arts-sciences interactions, we wish to mention Sharon Friedler, Julian Gresser, Paul Heltne, Scott Shanklin-Peterson, and Mark Slavkin. A number of people kindly read and commented on the manuscript. Thank you, Mort and Maurine Bernstein, Alan Brody, Stephen Edelglass, Linda Caruso Haviland, Richard Kaplan, Eric Oddleifson, and Todd Siler. We appreciate your time and effort.

Finally, we gratefully acknowledge close friends and family members who haven't minded our shoptalk too much. And especially we thank our teenagers for putting up with preoccupied parents, late meals, and a continuous gloss on dinner conversation. "Empathizing," we'd say in response to homework assignments, good books, or piano practice. "Pattern forming, body thinking, imaging." Meredith and Brian simply rolled their eyes, good-natured to the end.

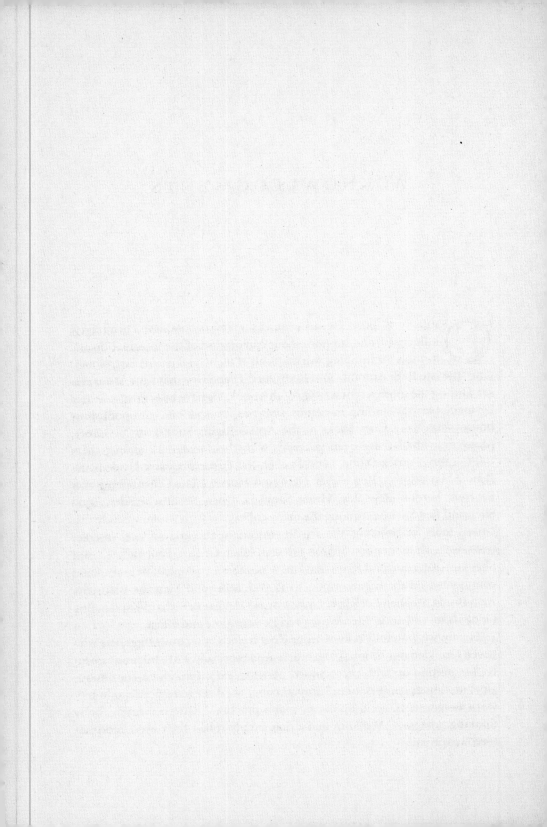

PREFACE

THIS BOOK IS ABOUT creative thinking. Creative thinking in all fields occurs preverbally, before logic or linguistics comes into play, manifesting itself through emotions, intuitions, images, and bodily feelings. The resulting ideas can be translated into one or more formal systems of communication, such as words, equations, pictures, music, or dance only after they are sufficiently developed in their prelogical forms. Regardless of the infinitely diverse details of the products of this translation (paintings, poems, theories, formulas, and so on), the process by which it is achieved is universal. Learning to think creatively in one discipline therefore opens the door to understanding creative thinking in all disciplines. Educating this universal creative imagination is the key to producing lifelong learners capable of shaping the innovations of tomorrow.

Because our approach to creative thinking is integrative and transdisciplinary, we have had to unravel certain strands of disciplinary knowledge in order to posit a new fabric of unified understanding. A new synthesis is necessary, not only in order to understand thinking itself, but for pedagogical and social reasons as well. Ever-increasing specialization is clearly leading to a fragmentation of knowledge. People today have so much information and so little grasp of its origins, meanings, and uses that overall comprehension has frayed beyond repair. Even as specialized knowledge increases, communication between fields decreases. Within fields experts address larger and larger problems in smaller and smaller bits. Modern society faces a dark age in the midst of intellectual plenty, a paradox that can be resolved only by reintegrating knowledge in new ways and by training a new generation of Renaissance people to weave new syntheses for themselves.

Such an intellectual enterprise requires both cognitive and educational foundations. Our project therefore has both warp and woof. We must comprehend the nature of creative thinking (the warp) if we are to devise an educational system capable of training creative thinkers (the woof). In the opening chapters we prepare the loom, discussing, first, current misunderstandings about the nature of creative thinking, then the barriers our current educational system raises to creative thinking.

We weave the fabric of the book from the experiences of the century's greatest minds, who explain how they think about thinking and how they learned how to think. People in every creative endeavor use a common set of general-purpose thinking tools in an almost infinite variety of ways. These tools reveal the nature of creative thinking itself; they make surprising connections among the sciences, arts, humanities, and technologies. At the level of creative imagination, everyone thinks alike.

By restructuring our cognitive categories to emphasize the unity of creative thinking, we formulate a new conception of knowledge and, correspondingly, a new form of education. In the concluding chapters of the book, which deal with the ways in which ideas are transformed and synthesized during the creative process, we demonstrate how the warp and woof yield an integral tapestry of understanding. The final chapter suggests concrete ways in which our cognitive restructuring can be implemented through specific educational reforms.

The wonder of the resulting intellectual fabric is that like real fabric, it can be transformed into an almost infinite number of things. Our new material is not, therefore, an end in itself, but the stuff from which future artists and scientists, humanists and technologists, will fashion their world.

One final note: following the Notes and Bibliography is a section of Minds-On Resources that will help readers to practice and develop the thinking tools we describe in the text. This book is but a beginning.

CONTENTS

Invention presupposes imagination but should not be confused with it. For the act of invention implies the necessity of a lucky find and of achieving full realization of this find. What we imagine does not necessarily take on a concrete form and may remain in a state of virtuality, whereas invention is not conceivable apart from its actually being worked out.

Thus, what concerns us here is not imagination in itself, but rather creative imagination: the faculty that helps us pass from the level of conception to the level of realization.

— Igor Stravinsky, *The Poetics of Music*

1

Rethinking Thinking

EVERYONE THINKS. But not everyone thinks equally well. For real intellectual feasts we depend on master chefs who have learned to mix and blend and savor an entire range of mental ingredients. It's not that what they do in the kitchen is any different from what we do, they just do it better. We like to suppose master chefs were born that way, yet even the most promising individuals spend years in training. It follows that we, too, can learn the tools of the trade and thereby improve our own mental cooking. This process, however, requires us to rethink what gourmet intellection is all about. And rethinking shifts our educational focus from *what* to think to *how* to think in the most productive ways possible.

Our tour of mental cookery begins in the kitchen of the mind, where ideas are marinated, stewed, braised, beaten, baked, and whipped into shape. Just as real chefs surprise us by throwing in a pinch of this and a handful of something else, the kitchens of the creative imagination are full of unexpected practices. Great ideas arise in the strangest ways and are blended from the oddest ingredients. What goes into the recipes often bears no resemblance to the finished dish. Sometimes the master mental chef can't even explain how she knows that her dish will be tasty. She just has a gut feeling that this imagined mixture of ingredients will yield a delicious surprise.

Gut feelings don't make obvious sense. Consider, for example, the experience of young Barbara McClintock, who would later earn a Nobel Prize in genetics. One day in 1930 she stood with a group of scientists in the cornfields around Cornell University, pondering the results of a genetics experiment. The researchers had expected that half of the corn would produce sterile pollen, but less than a third of it actually had. The difference was significant, and McClintock was so disturbed that she left the cornfield and climbed the hill to her laboratory, where she could sit alone and think.

Half an hour later, she "jumped up and ran down to the field. At the top of the field (everyone else was down at the bottom) I shouted, 'Eureka, I have it! I have the answer! I know what this 30 percent sterility is.'" Her colleagues naturally said, "Prove it." Then she found she had no idea how to explain her insight. Many decades later, McClintock said, "When you suddenly see the problem, something happens that you have the answer — before you are able to put it into words. It is all done subconsciously. This has happened many times to me, and I know when to take it seriously. I'm so absolutely sure. I don't talk about it, I don't have to tell anybody about it, I'm just *sure* this is it."

This feeling of knowing without being able to say how one knows is common. The French philosopher and mathematician Blaise Pascal is famous for his aphorism "The heart has its reasons that reason cannot know." The great nineteenth-century mathematician Carl Friedrich Gauss admitted that intuition often led him to ideas he could not immediately prove. "I have had my results for a long time; but I do not yet know how I am to arrive at them." Claude Bernard, the founder of modern physiology, wrote that everything purposeful in scientific thinking began with feeling. "Feeling alone," he wrote, "guides the mind." Painter Pablo Picasso confessed to a friend, "I don't know in advance what I am going to put on canvas any more than I decide beforehand what colors I am going to use. . . . Each time I undertake to paint a picture I have a sensation of leaping into space. I never know whether I shall fall on my feet. It is only later that I begin to estimate more exactly the effect of my work." Composer Igor Stravinsky also found that imaginative activity began with some inexplicable appetite, some "intuitive grasp of an unknown entity already possessed but not yet intelligible." The Latin American novelist Isabel Allende has described a similarly vague sense propelling her work: "Somehow inside me — I can say this after having written five books — I know that I know where I am going. I know that I know the end of the book even though I don't know it. It's so difficult to explain."

Knowing in such ambiguous, inarticulate ways raises an important question. McClintock put it this way: "It had all been done fast. The answer came, and I'd run. Now I worked it out step by step — it was an intricate series of steps — and I came out with what it was. . . . It worked out exactly as I'd diagrammed it. Now, why did I know, without having done a thing on paper? Why was I so sure that I could tell them with such excitement and just say, 'Eureka, I solved it'?" McClintock's query strikes at the heart of understanding creative thinking, as do the experiences of Picasso and Gauss, of composers and physiologists. Where *do* sudden illuminations or insights come from? How can we know things that we cannot yet say, draw, or write? How do gut feelings and intuitions function in imaginative thinking? How do we translate from feeling to word, emotion to number? Lastly, can we understand this creative imagination and, understanding it, can we exercise, train, and educate it?

Philosophers and psychologists have pondered these and related questions for hundreds of years. Neurobiologists have sought the answers in the structures of the brain and the connections between nerve synapses. Full answers still elude us. But one source of insight into creative thinking has been greatly undervalued and underused: the reports of eminent thinkers, creators, and inventors themselves. Their introspective reports cannot answer all our questions about thinking, but they certainly provide important and surprising new avenues to explore. Above all, they tell us that conventional notions of thinking are at best incomplete, for they leave out nonlogical forms of thinking that can't be verbalized.

Take the testimony of physicist Albert Einstein, for instance. Most people would expect Einstein to have described himself as solving his physics problems using mathematical formulas, numbers, complex theories, and logic. In fact, a recent book by Harvard psychologist Howard Gardner, *Creating Minds*, portrays Einstein as the epitome of the "logico-mathematical mind." His peers, however, knew that Einstein was relatively weak in mathematics, often needing to collaborate with mathematicians to push his work forward. In fact, Einstein wrote to one correspondent, "Do not worry about your difficulties in mathematics. I can assure you that mine are still greater."

Einstein's mental strengths were quite different, as he revealed to his colleague Jacques Hadamard. "The words of the language, as they are written or spoken, do not seem to play any role in my mechanism of thought. The psychical entities which seem to serve as elements in thought are certain signs and more or less clear images which can be 'voluntarily' reproduced and combined. . . . The above mentioned elements are, in my case, of visual and some of muscular type." In a kind of thought experiment that could not be articulated, he pretended to be a photon moving at the speed of light, imagining what he saw and how he felt. Then he became a second photon and tried to imagine what he could experience of the first one. As Einstein explained to Max Wertheimer, a psychologist, he only vaguely understood where his visual and muscular thinking would take him. His "feeling of direction," he said, was "very hard to express."

McClintock, for her part, talked about developing a "feeling for the organism" quite like Einstein's feeling for a beam of light. She got to know every one of her corn plants so intimately that when she studied their chromosomes, she could truly identify *with* them: "I found that the more I worked with them the bigger and bigger [they] got, and when I was really working with them I wasn't outside, I was down there. I was part of the system. I even was able to see the internal parts of the chromosomes — actually everything was there. It surprised me because I actually felt as if I were right down there and these were my friends. . . . As you look at these things, they become part of you. And you forget yourself. The main thing about it is you forget yourself." A similar emotional involvement played a critical role in the prelogical scientific thinking of Claude Bernard, who wrote, "Just as in other human activities, feeling releases an act by putting forth the idea which gives a motive to action." For Wolfgang Pauli, a mathematical physicist, emotional response functioned in the place of ideas that had not yet been articulated. Within the "unconscious region of the human soul," he wrote, "the place of clear concepts is taken by images of powerful emotional content, which are not thought, but are seen pictorially, as it were, before the mind's eye."

Some scientists insist that thinking in feelings and mental images can be rationally manipulated. Einstein suggested "a certain connection" between "the psychical entities which seem to serve as elements in thought" and "relevant logical concepts." Mathematician Stanislaw Ulam made the argument even more strongly. He experienced abstract mathematical notions in *visual terms,* so the idea of "'an infinity of spheres or an infinity of sets'" became "a picture with such almost real objects, getting smaller, vanishing on some horizon." Such thinking is "not in terms of words or syllogisms or signs" but in terms of some "visual algorithm" having a "sort of meta- or super-logic with its own rules." For William Lipscomb, a Nobel laureate in chemistry and, not incidentally, a fine musician, this kind of thinking is a synthetic and aesthetic experience. In his research into the chemistry of boron he found himself thinking not only inductively and deductively but also intuitively. "I felt a focusing of intellect and emotions which was surely an aesthetic response," he wrote. "It was followed by a flood of predictions coming from my mind as if I were a bystander watching it happen. Only later was I able to begin to formulate a systematic theory of structure, bonding and reactions for these unusual molecules. . . . Was it science? Our later tests showed it was. But the processes that I used and the responses that I felt were more like those of an artist." Gut feelings, emotions, and imaginative images do make sense in science, but, like the meaning of a dance or a musical theme, that sense is felt rather than defined.

"Intuition or mathematics?" asks inventor and science fiction writer Arthur C. Clarke. "Do we use models to help us find the truth? Or do we know the truth first, and then develop the mathematics to explain it?" There is no doubt about the answer: gut feelings and intuitions, an "essential feature in productive thought," as Einstein put it, occur well before their meaning can be expressed in words or numbers. In his own work, mathematics and formal logic were *secondary* steps: "Conventional words or other signs [presumably mathematical ones] have to be sought for laboriously only in a secondary stage, when the associative play already referred to is sufficiently established and can be reproduced at will." To Wertheimer he explained, "No really productive man thinks in such a paper fashion. The way the two triple sets of axioms are contrasted in [Einstein's physics book with collaborator Leopold Infeld] is not at all the way things happened in the process of actual thinking. This was merely a later formulation of the subject matter, just a question of how the thing could best be written . . . but in this process they [the ideas] did not grow out of any manipulation of axioms." As he told Infeld, "No scientist thinks in formulae."

Scientists may not think in mathematical terms, but the need to express intuitive insight in a form comprehensible to others compels them, in McClintock's words, to "work with so-called scientific methods to put it into their frame *after* you know." Other scientists confirm the two-part process of intuitive, imaginative understanding followed, necessarily, by logical expression. Metallurgist Cyril Stanley Smith of the Massachusetts Institute of Technology (MIT) has said, "The stage of discovery was entirely sensual and mathematics was only necessary to be able to communicate with other people." Werner Heisenberg, who formulated the uncertainty principle, wrote that "mathematics . . . played only a subordinate, secondary role" in the revolution in physics he helped to create. "Mathematics is the form in which we express our understanding of nature; but it is not the content of that understanding." Nobel Prize–winning physicist Richard Feynman, who also saw and felt things intuitively, noted, "In certain problems that I have done, it was necessary to continue the development of the picture as the method, before the mathematics could really be done."

So much for the myth that scientists *think* more logically than others. To think creatively is first to feel. The desire to understand must be whipped together with sensual and emotional feelings and blended with intellect to yield imaginative insight. Indeed, the intimate connections between thinking, emotions, and feelings are the subject of a startling book called *Descartes' Error* (1994), which revisits the famous philosopher's separation of mind (and thinking) from body (and being or feeling) more than three hundred years ago. The author, neurologist Antonio Damasio, finds that neurological patients whose emotional affect is grossly altered due to strokes, accidents, or tumors lose the ability to make rational plans. Because they are unable to become emotionally involved in their decisions, they fail to make good ones. Our feelings — our intuitions — are not impediments to rational thinking, they form its origin and bases. For Damasio, body and mind, emotion and intellect are inseparable. We agree. Not only do scientists feel their way toward logical ideas, but creative thinking and expression in every discipline are born of intuition and emotion.

For many people this may come as something of a surprise. Cognitive scientists such as Herb Simon and Noam Chomsky define thinking only as the logical procedures of induction and deduction or the rules of linguistics. Even Howard Gardner, who promotes the notion of more diverse ways of thinking in *Creating Minds* and *Frames of Mind,* argues that the thinking of creative people is best categorized by the one mode in which they express themselves. For Gardner and his colleagues, scientists such as Einstein, McClintock, and Feynman are logico-mathematical thinkers; poets and writers are characterized as highly verbal thinkers; dancers as kinesthetic thinkers; artists as mainly visual thinkers; psychologists as intrapersonal thinkers; and politicians as interpersonal thinkers. All of these characterizations seem to make sense, just as it seems to make sense that a baker will use yeast to make bread. But soda breads and flat breads are made without yeast, and yeast can be used to make many other foods, including beer and Grape-Nuts cereal. No single ingredient determines the outcome of a recipe, either in cooking or thinking. Characterizing individuals by a single element in their mental processes is as misleading as describing Einstein as — primarily — a logico-mathematical thinker.

Artists, for example, draw only partially upon visual stimuli. Emotions, kinesthetic feelings, philosophy, life itself, are other sources of artistic ideas. Painter Susan Rothenberg describes her process of painting as "really visceral. . . . I'm very aware of my body in space — shoulders, frontal positions. I have a body language that is difficult to explain. A lot of my work is about body orientation, both in the making of the work and in the sensing of space, comparing it to my own physical orientation." Sculptor Anne Truitt also feels her art in her body. In describing her apprenticeship, she writes:

It was not my eyes or my mind that learned. It was my body. I fell in love with the process of art, and I've never fallen out of it. I even loved the discomforts. At first my arms ached and trembled for an hour or so after carving stone; I remember sitting on the bus on the way home and feeling them shake uncontrollably. My blouse size increased by one as my shoulders broadened with muscle. My whole center of gravity changed. I learned to move from a center of strength and balance just below my navel. From this place, I could lift stones and I could touch the surface of clay as lightly as a butterfly's wing.

Similarly, painter Bridget Riley describes her paintings as "intimate dialogue[s] between my total being and the visual agents which constitute the medium. . . . I have always tried to realize visual and emotional energies simultaneously from the medium. My paintings are, of course, concerned with generating visual sensations, but certainly not to the exclusion of emotion. One of my aims is that these two responses shall be experienced as *one and the same.*"

Picasso, Gardner's prototype of the "visual thinker," clearly would have concurred. He believed that all sensation, all forms of knowing, are interconnected: "All the arts are the same: you can write a picture in words just as you can paint sensations in a poem. 'Blue' — what does 'blue' mean? There are thousands of sensations that we call 'blue.' You can speak of the blue of a packet of Gauloises and in that case you can talk of the Gauloise blue of eyes, or on the contrary, just as they do in a Paris restaurant, you can talk of a steak being blue when you mean red." Those who look at pictures and do not feel these (or other) associations miss the point. The mixture of feelings and sensations is what gives rise to the painting in the first place.

Because most artistic ideas begin nonvisually, artists also experience the process of translation that Einstein, McClintock, and others have described. Josef Albers may have expressed this process most succinctly when he wrote that art is "the discrepancy between physical fact and psychic effect . . . [a] visual formulation of our reaction to life." Sculptor Louise Bourgeois says, "I contemplate . . . for a long time. Then I try to express what I have to say, how I am going to translate what I have to say to it. I try to translate my problem into stone." Max Bill describes the object of art in similarly sweeping terms, as "the expression of the human spirit. . . . Abstract ideas which previously existed only in the mind are made visible in a concrete form." Paintings and drawings are "the instruments of this realization [by means of] color, space, light, movement." Georgia O'Keeffe wrote, "I long ago came to the conclusion that even if I could put down accurately the thing I saw and enjoyed, it would not give the observer the kind of feeling it gave me. I had to create an *equivalent* for what I felt about what I was looking at — not copy it." Thus the images of art are no more a direct reflection of the feelings, concepts, and sensations from which they arose than are a scientist's formulas direct expressions of his thoughts. All public languages are forms of translation.

Even those who express themselves in words find that they rarely think in words or generate their ideas in words. The poet E. E. Cummings, for one, challenged the assumption that poets are essentially wordsmiths manipulating the rules of grammar, syntax, and semantics. "The artist," he wrote, "is not a man who describes but a man who FEELS." Gary Snyder, also a poet, has expanded on that theme, saying that to write he must "revisualize it all. . . . I'll replay the whole experience again in my mind. I'll forget all about what's on the page and get in contact with the preverbal level behind it, and then by an effort of reexperiencing, recall, visualization, revisualization, I'll live through the whole thing again and try to see it more clearly." Stephen Spender provided an almost identical description of his own creative process:

> The poet, above all else, is a person who never forgets certain sense-impressions, which he has experienced and which he can re-live again and again as though with all their original freshness. . . . It therefore is not surprising that although I have no memory for telephone numbers, addresses, faces and where I may have put this morning's correspondence, I have a perfect memory for the sensation of certain experiences which are crystallized for me around certain associations. I could demonstrate this from my own life by the overwhelming nature of associations which, suddenly aroused, have carried me back so completely into the past, particularly into my childhood, that I have lost all sense of the present time and place.

The crafting of imaginary worlds, in both cummings's and Spender's cases, took more than a mastery of language; it took an ability to relive sense impressions almost at will. Other writers have said much the same. Robert Frost called his poetry a process of "carrying out some intention more felt than thought. . . . I've often been quoted: 'No tears in the writer, no tears in the reader. No surprise in the writer, no surprise for the reader.'" The American novelist and short-story writer Dorothy Canfield Fisher also needed to experience what she wrote in order to write well. "I have," she said, "intense visualizations of scenes. . . . Personally, although I never used as material any events in my own intimate life, I can write nothing if I cannot achieve these very definite, very complete visualizations of the scenes; which means that I can write nothing at all about places, people or phases of life which I do not intimately know, down to the last detail." Isabel Allende, too, plans her books "in a very organic way. Books don't happen in my mind, they happen somewhere in my belly. . . . I don't know what I'm going to write about because it has not yet made the trip from the belly to the mind. It is somewhere hidden in a very somber and secret place where I don't have any access yet. It is something that I've been feeling but which has no shape, no name, no tone, no voice."

At first the impulse, the vision, the feeling, is unspoken. But in the end it must come to words. Once the poet or writer has relived inspiring or troubling images and feelings, the problem is the same one shared by scientists and artists: how to translate these internal feelings into an external language other people can experience. Fisher described her "presumption" in trying "to translate into words . . . sacred living human feeling." T. S. Eliot, Howard Gardner's exemplar of a "verbal thinker," almost quoted O'Keeffe: "With a poem you can say, 'I got my feeling into words for myself. I now have the *equivalent* in words for that much of what I have felt.'" Gary Snyder has stated, "The first step is the rhythmic measure, the second step is a set of preverbal visual images which move to the rhythmic measure, and the third step is embodying it in words." William Goyen, a novelist, poet, and composer, characterized his writing process as "the business of taking it from the flesh state into the spiritual, the letter, the Word."

Science-fiction writer Ursula LeGuin points out the irony in this translation process for writers of fiction: "The artist deals with what cannot be said in words. The artist whose medium is fiction does this in words," which, she goes on to explain, "can be used thus paradoxically because they have, along with a semiotic usage, a symbolic or metaphoric usage." Words are, in other words, both literal and figurative signs of interior feelings, but not their essence. They are, as Heisenberg said of mathematics, expressions of understanding, not its embodiment. So Stephen Spender defines the "terrifying challenge of poetry" as the attempt to express in words that which may not be verbally expressed but may be verbally suggested: "Can I think out the logic of images? How easy it is to explain here the poem that I would have liked to write! How difficult it would be to write it. For writing it would imply living my way through the imaged experience of all those ideas, which here are mere abstractions, and such an effort of imaginative experience requires a lifetime of patience and watching."

"Can I think out the logic of the images?" Relive "the imaged experience"? Create in words an effort of the imagination? The speaker could as easily be Einstein or McClintock as Spender. If this logic of images, of muscular movement, of feeling, is anything, it is not the mathematical logic or the formal linguistic logic that we study in school. Formal logic is used to prove the validity of preexisting propositions. This new "logic" — perhaps Ulam's term, "metalogic," is more appropriate — can prove nothing; rather, it *generates* novel ideas and conceptions, with no assurance of their validity or utility. This kind of thinking, as yet unstudied and unaccounted for by modern theories of mind, is nonverbal, nonmathematical, and nonsymbolic inasmuch as it does not belong to a formal language of communication. Nevertheless, our challenge here is to describe and understand this metalogic of feelings, images, and emotions. If Ulam is right, the result might be as revolutionary and as fundamental as the rules of symbolic logic codified by Aristotle thousands of years ago. Such a metalogic might, indeed, explain the creative origins and character of the articulated ideas to which Aristotle's logic can be applied.

At present, the closest concept we have to such a metalogic is the vague one of intuition. Einstein said, "Only intuition, resting on sympathetic understanding, can lead to [insight]; . . . the daily effort comes from no deliberate intention or program, but straight from the heart." His colleague Henri Poincaré, perhaps the greatest mathematician of the late nineteenth century, wrote in *Science and Method*, "It is by logic that we prove, but by intuition that we discover. . . . Logic teaches us that on such and such a road we are sure of not meeting an obstacle; it does not tell us which is the road that leads to the desired end. For this it is necessary to see the end from afar, and the faculty that teaches us to see is intuition. Without it, the geometrician would be like a writer well up in grammar but destitute of ideas." Physicist Max Planck put it even more simply: the "scientist needs an *artistically* creative imagination." Indeed, scientist and artist are kin, for their insights begin in the same realm of feeling and intuition and emerge into consciousness through the same creative process.

And that is the point. It is too easy to look at the diverse things people produce and to describe their differences. Obviously a poem is not a mathematical formula, and a novel is not an experiment in genetics. Composers clearly use a different language from that of visual artists, and chemists combine very different things than do playwrights. But neither is all scientific thinking monolithic (physics is not biology) or all art the same (a sculpture is not a collage or a photograph). To characterize people by the different things they make is to miss the universality of how they create. For at the level of the creative process, scientists, artists, mathematicians, composers, writers, and sculptors use a common set of what we call "tools for thinking," including emotional feelings, visual images, bodily sensations, reproducible patterns, and analogies. And all imaginative thinkers learn to translate ideas generated by these subjective thinking tools into public languages to express their insights, which can then give rise to new ideas in others' minds.

A good many scientists and artists have noticed the universality of creativity. At the Sixteenth Nobel Conference, held in 1980, scientists, musicians, and philosophers all agreed, to quote Freeman Dyson, that "the analogies between science and art are very good as long as you are talking about the creation and the performance. The creation is certainly very analogous. The aesthetic pleasure of the craftsmanship of performance is also very strong in science." A few years later, at another multidisciplinary conference, physicist Murray Gell-Mann found that "everybody agrees on [where ideas come from]. We had a seminar here [the Aspen Physics Center in Colorado], about ten years ago, including several painters, a poet, a couple of writers, and the physicists. Everybody agrees on how it works. All of these people, whether they are doing artistic work or scientific work, are trying to solve a problem."

As one musician put it, the "absolute similarities" between the thinking processes of scientist and artist are true not only individually but on a social level, too. What the scientist perceives as common problem solving, the artist understands as shared inspiration — but the "answer" springs from the same creative act. As Nobel Prize–winning immunologist and writer Charles Nicolle put it, "[t]he disclosure of a new fact, the leap forward, the conquest over yesterday's ignorance, is an act not of reason but of imagination, of intuition. It is an act closely related to that of the artist and of the poet; a dream that becomes reality; a dream which seems to create." French physician Armand Trousseau agreed: "All science touches on art; all art has its scientific side. The worst scientist is he who is not an artist; the worst artist is he who is no scientist." Similarly, the constructivist sculptor Naum Gabo once wrote that "every great scientist has experienced a moment when the artist in him saved the scientist. 'We are poets,' said Pythagoras, and in the sense that a mathematician is a creator he was right." Stravinsky believed this too. "The way composers think — the way I think," he wrote, "is . . . not very different from mathematical thinking." No matter how expressed, the perspectives of Gell-Mann and Gabo, Stravinsky and Nicolle converge on the same point, aptly made by Arthur Koestler in his seminal book *The Act of Creation:* "Newton's apple and Cezanne's apple are discoveries more closely related than they seem." Both require reperceiving and reimagining the world from basic perceptual feelings and sensations.

While the universality of the creative process has been noticed, it has not been noticed universally. Not enough people recognize the preverbal, premathematical elements of the creative process. Not enough recognize the cross-disciplinary nature of intuitive tools for thinking. Such a myopic view of cognition is shared not only by philosophers and psychologists but, in consequence, by educators, too. Just look at how the curriculum, at every educational level from kindergarten to graduate school, is divided into disciplines defined by products rather than processes. From the outset, students are given separate classes in literature, in mathematics, in science, in history, in music, in art, as if each of these disciplines were distinct and exclusive. Despite the current lip service paid to "integrating the curriculum," truly interdisciplinary courses are rare, and transdisciplinary curricula that span the breadth of human knowledge are almost unknown. Moreover, at the level of creative process, where it really counts, the intuitive tools for thinking that tie one discipline to another are entirely ignored. Mathematicians are supposed to think only "in mathematics," writers only "in words," musicians only "in notes," and so forth. Our schools and universities insist on cooking with only half the necessary ingredients. By half-understanding the nature of thinking, teachers only half-understand how to teach, and students only half-understand how to learn.

This kind of half-baked education harms us more than we know. In our own experiences in school (and we both completed graduate school) no one ever even hinted that one could think about problems in any way but verbally or mathematically. It never occurred to us, and no one suggested that it might be possible, to formulate a math or physics problem as a set of images and feelings stewed in our minds or to plot a book or a poem as a series of images and emotions brewed in our bellies. No one ever mentioned that the stage of inventing an idea or solving a problem might be distinct from the stage of translating it into a disciplinary language. No one ever suggested, as this book will do, that the way we learned one subject or came to one insight might be the key to learning how to have insights in other fields.

If, however, the creative thinkers quoted in this chapter have accurately portrayed the manner in which they work — and we will argue that they have — it is obvious that education based solely on separate disciplines and public languages leaves out huge chunks of the creative process. Teachers work to hone students' mathematical and syntactical logic, but they ignore the metalogics of feelings and intuition. We are taught and tested with words and numbers, and it is assumed that we think in words and numbers. No schooling could be more misconceived. As William Lipscomb has said of current scientific education, "If one actually set out to give as little help as possible to both aesthetics and originality in science, one could hardly devise a better plan than our educational system. . . . One rarely hears about what we do not understand in science, and least of all how to prepare for creative ideas." The same can be said for training in the arts, humanities, and technologies. We master the languages of translation but neglect our mother tongue. Feasts are set before us that we do not taste. We honor chefs and refuse to emulate them.

Nothing could be more important, therefore, than recognizing and describing the intuitive "dialects" of creative thinking. As important as words and numbers are to the communication of insight, that insight is born of emotions and images of many sorts conjured within the imagination. Feeling as thinking must, therefore, become part of the educational curriculum. Students must learn how to pay attention to what they feel in their bones, to develop and use it. This is not pie in the sky. Various professions, including medicine, are beginning to recognize intuition as a necessary part of disciplinary thinking. Geri Berg, an art historian and social worker, formerly at Johns Hopkins University, believes that "emotional awareness, like observation and critical enquiry skills, is an important part of providing good health care." Dr. John Burnside, chief of internal medicine at the Hershey Medical Center in Pennsylvania, has argued this even more forcefully. "One of our educational failures," he writes, "is a lack of serious recognition and attention towards the 'gut feeling' or inclination of common sense. Perhaps because this inclination is non-numerical it is glossed over as the 'art of medicine,' implying instinct, passion, or the primeval. But I believe it can be defined and should be taught."

Whether we are attempting to understand ourselves, other people, or some aspect of nature, or simply provide excellent medical care, it is imperative that we learn to use the feelings, emotions, and intuitions that are the bases of the creative imagination. That is the whole point of gourmet thinking and education.

2

Schooling the Imagination

In *The Phantom Tollbooth* (1961), a classic fantasy by the architect and designer Norton Juster, a boy named Milo takes on an impossible quest. He seeks to reunite the kingdoms of words and numbers, which have been divided by what C. P. Snow called "the two cultures" problem, the inability of those in the sciences and those in arts and letters to communicate. In the course of his adventure, Milo journeys through the Forest of Sight on his way to the city of Reality, when suddenly he sees magnificent buildings towering in the distance. His guide, Alec Bings, informs him they are only a mirage: the city of Illusions. "How can you see something that isn't there?" grumbles the Humbug, one of Milo's companions. "Sometimes," replies Alec, "it's much simpler than seeing things that are. . . . For instance, if something is there, you can only see it with your eyes open, but if it isn't there, you can see it just as well with your eyes closed. That's why imaginary things are often easier to see than real ones." Then where, Milo and his companions ask, is the city of Reality? "Right here," says Alec, pointing. "You're standing in the middle of Main Street." But, says Milo, "I don't see any city."

Milo's ability to perceive Illusions but not Reality may seem like an artificial literary device, but we discovered many years ago that our educational system actually fosters this odd talent. The lesson was brought home in a particularly memorable way when we were undergraduates. We had a friend — we'll call him John — who was considered one of the most brilliant students in the history of our college. He completed unheard-of amounts of work, acing class after class. This was no mean intellectual feat, though John's feet, like those of many a mere mortal, turned out to be made of clay.

We made the disheartening discovery on the way out of the physics building, just a few weeks after a series of lectures on mechanics. John was a rather tall, lanky young man — no athlete, but no ninety-pound weakling either. Nevertheless, try as he might, he could not open one of the very heavy oak doors of the old lecture hall. One of us reached for the doorknob and gave the door a shove that swung it cleanly open.

"How did you do that so easily?" John asked.

"You're kidding, right?" we responded. "We just studied the physical principles that relate to doors a couple of weeks ago." John had mastered the relevant equations so thoroughly that he got one of the highest scores ever recorded on the midterm exam, but nevertheless he appeared puzzled. "No. Really. I don't understand," he said.

We gave him a clue. "You were pushing at the center of the door rather than the edge."

"So?"

"Well, why are doorknobs usually put at the edges of doors rather than in the middle?"

"It's easier to make the latching mechanism, I suppose," John essayed.

"Sure. But what *physical* principle is involved?" John shrugged his shoulders. He really hadn't the slightest idea. For all his genius, he wasn't putting us on. "Torque, John, torque!" we cried.

Torque is a rotational force. Most of us have a kinesthetic understanding of torque that we develop from opening and closing doors or using a wrench. We have learned by experience that the closer to the *unhinged* edge of the door we push, the easier it is to move; that the longer the wrench, the less force we need to exert to loosen a bolt. The principle is akin to that of the lever. Give me a fulcrum, a lever long enough, and a place to stand and I will move the world, Archimedes is supposed to have said. For torque, one might say, give me a wrench long enough and I'll loosen any bolt. Or, in terms of John's problem, let me push as far from the hinges as possible and I'll open any door.

Insight visibly dawned in John's face, and he proceeded to calculate — in his head, mind you — that if the mass of the door was x, and the distance from the axis of rotation to the point at which the force was applied was y (and so forth), then, indeed, it would take significantly less force to move the door if that force was applied at the outer edge rather than at the center. The problem was that John made no connection between this intellectual work and his personal experience of the physical world around him. Torque problems were posed by a physics professor and solved using mathematics during a test. John could see what one might characterize as the "illusions" of torque equations before his mind's eye as clearly as Milo and his companions could see the city of Illusions in the Forest of Sight. But it had never occurred to John that such mathematical problems existed in real life. He could not relate his incredible store of academic knowledge and his fantastic facility with numbers to everyday activity. His Illusions failed to connect with Reality.

Unfortunately, many good students experience the same disjunction between academic work and real life. Albert Einstein certainly believed this to be true for his eldest son. When he took Hans Albert sailing, for instance, he expected the boy to apply his school knowledge of physics to the challenge of harnessing the wind and was disappointed when he did not. The case is all the more interesting because Einstein himself had been discouraged from tying experience to academic studies when he had attended the gymnasium (or technical high school). Although rote memorization and thinking in words and numbers formed the bulk of gymnasium studies, Einstein had found it difficult to ignore his senses and intuition. He blossomed only after transferring to a high school in Arrau, Switzerland, run according to the principles of Johann Heinrich Pestalozzi, an educational reformer who placed nonverbal, nonmathematical forms of thinking at the center of education. Students at the Kanton Schule focused not on communication skills but on learning how to imagine what it felt like to be inside a physical system. They learned to draw, create models, pay attention to their intuition, see and feel things in their minds. Later, as a patent examiner, Einstein practiced these skills further. He carried them into his physics and into his daily life.

When Einstein went sailing he *felt* the forces at work on his boat through the lines and the hull. He became, as his daughter Margot explained, "a little piece of nature" — a physical embodiment of his understanding. He could also interpret these feelings as expressions of well-known physical laws. As far as he was concerned, an expert sailor was an applied physicist, and a physicist was someone who could act upon his understanding in real life situations. Whenever Hans Albert made a sailing error, Einstein perceived it as a failure on his son's part to connect book work with experience of the world. "Every time his son made what he thought was a mistake in the sailing of the boat," Einstein's friend Chaim Tschernowitz recounted, "Einstein would burst out about the educational system of the gymnasia — how inefficient it was, and how it was responsible for all the mistakes men make in later life."

At about the same time J. J. Thomson, winner of a Nobel Prize in physics for his discovery of the electron, found similar failings in physics training at Cambridge University. To reach students like our friend John, Thomson larded his courses with physical demonstrations of physical laws and theorems. "The demonstrations brought to light some interesting points," he noted in 1937. "We found many cases where men could solve the most complicated problems about lenses, yet when given a lens and asked to find the image of a candle flame, would not know on which side of the lens to look for the image. But perhaps the most interesting point was their intense surprise when any mathematical formula gave the right result. They did not seem to realise it [mathematics] was anything but something for which they had to write out proofs in examination papers." Henri Poincaré found the same to be true in France. "There is one thing that strikes me, and that is, how far young people who have received a secondary education are from applying the mechanical laws they have been taught to the real world. . . . For them the world of science and that of reality are shut off in water-tight compartments."

The same disconnection between academic knowledge and physical experience continues to plague education today. "I am told," Harvard psychologist Leon Eisenberg told a symposium on creativity during the 1970s, "that in so distinguished an institution as MIT, a student can have mastered calculus to the satisfaction of the teacher by having solved the problem set on the final examination. On entering the physics course he cannot see how to apply the calculus to the solution of problems in physics. There is something very much wrong about what has been learned when the skills are not transferable." No less a scientist than Richard Feynman, whose work revolutionizing quantum physics earned him a Nobel Prize, confirmed Eisenberg's observation. In *Surely You're Joking, Mr. Feynman!* (1985), he told of students in a mechanical drawing class at MIT who didn't know how to describe the French curve mathematically. They were sure that the plastic tool they used for drawing smooth curves had to have "some special formula." For Feynman their ignorance was a joke and so was his response. "The French curve," he told them, "is made so that at the lowest point on each curve, no matter how you turn it, the tangent is horizontal."

> All the guys in the class were holding their French curve up at different angles holding their pencil up to it at the lowest point and laying it along, and discovering, sure enough, the tangent is horizontal. They were all excited by this "discovery" — even though they had already gone through a certain amount of calculus and had already "learned" that the derivative (tangent) of the minimum (lowest point) of *any* curve is zero (horizontal). They didn't put two and two together. They didn't even know what they "knew."

Indeed, professors at MIT and the California Institute of Technology (Caltech) as well as research directors at major engineering firms have long realized that what eventually separates successful scientists and engineers from the rest of the students in their classes is the ability to *feel* or *see* what the equations mean. Every student in their physics classes has the mathematical ability to solve Einstein's equations describing relativity theory, but only a few can bring the equations to life. Only a few can translate back and forth between their mathematical and their physical understanding as Einstein, Feynman, Pauli, Cyril Smith, and so many other great physical thinkers have been able to do. Having learned mathematics as a language of communication without also learning what mathematics communicates, too many students are like those observed by J. J. Thomson and Henri Poincaré, like our friend John. As brilliant as they are, they are only half-educated.

The problem of living in Illusions rather than in Reality is not limited to the sciences. Verbal schooling received in the humanities also fails in an analogous way by teaching students communication and analysis without exercising feeling, observing, empathizing, and other ways of knowing reality directly. The result can be crippling to the artist or writer. The writer Virginia Woolf explored an all-too-perfect example of this failing in her father. Sir Leslie Stephen, eminent man of letters and editor of the impressive *Dictionary of National Biography,* yearned to be a great literary figure, though he produced no more than dry, analytical criticism. According to Woolf, her father was "conscious of his failure as a philosopher, as a writer," telling her at least once that despite his high academic credentials, he had "only a good second class mind." After her father's death, Woolf took a long hard look at the "disparity . . . between [Stephen's] critical and his creative powers. . . . Give him a thought to analyse, the thought of Mill, Bentham, Hobbes," she wrote, "and his [writing] is . . . acute, clear, concise: an admirable model of the Cambridge analy[tical spirit]. But give him life, a character, and he is so crude, so elementary, so conventional, that a child with a box of coloured chalks is as subtle a portrait painter as he is."

Woolf blamed her father's education, just as Einstein, Thomson, and Feynman attributed the failings of their students and colleagues to an incomplete schooling. "One would have to discuss the crippling effect of Cambridge," Woolf wrote, "and its one-sided education; . . . and the crippling effect of intensive brain work; and to illustrate that by his lack of any distracting interests — music, art, the theatre, travel; and one would have to discover how much of this intensification and narrowness was natural; how much imposed by circumstances." The highly competitive nature of the honors examinations at Cambridge and other British universities in the mid-nineteenth century certainly had something to do with Stephen's narrow analytical powers. These tests, known as the triposes, relied heavily on memorization of material and speed of regurgitation. Stephen "crammed" well in both mathematics and linguistics, taking twentieth place in the math exam out of a particularly brilliant group of 143 students. And when he himself became a Cambridge tutor, he advised his students "to stick to your triposes, grind at your mill and don't set the universe in order until you have taken your bachelor's degree."

Such constant intellectual overwork left Stephen little time or inclination for the arts, a consequence his daughter deplored. Aside from his professional concern with literary criticism, Stephen ignored painting, music, theater, and opera, calling himself in this regard a "Philistine" — literally, a person hostile to aesthetic refinement. He even seems to have viewed artistic endeavor in the literary field with outright suspicion. "The imaginative writer," he declared, "is bound to be emotional and personal; he has to work up his innermost emotions for exhibition, and is thin-skinned and self-conscious. . . . Let us hope he has his reward in the raptures of creation, and be thankful we are spared his temptations."

Stephen certainly spared himself. Woolf noted that "at the age of sixty-five he was almost completely isolated, imprisoned. Whole tracts of his sensibility had atrophied. He had so ignored, or refused to face, or disguised his own feelings, that not only had he no conception of what he himself did and said; he had no idea what other people felt." Unable or unwilling to take his own emotions and feelings seriously, he was unable to perceive the impact of his ideas on others or to invent work that could move others in the ways literature or poetry must do. In contrast, his daughter achieved literary fame not only for her stylistic excellence but for her many literary innovations. Where her father was "limited" and "conventional," Woolf was as adventurous and inventive as any writer ever has been. She may have fretted when her father refused to send her to university, but in later years she realized that her self-schooling had been invaluable.

Woolf learned at home in an eclectic but also synthetic manner. From an early age she listened to her father read from Sir Walter Scott's Waverly novels, as well as from Jane Austen, Shakespeare, and classics of history. She spent time in "the mechanical part" of the South Kensington Museum and "the insect room" of the Natural History Museum. Along with her siblings, she made up stories in bed, imitating the tales her mother made up and wrote down for them. She contributed avidly to a family newpaper. In all this, her experience of learning, like Einstein's, seems to have been somatic. She developed almost total recall for her sensations; she had an ability to empathize with characters in books she was reading and tended to disappear into their worlds, forgetting herself. She took in so much that her father recognized by the time she was eleven that she "will really be an author in time." From about the age of fifteen, she became an autodidact, reading essays, history, biography, travel and adventure, poetry, novels. In German lessons with her father, as well as in math, she failed miserably, but she did study bookbinding with a teacher who came to the house and took private lessons in Greek and Latin. She discussed literature with her brother Thoby whenever he was home from his university, for "I don't get anyone to argue with me now, and feel the want." She learned to write by mimicking the best literary models and watching her sister explore the making of art. In complete contrast to her father, Woolf learned not only the "what" of literature but the "how" as well. Novels were not just to be read; they were to be *made*.

Woolf was fortunate to have escaped the educational separation of "what" and "how." To look at a novel or a sculpture or to listen to a piece of music as if it were simply an object — a "what" to be analyzed — is to perceive only the Illusion. Reality can be experienced only when we understand how the art emerges from and relates to life itself. More than sixty years ago the educational philosopher John Dewey argued in his classic *Art as Experience* that conventional art education fails in exactly the same way science education fails — by concealing rather than revealing the links between theory and practice. For Dewey, the more we consider artistic objects distinct from the original experience that formed them, the more we cut art off into a separate realm and threaten it with irrelevance. The "refined and intensified forms of experience that are works of art" are thus disconnected from "the everyday events, doings, and sufferings that are universally recognized to constitute experience."

The problem with divorcing what and how in education is that *knowing* about things is not the same as *understanding* them. Feynman made the point when he said, apropos of the French curve, "I don't know what's the matter with people: they don't learn by understanding: they learn some other way — by rote or something. Their knowledge is so fragile!" John, a brilliant student, *knew* a great deal of physics, just as Leslie Stephen *knew* a great deal about literature. When it came right down to it, however, neither one *understood* his subject — how to use it practically, how to make with it or create something new. Their knowledge was, indeed, fragile and useless —

the result of an educational failure that all too often clothes itself in the garb of academic success.

An opposite kind of educational failure, in which Reality is perceived in the absence of Illusions, has also attracted attention over the years. Two decades ago, for instance, educational psychologist Jeanne Bamberger embarked on a study of children in Cambridge, Massachusetts, who did poorly in school despite their "virtuoso" ability to build and fix things in their everyday world. Very early on in her Laboratory for Making Things, Bamberger realized that these young students, like Einstein, had trouble learning disembodied principles of physics but understood them at a practical level very well. In the course of building mobiles, for example, they placed weights at appropriate distances from the fulcrum, even though they could not articulate any of the physical concepts involved. One student explained that he "just knew. . . . I had a feeling of it, like on a teeter-totter." His lack of Illusions, of theoretical knowledge, represented a "failure to perform" in an academic sense because he could not explain to others what he had accomplished or how. But he understood the Reality of the situation in the same sense that the scientists and artists quoted in Chapter 1 knew they had achieved some basic insight or arrived at some seminal idea but did not yet know how to express it. Bamberger concluded that this boy and children like him had a "hand knowledge" acquired through experience that was, in its own way, as powerful as the "symbolic knowledge" taught in school.

Experience-based understanding represents a "poorly understood, but well recognized phenomenon," in Bamberger's words, that has counterparts throughout the annals of innovative art and science. Many creative individuals — including Einstein and the graphic designer M. C. Escher — perform poorly in conventional schools. "In high school in Arnhem," Escher wrote, "I was a particularly poor student in arithmetic and algebra because I had, and still have, great trouble with the abstractions of numbers and letters. Things went a little better in geometry when I was called upon to use my imagination, but I never excelled in this subject while in school." Mathematics nevertheless played a role in his later design of artistic patterns. "Although I lack theoretical knowledge," he observed, "the mathematicians, and in particular the crystallographers, have had considerable influence on my work." The influence was mutual. Escher's intuitive grasp of tilings, dimensions, and symmetries proved so profound that academicians have used his art to illustrate many mathematical and physical concepts. Who could have predicted his achievement based on such an inauspicious beginning? Despite his poor performance in school, Escher *understood* mathematics, though in a way his teachers did not expect or appreciate.

This is precisely what Bamberger found in her Laboratory for Making Things. When the young boy spoke of a "feeling of it, like on a teeter-totter," his teachers did not understand the validity of his experience-based explanation. As Bamberger explains, "They had, of course, learned the formula of 'weight times distance' [for balancing different weights], but what they had been taught and what they had learned to *say* seemed disconnected from what they could directly see and feel. . . . The teachers themselves, like most adults, were used to keeping neatly separate their school knowledge and their everyday knowledge." Indeed, Bamberger found that many teachers in her project could not build the mobiles or other constructions that they assigned to their students. They knew the theory but could not apply it in the real world. Illusions and Reality were just as separate for them as for their students, but for a different reason.

We can see now what was wrong with the schooling of Leslie Stephen and our friend John. Both men excelled in "cramming" the thought of others in science, philosophy, literature, or history. Both men exhibited a complete lack of interest in practicing the arts, whether fine or mechanical. They had no hobbies; they did not build or fashion things with their hands or their minds. In short, they lacked imagination, that capacity to link mind and body, intellect and intuition. No one insisted that they learn by doing and making; no one encouraged them to meld "hand knowledge" and "symbolic knowledge"; no one pressed them to make connections between practice and analysis, or image and object. They acquired facts but could not imagine their meanings. Their brilliant minds — and the minds of so many like them — were blinkered by pedagogies that separated knowing and understanding, Illusions and Reality.

The result was a serious handicap. As we will show in subsequent chapters of this book, if you can't imagine, you can't invent. "Illusion," as Pulitzer Prize–winning author and artist Paul Horgan has written, "is first of all needed to find the powers of which the self is capable." If you can't conceive of things that don't exist, you can't create anything new. If you can't dream up worlds that might be, then you are limited to the worlds other people describe. You see reality through their eyes, not your own. Worse, having failed to develop your own illusory but insightful "eyes of the mind," the eyes in your head will not show you much of anything at all.

In *The Phantom Tollbooth*, Milo realizes this when he finds that the city of Reality is home to a great many people rushing in and out of buildings and up and down streets they — and Milo — do not see. "Hasn't anyone told them?" the boy asks, alarmed by the thought of people inhabiting a phantom reality, as blind to its existence as John and Stephen were to the realities they encountered. Alec replies matter-of-factly that telling does no good, "for they can never see what they are in too much of a hurry to look for." "Why don't they just live in Illusions," quips the Humbug, for then they might at least exist in a city they can "see." "Many of them do," Alec responds, "but it's just as bad to live in a place where what you see isn't there as it is to live in one where what you don't see is."

The trick, Milo finally figures out, is to live in Illusions and Reality at the same time. Fantasy and imagination suggest how the world might be; knowledge and experience limit the possibilities; melding the two begets understanding. Without the illusions of the mind, a clear grasp of reality is impossible, and vice versa.

The best scientists have always realized this, arguing, as so many do, that their Illusions must constantly be tempered with Reality. Theory is always tested by experiment and observation. Artists, writers, and professionals in the humanities say much the same thing, although the paradox of that interaction is, for them, never quite resolved. "Fiction writers, at least in their braver moments, do desire the truth: to know it, speak it, serve it," writes Ursula LeGuin. "But they go about it in a peculiar and devious way, which consists in inventing persons, places, and events which never did and never will exist or occur, and telling about these fictions in detail and at length and with a great deal of emotion, and then when they are done writing down this pack of lies, they say, There! That's the truth!"

LeGuin argues further that the writer's "tissue of lies" is credibly supported by all kinds of facts, a "weight of verifiable place-event-phenomenon-behavior." As the perceptual psychologist Richard Gregory points out, "It is a mistake to equate 'fiction' with 'false.'" By checking and crosschecking fiction with fact, experience with knowledge, by creating each in the image of the other, the writer ever more closely approximates recognized truths. Ultimately, however, the imagined fictions matter far more than the facts, for they fuel the creative process — not just in art but in science, too. "The illusions of the experimenter," wrote Louis Pasteur, inventor of the germ theory of disease, the first vaccines, and pasteurization, "form the greater part of his power." And Einstein stated categorically, "In creative work, imagination is more important than knowledge."

For the scientist, experimentation keeps imagination from going astray; for the artist, it is a dialectical dilemma. When LeGuin insists, "Distrust everything I say. I am telling the truth," she might just as easily say, Consider carefully what this fictive lens lets you see. Our perceptions of Reality depend upon the kind and quality of Illusions we conjure. This is what Picasso meant when he said, "Art is a lie that makes us realize the truth." Like so many artists and scientists, he understood that imagination does not simply discover truth, it shapes it. A wonderful anecdote concerning the painter illustrates the point. One day, Picasso took a train trip and, as happens on such occasions, engaged in conversation with the gentleman seated next to him. When the man learned to whom he was speaking, he began grumbling about the ways in which modern art distorts reality. According to one account, "Picasso demanded to know what *was* a faithful representation of reality. The man produced a wallet-sized photo and said, 'There! That's a real picture — that's what my wife really looks like.' Picasso looked at it carefully from several angles, turning it up and down and sideways, and said, 'She's awfully small. And flat.'"

Without imagination all the world is, indeed, as flat and small as the portrait Picasso examined. This was Leslie Stephen's problem, and John's. What we sense directly — a door, the sun and moon rising and setting, a photograph or drawing, the scribbled marks we call letters on a piece of paper — these things are not real at all or, rather, they are not real to us in and of themselves. We must interpret what we sense in terms of imagination to create understanding. All of science and all of art are demonstrations of this fact. The door is not just a piece of wood hung on hinges; it is also an example of torque and of mass; it is also a marriage of materials, manual skill, and utilitarian purpose; a work of artistic design; an exit, an entry. To think of it in these different ways requires us to perceive it in these different ways, as our friend John found out the hard way. Despite appearances, the earth turns, not the sun, and thus the sun, not the earth, is the center of the solar system. The photograph, the drawing, writing itself — these are nothing but paper with some ink or silver stains on it. What we make of each occurs in our minds in accord with our skill at recreating the sensory, emotional, and experiential feelings that they are meant to symbolize. Their meanings are invented fictions that have a ring of truth only if we carry the truth around inside ourselves. Productive thought occurs when internal imagination and external experience coincide.

This being the case, the task for educators, self-learners, and parents is simply put: to reunite the two. And the world's most creative people tell us how in their own words and deeds; in their own explorations of their own minds at work. What they find as individuals, when taken as a whole, is a common set of thinking tools at the heart of creative understanding. These tools include (but are not necessarily limited to) *observing, imaging, abstracting, recognizing patterns, forming patterns, analogizing, body thinking, empathizing, dimensional thinking, modeling, playing, transforming,* and *synthesizing.*

Initially, all knowledge about the world is acquired through *observing,* paying attention to what is seen, heard, touched, smelled, tasted, or felt within the body. The ability to recall or imagine these feelings and sensations is also an important tool called *imaging.* Just as observations can be made using any sense, so images can be recalled or created for any sense or sensation. Indeed, scientists, artists, and musicians alike report "seeing" in the mind pictures of things they have never actually seen, "hearing" sounds and songs that have not yet been made, and "feeling" the sensual properties of things they have never truly touched. Because sense experience and sense imagery are rich and complex, creative people in all disciplines also use *abstracting* as an essential tool. And whether one is an artist like Picasso, a scientist like Einstein, or a writer like Hemingway, the process of paring down complicated things to simple principles is the same.

Simplifying often works in tandem with patterning, a tool with two parts. *Recognizing patterns* is involved in the discovery of nature's laws and the structure of mathematics, but also the rhymes and rhythms of language, dance, music, and the formal intentions of the painter. Recognizing patterns is also the first step toward creating new ones. Novel *pattern forming,* whether in music, art, engineering, or dance, almost always begins with combining simple elements in unexpected ways. Even more interesting, there are patterns to pattern forming itself. Moreover, recognizing patterns in patterns leads directly to *analogizing.* The realization that two apparently different things share important properties or functions lies at the heart of the world's greatest works of art and literature and the most enduring scientific theories and engineering inventions.

Tools for thinking are preverbal and presymbolic, and none more so than *body thinking* — thinking that occurs through the sensations and awareness of muscle, sinew, and skin. Well before they have found the words or the formulas to express themselves, many creative people "feel" ideas emerging. Bodily sensations, muscular movements, and emotions act as springboards for more formal thought. Athletes and musicians imagine the feel of their movements; physicists and artists feel in their bodies the tensions and movements of trees and electrons, instruments and tools. *Empathizing* is related to body thinking. Many creative people describe "losing" themselves in the things they study, integrating "I" and "it." Actors learn to make the character they play a part of themselves. Scientists, doctors, and artists play-act "becoming" another person or an animal, plant, electron, or star. Yet another tool, this one rooted in the experience of space, is *dimensional thinking*, the imaginative ability to take a thing mentally from a flat plane into three dimensions or more, from earth into outer space, through time, even to alternate worlds. One of the least recognized of our thinking tools, dimensional thinking is essential to engineering, sculpture, visual art, medicine, mathematics, and astronomy — indeed, any activity that involves interpreting "pictures" in one set of dimensions as objects in another set.

Up to this point, the thinking tools we have outlined are what might be called primary tools. None is absolutely independent of any of the others. Body thinking cannot be separated absolutely from imaging; analogizing relies on pattern recognition and pattern forming; and patterning relies in turn on observing. Nonetheless, one can learn and practice each of these tools somewhat independently of the others. Our last four, however, are clearly higher-order tools that integrate and rely upon the primary tools. *Modeling* objects and concepts often requires some combination of dimensional thinking, abstracting, analogizing, and manipulative or body skill. Poets and writers pattern genres on the exemplars of earlier writers; artists make small sketches and maquettes in preparation for their masterpieces; dancers model their choreography on real people; doctors learn procedures by trying them out on specialized mannequins; engineers test their ideas on working models. *Playing*, another integrative tool, particularly builds upon body thinking, empathizing and play-acting, and modeling. Playing involves a childlike joy in the endeavor at hand, an irreverence for conventional procedure, purpose, or the "rules of the game." Playfully challenging the limitations of a science, an art, or a technology just to see what happens is one of the most common ways in which novel ideas are born.

Transforming, another integrative tool, is the process of translating between one tool for thinking and another and between imaginative tools and formal languages of communication. In real life we become aware of problems through feelings of mental or bodily discomfort, but we must express the solution logically in words, movements, or equations or as an invention. To move from feelings to communication always requires a series of steps: translating the problem into images or models, searching for patterns through careful observation or experiment, abstracting out the most important material from the patterns and modeling it, then playing around with various solutions using empathizing or play-acting, and finally searching for the language that can best express one's insight. Transformational thinking weaves the rest of the tools together into a functional whole, correlating each skill with the others in a workable fashion.

Finally, and most important, *synthesizing* completes the imagination's tool kit, for understanding is always synthetic, combining many ways of experiencing. There are two fundamental components to synthetic thinking. One is *synesthesia,* a neurological and artistic term for experiencing sensations in multiple ways at once. A sound may provoke colors; a taste may call up tactile sensations or memories. Synthesizing also supposes an integration of knowledge in which observing, imaging, empathizing, and the other tools all work together organically — not serially, as in transformational thinking, but simultaneously, such that everything — memory, knowledge, imagination, feeling — is understood in a holistic, somatic way. The equations that describe torque become one with the feeling of torque when opening a door. We call this unified understanding linking mind and body, sense and sensibility, *synosia,* and it is the ultimate goal of a tools-for-thinking education.

Six important points must be made about these thirteen tools. First, we emphasize that we have relied upon creative individuals to describe their own thinking. Artist Brent Collins is typical of the introspective individual who clearly understands his creative process in terms of these imaginative tools. In working to transform mathematical models of equations into sculptural allegories, he says, "I made [2-dimensional] templates exactly to scale. . . . The entire mathematical logic of the sculpture is inherently readable from the template. There are, however, many aesthetic choices. . . . The template serves as a guide for a spatial logic I somehow intuitively know to follow. Using common woodworking tools and proceeding kinesthetically, I am able to gradually feel and envision its visual implications. . . . The linear patterns issue as abstractions." Dimensional thinking, modeling, body thinking, visual imaging, abstracting, synthetic thinking — he uses all of these tools to imagine and to create, as do the many other individuals we cite and discuss on the following pages.

Second, we acknowledge that we are not the first to take note of some of these imaginative skills. A century ago Francis Galton undertook many studies of what he called "genius." He observed that many of his eminent contemporaries tended to visualize things, to think with their bodies, and to transform ideas such as numerical patterns into visual ones. His work, and that of many psychologists building upon his ideas, has provided valuable insights into certain aspects of creative thinking. In studying the creative individuals of our own and times past, we are expanding upon Galton's original conception of the creative imagination. The tools described in this book are what creative people themselves say they use and, equally important, what studies of their creative processes show that they use.

Third, we argue that these tools for thinking promise to bridge the gap between Illusions and Reality to create synthetic understanding. Metallurgist Cyril Stanley Smith, also a humanist and artist, understands that tools for thinking, by their very nature, forge abiding connections between what is real, what is imagined, and what is created. Visual imaging, pattern recognizing, and pattern forming, based as they are in the sensory input of the external world, compel us to channel our sense-making capacities toward what Smith calls the "shared duality" of mind and matter. "The principles of pattern formation, aggregation, and transformation," he has written, "seem to be the same in matter and in the human brain, and if properly formulated they may provide a kind of visual metaphor that will serve to join and mutually illuminate physics on the one hand and geological, biological, and social history on the other — with art in between." The concept of tools for thinking is clearly a unifying one.

Fourth, we are not making any claims of cognitive significance for our tools. These tools are not to be taken for distinct forms of inheritable "intelligence" to be used as educational tracking devices or for cognitive "domains" representing specialized brain functions. Nor are they meant to be localized in some anatomical region of the brain or some set of neuronal connections. Rather, tools for thinking are exactly what we have called them: tools. They are just like whisks, knives, graters, spatulas, mixers, and blenders — equipment available to anyone. With practice and determination anyone can learn to use them with some degree of skill. We fully expect them to be used with other analytical tools, such as logic, and with communication tools, such as words and equations. Our tools complement but do not replace other cognitive skills.

Fifth, just as mastery of kitchen utensils does not guarantee innovation in cooking, mastery of tools for thinking does not guarantee innovation in science, art, or any other endeavor. There are no easy recipes for originality. Nevertheless, neither the chef nor the thinker can be creative without thorough practice and exercise of his or her equipment. Thinking tools are necessary to creativity, but, like the tools of any trade, they must be used with individual, even idiosyncratic, vision to yield innovative results.

Finally, though people can use these tools in the workplace or the home, their most important role may be in education. Our educational system is the embodiment of our cognitive and creative understanding of ourselves. If we fail to understand creative thinking, we cannot hope to have an educational system that will produce creative individuals. Conversely, a society that understands the nature of creativity will be able to foster it in the classroom. Indeed, we intend that these tools be used to cultivate imagination along with intellect, to reintegrate knowledge of mind with knowledge of body, to reveal in glorious detail the ways in which artists, scientists, dancers, engineers, musicians, and inventors think and create, so that the most unexpected surprises may illuminate all our lives.

An impossible and quixotic task? Perhaps. Knowledge is fragmenting at ever-increasing speed; understanding becomes ever more rare. C. P. Snow's two cultures have now multiplied to hundreds of noncommunicating cultures. Technology feeds reliance on the mysterious and even magical workings of "black boxes." Even as more and more information becomes available, we understand and use less and less of it. If society cannot find ways to make integrated understanding accessible to large numbers of people, then the information revolution is not only useless but a threat to humane civilization.

The only failure is not to try, as Milo learns in *The Phantom Tollbooth*. Surviving numerous scrapes with the Demons of Ignorance, in the end he reunites Dictionopolis, the capital of Words, and Digitopolis, the capital of Numbers, within the Kingdom of Wisdom by returning to them the banished Princesses of Rhyme and Reason. In terms that Milo would understand, we, too, can try to unite Illusions and Reality into Understanding through the medium of Tools for Thinking. Our goal is no less lofty than Milo's, and certainly as difficult. But if we push on the door in the right place, it will swing open.

3

Observing

A LL KNOWLEDGE BEGINS in observation. We must be able to perceive our world accurately to be able to discern patterns of action, abstract their principles, make analogies between properties of things, create models of behaviors, and innovate fruitfully. Before you read this chapter, therefore, we'd like you to test your observational skills. Turn on the television and describe what you observe about it. We're not looking for details such as who is saying what to whom in which program, but rather the characteristics of a working television itself. Try to get beyond the obvious aspects such as its glass screen, plastic case, and push-button switches to its intimate properties. Make notes and sketches about your observations. Then read this chapter and see how you could have gone about your task differently.

Most people equate observing with visual perception, which, although myopic, is as good a place to begin as any. So what do you see in the photograph below? At first glance you might think it a nondescript scene of dried-up grass. But look carefully. This photograph appeared as an illustration in a groundbreaking book about visual phenomena, Gerald Thayer's *Concealing-Coloration in the Animal Kingdom: An Exposition of the Laws of Disguise Through Color and Pattern: Being a Summary of Abbott H. Thayer's Discoveries* (1909). As the book title suggests, the picture shows something camouflaged. A small dark blob in the upper left corner might be an eye. The black patch toward the lower right could be the shadow of a tail. Above and to the left of this shadow, an area of somewhat different texture is evident. When these elements converge, you recognize a bird — specifically a ptarmigan, a type of grouse.

Fig. 3-1. An example of animal camouflage.

Now, why didn't you see the bird right away? The fact that it is camou-flaged is no excuse. You see it perfectly well after you have spotted it, so ob-serving must involve more than just looking. The truly remarkable thing is that although people have looked at camouflaged animals since the dawn of history, no one recognized the existence of a general concept. It took the keen mind of Gerald Thayer's father, Abbott Thayer, a painter of angels and women and a dabbler in natural history, to understand the meaning of camouflage. Thayer's contribution to evolutionary theory was significant enough to earn him a place alongside Charles Darwin and Alfred Russel Wallace (the codiscoverer of natural selection) and Henry Bates and Fritz Müller (the two men who characterized mimicry) in the pantheon of those who have elucidated basic mechanisms of natural selection. Thayer also in-vented military camouflage.

The difference between passively looking and actively observing contin-ues to yield surprises in the hands of modern artists. The objects Jasper Johns paints — everyday things such as flashlights, light bulbs, and Ameri-can flags — are chosen precisely because it is so hard to *see* them. "What interested me was this," Johns says. "At a certain point I realized that certain things that were around me were things that I did not look at, but recognized. And recognized without looking at. So you recognize a flag is a flag, and it's very rare that you actually look at the surface of it to see what it is. This aspect of things interested me and I began to work with it, to see how I could look at things that I was accustomed to looking at, but not seeing." Johns's American flag series consists of various ghostlike apparitions and highly textured surfaces. By reiterating and altering an object we know so well, he forces us to look again, to think about what we see.

As Johns suggests, even artists have to learn how to observe, and many can recall a key moment when they learned the difference between looking and seeing. For the artist Georgia O'Keeffe, this moment occurred when an art teacher, during her second year of high school, brought to class a stunning purple jack-in-the-pulpit.

> Holding a Jack-in-the-pulpit high, she [the teacher] pointed out the strange shapes and variations in color — from the deep, and black earthy violet through all the greens, from the pale whitish green in the flower through the heavy green of the leaves. She held up the purplish hood and showed us the Jack inside. I had seen many Jacks before, but this was the first time I remember examining a flower. . . . She started me looking at things — looking very carefully at details. It was certainly the first time my attention was called to the outline and color of any growing thing with the idea of drawing or painting it.

The lesson was so powerful that O'Keeffe went on to see jacks, as well as other flowers, skulls, landscapes, and even skyscrapers in ways that no one had ever seen them before. Near the end of her life she distilled what she had learned about observing into a few sentences: "Still — in a way — nobody sees a flower — really — it is so small — we haven't the time — and to see takes time, like to have a friend takes time."

O'Keeffe's words are appropriate for observing in any field, for as the poet and arts advocate Herbert Read has written, observing "is almost entirely an acquired skill. It is true that certain individuals are born with an aptitude for concentrated attention, and for the eye-and-hand co-ordination involved in the act of recording what is observed. But in most cases the eye (and the other organs of sensation) have to be trained, both in observation (directed

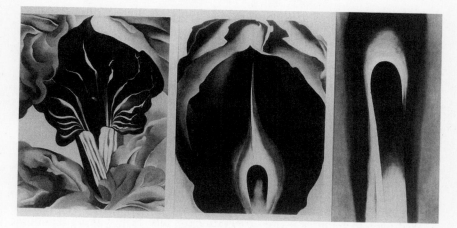

Fig. 3-2. *Left to right: Jack-in-the-Pulpit, No. 2; Jack-in-the Pulpit, No. 4;* and *Jack-in-the-Pulpit, No. 6* by Georgia O'Keeffe, 1930.

perception) and in notation." Such training takes what biologist Konrad Lorenz called "the patience of a yogi."

The patience to look and look again is therefore a trait that characterizes great artists. Pablo Picasso, renowned for his artistic abstractions, first learned as a young boy to draw realistically what he observed meticulously. "I recall my father saying to me, 'I am quite willing for you to become a painter, but you must not begin to paint until you are able to draw well, and that is very difficult.' Then he gave me a pigeon's foot to practise on. He came around later to look at my work and criticize it." The father, an art teacher who specialized in drawing pigeons, made his son draw the foot over and over. "At last the day came," Picasso continued, "when he gave me permission to go ahead and draw whatever I liked. . . . By the time I was fifteen I could do faces and figures and very large compositions — often without models — because, simply by practising on pigeons' feet, I had learned how to capture the mystery of lines, even of nudes." Having learned to observe one thing, he had learned the keys to observing and describing everything.

Artists past and present understand that manual facility is inextricably bound to observational prowess — and vice versa. In fact, many believe that what the hand cannot draw, the eye cannot see. This point was made by Henri Matisse, who taught himself to draw people in motion on the streets of Paris. He and a friend would sit outside and in just a few seconds try "to draw the silhouettes of passers-by, to discipline our line. We were forcing ourselves to discover quickly what was characteristic in a gesture, in an attitude." As Matisse knew well, observational facility was prized by his teacher, Eugène Delacroix. "If you are not skillful enough to sketch a man falling out of a window, during the time it takes him to get from the fifth storey to the ground," Delacroix is supposed to have said, "you will never be able to produce monumental work." Vincent van Gogh's goal, similarly, was to be able to draw "in such a way that it goes as easily as writing something down . . . to see in such a way that one can reproduce at will what one sees on a larger or smaller scale." The fact that van Gogh was able to produce some of his masterpieces within the space of a single afternoon demonstrates the acuity and facility he developed.

Writing also requires acute observational skills. E. E. Cummings once characterized himself as a "wily observer of everything-under-the-sun," and, according to John Dos Passos, as the two men walked about town "he [Cummings] would be noting down groups of words or scribbly sketches on bits of paper." Novelist W. Somerset Maugham believed similarly that "it is essential for a writer unceasingly to study men," and he meant not only their physical appearance but their conversation and their behavior. "You must be ready to listen for hours to the retailing of second-hand information," he advised, "in order at last to catch the hint or the casual remark that betrays." Indeed, according to writer Louise Morgan, Maugham was a "hunter" of human characters, interacting with people in much the way a scientist does experiments, to obtain more precise information. He was "winningly polite and attentive, but in an altogether impersonal way. . . . It is the sense of his catholic human interest that reconciles one to the scrutiny of his ruthless intelligence."

The importance of such observational powers in a writer should not surprise us. The development of a "true-seeming" plot depends upon a wide knowledge of how others respond to words, gestures, and deeds. The stimulation of sensation in the reader also depends upon an awareness of sensation in oneself. The writer not only lives experiences, he or she observes and analyzes them, too. The novelist Daphne Du Maurier once described a disturbing conversation she had in her teens when she suddenly realized she was operating on two planes of consciousness, one conversational and the other observational:

> Somewhere, buried in the unconscious of the eighteen-year-old, must have been the embryo writer observing, watching, herself un-

Fig. 3-3. *Women Picking Olives* by Vincent van Gogh.

moved, noting the changing moods of a woman [her schoolmis-
tress] dissatisfied with her mode of life and temporarily bored by her
young companion. The seed of an idea, sorting itself from others,
might take some five and twenty years or more to germinate and
come to the surface, fusing with later observations, these observations in turn blending with characters from long-forgotten books,
but finally a story or a novel would emerge.

Du Maurier's autobiographical volumes are, in fact, filled with events that
she witnessed, stored away in memory, and later transformed into the details
of her novels. A teenage crush on the much older Sir Basil Rathbone, for example, was worked into *Rebecca;* her homes, Ferryside and Menabilly, became the Manderley of that novel, and a real-life ship disaster that occurred
nearby provided the flavor and some of the details of the plot.

Observation is equally the bedrock of the sciences. And, like Georgia
O'Keeffe, many scientists believe that the secret to it lies in time and patience.
Karl von Frisch, who decoded the dance language of bees, wrote that his ability to observe came from simply lying "for hours between the cliffs, motion-
less, watching living things I could see on and between the slimy green stones

just below the surface of the water. I discovered that miraculous worlds may reveal themselves to a patient observer where the casual passer-by sees nothing at all." Konrad Lorenz, whose studies of geese, fish, and other animals revealed their hidden worlds, also commented on the need to indulge one's love of looking. "It is a pleasant urge. Those who have it want to look at animals, want to own them, to breed them. To really understand animals and their behavior you must have an esthetic appreciation of an animal's beauty. This endows you with the patience to look at them long enough to see something." Other scientists, such as geologist Nathaniel Shaler, at Harvard, were given exercises, much as Picasso was, that forced them to look at a specimen over and over until inobvious facts, for example, that in some fish the scale pattern differs on the two sides, became obvious.

However, simply looking, even patiently, is not sufficient. Part of seeing, as the camouflaged ptarmigan demonstrates, is knowing what to look at or for. Thus the real skill in hunting for fossils, according to paleontologist Elwyn Simons, is prompt and penetrating visual discrimination: "It's seeing order in a random background. . . . In the Egyptian desert where we hunt fossils, the desert surface is all covered with stones of all sorts and colours that have survived from wind erosion. It's called desert pavement or *serir* in Arabic . . . and if there's a bone with a tooth in it in that background it's not easy to see that in the pattern. I guess it's kind of comparable to some people who, if they're given a book in which some word occurs only once, can flip through and find it." Biologist Jared Diamond, an expert on tropical birds, believes that anyone who wishes to do fieldwork must "learn to . . . detect a bird just as a quick bit of motion that's different from the motion of a leaf in the treetops." Anyone who has gone bird watching in the woods, insect collecting through the fields, or fossil hunting on banks of shale will understand the point that he and Simons are making. Like Delacroix, Matisse, and van Gogh, scientific observers must learn to see the essence of things in an instant.

But observation, scientific and otherwise, goes well beyond the visual. As a scientist, Diamond depends greatly upon aural observation, too. "In the jungle in New Guinea, you hear most birds, you don't see them, and so you have to be good at identifying birds by sound. Since I'm musical, it happens that I have a good ear for bird sounds. . . . One morning I took [two colleagues] out into the rainforest. . . . We got out there before dawn, and by 7:30 A.M., I had identified fifty-seven bird species for them, but we had not yet seen a single bird." If this feat seems hard to believe, consider that composer Olivier Messiaen, who incorporated bird song into his music, could recognize at first hearing some 50 species of birds in his native France and another 550 species from around the world after a bit of reflection and consultation with his manuals. Most people learn to distinguish by sound at least fifty-seven different types of musical instruments and can identify all of their friends merely by their voice on the telephone. Professional musicians can even identify the "voices" of different examples of the same type of instrument. People who are deprived of sight — as Diamond was by the very density of the jungle — often do even better. The eighteenth-century novelist Henry Fielding had a sightless half-brother named John who, as a magistrate in London, was said to be able to identify more than three thousand criminals by their voices alone.

Being deprived of one sense can indeed sharpen our reliance on others, though not their actual acuity. We learn to use sensory stimuli that we usually ignore, and sometimes such heightened attention results in original insights. Biologist Geerat Vermeij's entire career is testimony to this fact. When Vermeij lost his sight as a very young boy, he was forced to rely upon his remaining senses. "The information they conveyed now meant something," he has written, "whereas previously I could afford to ignore it. My world was not black and hopeless. It sparkled as it did before, but now with sounds, odors, shapes, and textures. . . . Indeed, it is all these sensations that together provide a vivid, if nonvisual, picture of the world around me." Encouraged in his hobbies by family and teachers, Vermeij became particularly enamored of seashells and decided to become a professional conchologist. Now a professor of biology at the University of California at Davis, he makes frequent forays to the beaches of Africa, South America, and the South Pacific and is known worldwide for his evolutionary studies.

From the outset, Vermeij realized that his choice of profession required strong observational skills. "Much can be learned from books," he has noted, "but the knowledge thus gained is inevitably filtered through someone else's faculties. There simply is no substitute for making one's own observations in the wild." Vermeij replaced visual observation with tactile. "Observation by hand is particularly well suited to objects the size of most shells," he has noted, and it often leads to insights that can't be gained visually.

Vermeij's colleague Alfred Fischer remembers the day when Princeton professor Robert MacArthur was illustrating a lecture with the preserved skins of two birds. The birds looked virtually identical to sighted people, although one was from America and the other from Africa — an example of what evolutionary biologists call convergence. Vermeij, however, had no difficulty distinguishing them by touch. One of his secondary-school teachers had "felt strongly that we should know the shapes and characteristics of ducks, swans, owls, eagles, herons, gulls and other birds" by means of a collection of stuffed animals. "I don't find any resemblance," Vermeij said of MacArthur's specimens. "The beak and the feet are entirely different, and the very texture of the plumage sets them apart." So much for the objectivity of vision.

Vermeij has found that seashells hold secrets that only tactile observation can reveal. A sighted person will immediately observe that tropical shells tend to have bright coloration and intricate patterns, whereas shells from cold waters tend to be drab and unadorned. Vermeij, however, observes that tropical shells are chalky in texture while their cold-water cousins are hard and smooth. Why? he wonders. As Fischer says, Vermeij actually experiences shells differently from the rest of us: "Our eyes see mainly in two dimensions. Gary experiences form palpably in three dimensions, which provides him with a different, often advantageous perspective." Examples such as this should warn us against relying on any single sense as a basis for observation.

Fortunately, many disciplines train nonvisual observation skills. The nineteenth-century composer Robert Schumann believed that the ear's sensitivity to sound could be cultivated not only by musical training but by listening to everyday sounds. "Endeavor," he wrote to prospective students of music, "to distinguish tones and keys. The bell, the window pane, the cuckoo — seek to discover what tones they produce." Just as everyday visual observation can be useful to the artist, so aural observation can supply the musician with new musical ideas. Composer Georg Philipp Telemann recommended studying the improvisations of folk musicians, since "an observant person could pick up enough ideas from them in a week to last a lifetime." Many composers, including Zoltán Kodály, Béla Bartók, George Gershwin, Aaron Copland, and Darius Milhaud, not only observed folk musicians but perceived musical potentials in their themes that even their originators did not. Thus, Stravinsky argued that music itself, and modern music in particular, forces us to distinguish between hearing and listening in much the same way that modern art makes us look rather than simply see. "It obliges the *hearer* to become a *listener*, summons him to active relations with music." The hearing mind, like the seeing mind, must participate actively in observing.

Not surprisingly, looking and seeing, hearing and listening, have their equivalent in the distinction between passive movement and active motion in dance and other performing arts. Modern dance pioneer Doris Humphrey argued that the choreographer must be "a keen observer of physical and emotional behavior" and must have "a good eye and a sensitive ear" in order to create physical "images gleaned from close observation." "A dancer's art," agreed Martha Graham, "is built on an attitude of listening, with his whole being." Nor is this a skill to be practiced only in the studio, says dancer-choreographer Alwin Nikolais:

> In the final analysis the dancer is a specialist in the sensitivity to, the perception and the skilled execution of motion. Not movement but rather the qualified itinerary en route. The difference may be made even clearer by giving the example of two men walking from Hunter College to 42nd and Broadway [in New York]. One man may accomplish it totally unaware of and imperceptive to the trip, having his mind solely on the arrival. He has simply moved from one location to another. The other may, bright-eyed and bright-brained, observe and sense all thru which he passes. He has more than moved — he is in motion.

Actor-directors Konstantin Stanislavsky and Richard Boleslavsky argued similarly that the student of theater must, in Boleslavsky's words, learn "to notice everything unusual and out of the ordinary in every-day life. It builds . . . his sensory and muscular memory. . . . The only thing which can stimulate inspiration in an actor is constant and keen observation every day of his life."

Even smell and taste can have important roles in observation, as is clear in the cases of perfumers, aromatherapists, wine tasters, brewmasters, and chefs. Many other professionals also use these senses. Any baker can identify the pleasing smell of baker's yeast. It is less obvious that, as bacteriologist John Cairns admits, one of the attractions of his vocation is the smell of the bacterial colonies: "It is a rather nice smell. When you come into the laboratory in the morning there's this homely smell greeting you." In fact, many microorganisms can be identified by smell alone. One French microbiologist is famous among his colleagues for characterizing unknown cultures "by smell, sniffing at the culture tubes." You've done this sort of sleuthing yourself if you recognize the musty odor of mildew and the nauseating scent of rotten eggs. Chemists such as Primo Levi use their nose to identify chemicals, too. "I'm very glad that I educated my nose," Levi quipped once. Ecologist Tom Eisner agrees, having made dozens of discoveries by sniffing out the sometimes attractive, sometimes pungent chemical communication and defense systems of insects. "I'm essentially a nose with a human being attached," he jokes, noting that his father was a perfumer who taught him the importance of olfactory observation in their "redolent basement." Eisner even admits that as a child he would sniff strangers on meeting them, a habit some physicians, such as those at the Monell Chemical Senses Center in Philadelphia, also use for diagnostic purposes. Odors are clues to medical conditions as various as stress, which increases body odor; yeast infections; diabetic ketosis, in which the breath smells like acetone; and kidney disease, in which a person's breath may smell fishy from the buildup of ammonia-like compounds. We ignore such information at our peril.

Taste, too, can be diagnostic. Ancient physicians made a practice of tasting patients' pus and urine, which led to the discovery thousands of years ago that the urine of diabetics is sweet. Doctors nowadays verify this symptom with simple chemical tests, but as bacteriologist W. E. B. Beveridge recounted in *The Art of Scientific Investigation,* the old way still works: "A Manchester physician, while teaching a ward class of students, took a sample of diabetic urine and dipped a finger in it to taste it. He then asked all the students to repeat his action. This they reluctantly did, making grimaces, but agreeing that it tasted sweet. 'I did this,' said the physician with a smile, 'to teach you the importance of observing detail. If you had watched me carefully you would have noticed that I put my first finger in the urine but licked my second finger!'"

Of course, no physician today would dare put a body fluid of another individual in his or her mouth for diagnostic purposes, but taste is still sometimes used, purposefully or accidentally, in the laboratory and out in the field. One archeologist claims to be able to "date any Roman aqueduct by the flavor on her tongue of its crumbling masonry — she had tasted them all." Chemists discovered both saccharin and aspartame when they accidentally splashed these substances into their mouth or licked their fingers and realized how sweet their work really was.

The keenest observers make use of every kind of sensory information. In fact, the greatest insights often come to individuals who are able to appreciate the "sublimity of the mundane," the deeply surprising and meaningful beauty in everyday things. How many times have you gotten into the bathtub without really seeing that the water level rises? It took Archimedes to notice and connect the displacement of water with the density of objects. How many times have you hammered on something without really hearing the sound it makes? It took Pythagoras listening to blacksmiths at work to recognize the connection between the length of an object and its pitch, whether the material is an iron bar, the wooden bar of a marimba, or the string on a cello. And how many times have you looked at the sky and wondered why it is blue? This question led the eighteenth-century physicist John Tyndall to discover that the color of the sky is caused by light scattering caused by dust and other particles. He developed some of the techniques we use today to measure air pollution and water purity.

Biochemist Albert Szent-Györgyi discovered vitamin C by means of some equally mundane observations: "I suppose I was led by my fascination by colors. I still like colors; they give me a childish pleasure. I started with the question, 'Why does a banana turn brown when I hurt it?'" It turned out that plants have compounds called polyphenols that interact with oxygen to create the brown or black color — their equivalent of a scab. This observation led Szent-Györgyi to his next: "There are two categories of plants, you see — those that turn black on being damaged and those in which there is no color change. . . . Why no color in some damaged plants?" The answer was that those plants contained vitamin C, a sugarlike compound that prevents oxygen from oxidizing the polyphenols into brown or black protective compounds. You can actually gauge the vitamin C content of different fruits fairly accurately simply by noting which ones turn brown when damaged (for example, bananas) and which do not (oranges, say).

Discovering the sublimity of the mundane is not limited to scientific observers. Much of modern art has focused on rethinking the value of everyday phenomena. "The true creator," Stravinsky wrote, "may be recognized by his ability always to find about him, in the commonest and humblest thing, items worthy of note." In his pioneering choreographic work, dancer Merce Cunningham explored small-scale movements "found by watching people out the window of the studio in the street. . . . They were, mostly, movements anyone does when getting set to do a larger movement." Even awkward gestures have a beauty of expression begging to be discovered and exploited. Dancer Anna Halprin voiced the logical extreme of this view when she said, "Anybody's a dancer to me at any time when I am involved in communicating with that person through his movement." Mark Morris has made dances using everyday movements such as the gum-chewing, swagger-walking, ball-handling moves of a teenager on a basketball court. Morris makes us realize that all movement has a beauty and that everything has a meaning that is not necessarily obvious.

This is certainly the point of René Magritte's now classic painting "The Treason of Images" (1928–29), which depicts a pipe, with the written message "Ce n'est pas une pipe" (This is not a pipe). The apparent contradiction draws attention to the fact that the painting is not the thing itself any more than the word "pipe" is itself a pipe. For centuries Western art has had as its

Fig. 3-4. *Tea Bag* by Claes
Oldenburg, 1966. "I often
drop the bags I use when
drinking tea, and the effect
is that of a 'print.' . . .
I always try to establish
a corresponding effect
outside of art for what I
do in art."

goal a trompe l'oeil realism in which the retinal image created by the two-dimensional representation is identical to that cast by the three-dimensional reality. Nevertheless, the visual image is only a sign, not nature itself. Marcel Duchamp's "ready mades" — unaltered objects such as a snow shovel and a urinal — were an even more shocking reobservation of art. Think about what you see, his found objects say. Think most about what you tend to think about least. Many people claimed that Duchamp's objects simply poked fun at hundreds of years of artistic technique and development. Duchamp himself said, "I wanted to put painting once again at the service of the mind." If you bring your mind to it, you can see his point. In his wake, many artists, such as Jasper Johns and Claes Oldenburg, have asked us to look at flags, forks, plates, hamburgers, baseball bats, and tea-bag stains, not as everyday items but as things to be observed.

Observing, and rendering what we observe in some way, is indeed a function of the mind. We cannot focus our attention unless we know what to look at and how to look at it. As Harvard psychologist Rudolf Arnheim said in his 1969 book *Visual Thinking,* "The cognitive operations called thinking are not the privilege of mental processes above and beyond perception but the essential ingredients of perception itself." Consider an example. One day, preparing to go jogging, one of us (Bob) went to our closet for his typical name-brand white running shoes. On the closet floor he saw black dress shoes, brown shoes, sandals, pumps, slippers — everything except the running shoes. Clearly he must have put them somewhere else without thinking. But where? Then, just as he was about to ransack other closets, search under the beds, and crawl under the couch, the answer struck him. He was searching for something white, but the soles of his shoes were black! Instantly the shoes appeared, right where he had left them, invisible to a mind looking for something white. What he thought his shoes "looked like" influenced his ability to observe.

The mind's preconceptions can alter our other perceptual sensations, too. A simple example can be found in *Zap Science,* produced by the Exploratorium science museum of San Francisco. On page three of this stimulating book is a picture of a pizza covered with a removable piece of plastic labeled: "Mystery smell. Peel off and replace." The picture conjures in most people's minds the taste and smell of pizza. But, as the text says, "It doesn't smell like a pizza does it? It smells like . . . like . . . like . . . How come you can't think of the answer? Because we crossed up your mental wires. We put a picture of a pizza with the smell of a chocolate chip cookie. Messes up your brain." In fact, many who encounter the pizza picture find the cookie smell nauseating even though they like both pizza and chocolate chip cookies separately. Our mental expectations mediate perception just as certainly for touch, taste, smell, and hearing as for vision.

Because the "mind's senses" that control the "senses of the body" skew and filter what we experience, objective observation is not possible. As the novelist John Steinbeck and biologist Edward Ricketts wrote in their book on the marine life of Mexico's Sea of Cortez, "We knew that what we would see and record and construct would be warped, as all knowledge patterns are warped, first, by the collective pressure and stream of our time and race, second by the thrust of our individual personalities." Even in writing a nonfiction book, they understood that their version of the "truth" was just as subject to their preconceptions as was any novel. The same is undoubtedly true of this book. Our observations about what is significant about thinking are certainly filtered through our own mental biases and experiences.

So observing is a form of thinking, and thinking is a form of observing. In consequence, the purpose in practicing observation is to link sensory experience and mental awareness as closely as possible. As sculptor Beverly Pepper said, "I could draw anything, but drawing doesn't make you an artist. . . . Art is in your head. It's how you think, and what you think." Similarly, biochemist Szent-Györgyi argued, "Discovery consists of seeing what everybody has seen and thinking what nobody has thought." Observing is making sense of sensation.

Thus the mind must be trained to observe just as much as we train the eyes, the ears, the nose, or the hands. Clues as to how to do this come from one of the greatest fictional observers of all time: Sherlock Holmes, the violin-playing detective who, like a perfect artist, could size up a situation or an individual with a moment's glance. Holmes, the brainchild of physician Sir Arthur Conan Doyle, was based on the author's extraordinary pathology professor, Dr. Joseph Bell of the Edinburgh Infirmary. Bell was reputedly a man with the same wide learning, visual acuity, and deductive prowess of his fictional alter ego. It is therefore worth listening to Doyle when he has Watson say to Holmes in "The Greek Interpreter," "In your case, . . . from all that you have told me, it seems obvious that your faculty of observation and your peculiar facility for deduction are due to your own systematic training." The reader knows that this is true in part, because Watson explains in many of the novels and stories that Holmes relentlessly studied everything from types of tobacco and ink to poisons and soils, not to mention as many examples of the criminal mind as he could find. His mind was actively prepared to observe what his eyes saw, just as Bell's intense pathology studies prepared him to diagnose unusual causes of disease and death. But Holmes demurs. "To some extent," he answers Watson. "But, none the less, my turn that way is in my veins, and may have come with my grandmother who was the sister of Vernet, the French artist. Art in the blood is liable to take the strangest forms."

Indeed, there may be something to Doyle's tacit hypothesis that the arts train observational skills. As Herbert Read documented in his 1943 classic, *Education Through Art,* and as Maurice Brown and Diana Korzenik demonstrated in *Art Making and Education* (1993), teaching the visual arts has always been justified to some extent by its utility for increasing visual awareness. Some contemporary artists, such as Jasper Johns, continue to grant the arts such a role today: "Part of the activity of art is one of exercise, and an activity that keeps faculties lively, whatever the discipline touches on: the mind, the ear, whatever. And one hopes that by sharpening of such things and by an attempt to see the possibilities that are offered . . . that the senses we use in dealing with our lives will be in a state of readiness to deal with whatever may happen."

Personal accounts confirm this view. Louise Morgan once commented to artist and novelist Wyndham Lewis, "Your painting must help your writing." "It must of course do that," answered Lewis: "The habit of thinking of things in plastic and pictorial terms must have its influence upon the writer's art, when you practise both as I do. First of all, I *see!* The first — and last — thing that I do is to use my eyes. . . . The art of draughtsmanship is in the fullest sense a scientific study — it should help the writer of fiction. Anything that trains the mind to close observation should do that." Vladimir Nabokov similarly commented on the dramatic influence that learning to draw had upon his zoological and literary endeavors. The most rigorous of his drawing teachers, he recalled,

> made me depict from memory, in the greatest possible detail, objects I had certainly seen thousands of times without visualizing them properly: a street lamp, a postbox, the tulip design on the stained glass of our own front door. He tried to teach me to find the geometrical coordinations between the slender twigs of a leafless boulevard tree, a system of visual give-and-takes, requiring a precision of linear expression, which I failed to achieve in my youth, but applied gratefully, in my adult instar, not only to the drawing of butterfly genitalia during my seven years at the Harvard Museum of Comparative Zoology . . . but also, perhaps, to certain camera-lucida needs of literary composition.

It is not by accident, we conclude, that so many poets and novelists have had training in the visual arts, including William Blake, J. W. von Goethe, William Makepeace Thackeray, G. K. Chesterton, Thomas Hardy, the Brontë sisters, Mikhail Lermontov, Alfred, Lord Tennyson, George Du Maurier, Theodore H. White, J. R. R. Tolkein, Bruno Schulz, Ludwig Bemelmans, Henry Miller, and E. E. Cummings. Even when a writer's interest in the arts is limited to the observation of forms and styles rather than active practice, as in the poet Robert Lowell's case, "that study seemed rather close to poetry. And from there I began."

Numerous scientists have also advocated art as a way to train observation, reiterating the theme that "that which has not been drawn has not been seen." As Santiago Ramón y Cajal, the great turn-of-the-century neuroanatomist, explained, "If our study is concerned with an object related to natural history, etc., observation will be accompanied by sketching; for aside from other advantages, the act of depicting something disciplines and strengthens attention, obliging us to cover the whole of the phenomenon. . . . It is not without reason [therefore] that all great observers are skillful in sketching." Sir Francis Seymour Haden agreed completely. Not only was he one of the leading anatomists of his day, he was also the founder of the British Royal Society of Painter-Etchers and Engravers. Haden made all of his anatomy students study art (just as the artists of the time had to learn anatomy) to develop both observational and manipulative skills: "How much sooner would the eye learn to gauge the aberrations as the signs that make up the *facies* [the general appearances characteristic] of the disease," he wrote. "How much better would the hand trained to portray them accurately be able to direct with precision and safety the course of the knife."

Indeed, many of our greatest scientists had formal art training, including Louis Pasteur, Joseph Lister, Frederick Banting, Charles Best, Albert Michelson, Sir W. Lawrence and Sir W. Henry Bragg, Mary Leakey, Desmond Morris, Konrad Lorenz, and Bert Holldobler. Although classes in drawing for scientists and doctors are much rarer today than in the past, there is still widespread recognition that, in the words of physician Edmund Pellegrino, "The clinician's craft begins with the eye — his essential diagnostic tool. . . . Clinician and artist are united in their need for a special visual awareness. Each sees; but for each, sight must transcend appearances. As Paul Klee puts it: 'Art does not render the visible; it makes visible.' The clinician must penetrate beneath the images to comprehend what ails the patient."

The observational benefits of training in the arts do not stop with painting or drawing. Writing and reading literature can be valuable for those who deal with people, whether in the social, legal, or medical professions. Physician John Stone points to the dual medical/writing careers of such fiction masters as Arthur Conan Doyle, François Rabelais, Anton Chekhov, John Keats, Somerset Maugham, A. J. Cronin, and William Carlos Williams. Many physicians, such as Oliver Sacks and Jonathan Miller, excel as nonfiction writers. "Physicians and writers," Stone argues, "draw on the same source: the human encounter, people and their indelible stories. And the works of both depend on skillful use of the senses. As with [Sherlock] Holmes, success rests with the powers of observation. . . . Literature, indeed, can have a kind of laboratory function. . . . The medical ear must be properly trained to hear stories — a medical history, after all, is a short story." "I believe that the writing of poems makes me a better medical practitioner," says physician-poet

Jack Coulehan. "Poetry demands a style of seeing and responding that enhances my ability to form therapeutic bonds with patients."

Observational skills can also be nurtured by the study of music. Recall that Jared Diamond attributed his ability to identify bird songs to his musical training. Other bird watchers have trained their ears by listening over and over again to recordings of bird songs, comparing and contrasting until very subtle differences become apparent. Indeed, the publisher of the Peterson Field Guides has issued several volumes of *Birding by Ear* — audiocassettes designed to teach identification of birds solely by their calls. A great deal of research shows that the ear must be trained to hear just as carefully as the eye to see. Musicians tell us that although some people are born with perfect pitch, it can also be acquired through practice. And the music critic knows that only by listening to innumerable performances and by comparing, comparing, comparing can one begin to observe the subtleties of style and quality that differentiate the greatest performers from the merely competent. Studies of physicians have even found that those who are best able to draw useful information from using a stethoscope or palpating (thumping a patient's chest and abdomen) are those who have had musical training or who actively practice their listening skills. Some cardiologists play high-fidelity recordings of different heart anomalies as they drive from one place to another.

The art-improves-scientific-observation equation works in reverse as well. Writers and artists can often benefit from the careful study of natural history, medicine, or anatomy. Somerset Maugham once averred that "no education was more useful to the writer than a curriculum of medical study. Not only will he *see* human nature in the raw and all that sort of thing in the outpatients' rooms, but he will get enough science for his purpose as a writer so that he won't be entirely ignorant of a side of life that is most important in this age." Poet Marianne Moore, who majored in biology at Bryn Mawr, also felt that her scientific training influenced her work: "Did laboratory studies affect my poetry? I am sure they did. I found the biology courses — minor, major and histology — exhilarating. I thought, in fact, of studying medicine. Precision, economy of statement, logic employed to ends that are disinterested, drawing and identifying, liberate — at least have some bearing on — the imagination it seems to me."

For all these reasons we advocate explicit observational exercises in classes in every subject. All students need to develop sensory acuity. Some museums conceal natural or artificial objects in cloth-covered holes and ask the visitor to observe and identify them by touch alone, and such exercises can be adapted to home and classroom. Blindfolded, we can find out about things by feeling and smelling them, as Geerat Vermeij does, observing the bark, leaves, flowers, seeds, and nuts of trees, the feathers of birds, seashells, different types of cloth, buttons, and dozens of other common things. We can guess at the identity of objects sealed in small boxes by observing their weight, the way they roll, bounce, or slide inside the box, and the sounds they make when the box is shaken. We can learn what it means to really smell and really taste herbs and spices without seeing them. Another simple exercise is to close one's eyes and construct what is going on nearby through sound alone. Walking around in the dark also tunes a person in to the sense of space and the sense of touch. Listening to television without looking at it or, conversely, watching with the sound off is also an educational experience in observing; all too often either the visual aspect or the sound is irrelevant.

Collecting things, whether stamps, coins, insects, buttons, baseball cards, postcards, books, photographs, prints, or paintings, is another excellent way to improve visual observation. The serious collector learns to make finer and finer distinctions in variation and quality, thus training both the eyes and the mind to acquire and evaluate knowledge. You can train your other senses by collecting rocks, shells, feathers, bones, fabrics, yarns, and fountain pens that appeal to the sense of touch. You can record bird songs or other animal sounds in your backyard, in the woods, at the zoo. Or collect city sounds, folk songs, rock music, or jazz. Keep mental lists of smells at the perfume counter or the grocery store. Learning to identify cheeses or chocolates or coffees or teas or wines from taste and smell alone is no simple feat.

We also need practice in noting the sublimity of the mundane. Like an actor studying with Stanislavsky or Boleslavsky, "collect all of your attention." Select an object, notice its form, its lines, its colors, its sounds, its tactile characteristics, its smell, perhaps even its taste. Then remove the object and recall one by one as many details as possible. Write about what you perceived or draw it. Go back and observe it again. "Such an effort," Stanislavsky wrote, "causes you to observe the object more closely, more effectively, in order to appreciate it and define its qualities." Or, like Picasso and Shaler, observe and describe the same object again and again, over a period of days, weeks, even months, refining your vision through practice.

And so we return to our opening exercise, describing a television. Look at your notes and ask yourself how much you missed the first time. Are all your descriptions visual, as they are for most people, or did you think to observe more broadly? Did you observe the sounds of the TV set: the clicks of the buttons; the odd *poing* as the tube is turned on or off; the tiny crackles as the static built up on the screen? What can you tell about the materials and construction of the TV by tapping it in various places? What about smells: the ozonelike whiff of the electric charge and the odor of warm electronic components, perhaps the scent of new plastic? Did you feel the TV? How do the textures of the different components differ? Did you notice the way the hairs on your arm or head stand up from the static electricity formed when the screen is being turned on or off? How do the sound reverberations feel? Can you distinguish the different operations of the buttons by touch? And how close to the set did you get when you looked at it? Close enough to see the tiny red, green, and blue dots that form the images? (Wet your finger with water and flick a little on the screen to form miniature magnifying lenses.) Did you notice that the height of the screen divided by its diagonal is very close to the golden mean (0.616: 1.000)? Did you see how the screen distorts and alters the shape and colors of your reflected image when the power is off? Are you an acute enough observer to have drawn or noted these things down in the time it takes a TV to fall from a window on the fifth floor?

There is so much to perceive in a mundane object like a television set that only by patient cultivation of ever-new ways of observing will you discover the possibilities. As artist and choreographer Oskar Schlemmer realized in 1942, near the end of his life, observing is a skill that returns ever more, the more you invest in it. "I have recently completed a series of pictures, inspired by what I see right around me: views from my window into its neighboring window, done in the evening between nine and half-past nine shortly before the blackout. When night is falling and clashes with the scraps of interior beige-orange-brown-white-black, it produces amazing optical effects. I am experiencing with unfamiliar intensity the mystic effects of nature, and I observe that with the passing years one keeps learning to see in new and different ways." If one of the objects of education is to produce lifelong learners, what better recommendation for practicing the skill of observation could one want?

4

Imaging

THE NAME CHARLES STEINMETZ is not as well known as that of Alexander Graham Bell or Thomas Edison, yet his impact on modern life is as great. Steinmetz was the inventor of electrical generators, transformers, and other equipment that made possible the general distribution of electricity. Because of him, Bell's telephones and Edison's light bulbs became common household items. Colleagues at General Electric who knew his contributions intimately called Steinmetz "the Supreme Court" because, in their view, problems he couldn't solve were simply impossible. So in 1894 a couple of engineers approached him with a puzzler they had unsuccessfully worked on for weeks: "If you take a rod two inches in diameter and cut it [in half] by drilling a two-inch hole through it, what is the cubic content of the metal that's removed?" The problem was important; for any cost-conscious company, drilling holes in expensive metals means wasted material and monetary loss.

As the story goes, these men expected Steinmetz to sit down at his desk, pull out some paper, draw some figures, and begin a series of lengthy calculations. His first concern, they knew, would be to determine the shape of the core removed by the drill, which they had been unable to do. It isn't a ball and it isn't a rod; it's a sort of lozenge. Without knowing the shape, you can't figure out its dimensions or calculate its cubic content. Steinmetz's colleagues had every faith in him, but even they were surprised when the Supreme Court simply took a few extra puffs of his cigar and said, "The answer, gentlemen, is 5.33 cubic inches." Amazingly, he had seen the whole thing — the shape of the plug that would be produced, its dimensions, and the subsequent calculations — in his head.

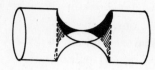

Fig. 4-1. The shape of the rod and hole imagined by Steinmetz.

Steinmetz had an extraordinary ability to visualize — to imagine the look of things not physically before his eyes. He shared this ability with other people of great accomplishment, such as his colleague and competitor Nikola Tesla, inventor of the first workable alternating-current motors and generators. Tesla related in his autobiography, "When I get an idea I start at once building it up in my imagination. I change the construction, make improvements and operate the device in my mind. It is absolutely immaterial to me whether I run my turbine in my thought or test it in my shop. *I even note if it is out of balance.*" More recently Elmer Sperry, the inventor of gyroscopic stabilizers and related mechanisms for ships and airplanes, has been described as typically "just looking into the air, when all at once he would pick up a pad and hold it at arm's length, then with a pencil in the other hand he would begin to draw. . . . 'It's there! Don't you see it! Just draw a line around what you see.'"

Inventor James Lovelock, best known for inventing the concept that the earth is a single interconnected organism, is also a skilled visual imager. Lovelock's interest in integrative systems began when he invented an ultra-sensitive instrument capable of analyzing the chemistry of atmospheric changes caused by living processes. Lovelock, like Tesla, credits his success to visual imagination: "What I tend to do is to wake about five in the morning — this happens quite often — think about the invention, and then image it in my mind in 3D, as a kind of construct. Then I do experiments with the image. . . . Sort of rotate it, and say, 'well what'll happen if one does this?' And by the time I get up for breakfast I can usually go to the bench and make a string and sealing wax model that works straight off, because I've done most of the experiments already."

Not surprisingly, numerous studies have found significant correlations between the aptitude for visual imaging and career success in engineering. Historian Brook Hindle described the role of visual imaging in his 1981 book *Emulation and Invention,* an examination of the invention process of men such as Samuel Morse and Robert Fulton — both of whom, significantly, were excellent professional painters. In *Engineering and the Mind's Eye* (1992) engineer Eugene Ferguson argues that nonverbal imagery plays a central role in invention in general, as does Henry Petroski in his 1996 book *Invention by Design*. Indeed, imaging benefits people in all professions.

Psychologists now recognize three basic types of visual thinkers. To determine what kind of visual thinker you are, try imagining a triangle. Do whatever it takes to image that shape in your mind. How did you do it? Some people cannot "see" a triangle in their minds until they draw it on a piece of paper or trace its outline on a table with the end of their finger. Some people need to close their eyes, apparently because seeing interferes with their visual imagination. When their eyes are closed, however, they can "project" the triangle on the inside of their eyelids. Did your eyeballs move as you drew the triangle? Some rare individuals can bring up the image of the triangle with their eyes open, superimposing the triangle on whatever they are looking at. A subset of this latter group can make the triangle change size, color, and perspective; they can make it twirl, jump, and pass through other figures. Steinmetz and Tesla clearly fell into this last category.

Triangles are simple, however. For those who really want to take a shot at Steinmetz's and Tesla's "thought," consider some additional problems that require the mental construction of three-dimensional visual images:

A. What object has a round profile from the top and from the sides?
B. What object has a square profile from the top and the sides?
C. What object has a triangular profile from all sides?

If you answered sphere, cube, and tetrahedron, you're on the right track. Keep going!

D. What object has a round profile from the top and square profiles from the sides?
E. What object has a square profile from the top and triangular profiles from the sides?
F. What object has a triangular profile from the top and square profiles from the sides?
G. What object has a round profile from the top and triangular profiles from the sides?

And now, for the really skilled visual thinkers, some more complex shapes.

H. What object has a round profile from the top, a round profile from one side, and a square profile from the other?

I. What object has a triangular profile from the top and circular profiles from the sides?
J. What object has a circular profile from the top, triangular from one side, and square from the other?

In case you are wondering, all of these objects do exist (even the last one) and we offer some of the possible answers as figures at the end of the chapter. In fact, H — an object that is square from one side and round from the others — describes the shape of the plug drilled out of the rod that Steinmetz had to imagine. The rod is round; the drill is round; but a vertical section of the plug viewed lengthwise along the rod is square. We strongly suspect that Steinmetz solved his rod problem with ease because he had played the kind of visual game we have just demonstrated and already knew the answer.

By visualizing various combinations of squares, rectangles, circles, ellipses, and many-sided polygons, you can generate every basic geometric solid that exists. And if you like this sort of thing you can try more complicated imaging problems, such as those proposed by Max Wertheimer in his 1959 book *Productive Thinking*. But if you find such exercises difficult, don't despair. Although some people have a greater proclivity for visual imaging than others, everyone benefits from practice. So even if you need to draw images or model them at first, working with these problems will train your visualizing ability. The more you practice, the more you will be able to partake of and understand the visual thinking process of countless inventors, mathematicians, physicists, artists, writers, and dancers.

Imaging, in its broadest sense, is a common thinking tool in many fields. Indeed, there is a statistically significant correlation between professional success and visual thinking among scientists as well as inventors. Ann Roe, who pioneered the study of visual thinking in scientists, reported that one of her famous subjects — probably her husband, George Gaylord Simpson — saw all of evolution in his mind as if it were a motion picture. Nobel laureate and biologist François Jacob reported that he began each day by mentally recreating his room, then his house, then his neighborhood, and eventually the entire world while lying in his bed with his eyes shut. Sir James Black, a pharmacologist and Nobel Prize winner, says that the focus of his thinking "is an imaginative sense, entirely open-ended and entirely pictorial. That is a vital part of my life. I daydream like mad. . . . You can have all these [chemical] structures in your head, turning and tumbling and moving." Another Nobelist, chemist Peter Debye, has written that "I can only think in pictures." Richard Feynman also noted the elaborate visions in his mind. "It's all visual," he explained to one interviewer. "[I see] the character of the answer, absolutely. An inspired method of picturing, I guess." As Feynman made clear, he worked at refining the visual image *as the answer to a problem* well before translating his solution into mathematical equations. "Ordinarily I try to get the pictures clearer, but in the end the mathematics can take over and be more efficient in communicating the idea of the picture. In certain particular problems that I have done [however] it was necessary to continue the development of the picture as the method before the mathematics could really be done." Similarly, astrophysicist Margaret Geller of the Harvard-Smithsonian Center for Astrophysics has said, "I think that not all scientists have to have a visual image, but I do. I can't do a problem unless I have a visual image. That's how I solve problems."

For many people, including scientists, being a good visualizer ties in with being artistic. Geller, for example, says, "I'm also generally visual. I'm very aware of visual cues in my environment. I have a good visual memory, and I am very observant. So it's not so separate from the way I am in general. I have an interest in the visual arts. I think that had I not been a scientist, I probably would have done something in design." Geller is far from rare among scientists in manifesting both visual ability and an interest in the arts, as we noted in Chapter 3. In fact, in a study of forty scientists, including several Nobel laureates, we found a high correlation between artistic avocation, visual thinking ability, and scientific success. Those who visualize well in their science often visualize in artistic pursuits as well, each activity feeding the other.

Not surprisingly, artists of all sorts also depend upon visual imaging. This may seem obvious in the case of painters, who express themselves with color, line, and form, but not all painters refer as explicitly as Georgia O'Keeffe did to their mental imaging of these elements. Shortly after meeting the photographer Paul Strand, O'Keeffe wrote to him that "I believe I've been looking at things and seeing them as I thought you might photograph them — Isn't that funny — making Strand photographs in my head." Ansel Adams's entire process of photography also relied on imagining what the final print would look like before the negative was ever exposed. But visual imaging in art is not necessarily tied to pictorial expression. It may deal with visual aspects of movement, for instance, or verbal description. According to the American choreographer Anna Sokolow, the dancer's visualizing "in terms of movement" was analogous to the painter's visualizing "in terms of color, line, mass." Countless of Martha Graham's students (and Sokolow was one of them) have described her teaching and composing as "flooded with imagery" meant to "awaken our imagination" and "guide the quality of the movement." Stuart Hodes, who studied and taught with Graham for many years, recalls her urging students to see "the French film *Farrabique,* a story of birth and death on a French family farm. She particularly wanted us to notice the stop-motion sequences of plants growing. 'Watch how they spiral upward toward the sun,' she said. 'Life flows along a spiral path.' Soon I noticed that spirals were being emphasized in many of our technical moves and introduced into others."

Imaging is also an important tool for thinking among writers. Poet Stephen Spender, who described writing poems as working through the "logic of the images," found that his poems often began with "a very vivid memory, usually visual, which suggests that it could be realized in concentrated written language." As we discussed in Chapter 1, such imagistic thinking is common among poets. Dryden declared that "imaging is in itself the very height and life of poetry," while the dreamy visionary Samuel Coleridge wrote to one friend that "a whole essay might be written on the danger of thinking without images." And Siegfried Sassoon said, "Thinking in pictures is my natural method of self-expression. I have always been a submissively visual writer." More recently, Pulitzer Prize–winner Donald Murray discovered by using himself "as an experimental rat" that he was not the "linguistic" thinker he had always supposed. Rather, he found his thinking to be "imagistic, a process of seeing, then recording the language."

Many writers of fiction are visualizers. Charles Dickens declared that he simply "saw" his stories and then wrote them down. By the same token, Tennessee Williams said that *A Streetcar Named Desire* originated from a single image: "I simply had the vision of a woman in her late youth. She was sitting in a chair all alone by a window with the moonlight streaming in on her desolate face, and she'd been stood up by the man she planned to marry." Vladimir Nabokov had a photographic memory, which allowed him in student days to absorb reading assignments in a matter of minutes. Later he would imagine, step by step, every aspect of his life, from the daily errands run by his mother when he was a child to the behavior of his characters and the unfolding of plot.

Indeed, as we noted in Chapter 3, it is not uncommon for writers who are also professional or amateur artists to foresee literally the action of a book. Thackeray, for example, made notes for his books not only in writing but with pencil and brush, as did the Brontë sisters, Antoine de Saint-Exupéry, Edward Lear, George Du Maurier, Wyndham Lewis, D. H. Lawrence, and J. R. R. Tolkien. G. K. Chesterton actually cartooned the action he wished to

Fig. 4-2. *Enraged Gentleman and His Victim,* sketches for a story, by G. K. Chesterton.

put into words, as his sketches for "Enraged Gentleman and His Victim" show. In the early stages of planning *Tropic of Capricorn,* Henry Miller, another artistic writer, visually charted the book's themes and events. And Marianne Moore, who went to college intending to become a painter, discovered she liked writing poetry and plays even better, especially since she "could visualize scenes." Imaging obviously goes beyond seeing simple geometric forms to recreating people and environments.

Clearly, inventors, scientists, and artists of all kinds find visualizing to be an important thinking tool. But conjuring visual images is only one of many types of imaging. In their 1990 book *Images and Understanding,* Horace Barlow, Colin Blakemore, and Miranda Weston-Smith make the point that images may be perceived and communicated not just as pictures, but in many other, nonvisual ways: "Artists, designers and engineers share an age-old problem, how to move facts and ideas from one mind to another: how are these mental transfusions achieved? Through the use of *images* — not just in the form of pictures and diagrams but with words, demonstrations, even music and dance." We not only see with the mind's eye, we hear with the mind's ear, imagine smells and tastes and body feelings — and any or all of these sensation pictures may be involved in the imagination and communication of images. To put it another way, if we observe with our eyes, we form a visual image. If we observe with our hands, we form a tactile as well as a hand-position, hand-movement image. If we observe with our nose, we form a smell image that may play a major role in scientific or artistic invention. What we can observe, we can imagine; what we imagine, we image.

Despite the fact that people use a wide range of images in their professional work, very little research exists documenting nonvisual imaging abilities, especially those involving smell and taste. Occasionally a perfumer discusses the smell ideas that went into a perfume. Occasionally a master chef like Charlie Trotter or Pierre Hermé reveals that the "finished taste" of a dish is cooked up in the imagination before it is cooked up in the kitchen. "When I create a cake," says Hermé, "I put the flavors and texture together in my mind. . . . I already know what it will taste like before it comes out of the oven." Occasionally a writer finds "the actual idea of a novel," as Nabokov put it, springing from "such actual sensations as the melting of a biscuit on the tongue or the roughness of a pavement underfoot." That the evidence of smell and taste imaging is meager only means that we tend to privilege vision over these senses in our imagination, as we do in observing things. The case for thinking in nonvisual images is much stronger for kinesthetic body imaging, explored in Chapter 9, and for aural imaging, considered here.

The same simple "test" that determines visual imaging capabilities can be applied to aural imaging. Can you "hear" the scream of Edvard Munch's image? Do you hear anything when you read: "Twinkle, twinkle little star"? Do the words sound in your mind? Do you hear a certain melody? Now try to

Fig. 4-3. An example of aural imaging. Cartoon by Tom Thaves.

Frank and Ernest

hear a scale of notes in your head. "Do, re, mi, fa, sol, la , ti, do." Did you hear silently? Did you have to hum or sing to get started? No doubt you are reading in a fairly quiet environment. Do you think you could hear the scale of notes with the radio on or at a crowded party? If you're one of those who have little "pure" aural imagery and have to hum a song or play the notes on an instrument to recreate sounds or tunes in your mind, you are in good company. As Aaron Copland pointed out, "The layman's capacity for imagining unheard sound images seems, by and large, to be rather poor." Few of us can read a musical score and hear the music in our minds. Casual musicians may be able to create a reliable internal image of music that they have played before. People without musical training may hear much less.

Some people, however, have no trouble hearing both notes and the words that go with them. And some, like those who can see triangles change color, move, and so forth, are able to hear the tune backward as well as forward, in different keys and different rhythms. Indeed, a few people who are highly skilled in aural imaging can hear entire symphonies in their mind in the same way great inventors can visualize entire machines. Wolfgang Amadeus Mozart, for example, once wrote, "The whole, though it be long, stands almost complete and finished in my mind, so that I can survey it, like a fine picture or a beautiful statue, at a glance. Nor do I hear in my imagination the parts *successively,* but I hear them, as it were, all at once."

Even Beethoven, who is often contrasted with Mozart as a slow, methodical, plodding, pen-and-paper composer, said, "I carry my thoughts about with me for a long time, often for a very long time, before writing them down. . . . I change many things, discard others, and try again and again until I am satisfied; then, in my head, I begin to elaborate the work in its breadth, its narrowness, its height, its depth. . . . I hear and see the image in front of me from every angle, as if it had been cast [like a sculpture], and only the labor of writing it down remains." Beethoven's mastery of mental imagery surely explains how he was able to compose some of his greatest music long after he had become profoundly deaf. He still heard sounds in his mind even if his ears no longer perceived them. Indeed, sonorous images seem very much the stuff of all composition, whether or not the composer ever actually hears his or her music performed. "The most perfect [musical] instrument in the world," the American composer Henry Cowell has said, "is the composer's mind. Every conceivable tone-quality and beauty of nuance, every harmony and disharmony, of any number of simultaneous melodies can be heard at will by the trained composer; he can hear not only the sound of any instrument or combination of instruments, but also an almost infinite number of sounds which cannot yet be produced on any instrument."

Thinking in sound also explains the "silent practicing" of top-notch musicians — they imagine performing their music much as athletes mentally rehearse their moves. Pianist Alicia de Larrocha says that when she is waiting in airports, "my mind is filled with music, and I'm hearing what I am going to play, and I'm practicing, every note, every phrase, every harmony, practicing my left hand." For much the same reason David Bar-Illan practices on a muted, soundless piano. "Do understand," he adds, "that during my soundless practicing I do hear the music in my mind." In similar fashion the dancer Martha Graham, after deep immersion in music, would practice her dances "in silence to the music I now felt in my body as well as heard in my mind."

As Graham makes clear, most imaging is actually polysensual. The dancer enacted the music she heard in her mind, as did de Larrocha and Bar-Illan. Moreover, kinesthetic and aural imaging is often accompanied by visual images. The American composer George Antheil, self-proclaimed "bad boy of Hollywood" during the 1930s, recounted that mental images and dreams were the primary sources of many of his musical compositions. A particularly prophetic dream accompanied by specific sounds of airplanes and giant factories found their way into his *Ballet Mecanique* (1924) in the form of airplane propellers, fans, sirens, electric bells, and other mechanical devices, all used to create "music." Stravinsky's compositions also began as detailed images of specific situations or actions. "In composing the music [for *Petroushka*]," he recalled, "I had in mind a distinct picture of a puppet, suddenly endowed with life, exasperating the patience of the orchestra with diabolical cascades of arpeggios. The orchestra in turn retaliates with menacing trumpet blasts. The outcome is a terrific noise which reaches its climax and ends in the sorrowful and querulous collapse of the poor puppet." When he wrote a polka dedicated to the ballet impresario Sergey Diaghilev, Stravinsky thought of his friend "as a circus ringmaster in evening dress and top hat, cracking his whip and urging on a rider." In both *Petroushka* and the polka, Stravinsky stated explicitly that musical themes accompanied his visions and provided the basis for his compositions.

For many musicians, visual and aural imaging involves mentally storing entire musical scores. Tenor Luciano Pavarotti recently confessed to an interviewer on National Public Radio, "I am studying with the music in my head, more than on the piano, singing the real stuff. . . . You have to see the music, you have to see the difficulty going on in a piece, so you have to put the thing in your head, photographically speaking, exactly like it is." Similarly, George Antheil had the ability — shared with Mozart, Beethoven, and many other composers — of hearing music and simultaneously seeing its written notation in his mind's eye. On one trip to northern Africa he wrote down local folk songs as they were played. "To hear was with me to see in music notes," he explained. "I needed only to hear a tune, however complicated rhythmically or melodically, to see it in my mind's eye on paper." Transcribing music "at sound" into notes usually strikes the layperson as nothing short of miraculous, as does the reverse, transcribing notation into music "at sight." Composer Arthur Honegger recalled that the question he was asked most frequently was, "You look at the notes and you really hear what is there?" For most musicians the answer is invariably yes. In fact, Copland believed that "the ability to imagine sounds in advance of their being heard in actuality" profoundly separated the professional from the amateur and especially from the nonmusician. In some cases, indeed, the talent can be almost supernormal. Henry Cowell actually preferred reading scores to listening to performances because he had complete control over the sounds in his mind in a way that he could not in real life.

Actually, there is no miracle here. Musicians and composers develop their aural-visual transcription abilities in much the same way that children and adults around the world learn to connect sounds to letters — by daily practice. Indeed, learning to read is a good model for aural imaging in general, since almost all people "hear" inside their mind their own voice speaking the words on the page. Writers often develop this skill to a high degree, as poet Amy Lowell did: "I always *hear* words even when I am reading to myself. . . . In writing, I frequently stop to read aloud what I have written, although this is really hardly necessary, so clearly do the words sound in my head." Taking internal speech several notches higher, Tennessee Williams imagined the different voices and speech patterns of his stage characters: "I have a good inner ear. I know pretty well how a thing is going to sound on the stage, and how it will play. I write to satisfy this inner ear and its perceptions." Williams took his imagery to extremes, often acting out all the parts as he developed his plays. "When I write," he said, "everything is visual, as brilliantly as if it were on a lit stage. And I talk out the lines as I write. When I was in Rome, my landlady thought I was demented. . . . 'Oh, Mr. Williams has lost his mind! He stalks about the room talking out loud!'" She didn't understand that Williams was simply expressing what he was experiencing in his mind.

Scientists also combine visual, kinesthetic, and aural images in their thinking. We noted in Chapter 1 that Einstein relied heavily on visual and kinesthetic images, but he appears to have relied on aural images as well. Many of his relatives recalled that he regularly played the violin or piano when he became frustrated with physics. "Whenever he felt that he had come to the end of the road or into a difficult situation in his work," wrote his son, "he would take refuge in music, and that would usually resolve all his difficulties." While developing the general theory of relativity, he frequently emerged from deep thought, played the piano, made a few notes, then disappeared back into his study. "There, now I've got it," his daughter Maja remembered him exclaiming as he got up from his piano. He even told his friend Shinichi Suzuki, the famous Japanese music teacher, "The theory of relativity occurred to me by intuition, and music is the driving force behind this intuition. My parents had me study the violin from the time I was six. My new discovery is the result of musical perception." In fact, Einstein called his piano "my old friend, through whom I say and I sing to myself all that which I often do not admit to myself at all."

The same multiple imaging is manifest in the work of Richard Feynman. When queried about his problem-solving techniques, Feynman listed visualizing, of course, but also kinesthetic imaging, "acoustic" — what we call aural — imaging and, like Tennessee Williams, talking to himself internally and verbalizing out loud. Family and colleagues often heard Feynman muttering, rhyming nonsense words, humming, or voicing clicks and whoops as he translated physical intuition and equation into sound. Presumably he heard but also felt the rhythmical nature of the physics in some way that was analogous to his experience as an avid bongo drummer.

We say presumably, because even though we know that imaging plays an important role in the thinking of many creative individuals, we do not necessarily know how it works in each case. Imaging is largely a private and personal shorthand of sights, sounds, and other sensations, ranging from realistic representations of phenomena to idiosyncratic abstractions and sensory associations. Moreover, different people rely more or less heavily on imaging. In some cases, a particular kind of imaging is so critical to an individual's way of thinking that he or she will purposefully choose work that draws upon that mental skill. Astrophysicist Margaret Geller says, "I have to have a visual model or a geometric model or else I can't do it. Problems that don't lend themselves to that I don't do." This sort of imaging proclivity may explain the styles and strengths of other inventive people as well.

In fact, Geller's choice of problems according to her imaging ability is known to apply to her peers as well. Physicist Peter Carruthers, also a visualizer, makes a broad distinction between those who are "pictorial" and those who are "mathematical." Physicists who are more mathematical don't share what Carruthers calls his "physical intuition" or his visualizing tendencies. In fact, about half of the eminent astrophysicists interviewed by Alan Lightman and Roberta Brawer in *Origins* (1990) said that they were not aware of using visual images. In various areas of the physical sciences, such as quantum mechanics, visualizing is actually discouraged by leading practitioners. Freeman Dyson has compared the strictly symbolic approach in this field to attaining fluency in a new, formal language; one understands quantum mechanics when one doesn't try to translate it into some other perceptual form or "tongue," but comprehends it directly, mathematically, the way musicians "hear" the meaning of written notes without the aid of an orchestra.

The dichotomy in science between those who think visually and those who do not was first noticed at least a century ago by Henri Poincaré. Poincaré, who wrote extensively on scientific creativity, used the example of four colleagues, Karl Weierstrass, Georg Riemann, Sophus Lie, and Sofya Kovalevskaya — a who's who of nineteenth-century mathematicians — to make his point: "Weierstrass leads everything back to the consideration of series and their analytic transformations; . . . you may turn through all his books without finding a figure. Riemann, on the contrary, at once calls geometry to his aid; each of his conceptions is an image that no one can forget, once he has caught its meaning." Lie "thought in pictures. Madame Kovalevskaya was a logician." The distinction in mathematics between imagers and nonimagers continues today. Feynman purposefully converted algebraic problems into geometric ones, asking himself, "Is there a way to *see* it?" In contrast, astronomer Fred Hoyle, who confesses to being a poor visualizer, has said, "I had to do all my geometry algebraically." (For a further discussion of algebraic versus geometric thinking, see the Appendix to this chapter.)

Poincaré realized that individual imaging preferences have important implications for the way we teach mathematics and other scientific subjects. "Among our students," he wrote, "we notice the same differences; some prefer to treat their problems 'by analysis,' others 'by geometry.' The first are incapable of 'seeing in space,' the others are quickly tired of long calculations and become perplexed. The two sorts of minds are equally necessary to the progress of science." Indeed, the two types of minds are necessary to every discipline. Moreover, if some people do algebra geometrically and others do geometry algebraically; if some people use equations to conceive reality and others use pictures; and if these pictures can combine visual with aural, as well as with olfactory and gustatory senses and bodily feelings, then we would do well to complement our usually abstract pedagogy with multi-imaging approaches to knowledge.

Everyone should be introduced to a wide range of imaging skills and be given the opportunity to master as many of these as possible. Fortunately, imaging skills can be learned and improved by exercise. At the Kanton Schule attended by Einstein, students practiced the ABC's of visual thinking as rigorously as the ABC's of language. The school's founder, Johann Pestalozzi, believed that visual understanding must in fact precede all other forms of education, and he argued in his classic didactic novel of 1801, *How Gertrude Taught Her Children,* that words and numbers must subsequently be firmly connected to this preestablished visual foundation. The young Einstein was thoroughly schooled in what modern scientists would call "thought experiments": seeing and feeling a physical situation almost tangibly, manipulating its elements, observing their changes — all of this imagined in the mind.

Other creative people have been encouraged to exercise their imaging skills by perceptive parents and supportive home environments. Margaret Geller's mother nurtured her artistic inclinations, and her father her ability to visualize three-dimensional objects. The imaging skills of Nobel Prize–winning chemist Peter Mitchell grew out of his interest in building things in his brother's workshop. "When I was a small boy . . . ," he has said, "I was always making little engines and things. I suppose that helped my development as a thinking person, because of the relationships between shapes. That's something I've kept in chemistry, of course. . . . You're concerned with the relationships in space of atoms." Such childhood experiences are common among many eminent scientists and inventors. Not everyone may have the extraordinary potential of a Steinmetz or a Tesla, but everyone benefits from the development of imaging technique that comes with hands-on experience in arts or crafts, or with simple mental practice.

Such lessons can be effective even after childhood. Engineering students at Auburn University in Opelika, Alabama, were tested for their visual thinking ability at the beginning of one semester. The tests revealed that the group was clearly divided between geometric or visual thinkers and analytical-algebraic types. All the students were then given an intensive course in two- and three-dimensional drawing as well as projection techniques. By the end of the course, those whose natural aptitude was analytical or algebraic tested nearly as high on the visual-thinking test as the "natural" visualizers. These results and similar ones from universities such as MIT, where Woodie Flowers teaches imaging skills, or Stanford, where Robert McKim teaches visual thinking, suggest that any kind of formal training in design, draftsmanship, drawing, painting, or photography can improve adult visualizing skills.

Sometimes the simple challenge to think concretely about abstract concepts can be effective. Caltech biologist James Bonner commented that he first learned how to visualize scientific situations from his chemistry professor, Roscoe Dickerson: "He told us this and he told us every day: 'You've got to really understand what you are doing.' . . . If we were plotting something, we had to see what this physically represents. All of a sudden, I learned to be able to physically visualize problems that would otherwise be abstract, or physically visualize the meanings of equations and things like that." Many teachers in the arts similarly exercise their students' visual imaginations. Nabokov counseled that good readers, who are as necessary to art as good writers, must actively "see" as they read; they must "visualize the rooms, the clothes, the manners of an author's people." One can learn to do this by paying close attention to visual, aural, proprioceptive, and other sensations daily. Imagination, after all, draws on experience.

Aural imaging skills, too, can clearly be learned by practicing. Roger Sessions notes that the degree to which one can mentally conceive a composition improves as one acquires musical skill: "The experience, I believe, is quite different for the mature and experienced composer from what it is for the young beginner. As he grows in practice and imagination it assumes an ever more preponderant role, and appears more and more to be the essential act of creation." To develop this aural skill, Harold Shapero advises would-be composers to begin by imagining accompaniments to well-known pieces and then comparing the results with the originals. Such training exercises the mind's ear and the mind's eye.

Listening to poetry and literature read out loud can also improve imaging skills, according to poet Amy Lowell. Perhaps this is one reason that reading to young children has been found to stimulate their intelligence. Listening to poetry and stories builds up their internal voices and frees their eyes from the page so they can concentrate on creating sensual images. Indeed, listening to literature read out loud is a good idea at any age, whether the reading is in person or on tape. As wonderful as television, movies, videos, and computer animation are in providing us with aural and visual "pictures," there is a corresponding danger that those who rely too completely on such prefabricated images will lose or never develop the ability to imagine their own.

Interestingly, aural practice with mathematical and scientific language can also result in a heightened imaging ability, as Norbert Wiener, inventor of cybernetics — the science of information theory — learned firsthand. As a child, he developed severe eye problems and was not able to read for six months. "Father went ahead teaching me mathematics, both algebra and geometry, by ear, and chemistry lessons went on. This period of ear training rather than eye training was probably one of the most valuable disciplines through which I have ever gone, for it forced me to be able to do my mathematics in my head and to think of languages as they are spoken rather than as mere exercises in writing." No one, of course, would recommend severe illness to improve imagistic thinking, but consider the advantages of learning a visual subject without seeing its symbols. Having once drawn a geometric figure on paper, draw it in your mind. When the images and feelings attendant in such imagining are connected with the sounds of the terms used to describe them, a deeper and broader understanding is awakened. If necessary, written and oral instructions and physical and mental drawing can be alternated, improving the connections among them.

Everything we have suggested here for the encouragement of imaging in education, from the earliest grades to the last stages of professional schooling, holds for individual self-training. Young or old, we can work on our imaging abilities just as we work on our observing skills. The steps are simple. First, recognize your own use of visual, aural, and other images. Do you see with your mind's eye just where you left your keys? Do you imagine the story you are reading as if it were a movie, as if you were acting in it, as if you were hearing it on the radio? When you imagine a banana or snow or a cat, can you see, hear, smell, and (even!) taste them all?

Second, indulge yourself. Image on purpose and to your heart's content. If you like to visualize, reimagine scenes from your favorite movie; better yet, rewrite and "resee" the movie so that it is perfect and perfectly your own. Try your hand at visual puzzles, such as those in the puzzle book *Pentagames*. If you like to think in images of sound, try to remember and hear in your mind not just the melody but the harmonies of your favorite song or concerto.

Third, take up an art. But don't just learn *about* music or dance or painting or cooking. Learn to make drawings, songs, poems, or gourmet dishes. In many of these activities imaging is part of the process of doing. Chances are you won't choose a color for your painting without thinking in color; you won't pick out a melody on the piano without thinking about and in sounds; you won't create a chicken dish without thinking about and in what tastes fair with fowl. Work at imagining these processes before you do them and at remembering them afterward. Finally, make up excuses to use your inner eye, your inner ear, your inner nose, your inner sense of touch and of body. Have someone pose math and science problems verbally for you; practice hearing different voices and seeing different physiognomies when you read a play; pay attention to what you feel and imagine as you listen to music. Like any skill, imaging becomes stronger and quicker with consistent and persistent practice.

There is, however, one downside to becoming a dexterous imager: the better one's skill, the more frustrated one may become in trying to present images directly to other people. The need to translate through another medium can be painful. This is why Henry Cowell preferred his mental renderings of scores to live musical performance and why Einstein found the formal communication of his ideas through mathematics to be, in his own word, "difficult." The immediacy and completeness of the original conception, with its attendant images, feelings, and emotions, is lost, attenuated, or distorted. Many creative people have consequently voiced a desire for ever more direct forms of communication. For artist Max Bill, the answer is a new form of art: "Mental concepts are not as yet directly communicable to our apprehension without the medium of language, though they might ultimately become so by the medium of art. Hence I assume that art could be made a unique vehicle for the direct transmission of ideas, because if these were expressed by pictures or plastically there would be no danger of their original meaning being perverted."

Composer Charles Ives was less sanguine about the ability of art, even musical art, to fill this role: "My God!" he wrote in his *Essays,* "why can't music go out in the same way it comes in to a man, without having to crawl over a fence of sounds, thoraxes, catguts, wire, wood and bass?" Novelist Margaret Drabble also questions the necessary translation of subjective images into objective forms of communication. "Writers, like painters, tend to think in pictures," she has written, and though visual art, literature, and film can "suggest . . . private, interior mental images," this communication, however skillful, is still indirect. Drabble imagines a kind of dream machine "that can record my dream pictures as they occur, so that, on waking, I can retrace the narrative." Nikola Tesla had the same thought with reference to real, waking time: "It should be possible," he conjectured, "to project on a screen the image of any object one conceives and make it visible. Such an advance would revolutionize all human relations. I am convinced that this wonder can and will be accomplished in time to come; I may add that I have devoted much thought to the solution of the problem."

Not to be outdone, numerous science-fiction enthusiasts have also envisioned a future of image-melding minds. Witness the numerous *Star Trek* episodes featuring "empaths," whose interpersonal communications are integral and instantaneous, or the disturbing film *Strange Days,* which explores the abuses of vicarious, virtual experience. But for better or for worse, no one has yet made such science fiction science fact. We remain in that "primitive" state in which all mental images must still be translated through other mediums, be they words, music, movements, models, paintings, diagrams, films, sculptures, or mathematical treatises. And perhaps we ought not to complain. To our lack of direct-imaging abilities we owe the human world of expressive artifacts.

Fig. 4-4. Solutions to geometric imaging problems. Note that some of the problems have more than one solution. You may discover yet more!

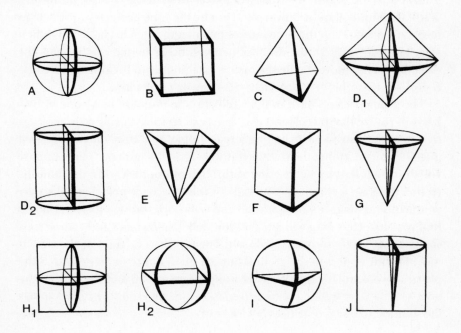

APPENDIX

On Algebraic versus Geometric Thinking

What are we to understand by Feynman's statement that he treated algebra problems geometrically and Hoyle's that he treated geometric problems algebraically? A concrete example may help.

A classic word problem concerns a man rowing a boat when his hat falls into the river, which is flowing at 3 kilometers per hour downstream. He is rowing upstream 2 km per hour faster than the stream is taking him down. He discovers his hat is missing one half-hour after it has fallen in the river. If he turns around and rows back at the same speed relative to the river to fetch his hat, how long will it take to catch up to it?

The algebraic approach to this problem is to abstract out the key parameters in order to set up an equation and solve for the unknown. The hat is dropped and moves at 3km/hr for 0.5 hrs, so it travels 1.5 km downriver. The man rows at 2km/hr upriver for 0.5 hrs, so he travels 1 km upriver. The man is therefore 2.5 km from his hat when he discovers its loss. He reverses course. In order to travel at 2km/hr upriver, he had to be moving at 5km/hr relative to the river, so if he rows at the same rate downriver, his total velocity will be 5km/hr plus the 3km/hr that the river moves, or 8km/hr. The hat, meantime, is still moving at 3km/hr downriver. Let t be the time necessary for the man to catch his hat. Then the time it takes the man to catch his hat is $(8\text{km/hr})t = 2.5\text{km} + (3\text{km/hr})t$, the distance between the man and the hat plus the distance the hat moves while the man is catching up to it. Solving the equation yields $(8\text{km/hr})t - (3\text{km/hr})t = 2.5$ km, or $t = 0.5$ hr.

The geometric approach to this problem is to visualize it. A good visualizer will realize that this class of problems can be solved using a simple relativistic trick. Instead of imagining a man riding on a boat moving upriver, imagine you are riding the river as if it were a swiftly moving train. Suppose you drop your hat as you are walking through one of the cars in the same direction the train is traveling. You walk for thirty seconds before you discover your hat is missing. You turn around and walk back through the cars till you find your hat. How long will it take if you walk that distance at the same constant speed? Thirty seconds, obviously. The fact that the train or the river is moving with respect to the ground outside turns out to be irrelevant to the physical problem. Treating the river as if it were a train and the man in the boat as if he were walking on the river/train quickly yields thirty minutes as the solution to our problem, as before.

Although the algebraic and geometric approaches clearly yield equivalent results, the methods are equally clearly different. Algebraicists might accuse geometricians of not having proven their answer, since no calculations or theorems are evident. Conversely, geometricians might accuse algebraicists of resorting to calculations when the answer is intuitively obvious. Most people prefer one method almost to the exclusion of the other.

Einstein's and Feynman's conundrum was that they thought as geometricians but needed to communicate their results in analytical, algebraic forms to satisfy the rigorous demands of physical proofs. Hoyle's problem was that his algebraic formulations had no obvious meaning for visual geometricians like Geller, whose astrophysical studies were meant to test his theories. Very few people can switch with ease or alacrity between the two approaches, although such transformations are often at the heart of new breakthroughs, a point we expand upon in Chapter 14, Transforming.

5

Abstracting

Abstractions are so common in our society that we rarely pay attention to them. We have all seen abstract art. We read abstracts of books and articles. We often label ideas or theories as abstractions because they lack the full body of real things. Nevertheless, the process of abstracting remains largely mysterious, and many of its products go unrecognized. A challenge will help you realize the truth of this statement. We would like you to put aside this book for a few minutes to abstract an orange in as many ways as you can imagine. Then abstract a human being. Again, create as many abstractions as you can. Once you've given our challenge some serious consideration, read on.

Don't feel bad if you had problems figuring out where to begin or how to proceed with this exercise. Experience has taught us that even professional artists, writers, and teachers often have difficulty with it. They can identify abstracting when they see it, but very few can actually tell you what makes abstract art abstract. Even fewer can create imaginative abstractions themselves. Most people who do this exercise come up with trite visual abstractions: oranges that are circles colored orange; stick figures or bodiless heads that look like happy faces. Few people try to abstract the motion or the sound or the smell or the tactile feel of an orange or a human being, let alone their chemical composition or their biological role in the web of life. Nor do they think to express these kinds of abstractions in music, dance, words, or numbers instead of drawings, though any and all of these mediums can be used to express abstractions. Clearly, the process of abstracting is neither perceived to be general nor generally understood.

Perhaps some masterly examples will help. The first emerged in 1927 as

Fig. 5-1. *Artist and Model, Cahiers d'Art* by Pablo Picasso, 1932.

Picasso sketched his companion, Marie-Thérèse Walter, while she was knit-ting. He drew himself drawing her, and included in the picture the canvas upon which he sketched as well. The picture is thus a drawing of the process of drawing, one of Picasso's favorite themes. It is illuminating, particularly as the portrait of Marie-Thérèse looks like little more than a series of appar-ently random lines and curves. What was Picasso after?

At about the same time, the physicist C. T. R. Wilson was taking photo-graphs of subatomic particles. Most of us would expect these particles to look like little bits of some larger mass. In fact, the pictures Wilson devel-

Fig. 5-2. Particle tracks in a bubble chamber, 1970.

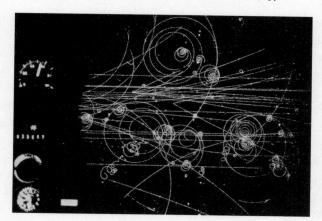

oped bear an uncanny resemblance to Picasso's portrait of Marie-Thérèse: a bunch of spirals and curlicues that in three dimensions might look like bizarre springs. Such photographs would eventually earn Wilson a Nobel Prize. But what had these images to do with atoms?

Several decades later, one of Picasso's fans and artistic followers, E. E. Cummings, produced a similarly puzzling work. In his case, the work was made of words rather than lines, and it looked like this:

I

l(a

le
af
fa

ll

s)
one
l

iness

A casual glance at Picasso's etching, Wilson's photograph, or Cummings's poem is likely to yield little more than confusion. The problem is that each is so incredibly simple that it is difficult to perceive its structure. But once you understand what the artist, the scientist, and the poet were about, the meanings become crystal clear. Equally surprisingly, one realizes that Cummings's poem is surely the verbal equivalent of Picasso's "Artist and Model," just as thunder is the aural equivalent of lightning. Moreover, Wilson's photograph is like an afterimage of each. All three men eliminated everything except one key element from their observation and thinking. They reduced complex visual, physical, or emotional ideas to bare, stripped images, revealing, through simplicity, the power of purity. In other words, they abstracted.

Physicist Werner Heisenberg defined abstracting as "the possibility of considering an object or group of objects under one viewpoint while disregarding all other properties of the object. The essence of abstraction consists in singling out one feature, which, in contrast to other properties, is considered to be particularly important." His definition applies to any discipline, as Picasso made clear in describing the purpose of one of his abstract paintings: "I want to say the nude. I don't want to do a nude as a nude. I want only to say breast, say foot, say hand or belly. To find the way to say it — that's enough." His goal, in other words, was to find the minimum visual stimulus that can be put on paper or canvas and still evoke recognition without spelling everything out. He searched for the essence of visual language, just as Heisenberg searched for the principles of nature.

The key to understanding Picasso's abstraction of Marie-Thérèse is to realize that abstractions may not represent whole things but one or another of their less obvious properties. Picasso decided to focus his attention not on his model but on the space she inhabited. It is essential to the interpretation of this picture that we recognize that, unlike most models, Marie-Thérèse was in motion. Her knitting needles swung back and forth, in and out. She had to adjust her skein of wool, perhaps reach down to pick it up if it dropped, look at her pattern. Picasso has therefore drawn the curves that her head, hands, elbows, shoulders, and body swept out as they moved through space. It is as if he had attached luminescent markers that left a trace in the air as she moved — an idea, by the way, that had already occurred to various other people interested in motion, as we shall soon see. The result is a complex picture. On the one hand, Picasso tells us from his realistic portrayals of himself and his model that he could have drawn her realistically if he had wanted to. He did not. There is, his portrait says, another reality that is also Marie-Thérèse, one that is just as interesting and significantly more unexpected. You are looking, Picasso admonishes us, but you are not seeing. Don't just look — think! Find the surprising properties hidden behind the obvious ones. See with your mind, not your eyes!

Seeing with the mind is also the key to understanding Wilson's photograph. In this instance, one must understand the technique he used to capture the odd images in his photograph. He had invented an instrument called a cloud chamber to study the formation of clouds. In essence, Wilson created a saturated atmosphere of water vapor in a special box to which was attached a large piston. When the piston was drawn out, the pressure and temperature dropped, causing the water vapor to condense. As a physicist, Wilson was interested in the conditions that best favored the formation of his clouds, and he soon realized that the presence of ions — charged particles — helped the process immensely. It then occurred to him that subatomic particles, such as electrons and protons, are charged and that they could cause the water vapor to condense in the cloud chamber, creating tracks of water droplets as they passed. If the entire cloud chamber was placed within a strong magnetic field, one could tell, by the direction in which the subatomic particles twisted in the field, whether they were positively or negatively charged. Thus his photograph shows not the particles themselves, but the tracks left by charged fragments of atoms moving through a magnetic field, much as Picasso's picture shows the tracks of his model through space. From both one can make certain inferences about the subject's physical and dynamic properties — but only if one recognizes that the experiment has yielded not a portrait, but an abstraction.

The poem by Cummings is as powerful an abstraction as Picasso's and Wilson's. In fact, it is related to them. Picasso, who was enamored of Chinese ideograms, once said, "If I were born Chinese, I would not be a painter but a writer. I'd write my pictures." Just as Wilson's reputation came from forcing subatomic particles to leave their handwriting on the wall, as it were, cummings's reputation as a poet rests largely on the fact that he figured out how to force words to write pictures — in English and without resorting to ideograms.

Consider Cummings's poem not just as letters and words but also as an image. The poem begins with the letter l, which can also be read as the number 1. This letter/number is the essence of Cummings's abstraction. He plays on both meanings. He also plays with the structure of the poem on the page, calling his creations "poempictures." The words must be seen as well as heard, and their pattern on the page studied as carefully as the syntax. Thus, when the poet says in parentheses, "a leaf falls," you are expected to notice that the fragments of words on the page mimic this falling, forcing the reader's eyes back and forth across the page as if one were following the pendular fall of the leaf itself. (This is a technique Cummings had used in other poems, such as "Grasshopper," in which the reader's eye must jump back and forth across the page.) Then the word "one" appears, reiterating the opening letter, followed by l again, and then "iness," which may be read, particularly in Cummings's lowercase alphabet, as "I-ness" — the I being one, alone, single, like a leaf falling from the communal home of the tree. Moreover, combining the initial letter l with the one, l, and iness at the end of the poem (in other words, deleting the parenthetical phrase) yields "loneliness" — the state of the leaf that has left its fellows in the tree; the state of the individual, alone. Or, knowing that Cummings often invented words, one can read just the letters after the parenthesis, which form the word "oneliness" — the state of being one. Perhaps equally profoundly, the whole poem appears on the page as a 1, with all of its connotations of oneness, loneliness, and I-ness synthesized in its form. So much meaning in so few letters!

Oddly, although all abstractions are simplifications, the best abstractions are like Picasso's, Wilson's, and Cummings's in that they yield new and often multiple insights and meanings, using simplicity to reveal inobvious properties and hidden connections. Moreover, experience suggests that the simplest abstractions are often the hardest to perceive or devise and at the same time yield the most important insights. Take mathematics, for example, a field that is nothing but abstractions. The very concept of number is as abstract as one can get, for it can be applied to anything, anywhere, anytime. It can be manipulated without reference to reality — hence the universal power of computing. "Nothing" itself is an abstraction, zero representing that which does not exist and yet holding the place of everything that could. Mathematical physicist Paul Dirac has argued, "Mathematics is the tool specially suited for dealing with abstract concepts of any kind. There is no limit to its power in this field." And mathematicians Philip Davis and Reuben Hersh go so far as to suggest that abstracting "is almost characteristic [of] or synonymous with intelligence itself."

Every scientific theory or principle is a surprisingly powerful and insightful abstraction. Just think about the implications of the fact that any object in a gravitational field can be represented by a point mass — an infinitely small point having all of the mass of the real object — regardless of the object's shape, size, density, color, texture, consistency, or constitution. Physicists can even treat a mouse as a point mass perched atop a spring, to represent its legs, and come up with an equation that very accurately describes how high that mouse can jump. Similarly, the concepts of velocity, acceleration, temperature, density, and so forth are abstractions so universal that

Fig. 5-3. Abstraction of a jumping mammal.

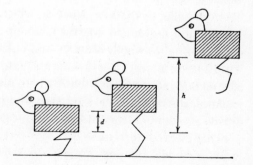

they can be applied to any object anywhere. And, like Picasso's portrait of Marie-Thérèse and Wilson's portrait of subatomic particles, these properties are not at all apparent. One must learn to see past the obvious reality that we observe through our senses to perceive them with the "eye of the mind."

Language, too, is shot through with abstractions. Many words, such as love, truth, honor, and duty, represent very complex concepts. The writer abstracts these and other words from a plethora of possible texts to make a singular statement. But the abstractions of literature run deeper than this. As Samuel Johnson said, "The business of a poet . . . is to examine, not the individual, but the species; to remark general properties and large appearances. . . . [To do so he] must neglect the minuter discriminations" that do not characterize the group. A great deal of literary abstracting leaves important things unsaid as well, novelist Willa Cather pointed out. "Whatever is felt upon the page without being specifically named there —" she wrote, "that, one might say, is created. It is the inexplicable presence of the thing not named, of the overtone divined by the ear, but not heard by it, the verbal mood, the emotional aura of the fact or the thing of the deed, that gives high quality to the novel or the drama, as well as to poetry itself." Elsewhere she concluded, "The higher processes of art are all processes of simplification. . . . That, indeed, is very nearly the whole of the higher artistic process; finding what conventions of form and what detail one can do without and yet preserve the spirit of the whole."

The language of the body is also abstract. Indeed, it is so basic that body talk, like arithmetic, can bridge the most disparate cultures. People all over the world resort to pantomiming whenever verbal language fails. We make faces, use gestures, act out our desires. We invent games such as charades to test our miming abilities — and often find our skills none too good. We therefore applaud the amazing abilities of a Marcel Marceau. We pay top dollar to see the purified languages embodied in a Japanese *no* drama or a Western ballet or modern dance, in which meaning has been reduced to a gesture or a movement. Martha Graham characterized her dance "Appalachian Spring" as wholly abstract, and Oskar Schlemmer wrote to his friend Otto Meyer, almost paradoxically, "I have observed that involvement with abstraction increases one's sensitivity to reality." In dance, as in all other disciplines, abstraction gets at essences and purifies concepts, yielding, in the words of sculptor Henry Moore, "the greatest directness and intensity."

That essential directness pervades every aspect of our lives. We abstract great orchestral and pop music when we whistle a tune — a bit of the main theme dissected from its rich tapestry of notes. We abstract when we give a quick summary of a good book we've just read. We use abstractions when we choose the television program we intend to watch from the one-line plot descriptions given in *TV Guide* or the newspaper. We rely on abstractions in the form of newspaper and magazine headlines to determine whether to read a particular article. Students often resort to the work of professional abstracters who provide brief summaries of classics such as Shakespeare's plays in the form of Cliff Notes and its competitors. Caricatures are abstractions; so are a person's initials. Even epigrams are a type of abstraction, embodying in a few words the experience and wisdom of ages: "A stitch in time saves nine."

All of these — numbers, words, gestures — are so basic, so simple that they seem unremarkable. Indeed, the essence of abstractions is that we say to ourselves, "My kid could do that." It is easy to forget that although we learn to use these abstractions, few of us could invent a new mathematics, discover a new law of nature, devise a new way of portraying perception, develop a new gestural language, or describe a fundamental truth about human feelings. Such triumphs are rare and difficult to achieve. Picasso commented repeatedly on how difficult it was for him to learn to draw simply and directly. He had to learn the process step by step. The notebooks of E. E. Cummings similarly show how hard he worked to achieve his simple effects. It is so much easier to see and convey the complexity and confusion of reality.

Indeed, abstracting is difficult for people in every discipline. Many famous novelists — Mark Twain and Ernest Hemingway come to mind — have written to their editors that they regretted the extreme length of their manuscripts; if they had had more time, the work would have been half as long. Winston Churchill is supposed to have said that he could talk for a day with five minutes' notice but needed a day to prepare if he had only five minutes in which to speak. The poet Edwin Arlington Robinson shifted from writing short verse to lengthy works as he got older, remarking, "I am over sixty now, and short poems require too much effort." The essence of writing, these individuals say, is not putting words on the page but learning to recognize and erase the unnecessary ones. Teachers know that preparing lessons for introductory students is much more challenging than teaching advanced students because the basics are so much more difficult to master and simplify. Similarly, when one reads a brilliantly simple paper in science, it is all too easy to pass it off as inconsequential. But as Harvard biologist George Wald once said to Nobel laureate Albert Szent-Györgyi after reading one of his typically lucid and simple papers, "This paper of yours is so lightly written that you must have sweated terribly."

There is much truth to Wald's words, not only for the writing of science but for its principles as well. Indeed, we point out at the start of every science class a very interesting fact: even the simplest textbooks written for secondary-school students are based on the achievements of the greatest names in science, such as Galileo, Newton, Darwin, Pasteur, Mendel, Curie, Watson, and Crick. If you think about it for a moment, this is truly surprising. One would expect the most important developments in science to be the most complex, but in fact, they are always the simplest. As physicist and inventor Mitchell Wilson wrote half a century ago, "I'll tell you what you need to be a great scientist. You don't have to be able to understand very complicated things. It's just the opposite. You have to be able to see what looks like the most complicated thing in the world and, in a flash, find the underlying simplicity. That's what you need: a talent for simplicity."

From fundamental simplicities spring basic theories. And each basic theory is exactly analogous to Cummings's poem in which the concept of I/l/1 has a multitude of possible interpretations and applications. Abstracting, by simplifying, yields the common links, the nexuses, in the fabric of perception and nature. But seeing through the complexity of reality to discover these simple principles often takes the greatest genius. As Picasso said, "Whatever is most abstract may perhaps be the summit of reality," and as Werner Heisenberg wrote, "The step toward greater generality is always itself a step into abstraction — or more precisely, into the next highest level of abstraction; for the more general unites the wealth of diverse individual things." Richard Feynman put it more simply still in one of his notebooks: "Phenomena complex — laws simple. . . . Know what to leave out."

Knowing what abstracting is and why it is so important, though, is only half the problem. The other half is learning how to find the simple concepts hiding among complex expressions. How do you do it? Fortunately, many creative people have left detailed records of how they invented their abstractions. One mistake many people make is to begin by ignoring reality. Bridget Riley, an artist famous for her nonrepresentational and op-art paintings, tells us that abstractions must evolve from something real. Bryan Robertson, a writer and art lecturer, once said to Riley, "I like Gertrude Stein's funny remark quoted in *The Autobiography of Alice B. Toklas:* 'I like a good view, and I like to sit with my back to it.' I think that's probably the best approach to nature for most artists working abstractly." Riley replied succinctly, "She should be shot." Observing that natural view is a first and important step for any artist. Even for someone like Riley, whose purpose in painting is to awaken "recognition of the sensation without the actual incident that

Fig. 5-4. *The Bull* by Pablo Picasso, 1946. *Clockwise from upper left:* second, fourth, eighth, and eleventh states.

prompted it," the sensation must first be experienced and understood and then purified.

Picasso also cautioned other painters, "To arrive at abstraction, it is always necessary to begin with a concrete reality. . . . You must always start with something. Afterward you can remove all traces of reality. There's no danger then, anyway, because the idea of the object will have left an indelible mark. It is what started the artist off, excited his ideas, and stirred his emotions." True to his word, Picasso began his well-known *Bull* series with a realistic image of a bull. Then he became interested in the planes defining the bull's form. But as he experimented with these planes, he realized that what defined them were their edges, which he then reduced to simple outlines. Finally, he eliminated most of these lines, leaving a pure outline that still conveys the essence of "bullness." Note that the head, which is massive in the original print, has become insignificant in the final print, yet we still have no difficulty recognizing the image as a representation of a bull. For Picasso, bullness was not in the size or shape of the head but in other very simple features, such as the horns. None of this was obvious at the outset. Other, less evident discoveries become manifest if one compares Picasso's bull series with another made many years later by Roy Lichtenstein, which can be seen in Randy Rosen's wonderful 1978 book, *Prints*. Lichtenstein used the same theme but developed his abstraction in a very different way, thereby revealing other aspects of bullness than Picasso's prints focus on.

Because abstracting is a tool, it has multiple uses. Just as two artists may find very different ways to represent bulls, so there may be many ways of abstracting any object or idea that will reveal different fundamental aspects of it. Often the result depends upon the properties that are observed and simplified. The painter Ellsworth Kelly, for example, tends to focus on color and plane, as in his 1973 painting *Yellow with Red Triangle,* which consists of a large oblique rectangle of bright yellow to which is attached a slightly smaller equilateral triangle in red. When asked how he came up with the idea for this apparently simple painting, Kelly explained that "the shape of the two panels was abstracted from something I observed in the architecture of a house near my studio. The sloping roof of a house became a yellow rectangle placed on a diagonal; the dormer window on this roof seen from the side became the red triangle. . . . Everywhere I look, I see relationships — forms and colors. And I break them down to the bare essential forms." The process of looking, drawing, and painting, often from various angles or viewpoints, always begins with "the world rather than my own invention." For Kelly, abstracting comes down to discovering the simplest relationships between form and color in things that he observes.

Henri Matisse also abstracted in his own way. Late in his life he was confined to his bed, unable to paint because of chronic illness. Nevertheless, finding that he could manipulate scissors with some agility, he produced his famous cutout collages. A set of snails particularly illuminates his methods. We know that Matisse, like Picasso, could draw realistic-looking snails if he wished. His scissors suggested novel ways of abstracting them. In one case he imagined what would happen if one cut a snail shell along the lines of its curvature, then flattened it out as if it were a piece of paper. Another inspiration led him to portray the essence of "snailness" as a spiral formed by a series of hinged blocks of paper. In both cases, his object was to focus our attention on the snail's articulation of a complex shape.

Fig. 5-5. Sketches showing basic abstractions employed in *The Snail* by Henri Matisse, 1952 and 1953.

Fig. 5-6. *Left: Stramonium,* showing the flower, the corolla, and a cross-section of the corolla; *right:* Transverse section of the apex of a seedling pine.

The lesson we may draw from Matisse, Kelly, Picasso, and Lichtenstein is that many abstractions are possible for any given object, each of which illuminates some hidden truth. One might even say that reality is the sum of all possible abstractions and that in coming to know these possibilities, we understand reality better. This is a lesson scientists, too, have learned. Like Matisse, biologists have often found it useful to "cut" — sometimes literally — the objects of their study into various forms to study their fundamental structures. Thus, nineteenth-century botanists such as Asa Gray frequently characterized flowers by means of a series of abstract sections, none of which, singly, looks like the flower as we view it. To understand the development of the structure of a fruit, such as a pineapple, botanists have followed the same procedure Matisse used with one of his snails: cutting through the outer surface and flattening it out (see Fig. 5-7). In this abstraction a previously hidden pattern suddenly emerges from the apparent randomness of the fruit's surface. Indeed, a mathematician can take this pattern a step further by writing an equation for it. In this case, the equation emerges from the ratio of two numbers in the Fibonacci sequence, which is generated by beginning with the numbers 0 and 1 and adding the last two numbers of the series to generate the next: 0, 1, 1, 2, 3, 5, 8, 13, 21, and so on. The sequence gives us some of nature's most common patterns. A pineapple can be described as

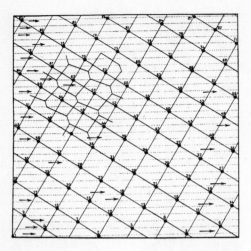

Fig. 5-7. Analysis of pattern arrangement in the pineapple.

the ratio of the number of times (eight) you must spiral around the fruit before its pattern repeats exactly (twenty-one sections): 8/21. Pinecones, flowers, and other natural objects can be described in similarly simple terms using the Fibonacci sequence.

Another example of abstracting, which involves a series of inventors, scientists, and artists, helps to demonstrate that not only is the process identical from one field to another but it transcends disciplinary boundaries. One of the most important, revolutionary, and, for many people, incomprehensible paintings of this century — Marcel Duchamp's abstract *Nude Descending a Staircase* — represents the culmination of a series of innovations that began more than a century ago with a man named Eadweard Muybridge. In 1878, Muybridge had taken up the challenge posed by a deceptively simple question: did a running horse ever have all of its feet off the ground at the same moment? The answer was not obvious. Observers could not agree, and there seemed to be no way to prove the issue until Muybridge came up with an innovative idea. He realized he needed to freeze time, which he could do with the newly invented camera. However, he needed to freeze time in a succession of instants to show a horse with all of its feet in the air simultaneously, if that in fact happened. No existing camera could do this, so Muybridge improvised. He set up a series of cameras, which he triggered with a timing mechanism so that each went off just a fraction of a second after the previous one. After many experiments, Muybridge succeeded in obtaining his answer: a galloping horse does indeed lift all four feet off the ground during one part of its stride. And he had the photographs to prove it.

Muybridge immediately recognized that his invention could be used to analyze motion of many kinds. He made serial photographs of people performing gymnastic tricks, getting in and out of bed, walking up and down inclines and stairs, running, jumping, and engaging in dozens of other activities. These pictures, which appeared in books widely reprinted and translated, fascinated people around the world.

Thus far there had been no abstracting; Muybridge simply recorded what he saw. His focus was on reality in all of its complexity. But some people, the most prominent of whom was the French physiologist E. J. Marey, saw other possibilities in his technique. Marey, a great innovator in recording and analyzing motion, immediately saw that Muybridge's pictures were too cluttered to serve a scientist's needs. Marey wanted to know only the positions of key parts of the body, such as the bones and joints, in order to study their motion. He dressed models in black suits from head to toe and drew white lines on the suits to represent the key bones in the limbs, with large white dots marking the position of the joints. He then photographed the models moving against a black background, so that they looked like disembodied ball-and-stick figures — abstractions (see Fig. 5-9).

Another French physiologist, Paul Richer, who was also an amateur artist, almost immediately recognized that the information in Marey's abstract photographs would permit scientists to analyze for the first time the exact physical dynamics of human motion. He traced some of Marey's photographs so that he could calculate the forces at work on the body as it moved,

Fig. 5-8. Photograph of a man descending stairs by Eadweard Muybridge.

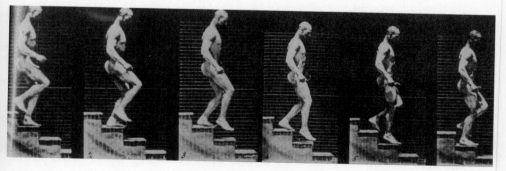

Fig. 5-9. *Above:* a man in black costume; *below:* a partial geometric chrono-photograph of the man in motion, both by Etienne-Jules Marey.

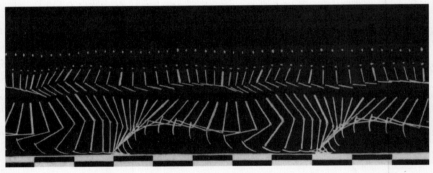

its center of gravity during various motions, its relative velocity, and so forth. Enlightenment philosophers had dreamed of man as a machine, an idea that represents both an analogy and an abstraction. Now physiologists could actually analyze the mechanics of the human form. Bodies became masses, limbs and joints levers, motion a mere function of force, velocity, and acceleration. Abstraction had moved beyond what can be seen to what can be imagined. Richer had created the physiologist's equivalent of Wilson's cloud-chamber photographs and Picasso's *Artist and Model.* In fact, he beat both men to the punch by several years.

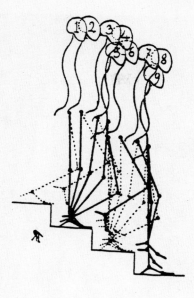

Fig. 5-10. *Figure Descending a Staircase* by Paul Richer.

The process held yet more surprises. Artists at the turn of the century became as interested in the problems of motion as Muybridge and the physiologists were. How could one portray moving objects effectively on a static canvas? they asked. Muybridge's work clearly provided some clues, but the most daring artists followed the physiologists' discoveries as well. One was Marcel Duchamp, whose work constantly challenged whatever the art world considered sacrosanct. Duchamp owned various volumes of the works of Muybridge, Marey, and Richer, and their influence is obvious in the final form of *Nude Descending a Staircase* (see Fig. 5-11). Compare the *Nude* with Richer's analysis of a person descending a stair, Duchamp's inspiration. If the problem that motivated the artist and the sources upon which he drew are unknown to the viewer, his painting appears both revolutionary and incomprehensible. But in context, his abstraction not only makes sense, it seems inevitable.

The logic behind the pictorial abstraction of motion was clear enough to contemporaries that they not only understood its principles but could mimic its results. Other artists, such as the Italians Giacomo Balla and Umberto Boccioni and the Russians Kazimir Malevich and Natalya Goncharova, soon began using multiple overlapping images to portray motion in their paintings. Picasso also experimented with the technique in a series of etchings. Today this static, two-dimensional representation of motion is so com-

Fig. 5-11. *Nude Descending a Stair-case*, #2 by Marcel Duchamp, 1912.

monly understood that we see it in comic strips and advertisements. Muybridge, Marey, and the investigations they set in motion have had quite an impact on how we see. Indeed, the photographic innovations of these two pioneers led to several technological inventions. The motion-picture industry developed equipment capable of taking — and projecting — serial photographs in such rapid progression that the resulting pictures seem to "move." MIT's Harold (Doc) Edgerton invented methods of stop-action photography for recording impressions of very fast motions. Film animators have developed "motion capture" technologies in which actors wear small sensors at key points on their bodies, just like the dots and rods on Muybridge's human models, that send spatial information to computers used by artists to create realistically moving animated figures. Choreographer Merce Cunningham has brought these developments full circle in his dance "Biped," in which dancers wear motion-capture sensors to create computer-animated figures that are projected on see-through screens behind which the dancers then perform live with their abstract, animated selves.

As the origins of *Nude Descending a Staircase* demonstrate, the process of abstracting is identical, and can be interactive, across disciplines. When an artist invents a new method for abstracting, scientists and technologists benefit, and when a scientist or engineer discovers another form of abstraction, artists may hurry to employ it. Every scientific experiment, every scientific theory, is just as much an abstraction as an abstract painting or poem. Scientist, artist, and poet alike all strive to find meaning in complex systems by eliminating every variable save one. Experimentation in science, like that in the arts, becomes a formalized process for discovering important abstractions.

Precisely because this process is universal, learning how to abstract in one discipline provides the key to understanding the abstractions of all disciplines. Albert Szent-Györgyi, known to many for his clear and lucid writing, believed that the clearest scientific papers ever written were those of biochemist Otto Warburg. When approached about his "secret," Warburg responded, "I rewrite sixteen times." Szent-Györgyi put his own twist on the advice. "When I write first, I write up everything that comes to my mind. Then I put the paper away and rewrite a month later without looking at my first text. If the second text is different from the first, then I rewrite again. So I may rewrite sixteen times, till the text does not change any more." As Szent-Györgyi went from one draft to another, whatever was unnecessary to his argument disappeared, leaving only the essentials.

The same winnowing process can be applied to verbal description of any sort. Consider, for instance, the following sequence of verbal statements written by one of us (Michèle) in which the initial welter of observations and ideas (I) is gradually refined and simplified, first by emphasizing or extracting related visual images or ideas (II), and finally by pulling out and exploring one of those ideas with an essential sequence of words (III):

OBSERVATIONS ON A WATER-WORN STONE

I

A smooth lake stone, roundly pitted across one surface. It looks as if another stone hides inside, the way one circular pit holds within it the flat protuberance of another color. Again on its side, the slightly darker gray black emerges through the round erosion of light gray skin. There is on one side a deep pit, like a cave or an orifice. It looks like a cell or an ameoba, nucleus at the center, and all sorts of "bodies" floating within its protoplasm. How did the waves of water mark these patterns? The stone is smaller than the palm of my hand, on the back are different marks, straight lines scratched in the rock shaped like South America or Africa, like a hatchet head, almost a boomerang. I don't know where it came from.

II

Where it came from, this round erosion of handed rock, like the moon pitted, the cold matter of stars, a map of the unknown world, the ancient compass of cells emerging from the deep.

III

The ameoba was made of stone and the nucleus at its center was made of stone and all its protoplasm stone cold stone.

As verbal description becomes increasingly abstract, it often merges into poetry, for each word takes on ever more reference and significance. This is true whether one writes for a literary or a scientific purpose. Many scientists have noted that technical words and concepts often have the austere purity of poetry. Chemist Cyril Hinshelwood said in his 1956 Nobel Prize lecture that his fascination with time and change in chemistry went "outside science into poetry; but science, subject to the rigid necessity of always seeking closer approximations to the truth, itself contains many poetical elements." His colleague and fellow laureate, Roald Hoffmann, is well known for similar poetical conceptions of chemistry, as was Sir Humphry Davy. Many of John Updike's poems explore this borderland, as does Joan Digby and Bob Brier's excellent compilation of poems and essays, *Permutations* (1977).

Santiago Ramón y Cajal demonstrated that the differences between scientific observation and art also disappear through abstraction. The artistically talented neuroanatomist, who studied painting as a teenager, eventually took the first Spanish color photographs at the turn of the twentieth century. He drew all his own illustrations for his studies of brain anatomy. Most people probably assume that he drew directly from what he saw, but they could not be more wrong. Ramón y Cajal explained that he would spend the morning preparing and observing dozens of sections of the brain or the spinal cord.

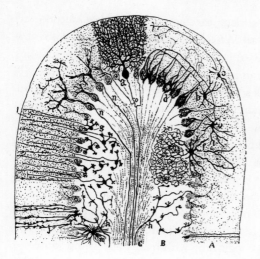

Fig. 5-12. Schematized transverse section of a typical convolution in a mammalian cerebellum by Santiago Ramón y Cajal.

Then, after lunch, he would draw what he remembered. Then he would compare his drawings to his preparations. He would analyze the differences, then draw again, repeating this process over and over and over. Only when the drawings he made from memory captured the essence of what he saw in an entire series of preparations would he consider them finished. The result was not a specific representation of a particular slice of a particular brain but a picture of what could be expected of any such slice of that portion of the brain taken from any individual — the abstract reality of the anatomy underlying the unique reality of each individual.

Ramón y Cajal's example puts the lie to the old adage that scientists simply record what they see. In fact, his drawings so accurately captured the essence of neuroanatomy that even in this day of sophisticated photography, high-tech stains, and three-dimensional representations of the brain's structure, many textbook writers still prefer his drawings for their clarity and conciseness. Unlike a photograph, which is an image of a unique specimen filled with unnecessary details, Ramón y Cajal's drawings show students what they should look for among the clutter of details in their own specimens. Matisse would have understood completely, for his method was exactly the same as Ramón y Cajal's: "I often told my students when I had a school: The ideal would be to have a studio with three floors. One would do a first study after the model on the first floor. From the second, one would come down more rarely. On the third, one would have learned to do without the model."

"It's abundantly obvious," notes Mitchell Feigenbaum, one of the inventors of the new mathematical science of chaos theory, "that one doesn't know the world around us in detail. What artists have accomplished is realizing there's only a small amount of stuff that's important and then seeing what it was. So they can do some of my research for me." He goes on to say, "I truly do want to know how to describe clouds," but the physicist's usual approach — using an enormous array of density measurements analyzed by differential calculus — "is wrong. It's certainly not how a human being perceives those things, and it's not how an artist perceives them. Somewhere the business of writing down partial differential equations is not to have done the work on the problem." What Feigenbaum is after, whether through artistic abstraction, mathematical abstraction, or a combination of both, is to find an abstraction that yields that sudden "aha!" so typical of great insights. Consequently, he does much of his scientific research in art museums.

Abstracting, then, is a process beginning with reality and using some tool to pare away the excess to reveal a critical, often surprising, essence. Artists do it; writers do it; scientists, mathematicians, and dancers do it. And they all do it in the same basic way. You can, too. Use one of the abstraction sequences discussed in this chapter — Picasso's *Bulls,* for example, or "Observations on a Water-Worn Stone" — as a guide. Choose your subject and your abstracting tool; think about them realistically; play around with their various properties or characteristics; get at what might be most essential; then consider and reconsider your results from a distance of time or space. Say your abstraction, mime it, sing it, write it in prose, write it in poetry, extract a concept or a metaphor. Practice with artwork, or, if you are scientifically inclined, practice with simple experiments or mathematical concepts. If you are a dancer, replicate the real movements of real people or of animals, then try to find the essence characterizing that personality or that species. Describe in music the distillation of birdness or windness or a carousel. Find the minimum vocabulary to convey the maximum amount of sense and sensibility.

It's never too soon or too late to start abstracting. Children in grade school can learn to search for and express what for them is the single most important thing about the room, a story, or the day. More mature learners can search for less obvious characteristics of objects and ideas that reveal more surprising and fundamental abstractions. Inspire yourself by collecting examples of abstracting by masters. Imitate. Test your progress by abstracting some object such as an orange or a human being over and over again. What abstractions have you discovered that you overlooked before? Orange juice? The heart's beat? A list of chemical constituents? Can you refine these and other abstractions even further than you first thought, engaging, like Picasso, in an abstracting process over time?

There are no "right" answers to these questions: only a never-ending quest for greater simplicity and more profound truths. Ultimately, what matters is finding the essence of abstraction itself to light your way wherever you explore.

6

Recognizing Patterns

L ET'S BEGIN THIS CHAPTER with a bit of fun. What do you get when you cross an owl with a female goat? How about crossing Lassie with a cantaloupe? Be careful: these are riddles, and the answers are puns. If you cross an owl with a goat you get a hootenanny. Cross Lassie with a cantaloupe and get, yep, a melancholy baby. And what do you get if you cross an abbey with a perfume factory? (Hint: the answer sounds like a well-known musical — nunscents!)

Lest you think *this* is all nonsense, be assured it is not. The subject of this chapter is recognizing patterns, and there is a pattern, a repetitive form or plan, to these "crossing" riddles. The riddle inventor finds a polysyllabic word whose parts sound like two other words: melancholy becomes melon and collie. The inventor then proceeds to make logical associations between these words and other well-known things. Melon becomes cantaloupe; collie becomes Lassie. The result is the question: "What do you get when you cross Lassie with a cantaloupe?" The pun or puns that result from the new joining of words create the surprise answer that makes the joke interesting. Once you get the pattern, it's not too hard to make up your own crossing riddle.

Of course, there would be no such thing as jokes if human beings weren't inclined to recognize patterns in the first place. As the psychologist P. C. Dodwell put it, "The ability to synthesize proteins, respond reflexively to a stimulus, get across the road, choose a mate, or decide among complex problem-solving strategies all depend on this skill." Every moment of every day we organize the random events we see, hear, or feel by grouping them. And as Horace Judson makes clear in *The Search for Solutions,* "To perceive a pattern means that we have already formed an idea what's next." Our ability to recognize patterns is the basis for our ability to make predictions and form expectations.

But patterns — and jokes — can be deceptive. Consider a few more riddles. What do you get when you cross the Atlantic with the *Titanic?* What do you get when you cross the Mafia? These seem to be crossing riddles, but the punch lines are of quite a different nature. Cross the Atlantic with the *Titanic* and get . . . very wet! (Or a ride in a lifeboat.) Cross the Mafia and get . . . cement overshoes. The surprise in these instances comes from the *breaking* of the pattern you have come to expect for answers to crossing riddles. All jokes in fact depend upon setting up the expectation of one pattern and then substituting another, a kind of bait and switch. As comedian (and mathematician) Tom Lehrer, who sets his droll lines to popular forms of music, explains, "Clearly it has something to do with expectancy. A well-known tune sets up a challenge. There's a template. Now, can he do it? The trick is to avoid what the listener has provisionally guessed. You have to satisfy the task but avoid predictability. That's what is creative, the surprise." If the comedian fails to create the necessary expectation in the audience (pattern number one), or if the audience fails to perceive the apt nature of the joke's resolution

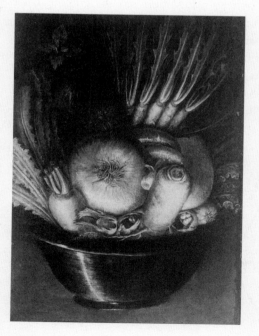

Fig. 6-1. *The Gardener* by
Giuseppe Arcimboldo (1527–1593).

(pattern number two), the joke falls flat. No expectancy, no surprise; no surprise, no fun.

According to Arthur Koestler in *The Act of Creation* (1976), the same patterns that are characteristic of jokes turn out to be characteristic of all creative endeavors, including science and art. We derive from patterns that we recognize general principles of perception and action and base our expectations on those patterns. Then we try to fit new observations and experiences into these expectations. Discovery occurs when, willy-nilly, something about our observations and experiences forces us to make another pattern. The still life by the Italian Renaissance painter Guiseppe Arcimboldo is the visual equivalent of a joke (see Fig. 6-1). At first, we see only a bowl of vegetables, but if we look at it upside down, we see quite a different pattern. When we finally perceive Arcimboldo's intent, we realize we've been focusing on only one set of characteristics. The new pattern yields connections between things previously perceived as being unrelated. The viewer has undergone what psychologists call a "gestalt shift," in which the same sensory information can take on two or more noncommensurate meanings. Another example of a simple gestalt shift is the interconversion of a hexagon into a cube. Is it a flat six-sided figure or a three-dimensional one made of squares? Can you make the pattern go back and forth between two and three dimensions?

One of the great masters of pattern recognition was the graphic artist M. C. Escher, who apparently practiced this skill daily. According to his son, George Escher, "The wall in the small downstairs washroom was decorated with irregular swirls of green, yellow, red and brown. . . . Father would take a pencil and emphasize a line here, a shade there . . ." and find a face, "laughing, sad, grotesque, or solemn." Over the course of many months the wall "came alive with faces." Escher also enjoyed identifying "animal shapes in

Fig 6-2. Two views of a cube.

Fig. 6-3. Complementary faces in wood grain.

seemingly random patterns like clouds or wood grain." In his art Escher married this kind of pattern recognition with formal tessellations or tilings. When we look at his interlocking animals we realize that no matter how complicated the figures, there is always a simple, symmetrical pattern underneath. Escher's genius was to see in a regular, repeating polygon the possibility of fish, birds, lizards, angels, devils, and other unexpected surprises — and to teach us how to see these things, too (see Fig. 6-4).

Recognizing patterns within patterns has stimulated many artists. The nineteenth-century French glass blower Emile Gallé searched for patterns in the unpredictable shapes and strange effects of blown glass, in the same way, he said, that one "transforms the marblings of wall-paper into thousands of strange figures, or the clouds at twilight [into] immense sheep folds." The surrealist painter Max Ernst, stuck indoors at a seaside inn because of heavy rain, found inspiration in the patterns of a wood floor. He placed paper on the roughened boards in his room and made rubbings of the wood grain using a lead pencil. There emerged a "dream-like succession of contradictory images," he later wrote. "Now my curiosity was roused and excited, and I began an impartial exploration, making use of every kind of material that hap-

Fig. 6-4. *Piranhas and Lobsters,* an Escher-style tessellation by Robert Root-Bernstein.

pened to come into my field of vision: leaves and their veins, frayed edges of sacking, brush-strokes in a 'modern' painting, cotton unwound from a cotton-reel, etc. etc."

Within a short time, Ernst parlayed his fascination with pattern recognition into several new techniques that revolutionized modern art: *frottage,* in which paper is placed over an object and rubbed with pencil or crayon to pick up the texture; *grattage,* in which paint is scraped onto a canvas placed over rough or textured objects; and *decalcomania,* in which images made, for instance, from random splotches of paint on one paper are transferred to another by laying the second piece on top of the first and gently rubbing. Rorschach-type blots are produced in this last way by placing ink or paint at random in the center of a piece of paper, folding it over, and then opening it up again. The resulting lines, textures, and shapes are subject to multiple interpretations. In essence, each individual observer makes the image he or she recognizes, as well as its meaning.

Add Leonardo da Vinci to the list of artists who used pattern recognition to come up with new ideas. In "A Way of Stimulating and Arousing the Mind to Various Inventions," Leonardo advised himself and others to "look at a wall spotted with stains, or with a mixture of different kinds of stones; if you have to invent some scene, you may discover a similarity with different kinds of landscapes, embellished with mountains, rivers, rocks, trees, plains, wide valleys and hills in varied arrangement: or, again, you may see battles and figures in action or strange faces and costumes, and an endless variety of objects which you could reduce to complete and well-drawn forms." Leonardo thought so highly of his inventive "device" that he used it aurally as well as visually. A fine musician who participated in opera improvisations and other musical amusements for the Italian courts, he knew that the ear was as subtle as the eye in discovering patterns. "It happens with this confused appearance of walls," he observed, "as it does with the sound of bells in whose jangle you may find any name or word you can imagine."

Aural pattern recognition is exactly the premise of that old Mother Goose rhyme "The Bells of St. Helen's," in whose many versions verbal phrases are "heard" in the chimes of various churches:

> *"You owe me five shillings,"*
> *Say the bells of St. Helen's.*
> *"When will you pay me?"*
> *Say the bells of Old Bailey.*
> *"When I grow rich,"*
> *Say the bells of Shoreditch.*
> *"When will that be?"*
> *Say the bells of Stepney . . .*

In fact, it is not unusual to hear patterns in all sorts of rhythmic and random sounds. Many people imagine the ringing of a phone in the water noise of the shower or hear the e-mail phone line say "golly-gee." Anyone who has heard the *chk-chk-chk* of a woodchuck or the *chick-a-dee-dee-dee* of a chickadee understands where their common English names came from. Every language has echoic or onomatopaeic words that originated in the imitation of distinctive noise: in English, brooks burble, snakes hiss, and iron clangs.

More complex patterns exist in everyday speech and writing. In colloquial English, many words consist of two syllables with the accent on the second; these two syllables make up the iambic "foot" or unit we hear in goodBYE, fareWELL, aDIEU. This rhythm may be particularly common because it mimics many natural sounds, such as the heartbeat and breathing — bah-BUM, bah-BUM, bah-BUM. Moreover, when we string a number of words together, the iambic foot often repeats itself in the rise and fall of our voice. It is fairly easy to say and write whole sentences in a regularly repeating iambic rhythm, as William Wordsworth did in "i WANdered LONEly AS a CLOUD." In trochaic rhythm, a two-syllable foot carries the accent on the first syllable, as in "WANder;" in anapestic a three-syllable foot carries the accent on the third syllable, as in "in the BREEZE;" in dactylic a three-syllable foot carries the accent on the first syllable, as in "DAFFodils;" and in spondaic both syllables are stressed, as in "HEAR! HEAR!" When you learn to recognize these patterns, you begin to "find" poetry everywhere.

"Found poetry" is, in fact, a literary form unto itself. Although it has no absolute rules, practitioners search for or stumble upon unintentionally poetic lines in prose texts of all sorts — news articles, advertisements, books — and then reorganize or slightly alter the lines to emphasize their poetic nature. The extraordinary thing about found poems is that the same words can often be organized in various ways to reveal quite different inherent patterns.

For example, take a look at the following passage from astronaut Michael Collins's book, *Carrying the Fire:* "I have been places and done things you simply would not believe. . . . I feel like saying: I have dangled from a cord 100 miles up; I have seen the Earth eclipsed by the Moon, and enjoyed it. I have seen the Sun's true light, unfiltered by any planet's atmosphere. I have seen the ultimate black of infinity in a stillness undisturbed by any living thing." One of us (Michèle) has rearranged and edited Collins's words to make three different poems, each illustrating a different rhythmic pattern. The first emphasizes syllabic rhythm, in which the line length is determined by a set number of syllables. The second features a kind of sprung rhythm, in which each line has the same number of stressed syllables but no regular pattern of measured feet. The third is a measured rhythm based on repeating iambs.

Astronaut I	Astronaut II	Astronaut III
Dangling from a cord	Dangling from a cord	I dangled from a cord;
I have seen the Earth	I have seen the Earth	I saw the Earth
by Moon eclipsed	by Moon eclipsed	by Moon eclipsed, the Sun's
		true light, the black
I have seen the Sun's	I have seen the Sun's	of stillness undisturbed
true light unfiltered	true light	by any living thing.
by atmosphere	unfiltered by atmosphere	
the ultimate black	the ultimate black	
of infinity	of infinity in a stillness	
in a stillness	undisturbed.	
undisturbed.		

The Teachers and Writers Handbook of Poetic Forms, compiled by Ron Padgett, urges students not to try to learn such rhythmic patterns through intellectual exercise or analysis alone. Rather, it suggests that "one good way to learn about rhythmic variation is to listen to bebop and modern jazz, and to dance. Rhythm is a skill that is best learned through the ears and legs, not through the brain." In fact, knowing how patterns in mediums as different as music, dance, and poetry are related is the first step toward recognizing meta-patterns — the patterns that link other patterns together. Photographer Ansel Adams, a phenomenal pianist, who as a teen aspired to a professional music career, could still remember many decades later the day when he suddenly connected musical pattern to the visual pattern of notes on the page. His piano teacher, whom Adams revered, asked him to consider how a phrase of rising and falling notes looked like "a hill to climb and descend," a thing "to lift and let fall," and urged him to "try it" on the keyboard. Adams did, and in his words, "Shape was born! If the notes were accurate, their volume should be in relation to their 'lift.'"

For musicians of all stamps, seeing the musical pattern can be as important as hearing it. And so can seeing or feeling the musical pattern as a series of movements, as a kinesthetic pattern. Pianist Mischa Dichter has described how he memorizes music. First he looks for aural and visual structures, such as intervals, that form the harmonic units of the piece. "My mind remains fixed on those big blocks . . . of harmonic structure or melodic pattern," he said, "because by then the hand has formed almost a visual image of those blocks and I have a picture not only of the harmony, but the hand relative to these main blocks." The purpose of practicing is to meld visual, aural, and kinesthetic patterns into one seamless meta-pattern. "All falls together in a grand, yet apparently simple creative pattern," wrote Adams, "that reveals high levels of memory, comprehension, and sensitivity."

Obviously, recognizing patterns and meta-patterns requires multisensory observation. It often requires conceptual analysis as well. Composer and conductor Leonard Bernstein provided a beautiful musical example in his book *The Unanswered Question*. As a student at Harvard, Bernstein recalled, he "made a startling discovery." A four-note pattern in Aaron Copland's *Variations* was also at the heart of other, very different compositions (see Fig. 6-5). As Bernstein described it,

> The first four notes of the piece [2], which are the germ of the whole composition, are really these four notes [3], with the fourth note displaced an octave higher [4]. And I suddenly realized that these same

[2]

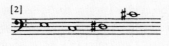

[3].

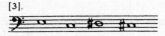

[4]

[5]

[6]

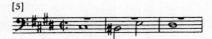

[7]

[8]

Fig. 6-5. Common patterns in music, as described by Leonard Bernstein.

four notes, in another order, formed the subject of Bach's C-sharp minor Fugue from the *Well-Tempered Clavicord* (Book I) [5]. Simultaneously I discovered the same four notes, transposed, with the first note repeated, germinating the variations in Stravinsky's Octet [6]. *And* the same four notes flashed through my mind, in yet another order and key, as the initial motto of Ravel's Spanish Rhapsody [7]. And on top of all *that* I suddenly recalled some Hindu music I had heard (I was a big Oriental music buff at the time) — and there were those same four notes again [8].

If the similarities that flashed through Bernstein's mind are not immediately apparent, don't worry. You may never have realized that the child's tune "Baa, Baa, Black Sheep, Have You Any Wool?" is really "Twinkle, Twinkle, Little Star," either. As in any form of pattern recognition, one must know what to expect and how to compare things before the patterns become evident. To begin with, you must realize that notes, for musicians, are like three-dimensional objects, as Arnold Schoenberg contended. "Just as our mind always recognizes, for instance a knife, a bottle or a watch, regardless of its position," he wrote, "and can reproduce it in imagination in every possible position, even so a musical creator's mind can operate subconsciously with a row of tones regardless of their direction." They can be looked at upside down, backward, inside out, and rearranged without losing their essential relations. Indeed, the composer is more interested in the *relationship* between notes than in the *order* of specific tones as read from left to right.

An analogy might help. Most of us know our own names backward as well as forward (Trebor = Robert; Elehcim = Michèle) and recognize that "dog" and "god" are composed of the same letters. One can rearrange letters to form new words: "Michèle" can be transposed into "ice helm," for example. With some thought we can also see that the word "add" is related to "bee," in that "add" is made up of the first and fourth letters of the alphabet and "bee" of the second and fifth. One can convert "add" into "bee" by simply moving the word down the alphabet in the same way a musician might change keys. The internal relationship of the letters to the alphabet order is still the same. Just so, musicians recognize relationships between musical patterns and relationships between patterns in different musical keys.

Now we can understand Bernstein's examples even without formal musical training simply by looking at the notes in Figure 6–5 as patterns. The Bach C-sharp minor fugue (5) is in a different key from the previous examples, but it retains the same intervals between the notes, just as "add" and "bee" do in the alphabet. The Ravel example (7) is in the same key as the Bach, but the notes are in a transposed order, like "arts" and "tsar." The Hindu music is simply a series of variations like "Michèle" and "ice helm," of the orders of the notes in the Bach and Ravel, in the same key.

Oddly enough, dyslexic individuals seem to process words and numbers the way musicians process music. Most people learn to read the equation $12 + 12 = 24$ by parsing the symbols linearly from left to right. Dyslexic individuals, however, often construe this statement in very different ways. The following figure shows the interpretation of $12 + 12$ according to eighteen

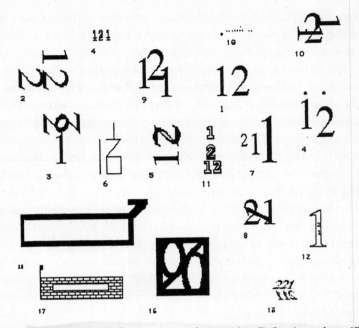

Fig. 6-6. Answers by dyslexic artists to the question "What is 12 plus 12?"

dyslexic artists. Rather than reading the statement as a two-dimensional one in a single linear direction, most of these artists process it in nonlinear and multidimensional ways. They alter the orientation, stack or overlap the numbers, invert them, alter their scale, typeface, and perspective, and in some cases (16–18) alter the formulation almost beyond recognition. Such artwork gives us clues not only to the possible visual-processing changes involved in dyslexia but also suggests how stereotyped our own pattern recognition tends to be. There are so many ways of looking at the same object or idea, yet most of us see only one way.

But not all of us do. Like musicians and dyslexics, mathematicians tend to excel at perceiving patterns in more than one way. And like musicians, mathematicians are good at recognizing patterns of relationship. A story about Carl Friedrich Gauss, one of the greatest mathematicians who ever lived, amply illustrates the point. As a young student, Gauss and his classmates were asked one day to add up all the numbers from 1 to 100. We can imagine the groans. But a few seconds later Gauss gave the correct answer. How could he possibly have performed such a feat? He had not done the calculation before, nor was he a phenomenal calculator. He was, however, an extraordinary pattern recognizer. What he noticed is that if you take a number at the beginning of the series 0 to 100 (0 being implied in the original problem) and add it to a number in the same position at the end of the series, it always adds up to 100. Thus, $100 + 0 = 100$; $99 + 1 = 100$; $98 + 2 = 100$; $97 + 3 = 100$; and so on, up to $51 + 49 = 100$. That leaves only the number 50 unpaired. So the 50 pairs of numbers that each add up to $100 = 5000$. Then add in the unpaired 50 and there's the answer: 5,050. Like the answer to many a joke, the solution to the problem was completely unexpected.

The solution of much more complicated problems can sometimes be reduced to similarly straightforward calculations. For example, what is the sum of the infinite series, $x = 1 + \frac{1}{2} + \frac{1}{4} + \frac{1}{8} + \frac{1}{16} \ldots$? This may look complicated or perhaps even impossible, but with a bit of clever manipulating, the problem is trivial. Given that x equals the series described above, then the series $x/2$ would be the sum of one half of each term, or $x/2 = \frac{1}{2} + \frac{1}{4} + \frac{1}{8} + \frac{1}{16} + \frac{1}{32} \ldots$. This second series bears an obvious resemblance to the first, which gives us an interesting option. We can subtract the second series from the first: $x - x/2 = (1 + \frac{1}{2} + \frac{1}{4} + \frac{1}{8} \ldots) - (\frac{1}{2} + \frac{1}{4} + \frac{1}{8} \ldots)$. Rearranging gives $x - x/2 = 1 + (\frac{1}{2} - \frac{1}{2}) + (\frac{1}{4} - \frac{1}{4}) + (\frac{1}{8} - \frac{1}{8}) \ldots$ All the fractional terms cancel, leaving $x - x/2 = 1$. It follows that $x = 2$. We have solved the original problem with a minimum of work by taking advantage of a number pattern. In fact, good mathematicians realize that whole classes of problems can be solved using this and other patterns. Half of mastering mathematics is simply recognizing the type of problem-solving pattern that applies to each problem. As Philip Davis and Reuben Hersh have written, "To some extent the whole object of mathematics is to create order where previously chaos seemed to reign, to extract structure and invariance from the midst of disarray and turmoil."

For mathematicians, a most frustrating situation occurs when no one can be sure that the pattern recognized is real. Goldbach's conjecture is a prime example. Christian Goldbach suggested, some 250 years ago, that every even number can be described as the sum of two prime numbers. For example, $24 = 13 + 11$. No exceptions are known, but no one so far has proven that exceptions cannot exist. Is the pattern real or imaginary? If it is real, why should numbers have this property? Such mysteries are what motivate mathematicians.

Mysteries also motivate scientists to look for patterns in the apparent chaos of nature. Most scientists believe that no matter how complex nature appears to be, the basic principles and laws are cogent and comprehensible. Sometimes all it takes to make a discovery is to recognize the patterns in front of our eyes. One could reasonably characterize medical diagnosis as pattern recognition, in which visual, tactile, auditory, olfactory, and technical information is combined and compared with existing descriptions of disease. Discoveries in medicine therefore often involve paying attention to new kinds of information or finding new ways to use existing information. For example, the field of epidemiology — the study of the origin and spread of disease — is often said to have begun when Dr. John Snow mapped the residences of people who died of cholera in central London in 1854. The map clearly showed that all of the deceased had drawn their water from a single contaminated water pump. In retrospect, we find it difficult to understand why no one had ever mapped deaths before, but they had not, and without data concerning the victims' time and place of death, no epidemiological patterns could be recognized.

In other cases, maps hold clues that people have seen and not understood. Many people in the past undoubtedly noticed that Africa and South America are similar in shape. Sir Francis Bacon recorded this observation almost as soon as the world had been circumnavigated and the shapes of the continents outlined. Geologically more important is the fact that the west coast of Africa seems to fit into the east coast of South America as if they were parts of a jigsaw puzzle. Several people during the nineteenth century, including Alexander von Humboldt and Antonio Snider-Pellegrini, pointed out this fact. The first person to take these observations seriously, however, was the geologist Alfred Wegener, who showed not only that Africa and South America fit together, but so did North America, Greenland, and Europe. Moreover, the rock strata and the fossils along the continental coasts, though separated by the whole of the Atlantic Ocean, also matched. Wegener theorized that once upon a time all of the continents on earth had been joined in one supercontinent he called Pangaea ("all earth"). Fifty years later, Harry Hess revolutionized geology by identifying the mechanisms of continental drift that broke Pangaea into the slowly separating continents we see today. Once properly assembled, the puzzle of continental drift allowed other patterns to fall into place: earthquakes shake, volcanoes erupt, and mountains form where the continental plates collide, buckle, or break.

In fact, the jigsaw puzzle, a broken pattern if ever there was one, is a powerful metaphor for scientists even when they apply it to theoretical or conceptual issues rather than to purely observational ones like a map. Nature provides tantalizing clues about the principles governing its operation — what Nobel laureates Chen Ning Yang, a physicist, and Christiane Nüsslein-Volhard, an embryologist, both call "pieces of a jigsaw puzzle." Scientists

Fig. 6-7. Drawing of Pangaea by Alfred Wegener.

must assemble the pieces to make sense of the big picture, which unfortunately is seldom available even in outline, as it was to Wegener. More often, scientists have pieces from many different puzzles all mixed together with no guide as to which pieces go together or what the various overall pictures might be. In cases such as this, Nüsslein-Volhard says, "The most important thing is not any one particular piece, but finding enough pieces and enough connections between them to recognize the whole picture." The most critical part of research is not getting the data, but making sense of it. To quote Yang, "This constant searching for new associations, subconsciously or consciously, is one important element of scientific research. You don't constantly attack one problem. If you have a lot of small linkages, you try to make them fit, and then once in a while you find one piece which can put five pieces together. That joy is indescribable." When enough data and concepts cohere, and conceptual puzzles become conceptual patterns or "pictures," scientists call them theories or natural laws.

Scientific puzzle solving is like jigsaw-puzzle solving in another way as well. When enough pieces have been fitted together, they may define either a whole or a hole. Both are valuable. The whole is a new structure that makes sense of the available data. But the hole — what is not there — is also useful because it is a valuable clue to the shape of our ignorance. Having defined that shape, we can now look for specific pieces to fill the hole. Our search for linkages is no longer random. We have a specific question to answer and definite criteria to use in evaluating possible answers. Almost every scientist of note has said something along the lines of "properly defining your question gets you more than halfway to its solution." Questions, from this point of view, are also patterns.

Knowing what you don't know, knowing the pattern of your ignorance, can be as valuable as knowing what you do know. "It is the mountain of the unknown that spurs scientific progress," writes Nobel laureate Thomas Weller. "The only interesting fields of science are the ones where you still don't know what you're talking about," said Nobelist I. I. Rabi. Fellow prize-winner Szent-Györgyi agreed: "A scientific researcher must be attracted to these [blank] spots on the map of human knowledge, and if need be, be willing to give his life for filling them in." One notable application of these words has been made by philosopher Ann Kerwin, an expert in the origins of ignorance, and surgeons Marlys and Charles Witte at the University of Arizona Medical School. They have developed a "curriculum on medical ignorance" specifically to train medical students how to ask questions and recognize blank spots in the map of medicine. Such a curriculum would obviously be useful in every discipline.

Eliot Hearst, a psychologist at Indiana University who also specializes in what we don't know, suggests an even more radical idea. In a fascinating paper titled "Psychology and Nothing," he points out that as important as nothingness is to musicians ("the rest is silence"), artists and architects (negative space, the gaps between objects), scientists (the perfect vacuum and absolute zero), philosophers (nihilism), and novelists (the famous Sherlock Holmes case in which the crucial clue is the dog who did not bark), we know almost nothing about nothing. "Recognizing and learning from absence, deletion, and nonoccurrence are surprisingly difficult," Hearst writes. "Animals and people, it seems, accentuate the positive." For example, everyone can remember occasions when a horoscope or a fortune cookie was right. Very few of us remember the myriad predictions that never came to pass. But Hearst surmises that in matters related to mind, in direct distinction to thermodynamics, it may be possible to get "something for nothing." The key is to build up, by means of predictions or even vague intuitions, a sufficient sense of what *should* be present in a particular situation so that absence becomes anomalous and therefore strikingly interesting. Hearst believes that if problems dealing with the absence, nonoccurrence, or deletion of events and information were incorporated into learning situations more rigorously and regularly, nothingness would become as useful a tool in perception, memory, and problem generation as any other.

The biggest problem posed by our ignorance of nothingness is how to determine when a pattern is absent because it doesn't exist and when it is present but can't be perceived. A visual puzzle used for many years by members of the Department of Natural Sciences at Michigan State University provides an apt illustration. The puzzle was accompanied by the caption "A Theory Is a Pattern of Data," and students were challenged to figure it out in order to grasp the concept that data per se — the puzzle pieces — are not sufficient to discover their meaning. The puzzle, reproduced here, provides all the data you need to solve it, but it is sufficiently difficult that significant numbers of students have concluded that there is no pattern.

In fact, there is a solution to the puzzle (see the end of the chapter), but in order to perceive it, you will probably need some clues. Culture influences pattern recognition in subtle ways, and in this case interferes with many Americans' solving of the puzzle. People around the world tend to recognize only those patterns favored in the arts and the sciences with which they grew up. Pattern bias exists in architecture and in art, in landscaping and city planning, in graphing data, even in the astronomical organization of the stars. American Indians and the Chinese do not see Orion or his belt — an ancient Western constellation — but pattern the stars in other ways.

Pattern differences also appear in games. For instance, hopscotch is played

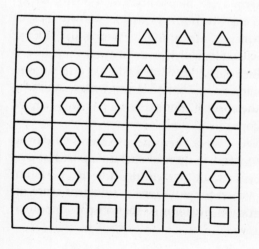

Fig. 6-8. Pattern puzzle.

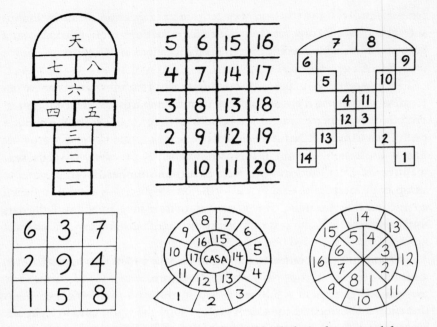

Fig. 6-9. Hopscotch patterns from around the world. *Clockwise from upper left:* Chinese; British name beds; Italian; British hop-round; Latin American and French snail; Danish *hinka.*

around the world in a considerable variety of forms, which, not incidentally, hold clues to solving our puzzle. Most of the variations work upon a common visual and kinesthetic pattern. The Chinese hopscotch board, for instance, is basically rectilinear, like the North American board, as are most of those from Europe, Asia, South America, Africa, and the West Indies. In England a somewhat different form, a rectangular array of twenty squares, is used to play a version of hopscotch called Name Bed. Similar grid patterns can also be found in India. In all cases, the rules are much the same, with players required to hop their way through the pattern along well-defined vertical and horizontal lines.

Some hopscotch games, however, break the general pattern. One of us learned to play Danish hopscotch (*hinka* or *Hinkerude*) on a board of nine boxes in which the numbers were laid out in a way that forced a nonlinear progression through the grid. A circular progression is mandated by the game board of hop-round, another British form of hopscotch supposedly derived from the cartwheel of the early Roman invaders. And in France and certain Latin American countries a form of hopscotch called the snail (*caracol* or *escargot*) is laid out in the form of a spiral.

A bit of reflection reveals that the truly unusual form is the French and Latin American one. While rectangular and rectilinear forms and even round ones are extremely common in Western cultures and can be found in everything from the shapes of our buildings to the tables and graphs on the nightly news, spiral forms — such as the Guggenheim Museum in New York City — are extremely rare. Although nature is full of spirals — snails, seashells, tornados, pinecones, the whorls of hair on your head — we tend to be blind to these shapes because very little in our man-made world mimics them. The pattern in our "Theory Is a Pattern" puzzle is, in fact, a spiral, even though the grid is rectangular. It just takes an eye for the culturally unusual to recognize it.

Cultural influences on pattern recognition also mediate what and how we invent. For example, Western science teaches us from a young age to think of the world in Euclidean geometric terms. We speak of "three dimensions" that can be described on the Cartesian x-y-z system of axes, each at right angles to the others. Nearly everything we see is built or described in these terms. This coordinate system becomes what Thomas Kuhn called a *paradigm,* a widely applicable pattern used to set up and solve problems within a particular field. But every paradigm has its limitations. Dimensional patterns that work in a fixed place on earth fail when it comes to navigating the globe. Think of longitude and latitude, which don't extend in straight lines as do Cartesian coordinates, but curve around the earth spherically. A different system of polar coordinates, which identifies location with regard to vectors in a spherical universe, is much more useful than geometric coordinates for applications such as celestial navigation and space flight.

Polar coordinates do not solve all problems left undone by geometric axes, however. Inventor Buckminster Fuller attributed his invention of the geodesic dome to his early rejection of both the standard x, y, z and polar systems in favor of a tetrahedral paradigm. Einstein similarly rejected Euclidean geometry for a non-Euclidian formulation that gives rise to his famous description of space and time curving in relativistic gravitational fields. Both Einstein and Fuller understood explicitly that Euclidean geometry is only one version of the world. Non-Euclidian geometries, spherical geometries, and many other mathematical formulations of space exist, each providing a different set of patterns for the use of inventors, builders, artists, and other

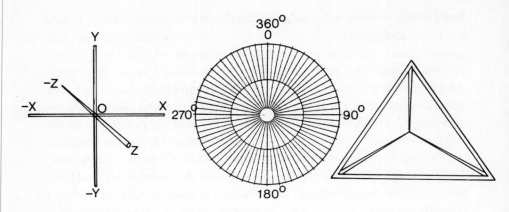

Fig. 6-10. Different patterns are associated with different coordinate systems of space. *Above, left to right:* Cartesian coordinates; polar coordinates; Buckminster Fuller's tetrahedral coordinates; each illustrated by a tessellation by M. C. Escher. As Doris Schattschneider and Wallace Walker have shown, it is possible to create tessellations called kaleidocycles on the surfaces of three-dimensional objects such as tetrahedrons. Kaleidocycles are a recent geometric discovery.

innovators. The problem is that we can't use what we don't know. Our pattern-recognizing ability benefits from practice with these different versions of space, just as it benefits from familiarity with different forms of hopscotch.

Given the complexity of pattern recognition, how can we exercise and enhance this imaginative skill? We can, of course, take advantage of the pattern bias of different cultures and systematically explore the unfamiliar ways in which people order seeing, hearing, dancing, feeling, doing. We can't recognize patterns we have never experienced. But there's more to it than that.

Recognizing patterns, whether from other cultures or from our own time and place, takes practice.

And practice we can — no matter what age we are. Physicist Richard Feynman began learning about patterns when he was "very small in a high chair." His father brought home some small bathroom tiles for him to play with and showed him how to set them up "in a more complicated way: two white tiles and a blue tile, two white tiles and a blue tile, and so on." In this way Feynman senior taught his son "what patterns are like, and how interesting they are. It's a kind of elementary mathematics." Such are the advantages for young and old alike of games as simple as dominos or as complex as chess. The key to tick-tack-toe, checkers, and chess is recognizing what patterns on the board are likely to win the game and what patterns are not. In fact, studies of top chess players have shown that much of their skill resides in pattern recognition rather than in application of rules, specific strategies, or exhaustive investigation of possible moves. Whereas computer programs designed to play chess calculate the odds of winning with any of millions of possible combinations of moves at each stage of a match, a chess master will instantly recognize the arrangement of pieces on the board as a pattern that suggests a particular strategy. Successful military commanders develop the same pattern-recognizing ability, though their purpose is hardly play.

Playing with jigsaw puzzles also exercises pattern recognition, as does puzzle making. One of the oddest things we have found in researching this book is how many eminent people in every field are puzzle addicts (like Napoleon Bonaparte) or puzzle inventors. Nüsslein-Volhard, the embryologist who compares her science to puzzle solving, designs "impossible" puzzles for her own and other people's amusement. Numerous mathematicians and physicists have designed puzzles as well, many of which can be found in Martin Gardner's mathematical recreation books. In some cases, the invention of a puzzle leads to the recognition of wholly new patterns. Designer Erno Rubik is justifiably famous for his cubes, which he developed to teach

Fig. 6-11. Invent your own puzzles.

Fig. 6-12. Why do we see faces or figures in inanimate objects?

three-dimensional color patterns to design students. Playing around with Rubik's cube became the basis for Alexander Frey and David Singmaster's book *Cubik Math* (1982), a look at the mathematics of permutations.

In addition to playing with puzzles and games, we can look for familiar patterns in unfamiliar places. Psychological studies indicate that infants in the first few months of life respond strongly to anything resembling the human face — in fact, the "need" to find faces stays with us through life. In 1997 two Swiss graphic designers, François and Jean Robert, produced *Face to Face,* a book filled with images of man-made objects — clocks, doorknobs, radios, handbags, cameras, bottle openers, and other diverse objects — that have in common their resemblance to faces. Look around and you'll see faces too, as well as entire bodies.

To help children see patterns, read to them Ludwig Bemelmans's *Madeline,* in which "a crack on the ceiling had the habit/ of sometimes looking like a rabbit." Or read them another children's classic called *It Looked Like Spilt Milk,* which enumerates a succession of things seen in a cloud configuration. In *A High Wind in Jamaica,* by Richard Hughes, a little girl kidnapped by pirates amuses herself by finding shapes and faces in the woodwork of her cabin. We can help children learn the ways of Escher, Ernst, and Leonardo simply by encouraging them to find images in doors, wood paneling, wallpaper, floors, tree trunks, window frost, and oddly shaped fruits and vegetables (see Chapter 13).

Both young and old can also look for patterns in words. The best children's books exploit verbal rhythms and rhymes, much to everyone's delight. Look for the same patterns in everyday speech or look for "found poems" in the newspaper. Older children can arrange the words they find in simple poetic forms, such as couplets, limericks, or haiku. They can write their own poetry in these forms, too. Teens and adults can work with the more complex poetic patterns described in books such as Padgett's *The Teachers and Writers Handbook of Poetic Forms* (1987) or Miller Williams's *Patterns of Poetry* (1986). Look for word games in Tony Augarde's *Oxford Guide to Word Games*. Make up jokes. Pun. Have fun.

And while you're having fun, look for meta-patterns. For instance, search for passages in contemporary dance music that sound similar to or have the same rhythm as phrases in classical music. Compare these musical rhythms to formal dance patterns, such as the waltz or the tango, and to their visual trace on the floor. Now compare these rhythms to patterns in language. Are such musical, kinesthetic, visual, or verbal patterns at all similar to patterns of knitting or weaving? Are the fabric patterns typical of different countries related to the patterns found in their art and music? Finding patterns among patterns depends most of all on posing your own questions about the repetitive order or plan of things — and on looking, listening, feeling for the answers.

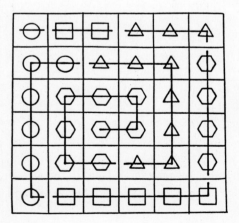

Fig. 6-13. Solution to the pattern puzzle in Fig. 6-8.

One last word: recognizing patterns sometimes requires a certain amount of tolerance for dawdling and play. Vladimir Nabokov reported that he was extraordinarily sensitive to patterns as a child, particularly when he was supposed to be preparing for bed. He began by moving the bathroom door back and forth to the sound of the "step, step, step" of the dripping faucet. "Fruitfully combining rhythmic pattern with rhythmic sound," he wrote, "I would unravel the labyrinthian frets on the linoleum, and find faces where a crack or a shadow afforded a *point de repère* for the eye." And throughout it all, he would be singsonging his "youthful verse." This experience of integrating aural, visual, and verbal patterns with patterns of movement and using each to augment the others was so important to him that he inserted in his memoirs a rare piece of advice: "I appeal to parents: never, never say, 'Hurry up,' to a child." At least, pause to consider the consequences when you chide a youngster, friend, or colleague. Like a good riddle, such nonsense at any age may be a nuisance that reveals new sense.

7

Forming Patterns

I N 1998 A RETROSPECTIVE EXHIBIT of paintings by the aboriginal artist Emily Kame Kngwarreye opened in Sydney, Australia. Two of Kngwarreye's works in particular explored simple visual patterns: the smaller one, a repetition of vertical strokes; the other, large enough to fill a whole wall, a meandering weblike pattern of lines (see Fig. 7-1). Two curators prepared to carry the small painting past the large one. And then something special happened, as we can see for ourselves, for at that moment a photographer snapped a picture. The *New York Times* attached the caption "Moving Lines," punning on the curators' activity as well as on the paintings themselves. But the photo really speaks for itself. Alone, each of Kngwarreye's paintings depicts a particular structure of lines, a particular rhythm. Juxtaposed by chance one upon the other, the two rhythms seem to take on a more complex meaning, echoing the human stride, the human head. An instant before the photo was taken, or an instant after, the curators' legs would not have formed repeating shapes, the painting they carried would have shifted askew, or only a portion of the painting on the wall would have been visible. Yet everything in the photo balances beautifully so that the act of moving lines makes these lines move in new ways.

Indeed, for a very few moments the two paintings and the two curators formed a new, synthetic visual pattern. Though the results were complex, the process itself was simple. Forming patterns is really nothing more than combining two or more structural elements and/or functional operations. Juxtaposing one element or operation with another in a consistent way yields a synthetic pattern that may be much more than, and far different from, the sum of its parts. In the case of "Moving Lines," this process was spontaneous

Fig. 7-1. Curators move one painting by Emily Kame Kngwarreye past another in a Sydney, Australia, art gallery.

and serendipitous. Pattern forming can also be planned and purposeful. Take, for instance, the kind of pattern we all make when we can't find a piece of graph paper and grid the lines ourselves with ruler and pencil. We combine the element of a straight line with the operation of repeating — or translating — it every quarter-inch or so. We make a much more complex pattern when we knit a sweater. Two different stitches — knit and purl — can be combined and patterned in thousands of ways. If we alternate the operation of two knits with two purls, we form a ribbed structure; if we knit one whole row and purl the next, we end up with a plain stocking-stitch weave.

Handicrafts such as knitting and weaving can teach us a lot about forming patterns, as we copy the operations and structures handed down by generations of skilled artisans. But in this chapter we want to focus on how original and innovative patterns are formed. Artists, musicians, dancers, physicists, mathematicians, and inventors imagine and make new patterns all the time and with almost any type of starting material, physical or mental. And as they invent new patterns, they often find that those patterns already exist but have previously been overlooked. To understand order it is often necessary to learn how to create it.

Painter Gene Davis, like Kngwarreye, began his artistic exploration of pattern with lines or, as he put it, "intervals." These intervals, he decided, could be defined through space by translating lines across the canvas and creating a grid. They could also be defined through color or through space and color. "I'll start with a matrix of vertical pencil lines," Davis says. "And while it sounds mechanical to describe it, I take colors and in my own particular way, begin to fill in these bands. And I keep working at it until I think I've filled in enough of the holes in the painting. . . . There's a system there — an order — which I discover after the fact."

Davis's work is in color and can't adequately be reproduced here, so imagine a set of vertical window blinds spanning a window four meters long and composed of thirty-seven panels, each about ten centimeters (four inches) wide, running from ceiling to floor. Each is painted in one of eight colors: dark blue (B), light blue (b), white (W), lime green (l), olive green (O), red (R), yellow (Y), or grass green (G), forming the pattern OBbWlBOBOBObBWOBOBOlBWRYGWBObBOWBlBOBO. This is the basis of Davis's 1962 painting *Citadel*. The syncopated rhythm of the dark blue and olive stripes is immediately evident in the repeated variations on the BOBO theme, broken with light blue (b) and white (W) panels. The entire painting actually revolves around the three colors that appear only once each: red, yellow, and grass green (RYG). Rather than stand out from the other panels, they focus the pattern because mixing red, yellow, and green paint creates the color olive. Thus, juxtaposition of these colors in the painting "explains" the repeating olive stripes. Using a set of colored pencils, pastels, or crayons, try making a small rendition of the pattern so you can see for yourself. Then try eliminating or changing one or more of the colors and see how dramatically the effect changes. Making such alterations is often the only way to really appreciate the ingenuity of simple patterns.

Davis notes that his artistic patterns bear resemblence to patterns in music. Indeed, our use of the term "syncopated" to describe Davis's painting is purposeful, for visual patterns can take on a rhythmic movement. The op artist Bridget Riley has also explored the movement in lines, but hers zigzag or undulate, seeming to move right before the eyes. She, too, associates her images with music. But for Riley, the rhythmic analogy begins in the pattern-forming process itself. Says Riley, "Painters have always been aware of a correspondence between music and painting. I think it is because painting is basically an organisation — or 'manipulation,' as you would say — of abstract qualities that bear no direct relationship to the physical world. . . . Being both a sensual and an abstract thing, music does provide a model." She goes on to say, "It's inevitable that one will in part carry one's interests over into another work. One always begins by understanding the things one has already experienced. That's how one starts to find out something new." Artist Stuart Davis agreed: "Jazz music always plays a part in my inspiration, because I always think of it as art. And I think, well if they can do it maybe I can too. Only I'm making a painting."

These statements suggest that there are patterns to pattern forming that allow one to cross disciplinary boundaries and transfer simple ideas in one realm of human experience to another realm. By comparing the pattern-forming processes of artists and musicians we can begin to unravel some of these and get a more general grasp of the underlying principles. So consider the amazingly complicated rhythmic structures of ethnic African music, which for some time greatly puzzled Western observers. Despite its complexity, the music is performed by ordinary members of the community, who acquire their musical training in the same way they acquire spoken language — by informal imitation and participation in social life. This is a far cry from the practice of Western societies, where specialized artists study composition and performance intensely and audiences tend to be passive. Moreover, it is a given in Western music that the score must be written down or it will be lost. Because the African musical tradition is largely an aural one, little of it is written. The question is, how do informally trained amateurs spontaneously produce sophisticated, unannotated music? Figuring that out gives us important information about pattern forming in general.

An important clue to understanding African rhythms has been provided by musicologist Simha Arom, whose careful analysis of several hundred audio and video recordings of polyrhythmic music from central Africa revealed that a simple principle — a strict periodic structure imposed by repetition of a pattern of beats — underlies much of it. Each musician has to master only a very limited set of beats or notes that is repeated over and over again, just as in the lines in Kngwarreye's aboriginal paintings. The complexity of the music derives from the juxtaposition of several of these patterns, like the accidental pattern that occurred when the curators carried one painting past the other.

One might expect music based on repetition to sound extremely boring.

Fig. 7-2. Aka men striking the *mo.kongo.*

It does not, because each musician produces a different pattern of beats that repeats over a different interval of time. While one musician is repeating a pattern over eight beats, say, another may be playing a pattern that repeats every nine beats, while a third plays yet a different pattern that repeats every twelve. In consequence, each pattern is out of synchrony with the others almost all of the time. The overall composition repeats only when the individual patterns have all returned to the original synchrony, which in this case will be after seventy-two beats (the smallest common multiplicand). During those seventy-two beats, what the listener hears varies continually, despite the fact that each performer has repeated his or her pattern many times over. Arom points out that the synthetic pattern is made more complex because each musician emphasizes or accents different elements of the rhythm or creates subtle variations upon it. In this way, a piece that never repeats in detail may be created from elements that vary little within an extremely repetitious formula.

Arom describes, as an example, Aka Pygmy music in which instruments such as rattles, bells, and iron strips beaten together provide the different rhythms. Bondo music is a form used by the Aka in various rites preceding

	1	2	3	4	5	6	7	8	9	10	11	12
First part	●		●	●		●		●	●		●	
Second part	❙			❙			❙			❙		

Fig. 7-3. A two-part Aka pattern.

hunting expeditions. In its simplest form, it consists of four instruments beating out two basic parts according to two distinct rhythms that repeat every twelve beats. Both sets of instruments are silent at beats 2, 5, and 12. The parts coincide only on beats 1 and 4. One set of instruments is heard alone at beats 3, 6, and 11, while the other set is heard alone at beats 7 and 10. This is an amazingly complex result for such simple ingredients.

The Aka Pygmies also play a more complex musical form, called Yombe, to celebrate successful hunts, important visitors, mourning, or festivity in general. Yombe songs tend to have repeating figures of three, twelve, and twenty-four beats. The complexity of the resulting rhythm can be appreciated in Figure 7-4, which shows a four-part Yombe. Oddly, the four instruments never strike a beat all together at the same time. Silences occur at beats 4 and 13. A single instrument is heard at beats 1, 10, 15, 16, 19, 21, 22, and 24. Two instruments are heard in common at beats 2, 3, 6, 7, 8, 9, 11, 12, and 17. And three instruments are heard together at beats 5, 14, 18, 20, and 23. One can imagine Gene Davis's stripe paintings as the visual equivalent of such music.

If these examples seem confusing, it is worth noting that Bondo and Yombe are relatively simple. Some African tribal music involves more than a dozen different instruments, each playing its own rhythm. It is mind-bog-

Fig. 7-4. A four-part Aka pattern.

	1	2	3	4	5	6	7	8	9	10	11	12	13	14	15	16	17	18	19	20	21	22	23	24
è.ndòmbà		●			●			●			●			●			●			●			●	
dì.kpàkpà			❙			❙			❙			❙			❙			❙			❙			❙
nguè			▲		▲	▲	▲	▲			▲			▲		▲	▲	▲		▲			▲	
dì.kétɔ	*	*			*		*		*	*		*		*				*	*	*		*	*	

gling in its complexity. Western musicologists have had difficulty understanding it because we expect our music to have a single dominant melody measured out in rhythmic units, such as 4/4 time, that are related to known mathematical patterns. African tribal music, however, has no identifiable melodic line and no bars. And what Westerner ever heard of mathematical series such as those in the Yombe that relate 1, 10, 15, 16, 19, 21, 22, and 24 or 5, 14, 18, 20, and 23? Unfamiliar with such patterns, we have trouble comprehending and analyzing them.

Our difficulty in understanding African tribal music probably has a deeper root as well. In the West, an individual composer writes the music long before it is performed. The patterns and melodies we hear are preplanned and intended. Some tribal music, however, results from collaboration by the players on the spur of the moment. The patterns heard, whether they are the silences when all players rest on a beat or the accented beats when all play together, are not planned but serendipitous. When an overall silence appears on beats 4 and 13, it is not because each musician is thinking, "On beats 4 and 13, I will rest." Rather, it occurs randomly as the patterns of all the players converge upon a simultaneous rest. The musicians are probably as surprised as their listeners to hear the silences at beats 4 and 13. Surely that surprise is one of the joys tribal musicians experience in making their music.

African polyrhythms have had well-documented effects on the innovative music of black Americans and the rag, jazz, and swing that flowered from their grass-roots genius. In addition, some modern Western composers have more formally rediscovered African musical techniques. Prominent among these was Joseph Schillinger, a Russian-born composer and music theorist whose students included George Gershwin, Oscar Levant, Glenn Miller, Benny Goodman, Tommy Dorsey, and Paul Lavalle. In his book *The Mathematical Basis of the Arts,* Schillinger describes rhythm as resulting from "synchronized component periodicities" and illustrates his definition with examples that are completely analogous to those described by Arom. In Figure 7-5, one player alternates notes every four beats, while the other alternates notes every three. This pattern of a four-beat alternation and a three-beat one is repeated every twelve beats, according to a formula of beats that sounds like: 3, 1, 2, 2, 1, 3. More complicated patterns emerge from combinations of synchronous beats such as 3:4:7. Schillinger, who was also a designer, provided extensive descriptions in his book of how to translate such musical patterns into visual patterns, making explicit some of the similarities be-

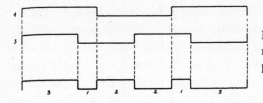

Fig. 7-5. Periodicities in time resulting from a four-on-three pattern.

tween music and art that Gene Davis, Stuart Davis, and Bridget Riley have mentioned.

Composer Steve Reich has carried out more recent experiments with elements of African tribal rhythm. In his 1978 piece *Music for 18 Musicians,* changing harmonic patterns cycle against constant melodic patterns to create a sense of varied accent in "that which is in fact unchanging." And Philip Glass, drawing on the principles of ancient Hindu music, has created amazingly variegated compositions. In his *Glassworks* of 1982 and *Koyaanisquatsi* of 1983, the human voice, saxophones, synthesizers, and many other instruments turn simple repetitions into marvels of complex sound. Even when Glass composes for a single instrument such as the piano, he employs the same principles. Like Scott Joplin in many of his rags, Glass often requires each of the pianist's hands to count in different beats. "You have to be able to play in five in one hand and four in the other. Or, what regularly happens in my music is that I'll set up a recurring cycle of meters of three in one hand and a cycle of meters in the other, so that against the three you'll have nine, eight, six, five, four, three, four, five, six, eight, nine, and twelve, all worked out so that they fit the basic cycle of three, but nevertheless require a good rhythmic feeling to carry them off."

As close as Reich's and Glass's pieces come to the fundamental structures of ancient polyrhythmic music, even closer is the work of the dance-percussion performance group Stomp. Banging on cans, pots and pans, hubcaps, kitchen sinks, and boxes with sticks, tire irons, hands, and feet; stomping on or hitting the floor repeatedly with brooms, trash cans, and crates; snapping fingers, crinkling paper bags, clapping hands, stomachs, and each other, the Stomp performers create sounds and rhythms that are both as old as humanity and as new as skyscrapers and recycling. Their "instruments" may not be those used historically in Africa or India, but the collaborative process is just as kinesthetic and just as exciting as it was at the dawn of music.

Surprisingly, even the most "sophisticated" music in the Western classical canon is based on pattern-forming concepts that are not much more complicated than those of the Aka Pygmies and Stomp. J. S. Bach, for example, often played simple games of counterpoint, contrasting two different melodies or themes instead of rhythms. Bach also used the method of inversions. A good example is his Two-Part Invention no. 8. After the basic theme is introduced (a), Bach reverses it (b), turns the reversed theme upside down (c), and inverts the reversed, upside-down theme (d). The final version (d) is now the upside-down version of the original theme (a), a curious result of pattern symmetry. A significant part of the Two-Part Invention is then an exploration of the various ways in which these variations on a theme can be strung together. While writing music looks trivially easy when described like this, inventing patterns that make musical sense when transformed through all these operations can be a tricky business. An enlightening example of inversion invention can be found in the audio recording *Mr. Bach Comes to Call,* in which Walter Babiak creates step by step a fugue called "Adventure in Music" on the theme of "Pop Goes the Weasel."

The sorts of inversions employed by Bach are related to a more general mathematical concept called combinatorics, which explores every possible combination of elements of a system. For instance, there is only one way to combine two identical elements, but there are four ways to combine two different ones and twenty-seven ways to combine three. Not all of the combinations may be of interest, but until you have tried them all, you can't tell. Thus, composer Darius Milhaud explicitly used combinatorial thinking as a way to explore polytonal music (that is, music written in more than one key simultaneously): "I set to work to examine every possible combination of two keys superimposed and to study the chords thus produced. I also studied the effect of inverting them. I tried every imaginable permutation by varying the mode of the tonalities making up these chords. Then I did the same thing in three keys." As he grew more and more familiar with his new combina-

Fig. 7-6. Inversions in Bach's Two-Part Invention no. 8.

tions, Milhaud discovered that some satisfied him by being more "subtly sweet" than usual harmonies, others by being more "violently potent." In both instances, his combinations yielded new compositional patterns to build upon.

Juxtaposition of simple patterns yields interesting results in the pattern-forming processes of the sciences as well. Indeed, it is impossible to categorize most patterns as belonging exclusively to any one art or science. Take, for instance, the moiré patterns originally associated with the "watered silks" first made in China many centuries ago. Such fabrics are produced by repeatedly folding the fabric upon itself at a slight angle to the dominant thread lines and then ironing it under intense pressure or by mechanically rolling an engraved pattern over the fabric. In either case, the fabric now has two offset patterns, the original pattern of the woven threads themselves and the impressed pattern. And just as offset musical rhythms produce novel musical effects, so do these offset visual patterns create novel visual effects. Light reflected off the intersection of the patterns yields a shimmer that often reminds people of the waves in a pond. You can also observe moiré effects by looking through two or more wire screens, the folds of a sheer curtain, or pairs of chainlink fences. In fact, you can make your own moirés by drawing any regular grid of lines (straight, wavy, circular — it doesn't matter), xerographically reproducing the grid on clear acetate, then laying the acetate over the original pattern and rotating it slowly through a small angle. What you see in these instances is a perfect visual analogy to what Aka Pygmies, Stomp dancers, Steve Reich, and Philip Glass are doing in music.

Moiré patterns have technological and scientific applications, too. By using optical grids to examine metals and crystals, one can easily see the stress lines. Irregularities in the surface of anything that has a defined pattern, from fabric or wire mesh to brickwork, can be spotted through a grid. Perhaps most important, as Gerald Oster and Yasunori Nishijima pointed out in their classic *Scientific American* article on the subject, "A moiré pattern can be regarded as a mathematical solution to the interference of two periodic functions; hence the moiré technique can be used as an analogue computer" — that is to say, a computer that "calculates" without numbers by directly adding images. If each grid represents one mathematical function, then the intersection of multiple grids represents the solution to a multifunctional mathematical problem. Electromagnetic, acoustical, and water waves create natural moirés, and their intersections can be solved not just by numbers but by the visual pattern itself.

The mathematical description of electromagnetic, acoustical, and water

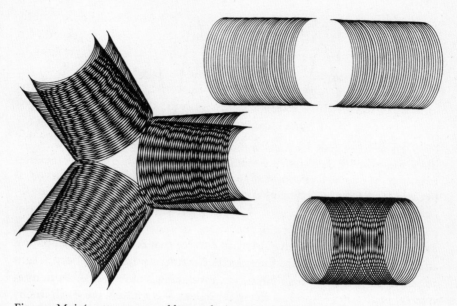

Fig. 7-7. Moiré patterns created by overlaying pairs of simple patterns like those at upper right.

waves — what is now known as Fourier analysis — also required an intimate understanding of how complex patterns might result from the combination of simple elements. When a record or a compact disk is played, the vibrations of the needle or laser light are transformed into an electrical current, which is then converted into sound by one or more speakers. The oscillations in the current contain all of the information necessary to make the speaker vibrate as if it were every instrument and human voice in an entire orchestra, choir, or rock band. When the electrical wave is made visible by an oscilloscope, it is obviously very complex. Working in the early 1820s, well before synthesizers or electronic equipment were available, Joseph Fourier wanted to describe such complex waves, whether they represented sound, electricity, heat, or any other physical agent or process. Like musicologists trying to address the complexity of African tribal music, most mathematicians were stumped by this problem. But just as Simha Arom discovered that tribal music is based on the juxtaposition of simple repeating elements, so Fourier discovered that any complex wave function can be described — or generated — by combining a series of simpler functions.

To understand what Fourier achieved, turn the problem on its head. In-

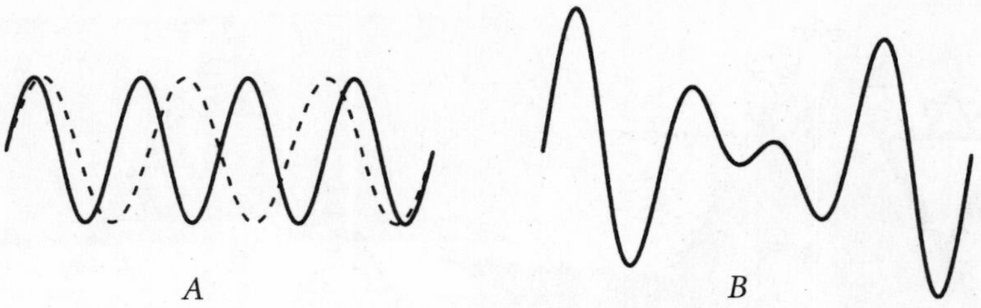

Fig. 7-8. Fourier analysis of a four-on-three pattern (see Fig. 7-5) made by two sine waves, one of which oscillates three times in a given period while the other oscillates four times. The figure on the right *(B)* is formed by adding the two sine waves on the left *(A)*, so *B* can be decomposed into its constituent sine waves, as shown in *A*.

stead of trying to analyze the electrical current that is carrying a symphony, imagine trying to synthesize the current. Creating a pure tone is easy. A tuning fork vibrates at a single frequency, producing a pure sound. Its mathematical expression — and its electrical signal — is a sine wave. Each different pitch will be expressed by a sine wave of different periodicity, as every mathematician of Fourier's day knew. Unlike others, however, Fourier asked what would happen if one combined a number of these pure tones, these pure mathematical functions. One could, he reasoned, theoretically create any sound imaginable by modulating with sufficient precision a wide range of tuning forks. And since every pure tone is describable as a sine wave, every complex sound must be some combination of sine waves. Conversely, every complex wave form, and every complex mathematical description of such a form, must be decomposable into its elementary wave functions.

Applications of Fourier analysis extend from thermodynamics (which Fourier himself helped to define) to electronics, from cybernetics to magnetic resonance imaging and beyond. The application most people will recognize is music produced by electronic synthesizers. During the latter half of the nineteenth century, Hermann von Helmholtz gave a physical "proof" of Fourier's reasoning by producing complex musical sounds using a machine that consisted of electrically controlled tuning forks. That machine is the direct ancestor of modern electronic synthesizers, and the music they generate is a modern demonstration of the power of Fourier's insight. The same synthesizer can reproduce a Bach cantata, sitar or sarangi music from India, shamisen or koto music from Japan, or the heaviest of heavy metal bands. And it does so by adding trigonometric functions. Now *that's* universality.

Fig. 7-9. *Left:* a Koch curve; *right:* a Sierpinsky carpet.

Modern mathematicians have discovered that other simple operations can generate complex patterns with surprising properties. As an example, let's see what happens when you apply a simple operation to a triangle. First draw an equilateral triangle about nine centimeters (or three inches) on a side on a sheet of paper. Divide each side of the triangle into three equal segments. Now draw an equilateral triangle on the outside of the central segment of each side. Each side of these three new triangles will be one-third the length of the sides of the original triangle. Now perform the same operation on each external side of the three new triangles. That is, divide the sides of the new triangles into three and draw a new equilateral triangle on the middle segment of each. One can continue to apply this process indefinitely, the result being a unique-looking star shape called a Koch curve, after the Swedish mathematician Helge von Koch, who invented it. The Koch curve has the surprising and bizarre property of having a finite area and an infinitely long perimeter. You can perform a similar operation on a square. See what happens when you do.

The inverse operation yields equally odd results. Again draw a moderately sized triangle, but this time bisect the sides. Inside the triangle, draw another triangle whose vertices are at the points bisecting the sides of the original one. Imagine that you have cut out the central triangle. That space is now a hole. In each of the remaining corner triangles, bisect the sides and cut out another triangle as before. Continue to perform these operations until you get bored. The result is what is known as a Sierpinski carpet. Its properties are exactly the opposite of the Koch curve: the carpet is so "moth-eaten" that although it has a finite perimeter, it no longer has any area. As with the Koch triangle, it is interesting to see what happens when you also cut square holes out of a square.

Both the Koch curve and the Sierpinski carpet belong to a huge set of mathematical objects called fractals, first explored systematically by Benoit Mandelbrot in the mid-1970s. Fractals have extremely odd characteristics. One concerns the unexpected relationships between area and perimeter; another is that the pattern in a fractal is exactly the same regardless of the scale of observation. The structure of the smallest part is identical to the structure of the entire fractal. Oddly enough, physicists and artists alike have found that fractal images aid the structural understanding and computer generation of objects as diverse as mountains and clouds. Botanists have discovered fractals within the structures of trees, and physiologists have found them in the structure of the branching bronchi of the lungs. A few musicians have even begun to experiment with fractal music. Once again, tremendous complexity and unexpected surprises result from the simplest operations.

Everything we have said so far about pattern forming in art, music, and mathematics applies to other disciplines as well. Writers obviously work their magic by combining a relatively small number of words into sentences, paragraphs, poems, stories, and books. Less obviously, they structure their works by forming patterns out of diverse experiences. When Virginia Woolf worked on scenes and characters, for instance, she felt keenly that she "put the severed parts together. . . . *in writing I seem to be discovering what belongs to what. . . .* From this I reach what I might call a philosophy; at any rate it is a constant idea of mine; that behind the cotton wool [daily events lived unconsciously] is hidden a pattern." The purpose of literature, for Woolf, was to make that pattern manifest, to let it sing.

Nabokov, too, called writing the "art of forming sudden harmonious patterns out of widely separate threads." Significantly, Nabokov came to prose through poetry, perhaps the most highly structured of the literary arts. He also invented chess problems, an activity he likened to creative writing, involving as it did rules, intricate patterns, and strategies for their use. In fact, his novels are as intricate as a chess game and as well planned. In Nabokov's early novel *Mary,* a rather simple story about a young man awaiting the unforeseen and dreaded arrival of a long-lost sweetheart becomes a narration of patterned experience. The action takes place over seven days in a Berlin boarding house with six rooms, each "numbered" with a leaf from an old calendar — showing six of the days in years past when he had trysted with his lover. In the course of the week the young man enters one of these rooms each day, and when the seventh day arrives and there are no more rooms, he leaves the boarding house, Berlin, and all possibility of seeing his old flame. By boxing the events into days and within rooms, Nabokov forms a repetitive structure for his story that is visual and spatial and marked by the regular passage of time. By juxtaposing memory and anticipation, he sets up a bittersweet counterpoint. According to Alex de Jonge, who has studied Nabokov's uses of pattern at length, the organization of *Mary* is simple compared with his later explorations of how human experience mirrors the natural order of things.

We need not be novelists to appreciate some of these patterns. Our very conversations are exercises in pattern forming. As in the creation of African tribal music, each of us controls only a part of the pattern, the overall effect resulting from the interplay of independent yet interwoven intentions. Just listen sometime to a conversation as sound — not to the specific words but to the patterns, the rhythms of the voices as they rise and fall, intersect and diverge, beat and syncopate. In the late 1960s the pianist and composer Glenn Gould actually made conversational music when he experimented with a "trio sonata" of voices in his radio program "The Idea of North." First we hear a woman's voice describe the solitude of living in Canada's far north. About thirty seconds later a man's voice comes in, overlying the woman's, describing the same subject but in different words and at a different pace. Then the voice of yet another man joins the first two and all three speak at once. The result is something less than clear conversation and more than sound; it is contrapuntal music without notes or a melody, communication *in* words that is not *by* words. Similar contrapuntal experiments are typical of the music and lyrics of Stephen Sondheim. In his musical *A Little Night Music,* for example, several voices sing simultaneously to create layers of sound and meaning that no single melodic or poetic line could carry. Paul Fleischman has also created many "musical duets" in his Newbery Award–winning poetry book, *Joyful Noise.* The poems require two people reading aloud at once.

Conversational music, whether electronically manipulated, sung, or recited, makes us realize that there are patterns to speech other than the verbal communication we expect to hear. In dance, choreographers such as Merce Cunningham have explored all the possible combinations of a limited vocabulary of movements and also have tried to break the expected patterns of dance so that we see and feel new kinesthetic patterns. Cunningham looks for pattern-forming inspiration in nature, randomly mixing dance elements in the same way that new gene combinations are generated with every throw of the reproductive dice. He begins by abstracting various aspects of dance: movement, timing, spacing, number of dancers, types of patterns. He then assigns each a different variable and generates their combinations by some random means, such as the flip of a coin. As Carolyn Brown, one of Cunningham's dancers, has said, "The dances are treated more as puzzles than works of art; the pieces are space and time, shape and rhythm." Cunningham's choreography, like Milhaud's polytonal music, avoids traditional preconceptions and explores all possible patterns inherent in a set of dance elements. As Cunningham says, "You can see what it is like to break these actions up in different ways" and then see what surprises new combinations may hold.

Cunningham's imitation of nature is scientifically accurate as well as insightful and stimulating. The entire theory of evolution is based on random modifications of existing genes, leading to an ever-ready supply of biological novelties, a few of which are more interesting and more adaptable than the existing ones. The human immune system is thought to produce all the possible antibodies needed to fend off infection by randomly combining a handful of genes into all possible permutations. Chemists have recently learned how to mimic this process in their laboratories, using a technique called polymerase chain reaction (PCR) to create millions of related sequences of DNA, from which those with specific desirable properties can be fished out and replicated. They have learned how to produce new drugs and synthetic materials by making every possible combination of any small set of chemical reactants, literally churning out millions of novel compounds each year.

Indeed, the principle that complexity results from combinations of simple elements characterizes pattern forming universally. All of the colors we can see are some mixture of red, blue, and green light or red, blue, and yellow pigment. Most music can be written with a dozen basic units. Combinations of only four nucleic-acid bases encode all the genetic information in every living thing in the world. All of the proteins known to nature are made up of an "alphabet" of twenty amino acids. All of the hundreds of millions of known chemicals in the universe are combinations of less than a hundred elements. Perhaps most astounding, all language can be transcribed using as few as two symbols — the dot and dash of Morse code — and virtually any kind of information can be translated into zeros and ones and fed into a computer. The striking thing about pattern forming is not the complexity of the elements that are combined, but the cleverness and unexpectedness with which the combinations are made.

We emphasize that the cleverness, unexpectedness, and even diversity of patterns formed in the arts are also typical of the sciences. The importance of this statement can be appreciated in light of a common myth embodied in the assertion "Give ten artists a scene to paint and you will get ten different paintings, but give ten scientists the same problem to solve, and if they solve it correctly, you will get ten identical answers." In fact, creative scientists, like artists, often take different paths and reach different solutions. There are more than three hundred ways to prove the Pythagorean theorem, each distinct in form and content from the others. The final answer may be the same, but that is saying no more than that ten artists have all painted the same tree in different styles. A recent review of theories of human evolution shows that at least seven different evolutionary trees are consistent with the available evidence. Similarly, chemist Edward G. Mazurs has documented, in his amazing book *Graphic Representations of the Periodic System During One Hundred Years,* more than 450 valid representations of the periodic table of elements, most of which are not tabular at all. Mazurs points out that although each version presents the elements in the same basic order and displays the same regularities in atomic weights, bonding affinities, and so forth, each emphasizes different features of the periodicities and different kinds of chemical in-

Fig. 7-10. Three of the hundreds of valid versions of the periodic table of elements. *Left to right:* De Chancourtois, 1863; Reynolds, 1886; Schirmeisen, 1900.

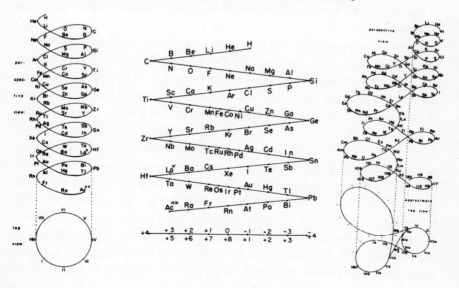

formation. Because our knowledge of chemistry continues to grow, new periodic structures are being invented even today. We have copiously illustrated other multiple solutions to scientific problems in a previous book, *Discovering*.

The issue involved in multiple formulations of scientific and mathematical solutions is not merely their creativity but what they allow us to do. Different solutions permit different uses. Think about the words "one and a half" and the number formalisms $1\frac{1}{2}$ and 1.5. These are all logically equivalent, but only one can be entered into your calculator. Similarly, it is easy to multiply 157 times 339 using Arabic numerals, but try it using only roman numerals: CLVII times CCCXXXIX. It's not so obvious how to proceed. You certainly can't multiply each "digit" in each number by the "digits" in the other, as we do in arabic notation, so what do you do? The specific patterns we invent to embody our understanding of things have different limitations and different strengths — no single pattern is ever the end all or be all of a subject. The nature of the objects or concepts combined alters the outcome.

Precisely these sorts of differences are evident in other disciplines. The twelve-tone scale invented by Arnold Schoenberg permits different possibilities than does the standard Western musical scale. The alphabet of movements allowed to a classical ballet dancer defines one universe of possibilities; the alphabet of movements devised by modern dancers another; and those culled from gymnastics or the martial arts yet others. Obviously, the more patterns we invent to circumscribe, define, and express our experience of the world, the more real knowledge we possess and the richer we are in understanding.

Learning to create patterns is therefore one of the keys to innovating in every discipline, and it is wise to learn this skill early on. You can do this easily in writing by taking a very limited number of words and exploring all the possible ways of making sense with them. Mary Ann Hoberman's poem "Combinations," which can be found in the *Oxford Book of Children's Verse in America,* is a good model. It starts, "A flea flew by a bee. The bee / To flee the flea flew by a fly," and goes on for another twenty-eight lines without repeating itself, using only the words introduced in the first two lines.

Similar exercises can be performed with kinesthetic and auditory patterns and rhythms. All of us have probably been challenged to pat our head while rubbing our stomach in a circular motion, but this exercise is trivial compared to the possibilities. Try patting your head not once with each rub of the stomach, but with three pats for each rub. If you can master that, try three pats for every two rubs. Or three on four. Don't expect this to be easy!

The same kinds of exercises can be done with hands or feet, as drummers do; the best can play four different rhythms simultaneously. You can explore this skill yourself. Take a pencil in each hand and tap out two beats per unit of time with one and three with the other; or three on four, three on five, and so on. Many piano pieces have three-on-two motifs, and once you grasp the idea, you can try any combination. Or you can do a simple two-step with your feet while clapping out three beats with your hands and learn complicated combined rhythms in this whole-body manner. All of these exercises are even more fun (and just as difficult to execute) in groups. The drum section of our local middle-school band recently learned some African polyrhythms from a university professor and experienced the difficulties of keeping to individual patterns in the face of the overpowering effects of the combined effort. Anyone who has sung a round has experienced the urge to conform to a dominant pattern rather than to maintain one's own. Collaboration takes effort.

People who have difficulty with the physical elaboration of multiple, contrasting patterns may find it easier to explore such patterns graphically. As a starting point, we highly recommend René Parola's *Optical Art: Theory and Practice,* which provides examples and guidelines for designing a wide range of regular and irregular patterns. Parola's book provides a history of this art as well as some of the science behind it. Even those without much drawing ability can explore such combined patterns by using ready-made materials. Rummage in the trash or go to the hardware store and buy a variety of filters, screens, and other regularly patterned woven materials. Then cut them up and lay them on top of each other to create collages or more complex arrangements in which moiré patterns emerge. If you lay your creations on a xerographic copier (take care not to scratch the glass) you can transform them into graphic images. You can even use such materials to make mobiles designed so that as one part of the mobile moves past another, moiré patterns are formed.

Combinatorial and visual pattern forming can be enhanced by playing with puzzles such as the ancient Chinese tangram puzzle. The tangram is a square cut into five triangles, a square, and a rhomboid. The pieces can be arranged in an infinite variety of ways to look like houses, animals, people, and almost anything else the imagination suggests. Particularly relevant to our current point is that some tangram shapes have multiple solutions. There are, for example, at least nine ways of forming a square with two, small triangular gaps in it. If we think about these squares analogically, we can imagine them as being nine logically equivalent but structurally and aesthetically dif-

Fig. 7-11. Forming tangram squares using puzzle pieces shown at the top.

ferent solutions to the same problem — how to build a square of a certain size and with particular characteristics with the pieces supplied. Thus, devising one solution to a tangram puzzle is often only the beginning. There may be more!

The same principle of diversity in simplicity also characterizes engineering. All complex machines are built from simple machines: levers, wheels, screws, cogs, and so forth. Invention is the process of putting together these components in a new way — that is, devising a novel pattern from them. The classic construction toys of childhood, from Tinkertoys and Erector and Mechano sets to the current rages, Legos, K'NEX, and Zoob, embody these principles. Legos, of course, are based on the idea that a limited number of structural units can provide almost unlimited opportunities for the imagination. Mitchel Resnick, a writer/inventor at the MIT Media Lab who has degrees in physics and computer sciences, collaborated with the Legos Company to produce Mindstorms — a synthesis of computer-driven motors and the standard Lego building blocks. "We're trying to bring together the best of the digital and the physical world," says Resnick. "Our point is not to give kids prebuilt toys, but to give them the parts to build their own toys. . . . We want to help children become designers and inventors. By building things, kids can take their theories and test them out in a very personal way." Other building toys are based on the same philosophy. Zoob, for example, has only five basic units, which the toy's inventor, Michael Grey, an artist with a degree in genetics, compares to the structural units of DNA. "Zoob is a parallel to a language or an alphabet," he says. You can build almost anything with it, including models of DNA. K'NEX is also based on a limited set of interactive parts, which artist-businessman-inventor Joel Glickman describes as "three-dimensional crayons." What you can "draw" in 3-D is virtually unlimited.

We draw two lessons from these toys. First, each inventor utilized a wide variety of training in the arts and sciences, which observation, along with our earlier discussions in this chapter of Gene Davis, Stuart Davis, Bridget Riley, and Joseph Schillinger, suggests that pattern forming crosses disciplinary boundaries in both its origins and its meanings. And second, in the pattern-forming possibilities of these toys, as in those of the visual arts or music or computer programming, the complexity of the final product doesn't reside in the complexity of the components but in the cleverness with which a handful of simple elements is used to generate diverse surprises.

We would like to see this lesson applied even in the sciences, where all too often a single answer is expected. Given the availability of Mazurs's book on multiple periodic tables of elements, we suggest that an effective way to teach chemistry students the periodic table would be to challenge them to devise their own schema for representing the periodicities instead of simply memorizing a structure invented by someone else. Similarly, students learning geometry should be encouraged to invent their own ways of proving theorems, rather than following the one in the book or that favored by the teacher. In fact, looking through the history of almost any scientific field or studying any scientific controversy will show that scientists always try many ways of expressing their insights before some standardized textbook formulation ossifies thinking in that area. Making patterns for oneself is a lot more fun than memorizing — and a lot more valuable. Teasing apart one pattern and composing another requires real understanding of the basic elements of phenomena and processes. More, it opens up whole new worlds of knowledge.

8

Analogizing

D URING THE FIRST TWO DECADES of the twentieth century, physicists began talking about atoms as if they were organs or grand pianos or "a clarion of bells." There was more than poetry to such prose. The suggestion of similarity between atoms and musical instruments stemmed from various unexplained observations that atoms, when struck by energy such as heat, gave off wavelengths of light. Spectroscopes, which broke up the light much as a prism does, showed that the spectra making up the colors characteristic of each element were more complicated than the eye could see. Like organs or pianos, each atom sounded a series of notes simultaneously, each resulting chord being characteristic of only one element. Clearly there was some connection between an element's energy spectrum and its structure. But what?

The German physicist Max Planck tackled the problem. One puzzle was that even an atom like hydrogen, with a simple nucleus and only one pair of electrons, had a complicated spectrum. The standard model of the atom proposed by the Danish physicist Niels Bohr, which showed the electrons orbiting the nucleus like planets around the sun, provided no obvious clues to the complexity of the spectra. As far as anyone knew, the orbits were continuous and could occur at any distance from the nucleus, so why was the energy given off by atoms limited to specific frequencies? What "tuned" the atoms, keeping their electrons in certain paths with certain amounts of energy? How was it that they could jump from one path to another, as from the note A to C, but never performed a glissando in between? Planck found that he could answer this set of questions by taking the musical analogy a step

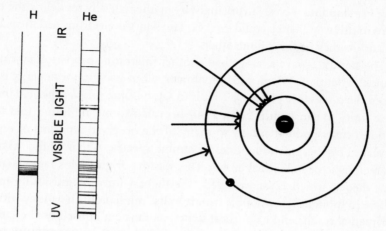

Fig. 8-1. The emission spectra of even simple atoms such as hydrogen, with one electron, and helium, with two, are as complex as chords played on a piano or an organ. Niels Bohr explained these spectra by postulating that the electrons orbited the nucleus the way planets orbit the sun. If an electron fell, as shown by the arrows, from a higher-energy orbit (farther from the nucleus) to a lower-energy one (nearer the nucleus), it would release a quantized unit of light energy, or photon. The possible orbit changes correspond to the observed energy lines in the emission spectra.

further: he treated the electron orbits in an atom mathematically *as if* they were vibrating strings.

In its most general sense, analogy refers to a functional resemblance between things that are otherwise unlike. Planck, a pianist who had once considered a musical career, did not mean to imply that the electrons really were vibrating strings, but when he treated them mathematically *as if* they were, he learned some very interesting things. He found, first, that only when the electrons behaved like standing waves was the energy of orbital vibration conserved. Whether they are vibrating strings or waves in a pool of water, standing waves resonate with themselves; the high-energy areas, or peaks, overlap and reinforce each other. Waves that do not synchronize in this way dampen themselves; the high-energy and low-energy areas, peaks and valleys, average each other out. If damping were to happen in atomic orbits, the electrons would all collapse into the nucleus and matter would cease to exist as we know it. Since electrons do not collapse, Planck realized, they must *behave like* standing waves. Surprisingly, by mathematically modeling the electrons in this way, Planck could even explain why the electrons had the particular orbits they had and none other.

The standing-wave analogy had another interesting property that caught Planck's attention. When a string vibrates, all of its vibratory energy is between the nodes (see Fig. 8-2). That is to say, it is *quantized,* packaged in discrete units. When Planck carried out his calculations, he found that these bundles corresponded exactly to many of the observed amounts of energy displayed by the individual lines of atomic spectra — that is, the "chords" characteristic of individual atoms. This was the origin of his famous quantum theory, which Einstein called "the highest form of musicality in the sphere of thought" — a double tribute to its "miraculous" harmony with experimental results and its musical structure. Einstein himself used quantum theory to explain how light waves also act like particles or, as we now call them, photons. As Planck and Einstein predicted, the amount of energy contained in each photon packet, or quantum, was a function of its wavelength, or color of the light. Planck won a Nobel Prize in 1918 and Einstein in 1922 because of these insights.

For Planck, the analogy between vibrating strings and atoms was a convenience, a mathematical formalism adopted because it made a complex problem tractable. For another scientist, however, it meant more than that. Louis de Broglie, a professional physicist and one of the finest amateur violinists in France, not only took the musical analogy of quantized electrons seriously, according to his colleague George Gamow, he actually thought of atoms as tiny stringed instruments. By doing so, he realized implications that Planck and Einstein had not explored. If the circular strings of these tiny musical in-

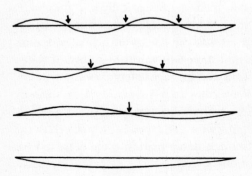

Fig. 8-2. Max Planck's equations for the behavior of electrons describe vibrating strings like these. Note that at the points indicated by the arrows, the strings do not move. All movement, and thus all kinetic energy, is quantized between these unmoving nodes.

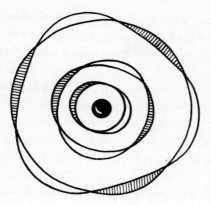

Fig. 8-3. In order to explain, as Bohr could not, why only certain orbits around the nucleus were possible, Louis de Broglie proposed that electrons were both particles and energy waves that behaved like vibrating strings. He predicted that such vibrating energy waves should have harmonics and overtones just as vibrating strings do (see Fig. 8-2).

struments vibrated, then it followed that they should have harmonics and overtones, just as the real strings on real musical instruments do.

On a piano or other stringed instrument you can verify what de Broglie was referring to. When you strike an A at one place on the piano keyboard, other A strings octaves away are set to vibrating as well. (Make sure you depress the damper pedal so that the strings can vibrate freely.) The same sympathetic vibrations occur on all stringed instruments. And if you pluck the string of a bass, tympani tuned to the same note will sound — and vice versa. These sounds are harmonics, and they occur because the vibrations of the first string exactly match those of the others — the strings *resonate*. Some strings other than the A's will also begin to vibrate (though less energetically) because their energy patterns overlap sufficiently that partial resonances are set up. De Broglie imagined analogically that these same harmonics and overtones would exist for atoms, too. Using standard mathematical techniques worked out centuries before to describe the harmonics and overtones of real strings, de Broglie calculated what these would "sound" like for atom-sized instruments.

De Broglie's predictions were initially met with scorn or dismissed as foolishness. Electrons were particles, which don't vibrate or have wavelengths. Physicists generally used Planck's wave functions as a mere mathematical formalism, not reality. If electrons literally behaved like strings, it would mean that electrons were both particles and waves. The implications were ridiculous: if de Broglie was right, then *any* particle, even a baseball, would have a "wavelength." Too absurd. But in 1927, when a pair of American physicists, G. Davisson and L. H. Germer, developed the tools necessary to "listen" for de Broglie's atomic harmonics, they found them, and Davisson,

Germer, and de Broglie were awarded Nobel Prizes in 1929. It was subsequently shown that irradiating atomic nuclei with energy produces harmonics, a finding that led to nuclear magnetic resonance spectroscopy, whose offspring, magnetic resonance imaging, or MRI, is now a standard medical diagnostic technique. By generating specific amounts of energy and tuning in on various frequencies at which atomic nuclei resonate, we can "hear" some of the atoms that compose our bodies and convert the "sound" into a visible image. And, by the way, de Broglie's calculations *do* apply to baseballs, as anyone who has taken college physics has probably had to demonstrate. Too absurd, but too true.

Perhaps the most amazing thing about this story is that the basic physics still holds, even though our view of atoms has undergone a fundamental change since the 1920s. Erwin Schrödinger's equations and subsequent developments in quantum mechanics have vanquished the orbital model of the atom forever. The analogy between atoms and tiny musical instruments is no longer viable. Yet Planck's and de Broglie's work still stands at the heart of modern physics. Why an analogy that we now "know" to be "wrong" could yield such basic and empirically verifiable insights is a mystery — a mystery that lies at the heart of *all* analogies. How and why do things that correspond only inexactly to whatever we are trying to explain nonetheless provide us with useful insights into real phenomena?

Let us go a step further. How is it possible to learn about things such as quantum mechanics or logic or democracy or goodness in the first place? How can we learn about or explain anything that we can't directly, physically sense? And how is it possible to apply knowledge learned in one context to another very different one? How do we realize that musical resonance has some application to atoms, or atomic resonance to medicine? The answers seem to lie in yet another version of the resonating-atom analogy. Without being identical, ideas can resonate, too, just like the strings of musical instruments or the electrons and nuclei of atoms. More than two hundred years ago the French philosopher Denis Diderot compared the sentient "fibers" of human beings to "sensitive vibrating strings" and argued that vibrating strings have the property of "making others vibrate, and it is in this way that one idea calls up a second, and the two together a third, and all three a fourth, and so on." For Diderot there was no limit to the number or range of ideas that might be linked in this way. The mind-instrument, he observed, "can make astonishing leaps, and one idea called up will sometimes start an harmonic at an incomprehensible interval." To carry the analogy into the modern age and nuclear physics, we might say that if we irradiate a set of concepts with an idea of the proper wavelength, we may pick up the harmonics and overtones that illuminate some previously confusing or even unsuspected phenomenon.

One of the strongest testimonials to the power of analogizing to illuminate inaccessible worlds comes from Helen Keller. How could a woman relying solely on touch, taste, and smell learn anything about the world of the seeing and hearing, let alone understand and contribute to it? Her challenge was, in many respects, no different than that faced by Planck or de Broglie or anyone else trying to understand a world that can be sensed or conceived only indirectly. We are just as handicapped as Keller when we study an atom by looking at its tracks or its radiation spectrum, locate a black hole in outer space by its effects on the path of light from other stars, examine life by reading a genetic script, understand love by reading the words of poets and novelists or justice by examining how different cultures respond to particular acts or God by reference to imperfect earthly evidence. What we can know directly with our eyes, nose, ears, mouth, and skin is so limited as to be truly humbling. Indeed, many living creatures can sense things we cannot: the magnetic fluxes of the earth, electrical fields, atmospheric or water pressure. Many can sense light in the ultraviolet or infrared ranges to which we are blind. Whole realms of taste and smell exist beyond our knowledge or imagination, and other senses may still be discovered for phenomena we have yet to uncover. Even our best instruments are limited in their ranges and sensitivities and can communicate their findings to us only by converting them into forms accessible to one of our limited senses. So even those of us with a fully functional set of human senses are insensate to some — arguably the vast majority — of our universe. Yet we cope. We learn.

So did Keller. And as she makes clear in her autobiographical writings, a key to her learning was analogizing. Shortly after her teacher, Annie Sullivan, taught her to communicate by associating the sign for water with the desire for it and the feel of it, Keller says, "I examined as I had not before my impressions arising from touch and smell, and was amazed at the ideas with which they supplied me, and the clues they gave me to the world of sight and hearing." Keller's analogizing depended heavily upon her ability to form "numberless associations and correspondences" between what she tasted, smelled, and felt and what she could not see or hear.

> I observe, I feel, I think, I imagine. . . . I associate the countless varied impressions, experiences, concepts. Out of these materials Fancy, the cunning artisan of the brain, welds an image . . . for there is an inex-

haustible ocean of likenesses between the world within and the world without. . . . The freshness of a flower in my hand is analogous to the freshness I taste in an apple newly picked. I make use of analogies like these to enlarge my conceptions of colors. Some analogies which I draw between qualities in surface and vibration, taste and smell, are drawn by others between sight, hearing, and touch. This fact encourages me to persevere, to try to bridge the gap between the eye and the hand.

Making analogies between what she could sense and what she could not became her primary tool in acquiring a huge range of information to which she had no direct access. "For example, I observed the kinds and degrees of fragrance which gave me pleasure, and that enabled me to imagine how the seeing eye is charmed by different colors and their shades. Then I traced the analogies between the illumination of thought and the light of day, and perceived more clearly than I ever had the preciousness of light in the life of the human being." Her writings are full of similar analogies.

That Keller learned to speak without being able to hear, that she learned to write and type without being able to see, to read half a dozen languages purely through the intermediary of Braille, to provide some of the most cogent thoughts ever written on thinking, and to bridge the worlds of the seeing-hearing with the blind-deaf is surely extraordinary evidence of the analogical imagination at work. If we agree with various psychologists and philosophers that "the power to recognize analogies is an excellent test of intelligence," then Keller certainly ranks as one of the most intelligent people who has ever lived. By comparing her methods with those of de Broglie and Planck, we begin to realize that it is not our senses that limit or liberate us, but our ability to illuminate the unknown by means of analogies to the known. Learning itself depends on analogizing.

It is critical to this process that analogies not be confused with similarities. Analogies recognize a correspondence of inner relationship or of function between two (or more) different phenomena or complex sets of phenomena. In fact, we limit the use of the term "analogy" to such comparisons. Similarities, on the other hand, are resemblances between things based upon observed characteristics such as color or form. A typical simile in a poem, such as "her lips were red as berries," is an example of similarity rather than analogy since the comparison simply links the observed property of redness. Children who say "An orange is like a grapefruit" or even "An orange is like a baseball" are also creating similes — the items are alike in their round appearance. A child or poet who compares a baseball to the sun might, however, make a valid analogy based on the fact that each rises and falls through the sky in an arc. Comparing an orange to the sweetness of life would also represent an analogy since life may be metaphorically "sweet" in that we desire and are pleased by it even though it is not literally sensed by our tastebuds. By the same token, Keller's comparison of the variety and intensity of flower fragrances with the varying colors and their intensities of things seen, such as paintings, constitutes a proper analogy. She compared the *relationship* between observed properties and our senses of them, not the actual shared properties. De Broglie's comparison of atoms to stringed instruments is also a valid analogy, since atoms obviously do not have strings yet *function* as if they do.

The critical part of interesting analogies is that they reveal not mere resemblances but inapparent relationships between abstract functions, one of which is understood, the other not. Atoms are not *really* (like) musical instruments. Smell is not *really* (like) color. A baseball is not *really* (like) the sun, but the comparisons reveal unsuspected shared properties. In fact, these comparisons are inexact and in many ways inaccurate. In some cases, useful analogies are literally wrong. For example, in 1816, physician René Laënnec, who was also a flutist, needed to listen to the heart of a woman so obese that he could not hear her heartbeat. "I recalled a well-known acoustic phenomenon," he wrote, "namely if you place your ear against one end of a wooden beam, the scratch of a pin at the other extremity is most distinctly audible. . . . Taking a sheaf of paper, I rolled it into a very tight roll, one end of which I placed over the praecordial region, while I put my ear to the other. I was gratified at being able to hear the beating of the heart with much greater clearness and distinctness than I had ever done before." Thus was the stethoscope invented. In fact, Laënnec's analogy is wrong. Wood *transmits* sound; the hollow tube of the stethoscope *focuses and reflects* it. The difference was not important to Laënnec: the analogy was *functional*. A logician, on the other hand, would be disgusted. And, in fact, many serious philosophers have spurned analogies as generally misleading and illogical. But truth be told, it is the inexact, imperfect nature of the analogy that allows it to bridge the known and the unknown in the first place. Analogies, as imperfect correspondences presumed in spite of difference, help us make the leap from existing knowledge to new worlds of understanding that no other mental tool allows.

No wonder analogizing is one of the imaginative tools of people in all walks of life. According to a recent book, *Mental Leaps: Analogy in Creative*

Thought, analogical thinking pervades every aspect of our lives, including religion, politics, social organization, and cultural activity. The authors, Keith Holyoak and Paul Thagard, argue that making analogies may lie at the core of human thinking. It certainly lies at the heart of what it means to think creatively. Many scientists rate analogizing as one of their most important mental skills. Biologist Agnes Arber wrote, "So long as their peculiar nature is borne in mind, they [analogies] are irreplaceable tools." The philosopher A. E. Heath argued that "it must be gently but firmly pointed out that analogy is the very corner-stone of scientific method. A root-and-branch condemnation would invalidate any attempt to explain the unknown in terms of the known, and thus prune away every hypothesis." Stanislaw Ulam argued more particularly that a good mathematician is one who finds analogies between things; a great mathematician is one who finds analogies between analogies.

In fact, analogizing has played a role in the generation of many important ideas in science. In *Mental Leaps,* Holyoak and Thagard compile a short list of these breakthrough analogies, including the ancient Greek analogy of sound to water waves, the European analogy of light to sound, William Harvey's analogy of the heart to a pump, Benjamin Franklin's analogy of lightning to electricity, James Clerk Maxwell's analogy of electromagnetic forces to continuum mechanics, and, more recently, analogies comparing chromosomes to beads on a string and the mind to a computer.

Analogies underlie many other fundamental scientific insights. Newton's theory of gravitation originated when he suddenly realized that the moon, like an apple dropping from a tree, must be falling. The same force that draws the apple to the ground must reach up into the sky and tug at the moon as well. But like a rock (or a rocket) thrown so hard that it falls over the horizon, the moon falls in such a way that it orbits. This analogy between the behavior of everyday things and celestial mechanics was so profound that it revolutionized the physical sciences. It asserted that we can understand the processes by which the entire universe operates by analogy to the processes we can study here on earth. The moon, the stars, matter itself — and here is the grandest metaphor of all — are all functionally the same.

Darwin's theory of evolution is also based on several analogies. One links the effects of breeding plants and animals for particular traits — artificial selection — with the effects of different environmental conditions, predation, disease, and similar factors on populations of organisms — natural selection. If, Darwin argued, human beings have generated all of the different breeds of pigeons, dogs, cats, cattle, and horses within the time recorded in human history, how much more profound might be the changes wrought upon living things by innumerable years of modifications? His second analogy is equally profound. The early-nineteenth-century British economist Thomas Malthus had noted that populations are limited by resources and that reproduction beyond the limits of those resources must result in starvation. Because the poor and the weak are most likely to starve, the result is nonrandom. Darwin realized that the same sort of process must occur in nature. Fish lay thousands of eggs, trees spread millions of seeds, yet only a few of these will reach maturity. If, he reasoned, the selection of who dies and who survives in nature is as nonrandom as it is in human populations, selection for the "fittest" would occur throughout nature. This analogy has now been extended by biotechnology and pharmaceutical companies that "evolve" new drugs by processes based on natural selection.

Many products of engineering and invention are similarly based on analogies to nature. Surgical staples used today for closing wounds originated in the use by tribal people of biting ants to fasten the sides of wounds together. Modern vacuum forceps and breast pumps derive from nineteenth-century mechanical analogues to real blood-sucking leeches. The design of Velcro, increasingly used to fasten everything from shoes to clothes to satchels, was inspired by the grasping properties of the humble bur. Such analogies from nature have become so widespread in recent years that biomimicry — the use of nature as a source of ideas — has become a well-recognized method of innovation. A recent drawbridge design by Chris Wilkinson Architects in Great Britain took the human eyelid, of all things, for its analogical model (see Fig. 8-4). The curvature of the bridge provides structural stability, just as it does for the eyelid. When the "lid" is closed, the bridge is down and people and cars can move across it. When a ship approaches, the lid is raised.

Analogies are just as fecund in artistic design as they are in engineering and science. Scientists and artists, technicians and craftspeople, all analogize in the same way and for the same reasons. As Jacob Bronowski, physicist, poet, and humanist, put it, "The discoveries of science, the works of art are explorations — more, are explosions, of a hidden likeness." By means of analogy, the discoverer or artist juxtaposes two phenomena, "two aspects of nature," in Bronowski's words, and "fuses them into one. This is the act of creation, in which an original thought is born, and it is the same act in original science and original art." Many artists, poets in particular, understand this explicitly. William Wordsworth wrote of "the pleasure the mind derives from the perception of similitude in dissimilitude." And Robert Frost once confessed that "I have wanted in late years to go further and further in mak-

Fig. 8-4. *Top:* "Closed/open" sketch of a possible bridge structure based on an analogy to the eyelid; *bottom:* the Gateshead Millennium Bridge design.

ing metaphor the whole of thinking." He argued that "education by poetry is education by metaphor." Like the scientist, the poet hopes to enlarge human understanding, not of an objective but of a subjective world, searching for analogical connections between the known and the unknown that ripple with emotional as well as intellectual associations. This is what makes a metaphor different from a simple analogy.

Powerful metaphors are found in all enduring literature. One common literary metaphor is that of life as a labyrinth or maze in which we are trapped and which can be navigated successfully only with the greatest care and sagacity. This metaphor is found in writings from the myths of Theseus and the Minotaur in ancient Greece to Umberto Eco's *In the Name of the Rose* and the novels and stories of Jorge Luis Borges. Many writers have also compared life to a journey and the novel or poem itself to a "rugged and steep mountain, beyond which is situated a most fair and delightful plain," as Boccaccio characterized his *Decameron*. The analogy informs Homer's *Odyssey*, Chaucer's *Canterbury Tales*, and Dante's *Divine Comedy*, Cervantes's *Don Quixote*, Defoe's *Moll Flanders*, and Fielding's *Tom Jones*. In these books we are metaphorically faced with temptations and dangers to which we can respond with our passions or our intellects, do what is right or do what is wrong. And the metaphor still holds meaning for twentieth-century literature; witness Mark Twain's *Huckleberry Finn* and J. R. R. Tolkien's *Lord of the Rings*. Stephen Spender wrote quite seriously of the "stations on the journeys of poets through life," and Frost reaffirmed the metaphor in "The Road Not Taken" in the lines "Two roads diverged in a wood and I — / I took the one less traveled by." For all its ancient lineage, this fundamental metaphor never grows stale, for in each instance of use it resonates with a new and unique set of associations.

Analogizing shapes the literary endeavor itself as much as it shapes what is written. Poets, supposing that the minds of other people are like their own, manipulate images of sight, sound, smell, and feeling to create in their readers an emotional experience akin to their own. It is the purpose of their work, in the words of the French poet Paul Valéry, "to set up an analogous state of being in someone else." Moreover, the moments of insight that poets wish others to experience often come to them, as Bronowski understood, in explosions of hidden likeness, of analogy. In an essay discussing his development of poetic ideas, Spender described how, traveling in the early 1940s through an industrial region of Great Britain, he suddenly compared the slag heaps, smoking chimneys, and slums of that wounded landscape to a confused kind of language in which manufactured objects take the place of words. Yet, he wondered, if people really spoke with the things of this world, was this wasteland the speech they truly yearned for? "All this sequence of thought," Spender recalled, "flashed into my mind with the answer which came before the question: *A language of flesh and roses*." In an experience common to many poets, the phrase dropped into his mind fully formed, a fusion of images, an analogy, "a way," he wrote, "of thinking imaginatively."

Not all analogies lend themselves to development, however. Spender never turned "a language of flesh and roses" into a poem, as he did other analogies, such as the inspiration that "some days . . . the sea lies like a harp." In the same essay, Spender demonstrated how, in draft after draft, he built upon his comparison of the sea with a musical instrument, the lines of its waves like the strings of a harp, and in between the waves, the cliffs, the fields, the houses of the land reflected in the mirror of water like "a seen music," a fusion of brief life and endless eternity. The metaphor worked for Spender, just as de Broglie's had worked for physicists, because of the manifold associations he was able to draw from it and use to craft his vision.

At times, analogizing proves critical not just to the content but also to the structure of poems. Gary Snyder builds his poetry upon an analogy with the traditional music of India. "There are some idea or image lines," he has said, "that are equivalent to the melody line, and some idea or image lines which are like a recurrent chorus or a recurrent subtheme, or repetitions that revolve in various ways, bring different facets to light in the unfolding of a poem." In his "Burning the Small Dead," we can see the structural analogy at work:

> Burning the small dead
>   branches
> broke from beneath
>   thick spreading
>   whitebark pine.
>
>   A hundred summers
> snowmelt   rock   and air
>
> hiss in a twisted bough.
>
>   Sierra granite;
>   Mt. Ritter —
>   black rock twice as old.
>
> Deneb, Altair
>
> windy fire

The poem opens with the image, the melody, of a small camping fire consuming dead branches of pine. The melody modulates with the idea of "a hundred summers," time itself, hissing "in a twisted bough." Yet the subtheme or chorus has already sounded: in a simple beat of words spaced rhythmically upon the page, the branches are linked to the elements, to the mountain of metamorphic rock seen in the distance, to the stars Deneb and Altair, light-years away. Burning branches, molten rock, fusing star, and we, ourselves, are all the same "windy fire," the poem itself a combustion and a release of organized time. Even the layout of the poem on the page resembles smoke.

The best art is often founded on analogies and metaphors as profound as those of the best literature. Sculptor Isamu Noguchi based some of his work on the multiple meanings of light, tracing the origins of his light sculptures to his fascination with the making of Japanese lanterns. "I was much interested as a sculptor in their methods of manufacture," he wrote, "the frames upon which are wound the bamboo and paper; the flexibility and simplicity of which immediately suggested new possibilities of sculptural forms — light sculpture, translucent and collapsible." Noguchi developed his analogy by working in two parallel directions (see Fig. 8-5). First, he went to Gifu, Japan, to study and master the craft of making the lanterns, or *akari,* which means light or illumination in Japanese. His efforts were so successful that examples of his akari are in design collections such as that of the Museum of Modern Art in New York. At the same time, Noguchi worked analogically, developing new sculptural forms based on the same principles of construction as his *akari* and illuminated from within like a lantern, but intended as artistic exploration of form and light, not as functional objects. These are among the first light sculptures ever created.

Sculptor Henry Moore is well known for drawing structural inspiration from bones, rocks, and other common natural objects (see Fig. 8-6). He also drew upon his understanding of how nature physically alters these objects. "Pebbles and rocks show nature's way of working stone," he once wrote. "Smooth sea-worn pebbles show the wearing away, rubbed treatment of stone and principles of asymmetry." By studying how nature "sculpts" — a pregnant metaphor — Moore learned new ways of sculpting for himself.

For his part, the great Spanish sculptor Eduardo Chillida draws analogies to the biological processes of nature to inform his art. "I can copy life — not the appearances of life, but life, the steps that life takes in evolving across time. Things change, evolve. I can copy this evolution . . . in my work. . . . It's

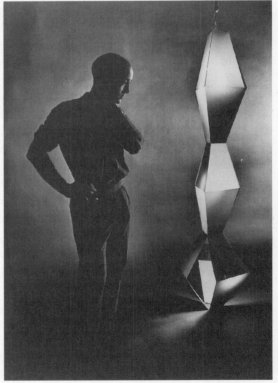

Fig. 8-5. *Top*, Isamu Noguchi with *akari* lamps; *bottom*, Noguchi with *Column of Light*.

Fig. 8-6. *Left:* Working model for *Mother and Child with Hood* by Henry Moore; *right:* found object (a bone) given to Moore by Nathaniel Friedman.

. . . a very free parallel, you understand, but very useful all the same." Chillida has learned to let his artistic ideas grow, by questioning how form develops naturally. By pondering the steps by which natural forms grow and change, he learns new ways to bring his sculptures into being. He has, for instance, mimicked the maturation of trees and has observed, "I act just as a tree acts. But it's not that I want to make a tree; I want to make something else. . . . I am a great *amateur* of the natural sciences." His art reflects this passion.

Diverse interests are a frequent source of fruitful analogies for innovators. Just as Chillida has used his knowledge of biology to enhance his crafting of sculpture, biologists Don Ingber and Steven Heidemann have used their interest in sculpture to inform their research. As graduate students, both men became fascinated with Kenneth Snelson's tensegrity sculptures and actually built some to decorate their dorm rooms. Tensegrity, a principle elaborated by Snelson and Buckminster Fuller, produces structural integrity by placing tension on independent units. Snelson's sculptures consist of hollow metal rods, none of which touch one another, connected by means of a continuous

Fig. 8-7. Spanish sculptor Eduardo Chillida makes analogies between the ways the trees outside his studio grow and his sculptures "evolve."

wire cable that is tightened until a stable structure is achieved. (The children's toy Skwish is a tensegrity structure based on Snelson's idea.) Then, about 1990, Ingber and Heidemann realized that the proteins that give cells their structural integrity have many of the properties of Snelson's sculptures. These proteins are also made of alternating rigid rods linked by flexible regions. They proposed that proteins may have the properties of tensegrity sculptures, an idea sufficiently provocative to have illustrated the cover of *Scientific American* in January 1998.

Many other useful analogies have equally inobvious origins. Kathy Tosney, an embryologist at the University of Michigan, teaches the development of birds by means of origami, drawing an explicit analogy between the way that paper and embryos undergo a series of foldings that form the final developed structures. Embryologist Scott Gilbert, on the other hand, uses an analogy between the development of a fetus and a particular form of Balinese music. As an undergraduate at Wesleyan University, Gilbert became interested in *gamelan,* a word that refers to Balinese drums, xylophone-like instruments, and gongs and also to the group of people who play the instruments. Like the African drummers discussed in Chapter 7, each player in the gamelan is given a more or less simple rhythm to follow. Gamelan music differs from its African cousins, however, in that the instruments are tuned in pairs, one above the pure note, one below. When played together, these pairs of offset frequencies create an interference pattern resulting in a third tone and also a beat not found in either of the original notes. (Whistles used by police and by sports referees in Western countries use the same mechanism of two offset notes to produce the unusually shrill, beating sound that gets our attention.) The result in gamelan music is extreme complexity by very

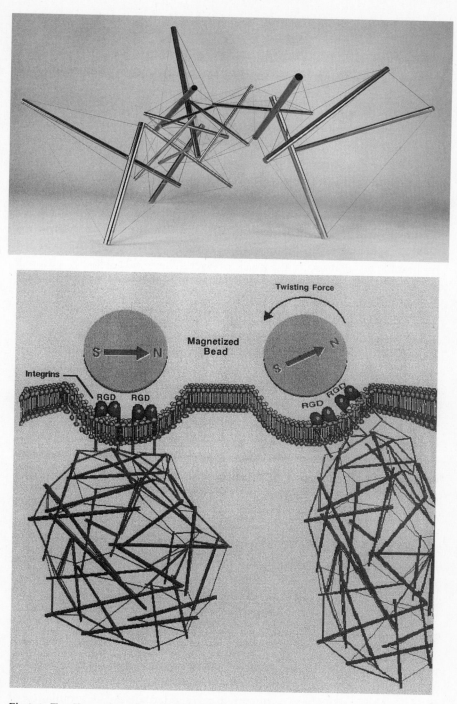

Fig 8-8. *Top:* Kenneth Snelson's tensegrity sculptures, such as *Wing I* (1992), are the basis for a theory developed by Don Ingber and Steven Heidemann that structural proteins in cells *(bottom)* may also obey the principles of tensegrity.

simple means, first by the pairing of slightly offset instruments to achieve multiple tones and then by the contrast of several simple rhythms that combine, as in African drumming, into something intricate and ever-changing. Gilbert has drawn an analogy between these processes and those that form the cell into an embryo and then an adult. If the cellular program is like gamelan music, the cell's complex development may actually be the result of only a handful of different cyclical processes occurring at different rates, intersecting to produce an evolving set of molecular or biochemical "music." Such a "program" or developmental "composition" would require the interaction of only a limited number of genes and so leave ample room in our chromosomes for other types of structural and functional information.

Musical analogies are common also in the arts. M. C. Escher once likened his graphic tessellations to the music of Bach. There was, Escher discovered, an "affinity . . . between the canon in polyphonic music and the regular division of a plane into figures with identical forms. . . . The Baroque composers have performed manipulations on sounds similar to the ones I love to do with visual images." Anyone who has sung a round has an idea of what a canon is — a musical form in which the successive parts repeat a given melody at stated intervals. If we simply alter the previous sentence to read "a canon is an *artistic* form in which the successive parts repeat a given *theme* at stated intervals," we can perceive the basic analogy that Escher recognized. The pattern in a tiling repeats regularly just as the pattern in a round does. In both arts there are rules — which is another meaning of the word "canon" — that determine the periodicity. In the same way that musicians take a musical motif and invert it, reverse it, invert the reversal, and so forth (see Fig. 7–6), artistic tilings such as Escher's perform the same kinds of symmetry operations in the service of visual pattern. Moreover, in both fugues and tilings, creating a line (musical or visual) results in two figures, as is evident in Escher tilings. It is less obvious in music, where the inverse or reverse of the musical figure appears not simultaneously with the original figure but later in time. By listening to Bach's canons and fugues, Escher said that he learned from one of the greatest, most clever patternmakers ever to design complementary figures. "Father Bach has been a strong inspiration to me, and . . . many a print reached definite form in my mind while I was listening to the lucid, logical language he speaks."

There is so much to be learned by analogizing that we must not neglect to learn how. Like every other tool for thinking, the capacity within ourselves and our children ought to be nurtured, exercised, trained. The stimulation of analogical thinking can begin in one's earliest years. Writer Geraldine Brooks

Fig. 8-9. *Snowflakes,* an Escher-style tessellation. Can you imagine this as a Bach fugue?

attributes her own facility at analogizing to the kind of play her mother encouraged almost as soon as she could walk. Her "most memorable playthings," she has written, " . . . were the creations of my mother's spontaneous invention. . . . 'Let's tour our estate,' she would say, and we would linger to learn the stories that each plant or rock had to tell. . . . The lizard basking on a brick was the hero of a quickly conjured tale of dragons. The serrated fungus on a fallen branch was a fairy's staircase leading to a secret realm." A daisy became a doll to be dressed in an azalea-gown or a fuchsia-suit. Any object had resonances that allowed it to stand in for some other. Everything was metaphor in the way that Robert Frost advocated. Of her mother, Brooks said, "There was poetry in the way she saw the world. . . . By the time I was 5, our small yard encompassed a parallel universe."

Brooks urges us to help every child discover parallel universes of possibilities. When a flower can be a person or a fungus a fairy stairway, we ought to wonder what damage we do to children's imaginations when toys are too "real." As Brooks says, "Modern toys don't leave much margin for imagination. Computer chips do the thinking. Characters come pre-scripted from cartoon shows. Every doll trails a comet tail of must-have accessories." Such prefabricated experiences stunt the poetic and artistic imagination. They also crimp the inventive mind, for the child who never has to make or make do will never perceive the possibilities of materials or the purposes in objects originally designed for some other use. Only when we can see things for what they *might be* and not just for what they are can we begin to use them in novel ways.

So we should give children toys that they can use in many ways. Let them adapt blocks, simple dolls, paper, cloth, and household items to as many scenarios as they can imagine. Encourage them to imagine a stick to be a sword, a scarf a river, a pair of alphabet blocks a pair of dice. And incorporate such analogizing into the classroom through materials such as those used in the Private Eye Project initiated by Kerry Ruef and piloted in the Seattle public schools. With the aid of a loupe, or jeweler's magnifying lens, children of all ages are taught to concentrate on observing, to ask "What does this remind me of?," to draw it, ask again, generate lists of comparisons, critique these visual analogies, search for functional relationships and, finally, to theorize why it is like that. The Private Eye guide suggests numerous exercises that incorporate thinking by analogy into every grade and nearly every grade-school discipline, including writing, art, science, math, and social sciences.

Teach and learn by analogy and metaphor. As a character in an ancient Chinese story says when ordered to stop using analogies, "A man who explains necessarily makes intelligible that which is not known by comparing it with what is known. . . . [To abandon analogies] would make the task impossible." Start with what you know or what the person you are teaching already knows, then find the functional analogy that bridges this known thing with the unknown one that needs to be understood.

The works of artist-inventors such as Leonardo da Vinci and Todd Siler provide masterful models upon which to build. Leonardo's notebooks are littered with analogies rendered in words and visual images. The swirling of water in the pool around a water wheel is juxtaposed with the swirling of the blood as it courses through the heart — not quite Harvey's pump analogy, but almost. Leonardo compares the eddies in water with the movements of wind. He compares the processes by which light, heat, and odors are dispersed with distance — analogies that we now know to be inaccurate. But his analogies between waves in water, wind, and sounds carried on the air are still recognized as valid in modern physics. He compared the structure of

Fig. 8-10. *Left:* Leonardo da Vinci (1452–1519) drew an analogy between the structure of the brain and those of the eye and the onion; *right: Our Perpetually Flowering Minds* (1993), by Todd Siler, compares the brain stem to a flower bud. His text reads in part: "The ultimate bulb of intelligent life forms. 'Consciousness and Imagination.' Our perpetually flowering minds. Metaphorm on . . . annual rings . . . growth cycles . . . development."

the eye with that of the mind and also of an onion, portraying each as a visual analogy of the others.

Todd Siler greatly expands this approach, comparing the growth of our minds to the growth of trees and onions, a bulb that flowers with ideas, a cerebroreactor that fuses information like an atomic reactor to produce psychic energy, a collider in which oppositely charged ideas explode to reveal their underlying particle/assumptions. Siler argues that the structure of the universe and the tools we use to understand that reality are reflections of the structure of the mind and the tools we use to explore ourselves. Ultimately, he transforms his metaphorical fusions into compelling works of art, practical inventions (he has many patents), intriguing speculations about thinking, and connections between art and science, as shown in his book *Breaking the Mind Barrier.* Siler has revealed the bases of his thinking, subsumed under the rubric "metaphorming" in *Think Like A Genius*, which provides dozens of exercises, some of which specifically develop analogical and metaphorical thinking. Siler suggests, for instance, that we compare the mind with a garden and explore metaphoric figures of speech, imagine stories, form hypotheses, search for puns, following up every image, feeling, and association these provoke. This approach can be used with any set of materials to open worlds as unexpected and otherwise unknowable as those explored by Helen Keller or Louis de Broglie.

So try a bit of "metaphorming" yourself. Compare the figures by Leonardo and Siler shown on the previous page and think about all the verbal, visual, and scientific ideas they bring to mind. How would Keller think about them, or de Broglie, or Robert Frost? Or think about the game of life that we must all play, as the Persian poet Omar Khayyám did in a *rubaiyat* — an epigram written as a quatrain — over eight hundred years ago:

> *Tis all a Chequer-board of Nights and Days*
> *Where Destiny with Men for Pieces plays:*
> *Hither and thither moves, and mates, and slays,*
> *And one by one back in the Closet lays.*

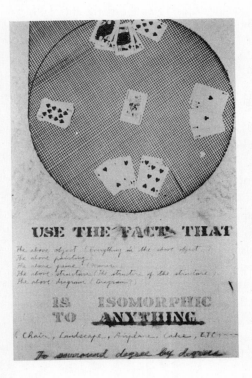

Fig. 8-11. *The Degrees of Meaning,* by Shusaka Arakawa, *1972.* The text reads: "Use the fact that the above object . . . painting . . . game . . . structure . . . diagram is isomorphic to anything. (Chair, landscape, airplane, cake, etc.) To surround degree by degree."

Now compare this with a print about a card game, *The Degrees of Meaning,* created in 1972 by the Japanese artist Shusaka Arakawa. Both men are clearly telling us that life is a game, which should bring to mind other game analogies ("The leaders of Britain are formed on the playing fields of Eton;" "Games mimic life;" and so on). Many of these associations will be trite, but finding the analogies between their analogies — by metaphorming — reveals deeper meanings. Are we pawns moved by fate (the joker in the center of Arakawa's table) or are we dealt random hands (our genetic, personal, social, economic lot) that we must play? In checkers and chess, the outcome of the game can be altered by strategy, but if you are a pawn being moved at the whim of another player, it cannot. Perhaps it is best to enjoy life as much as possible before it is too late. Or perhaps it doesn't matter. What will be will be. In poker, knowing the odds can make all the difference between winning and losing, and sometimes you can bluff your way to winning, but by the time the cards are face up (as they are in Arakawa's print), and we know what cards each player holds, the game is over. Obviously there are more possibilities here: lost causes, journeys, life, fate, destiny, death. Whether a card game is a thing, an intention, a process, a map, a form, Arakawa and Khayyám tell us that it can be likened to anything. They might as well be referring to analogizing itself. When we seek out and find hidden identities of function and purpose, "degree by degree" we "surround" our perception of world and self with meaning. And then, suddenly, we understand.

9

Body Thinking

IN 1925 PRIMATE EXPERT Wolfgang Kohler published the results of
more than a dozen years of research on the intelligence of chimpanzees.
Perhaps the most famous of his experiments involved placing chimpanzees in a room empty except for sticks of different lengths, some crates, and a banana hanging from the ceiling out of reach. The chimps figured out how to obtain the banana by knocking it down with sticks or by stacking enough crates to reach it directly. There is a story, possibly apocryphal, that one chimpanzee was smarter than Kohler anticipated, solving the banana problem while he was still in the room, within seconds of his hanging up the fruit. Most impressively, the chimp did it without the aid of any of the available tools. But how? To figure this out, you have to move. Actually, you have to move like an ape. Or, if you can't quite imagine moving like an ape, try remembering how you moved as a child. Remember the *feel* of hopscotch, leapfrog, cartwheels, piggyback rides, playing ball, turning somersaults, climbing trees, twirling till you fall down dizzy, hopping on pogo sticks, swinging and leaping out of swing sets, and spinning Hula Hoops — physical games that people, as children at least, share with their evolutionary cousins. How you move — indeed, if you move — will determine whether you can think like a chimp.

Aha! you say. The solution lies in those hints about piggyback rides and climbing trees. In a sudden reversal of expected behavior, the chimp jumped on Kohler's back as he passed under the banana, climbed up on his shoulders, grabbed the banana, and leaped triumphantly down. We humans tend to overintellectualize, forgetting that our bodies "know" how to do things that we understand only after we have done them.

Fig. 9-1. Chimpanzee using boxes to reach a banana.

Thinking with the body depends on our sense of muscle movement, posture, balance, and touch. This general sense, discovered in the 1890s by the neurobiologist C. S. Sherrington and called proprioception, is fundamental to our experience of the body. As we walk or run or jump we are constantly aware of how our body feels; and we know where we are in space. Most of the time we have this awareness without realizing it. According to neurologist Oliver Sacks, "that continuous but unconscious sensory flow from the movable parts of our body" has been called our "sixth" or "secret" sense. We continually monitor our muscles, Sacks notes, and adjust their "position and tone and motion . . . but in a way which is hidden from us because it is automatic and unconscious."

That is, it is *usually* hidden from us. We are very aware of our proprioceptive senses when we are learning a new skill, such as riding a bike, hitting a baseball, using a hammer or screwdriver, playing a new instrument, knit-

Fig. 9-2. "Vivian just read how different ways of moving can produce different ways of thinking." Cartoon by Jerry van Amerongen.

ting a sweater, or blowing glass. Each of these skills requires long periods of conscious learning and practice. As you master the movements involved in bike riding or piano playing, you do them increasingly without awareness. When you no longer have to think about how to hit the ball, you can actually start to enjoy playing tennis. When you no longer have to remember where and how to move your fingers to play a piece, you can begin to make real music. Pianists speak of muscle memory for the notes and dynamics of a sonata; they store these memories in their fingers, just as actors store memory of pose and gesture in all the muscles of their body. When actors improvise a character's behavior, the remembered gestures come easily and naturally, as they do for the musician. If the musician is also a composer, he or she may imagine musical phrases as the movements involved in playing an instrument or singing — Mozart, for instance, often composed in public with movements of his hands and mouth. This is body imagination at work, when the feel of muscle movement or physical tension or touch is enacted in order to think and create.

It is possible to conjure up feelings of body tension or touch or movement in the mind, but most of us overlook these imaginative feelings because we are trained so early to see them or translate them into descriptive words. Sometimes it takes a person like Helen Keller, unencumbered by competing visual or auditory information, to understand just how clearly the body speaks. On several occasions in the 1930s, Keller visited Martha Graham's dance studio. Keller was used to "hearing" music by placing her hand on a piano or some other instrument and feeling its vibrations. Similarly, she "saw" Graham's troupe dance by feeling the vibrations of the floor through her feet and the stirring of air on her face and hands. Still, Keller knew some aspect was eluding her. Certainly she had no visual sense of ballet or of the revolution Graham was creating in modern dance, but she had no physical sense of it either. How could she? She had never run, jumped, or twirled about as most sighted people do; such activities were considered too dangerous for a blind girl. This lack of internal body images became clear one day when she said, "Martha, what is jumping? I don't understand." Graham responded at once by calling one of her dancers, Merce Cunningham, to the barre and placing Keller's hands on his waist. As Graham tells the story, "Merce jumped in the air in first position while Helen's hands stayed on his body. Everyone in the studio was focused on this event, this movement. Her hands rose and fell as Merce did. Her expression changed from curiosity to one of joy. You could see the enthusiasm rise in her face as she threw her arms up in the air and exclaimed, 'How like thought. How like the mind it is.'"

With these words Keller movingly validated what Graham and many dancers had long known, that jumping is a kind of thinking. As Jean Cocteau said of the great dancer Vaslav Nijinsky, "His body knew; his limbs had intelligence." According to Cocteau, Nijinsky seldom articulated his dance innovations in words; he simply placed his foot where it had never been placed before or jumped higher and farther than anyone ever had. For her part, Graham once wrote that the logic of dance — "such as it is — occurs on the level of motor activity." This was not to deny that dance may be born of explicitly articulated intellectual concerns. Graham larded her notebooks with verbal analyses of the texts and symbols that stimulated her work. It did mean that the stuff of dance — the body's use of space, force, and time — had to make sense on a purely physical level.

Because of their long training in the way one movement leads to another in human locomotion, Graham and her dancers fully understood how moving can be thinking. After all, choreographers necessarily compose through their own and their dancers' bodies. "You have to make it up in your body," choreographer Eliot Feld has said. "You do not make it up in your mind." But for Keller, body thinking also had a wholly mental dimension. The gathering of physical energy and its sudden release in the dance jump reminded her of the manner in which ideas burst into consciousness. She herself experienced this kind of mental jump many times, most famously when the string of letters *w a t e r,* spelled into her hand by her teacher, mysteriously and suddenly revealed itself as the name for the cold liquid spilling from the pump. Moreover, she realized that many of the ideas that burst upon her consciousness were not actual sensations but memories or imagined perceptions of body movement and feeling. During her years of silence and darkness, before her first "vision" of language at the age of seven, Keller knew herself and her world primarily through sensations of the body, including touch. "When I wanted anything I liked, ice cream, for instance," she later wrote, " . . . I had a delicious taste on my tongue (which, by the way, I never have now), and in my hand I felt the turning of the freezer. I made the sign [presumably a rotating motion as if she were turning the freezer handle], and my mother knew I wanted ice cream. I 'thought' and desired in my fingers."

In later years Keller referred to such vivid body sensations recalled from early childhood as thoughts — "if," she modestly asserted, "a wordless sensation may be called a thought." We certainly think that, individually or together, sensations of muscle movement, body feeling, and touch act as a powerful tool for imaginative thinking. Indeed, many researchers have already made a case for kinesthetic thinking, that is, thinking in terms of the body's motor images or remembered movements. In 1959 Eliot Dole Hutchinson argued that creativity in any endeavor requiring great physical skill or dexterity would likely involve imagined body sensations. "By no means all insights express themselves in verbal form," he wrote. "To the pianist and sculptor, the instrumentalist, dancer, surgeon and manual artisan, they [ideas] burst upon awareness in a kinesthetic form, feeling their way into varying types of muscular expression. Fingers 'itch' to play; music 'flows from the hands'; ideas 'flow' from the pen. Movement expresses the 'idea' of the dancer or orchestra conductor; the almost sensuous desire to model plastic form becomes compulsive in sculpture."

More recently psychologist Howard Gardner, in his book *Frames of Mind* (1983), has made the case for a similar concept of kinesthetic thinking. Gardner argues cogently that the body harbors an "intelligence" all its own, and he reiterates the analogy between skilled body use and thinking that other psychologists, such as Frederic Bartlett, have drawn. Psychologist Vera John-Steiner also views the body "as an instrument of thought" and explores it as such in *Notebooks of the Mind* (1985). Even researchers who seek hard and fast answers about the biological bases of motor memory, such as the neuroscientist Marc Jennerod, hope to tease out the relationship among perception, imagery, and cognition.

We believe, however, that psychologists and neuropsychologists limit their studies and therefore their understanding of body thinking with two erroneous assumptions. First, they assume that body thinking has only to do with movement, whether it is the movement itself or the imagined sensation or image of movement. But as physiologist Walter Cannon pointed out fifty years ago, proprioception also includes how we feel *viscerally and emotionally.* Our posture and movements reflect our moods, and our moods are related, in turn, to how we feel in what Cannon called our "internal milieu," our gut and mind. People can "think" in nonmuscular physical sensations, too. The second error, which follows from the first, is thus to assume that body thinking *can only be expressed* as movement and is therefore best studied in dancers, athletes, and other performers. Movement sensations certainly make up a large part of body thinking, but not to the exclusion of other proprioceptive and tactile sensations. Musicians are proprioceptive thinkers, but so are mathematicians — and not just because they move, but because they feel with their skin and in their gut.

Body thinking in all its manifestations is often a fundamental part of creative expressions we don't normally associate with movement or touch or

Fig. 9-3. Jackson Pollock painting, circa 1950, photographed by Hans Namuth.

inner tensions. Take, for instance, the *making* of paintings, drawings, and etchings. The motor aspect of creation is particularly obvious in Jackson Pollock's work. Art museums often hang his "drip" paintings on the wall as if they were simply canvases to be experienced visually. But Pollock's work cannot be fully experienced just by looking — it is necessary to feel as well. To make his paintings, he took the canvas down from the artist's easel and placed it flat on the floor, changing the usual physical relationship between the artist and his material. He then literally *danced* around the canvas, flinging paint as he went (see Fig. 9-3). Each canvas is, therefore, a *record* of his movements, an action painting. If you do not feel the physical sensations involved in Pollock's artistic process, then you do not understand his art.

Pollock is hardly alone among visual artists in privileging the thinking body. Neuroscientist and painter Jacques Mandelbrojt says that "an artist creates signs by an interior muscular identification with the object he wants to represent." Mandelbrojt lived in Aix-en-Provence, France, for several years "and when I painted outdoors I *identified* myself . . . either with the simple and pure shapes of trees or with the entangled shapes of bushes. My memory

Fig. 9-4. *Bushes*, ink on paper, by Jacques Mandelbrojt, 1993.

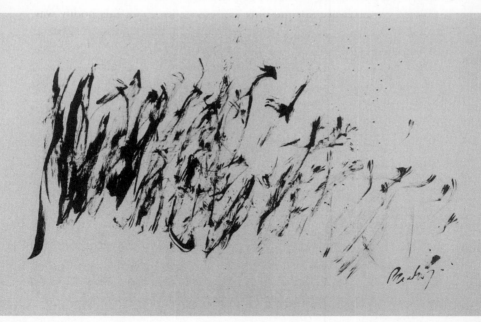

Fig. 9-5. *Thistle* by Gunta Stolzl-Stadler, drawn while she was Itten's student.

and muscles still retain these internal muscular identifications and my recent generally abstract paintings or drawings often express this identification. This drawing is a remote memory of my identification with bushes."

Abstract painters are not the only artists who think in this bodily way. Johannes Itten, a master teacher at the German Bauhaus, felt what he drew as both movement and touch and taught his students to incorporate these feelings into their art. "I have a thistle before me," he wrote in 1921. "My motorial nerves experience a lacerated, spasmodic movement. My senses, touch and sight, record the sharp pointedness of its form movement and my spirit sees its essence. I *experience* a thistle."

Proprioceptive thinking is even more evident in sculpture. As Isamu Noguchi said, "The man who really sees sculpture must move physically to realize its form." Centuries ago the Renaissance sculptor and architect Lorenzo Ghiberti remarked that the feel of that form "could not be discovered by sight, but only by the touch of the hand passed over it" (see Fig. 9-6). What a disservice to the public, then, that art museums so often place "Do Not Touch" signs on sculptures or make it difficult to walk around them. Because sculpture is a wholly physical expression of a physical experience, viewing it without proprioceptive interaction is like watching an orchestra play silent music. Indeed, for many sculptors a love of the medium stems from the body's interaction with manipulated materials. Claes Oldenburg was drawn to sculpture by the physical feel of its creation: "I started as a painter but after a while I didn't like the flatness. I want to touch the object." Charles Simonds decided to become a sculptor after working with some Plasticine given him as a boy: "One night I took some of it and made a sculpture of a lying-down wrestler, with all of the musculature. I remember the sensation of working with the clay was overwhelming. The feeling of the clay, the sense of connectedness, that my hands could do this was stunning."

Some sculptors try to turn this heightened physical awareness into sculpture itself. Perhaps the most famous was Auguste Rodin, who recognized that sculpture had to be made from the inside out. He made numerous drawings of his subjects before modeling them in clay, in order, he said, "to test to what extent my hands already feel what my eyes see." Understanding plastic form was, for Rodin, almost entirely a function of the feeling body. "Don't you see," he remarked in his *Personal Reminiscences,* "that, for my work of modeling, I have not only to possess a complete *knowledge* of the human form, but also a deep *feeling* for every aspect of it? I have, as it were, to *incorporate* the lines of the human body, and they must become part of myself. . . . Only then can I be certain that I understand." When Rodin created

Fig. 9-6. Henry Moore with Sir Kenneth Clark, feeling a statue in the British Museum, circa 1950.

Fig. 9-7. *Le Penseur* by Auguste Rodin (photograph by Victor Pannelier).

The Thinker, perhaps one of the best-known public sculptures in the world, he gave physical form to his own proprioceptive imagination. A nude man, whom Rodin meant to represent all poets, all artists, all inventors, sits upon a rock in tense and intense contemplation. "What makes my *Thinker* think," Rodin wrote, "is that he thinks not only with his brain, with his knitted brow, his distended nostrils, and compressed lips, but with every muscle of his arms, back and legs, with his clenched fist and gripping toes."

Henry Moore also worked from a "deep feeling" for the forms he sculpted, though these were abstract and often nonrepresentational. He wanted to express the inner vitality, the sense that a "form is pressing from the inside trying to burst . . . trying to make itself come to a shape from inside itself." This desire to project body in sculpture drew Moore to many organic objects, particularly bones. Bone, he said, is "the inner structure of all living form. It's the bone that pushes out from inside; as you bend your leg the knee gets tautness over it, and it's there that the movement and energy come from." Thinking with his body, Moore often tried to feel the inner strength and pressure of forms he found interesting. "Try positions oneself," he jotted in a notebook, as an "aid to physical understanding." This could as well have been Henri Matisse speaking to his students about how best to use a human model: "Close your eyes and hold the vision, and then do the work with your own sensibility," Matisse told his students. "If it be a model, assume the pose of the model yourself; where the strain comes is the key of the movement." This was also the key to dance for Martha Graham, who told her students to "feel the inner skeleton of the body as part of the whole movement." She urged them to move "like a piece of sculpture with holes, such as in a Henry Moore sculpture. That is, we should have the feeling of air going through the holes in our bones." We suspect that Moore would have been pleased that his expression of deep proprioceptive feeling had been so well understood.

Music, too, is born of proprioceptive thinking. And just as it is impossible to appreciate a Jackson Pollock drip painting by simply looking at it, it is impossible to understand the performance of music fully without feeling the physical activity it entails. Seiji Ozawa, director of the Boston Symphony Orchestra, has been described as conducting "with his whole body; he dances the shape of the music." And Leonard Bernstein, as conductor of the New York Philharmonic, had an intensely kinetic style that melded passion and movement into sound. Performers also make music with bodily imagination. According to Yehudi Menuhin, the violinist must learn how to stand as well as how to hold the violin, how to wield the bow, how to move the fingers on the fingerboard — a physical progression that takes years to master. Composer and pianist George Antheil emphasized that the pianist's skills are also primarily muscular: "You practice slow trills until it almost kills you, until your two forearms are like sore throbbing hams, twice, three times their normal size, or so they seem." Antheil compared playing a concert to going fifteen rounds with a boxer. One sweats as much and works as hard. As the well-known concert pianist Ruth Laredo put it, "It isn't just your hands that are busy and working hard. Playing the piano is a total physical involvement, it involves your entire body . . . and you have to use your body in a special way for each different kind of music."

The musician's physical feel for a piece of music is ultimately enacted as a complex sequence of highly skilled movements. And, like athletes and dancers, musicians learn to maximize their performance by mentally rehearsing the body's experience of the music. One of the most eccentric students of such "mental practice" was undoubtedly Glenn Gould, who claimed to work at the keyboard a mere hour a day, even in preparation for recording. Instead of playing his instrument, he intensively "studied the score," developing "a very clear conception of how I wanted to approach the [music]." When queried by a skeptical interviewer that such minimal practice must result in loss of coordination, Gould replied, "On the contrary, when I do go back [to the piano] I probably play better than at any other time, purely in a physical sense, because the image, the mental image, which governs what one does is normally at that point at its strongest and most precise. . . . What it all comes down to is that one does not play the piano with one's fingers, one plays the piano with one's mind." Of course, such mental practicing depends upon having already created through prior physical practice a ready store of body movement and body feeling images. Only thus can one imagine well the body sensations of performance.

Surprisingly, muscular feeling, physical sensations, manipulative skill, and their mental imaging play an important role in scientific thinking, too, which may be related to the fact that many eminent scientists are also excellent artists or musicians. Scientists "play" laboratory instruments and develop a kinesthetic feel for their experimental work. As embryologist C. H. Waddington wrote, "Outstanding execution in scientific experimentation and painting have in common a dependence on ability — probably ultimately muscular — to handle the physical stuff of the world." Indeed, Cyril Stanley Smith purposefully studied graphic arts to develop his sense of the structure of metals. And he meant the word "sense" literally, for "in the long gone days when I was developing alloys," he wrote to a friend in 1972, "I certainly came to have a very strong feeling of natural understanding, a feeling of how I would behave if I were a certain alloy, a sense of hardness and softness and conductivity and fusibility and deformability and brittleness — all in a curiously internal and quite literally sensual way." This sounds very much like the proprioceptive and kinesthetic imaging of Einstein and Feynman discussed in Chapter 1. For Smith, these feelings were not beside the point; his scientific work actually depended upon "aesthetic feeling for a balanced structure and a muscular feeling of the interfaces pulling against one another."

Physicist and inventor Mitchell Wilson similarly explored the tactile knowledge gained from handling materials and objects in his novel *Live with Lightning*. The character Erik recreates Wilson's own experience learning to use the lathe, drill press, and other machinery and discovers, in the novelist's words, the "working nature of the various metals as though they were the personalities of old friends. Copper was so soft and chewy that one had to be tender with it. Brass was good and brittle and could be worked with relaxing ease. Steels were unpredictable: some tough, and others soft with knots of hardness spread throughout like seasoning." Wilson makes clear that such tactile knowledge of materials was as critical to the design and assembly of equipment as the equipment itself was to the design of an experiment.

By the same token, a muscular and tactile feel for materials is essential to the building of machines, buildings, and other structures. According to Eugene S. Ferguson, author of *Engineering and the Mind's Eye,* the building of machines and structures designed by engineers depends more than is commonly realized upon the manual knowledge of mechanics. "In erecting a machine, such as a large steam turbine-driven electrical generator," he writes, "not only visual but also tactile and muscular knowledge are incorporated into the machine by the mechanics and others who use tools and skills and judgment to give life to the visions of engineers." The work of machinists, carpenters, and other skilled labor, Ferguson concludes, "involves the laying on of knowing hands." Such hands know how tight is tight, when one more turn will strip a screw or crack a nut. They know how far they can bend different woods and metals before they crack. They know when glass is ready to fuse or blow and when it will not cooperate. Such knowledge cannot be written down or specified in blueprints, it can be learned only through direct physical experience.

Muscular, tactile, and manipulative thinking skills play an important role in understanding biological, chemical, and physical systems. They also figure noticeably in mathematics. The mathematician Kalvis Jansons, for instance, has a "feel" for knots. "Knots," he writes, "are examples of things that are extremely hard to describe and remember in words, and people who attempt to do so usually forget them very quickly and are poor at spotting similarities between complicated knots." Knowing hands, however, can help. Indeed, when Jansons, who is severely dyslexic, doesn't have a piece of rope in his hands with which to think about his knots, he does not try to see or describe them. Rather, he creates an internal bodily feeling for space, much like the blind man who gauged his position on the street by feeling some wooden railings: "As I touch them," the man remarked, "a shudder runs ahead, marking their pliant length, and jerks suddenly to a tension at the concrete post." These images are not seen but *felt.* In the same way, Jansons "imagine[s] the finger movements involved and the feel of the knot being tied without picturing it in my mind or moving my hands at all." He is like Glenn Gould, practicing the mathematical manipulations in his mind before committing to the performance of symbol expression.

Stanislaw Ulam goes a step further as a mathematician, actually *calculating* "not by numbers and symbols, but by almost tactile feelings combined with reasoning, a very curious mental effort." In his work on the atomic bomb at Los Alamos he apparently imagined the movements of atomic particles visually and proprioceptively. "I found out that the main ability to have was a visual, and also an almost tactile, way to imagine the physical situations, rather than a merely logical picture of the problems. . . . Very soon I discovered that if one gets a feeling for no more than a dozen . . . radiation and nuclear constants, one can imagine the subatomic world almost tangibly, and manipulate the picture dimensionally and qualitatively, before calculating more precise relationships." When we were in graduate school we heard about another physicist, whose name we've unfortunately long forgotten, who was said to have Ulam's capacity for "feeling" quantum equations with his whole body. During seminars, if a speaker presented equations resulting in atomic interactions that were too loose, the man would slump in his chair. If the equations forced the atoms to pack too tightly, he would scrunch up as if desperately in need of the men's room. Speakers could "read" his opinion of their work long before he ever opened his mouth to comment.

Mathematician Norbert Wiener employed an even more bizarre set of bodily feelings. After spending months working fruitlessly on a difficult problem that led him into controversy with his Harvard colleagues, Wiener became gravely ill with pneumonia. Throughout the course of the feverish disease his mind conflated bodily discomfort with mental anxiety. "It was impossible for me to distinguish among my pain and difficulty in breathing, the flapping of the window curtain, and certain as yet unresolved parts of the potential problem on which I was working." For Wiener, the physical pain represented the mathematical tension worrying his mind, and the mathematical tension represented the pain; "I became aware of the possibility that almost any experience may act as a temporary symbol for a mathematical situation which has not yet been organized and cleared up." Vladimir Nabokov experienced similar conflations between mathematical cerebration and illness: "As a little boy, I showed an abnormal aptitude for mathematics. . . . this gift played a horrible part in tussles with quinsy or scarlet fever, when I felt enormous spheres and huge numbers swell relentlessly in my aching brain."

While most people would probably find such feelings unwelcome, Nabokov later drew on the memories for greater insight into how he experienced the world. Wiener also reflected on his experience of illness and realized that much of his mathematical thinking — even when he was not sick — took the form of physical tension. The "discomfort or even the pain of an unresolved mathematical discord" actually motivated his search for a mathematical solution. Indeed, he used bodily feelings as a kind of shorthand for various mathematical difficulties and came to believe this kind of thinking absolutely essential to his field. "If there is any one quality which marks the competent mathematician more than any other," he wrote, "I think it is the power to 'operate' with temporary emotional symbols and to organize out of them a semipermanent, recallable language. If one is not able to do this, one is likely to find that his ideas evaporate from the sheer difficulty of preserving them in an as yet unformulated shape."

The experiences of Wiener, Nabokov, Gould, and others discussed in this chapter lead us to conclude that to think is to feel and, conversely, to feel is to think. How, after all, do we know when something represents a problem for us? We become physically uncomfortable. And when we have resolved the problem, we feel physical well-being — not just a sense of elation, but a literal spring in our step, a smile on our face, a laugh in our voice. It is not surprising to find Nabokov writing of the "mellow physical satisfaction" of composing novel chess problems, "a feeling of snugness (which goes back to one's childhood, to play-planning in bed)." Nor are we surprised when the mathematician and philosopher Bertrand Russell writes, "In all the creative work that I have done, what has come first is a problem, a puzzle involving discomfort." We have all experienced bodily pleasure or pain from purely mental ideas and vice versa. And, as it turns out, there are strong anatomical connections between mind, gut, and facial features. Sylvia Bensley, an anatomist, once pointed out that "our emotions are expressed largely by our facial muscles; every one of them is [embryologically] a gut muscle derived from the first or second visceral arch and innervated by a gut nerve. The anatomical association is direct; the psychical association between our emotions and our viscera is closer perhaps than we realize or would like to admit." When we feel good or bad, happy or sad, our minds really do communicate with our gut, and our gut with our mind and muscles. Mind and body are one, and we must learn how to facilitate and make use of the interconnections.

Perhaps the most surprising aspect of proprioceptive thinking is that it is not limited to what we feel in our own bodies, but extends to our experience of other people and even of other things. According to dance critic and historian John Martin, the recognition and imitation of proprioceptive states in others make possible the arts of dance and mime. "It is the dancer's whole function," he has written, "to lead us into imitating his actions with our faculty for inner mimicry in order that we may experience his feelings. Facts he could tell us, but feelings he cannot convey in any other way than by arous-

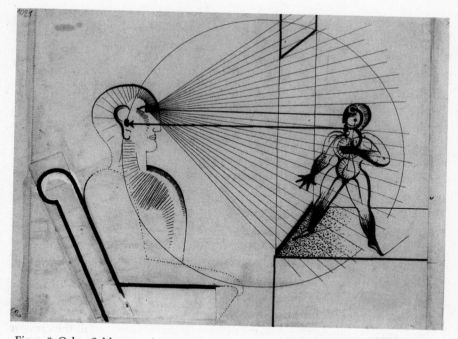

Fig. 9-8. Oskar Schlemmer images inner mimicry in *Man the Dancer I: Performer and Spectator II*, circa 1924.

ing them in us through sympathetic action." Oskar Schlemmer made the same point in his drawing *Man the Dancer*. Dance communicates only when the proprioceptive experience of the dancer resonates bodily within the viewer.

Consider, too, that people around the world know what Charlie Chaplin's Little Tramp means when he lifts his hat or looks shyly at his feet in the presence of a beautiful woman, because they recognize in themselves the feelings that accompany the body language. Indeed, the *Encyclopaedia Britannica* defines mime as the first and only truly universal language. No wonder, then, that Stanislavsky argued that every actor should have the skills of the mime: "An actor must possess so keen a sense of observation and such a well-developed memory in his muscles as to be able to reproduce not only pose and gesture but also harmoniously moving thoughts and body." Our only objection to Stanislavsky's statement is that he limits it to actors. Surely this is a skill that would improve everyone's ability to understand and communicate with others.

Our proprioceptive sense can extend to missing body parts and to inanimate objects as well. Neurologists have long known that amputees and people who lose their sight or hearing experience what are called phantom limbs or phantom senses. People who have lost a leg will continue to experience pain, itching, and even movement in the absent limb for months and sometimes years afterward. Someone without a hand can still imagine using it to reach for a cup of coffee. People who have gone deaf or blind will continue to think that they hear or see things. Apparently the mind creates an internal image of the body and its senses so that even when some part of these are physically lost, the mind continues to operate as if all were still there. The persistence of this proprioceptive image is so critical to the successful use of any prosthesis that some doctors recognize that an artificial limb will be relatively useless unless and until the phantom is incorporated into it. The amputee learns to invest the prosthesis with the "feelings" of his mental image, just as we invest a dancer or mime with feelings that we imagine. A neurologist recently told us about teaching a patient to pick up a pencil with his new artificial hand and to draw with it. When asked how he knew the pencil was in his "hand," the man immediately replied, without thinking, "I feel it." There was a pause and then he added, with a puzzled look on his face, "But I can't really do that, can I?"

He can, but not in the way most of us think of "feeling." What he has created is not a phantom limb — the feelings of a limb that is not there — but its inverse, a limb phantom that provides feelings to a prosthesis. People can project limb phantoms even when their arms and legs are intact. Matthew Botvinick, a psychiatry resident at the University of Pittsburgh Medical School, recently ran an experiment in which full-bodied individuals were seated so that they could not see their own hand but could see an artificial, look-alike hand that was in no way attached to themselves. Using a paintbrush, the investigator stroked the real and the fake hands at the same time. Subjects reported responding to the prosthesis as if it were their own hand, and when the fake hand was stroked *but not the real hand,* they reported feeling "numb." Botvinick describes the effect as tactile ventriloquism. "You have something going on over here, namely the visual input of the brush touching a hand, and something going on over there, which is the tactile input from your own hand being touched," he writes. "The brain sometimes will simply override the discrepancy, and say, 'I see a touch, I feel a touch. Something must be wrong with my calibration of space. I'll just gloss over that and put them together.'"

Actually, we all create limb phantoms all the time — in order to use tools, equipment, and instruments of many kinds. The tennis racket, the paintbrush, the cello and bow become extensions — indeed, prostheses — of ourselves that we use to manipulate the world. Even the most unwieldy of extensions can, in time, be invested with a body phantom. Take the twelve white wooden poles, some as long as ten feet, that were strapped to the limbs of dancer Amanda von Kreibig in Oskar Schlemmer's *Pole Dance* of 1927. How von Kreibig felt was never recorded, but a reconstruction of the dance by Debra McCall in the mid-1980s suggests that the dancer must eventually project a sense of body into the farthest reach of every pole. "As the dancer began rehearsals with the twelve white poles attached to his limbs and torso," she wrote, "he had difficulty breathing and fought the confinement. Gradually he came to feel less encumbered by imagining the poles as naturally exaggerating his movement. Next he sensed his body interacting with and

Fig. 9-9. Dancer Amanda von Kreibig performing Oskar Schlemmer's *Pole Dance*, 1927.

defining the surrounding space. Only then did the dance become three-dimensional and sculpturally alive." The poles, in other words, became "extra bones and flesh," in the words of Alwin Nikolais, who has also experimented with props "to extend [the dancer's] physical size in space." With practice, such props can be maneuvered just as the body itself is maneuvered, and the feeling of separateness is overcome. The mental image of one's body changes, incorporating the extensions both kinesthetically and proprioceptively.

Incorporating extensions of the body is crucial for success in many other arts as well. Yehudi Menuhin has written that "a great violin . . . is alive" and the violinist "is part of his violin." When he plays, he said, "the body becomes a kind of aural intelligence, an instrument perfectly tuned and playing independently of me, a 'pure' voice" that is indistinguishable from the violin itself. In *The Hand,* Frank R. Wilson records an interview with the German puppeteer Anton Bachleitner, who projects body sensations into his tool, the puppet. "The most difficult job technically is to be able to feel the foot contact the floor as it happens. The only way to make the puppet look as though it is actually walking," the puppeteer says, "is by *feeling* what is happening through your hands." This requires a kind of shift in perception, so that the puppeteer sees through the eyes of the puppet. As Bachleitner puts it, the puppeteer "must learn to be *in* the puppet."

The same fusion of body and tool takes place in medicine and science. The Pentagon has recently developed a Telepresence Surgery System (TeSS), a virtual-reality machine that will enable surgeons to operate on people with life-threatening injuries from miles away by electronically manipulating a surgical robot. Surgeons testing TeSS on dummies, cadavers, and anesthetized animals report that they quickly begin to "feel" as if they are doing the operation without an intermediary. "The pincers respond instantly to your hand motions," said one, "and open or close when you manipulate the handles. Most startlingly, you feel what they feel. When a pincer bumps something or pulls the surgical thread taut, you sense the resistance." Equally startling reports have come from physicists working with specially adapted atomic-force microscopes that magnify the pull experienced by a microscopic needle in the presence of a layer of atoms. Users claim that you can actually *feel* the texture of a single layer of atoms and *sense* the physical attraction of individual ions.

No matter the purpose or the size, people project bodily senses into every kind of tool that requires skilled use. We even develop body phantoms for the instruments we drive. It may come as a surprise to hear construction workers speak of communion with their big machines, expressions more typically associated with musicians and artists, but the physical bonding they experience is real. "You must empty your mind and think of nothing so that the backhoe becomes an extension of your arm," said one machine operator quoted in the *Wall Street Journal*. "You're part of the machine. It's part of you," reported another construction worker. Many people embody their cars in the same way. Think about how you know the size of your car well enough to park it in a small space or pull it into your garage without hitting anything. You can't actually see the car's outer dimensions, yet you know the size and shape of your extended "body" — a fact that becomes apparent when you hop into an unfamiliar car or take one for a spin in a country where people drive on the "wrong" side of the road. Without doubt you find yourself making countless conscious adjustments until your body phantom re-forms in the image of your new car body.

Like all the other types of thinking discussed in this book, body thinking combines objective and subjective ways of knowing. Only when the thing we manipulate is no longer "other" but an extension of "I" does it obey our will and desires. Only when we feel our way into the space around us, as Picasso did in his drawing of Marie-Thérèse knitting (Fig. 5-1) and as Schlemmer did in his 1924 drawing *Figure and Space Delineation* (Fig. 9-10), do we truly sense and interact with it. Unfortunately, as dancer Doris Humphrey once wrote, "Kinesthesia is a rudimentary response in most people, and there is a great need for a fuller consciousness of this special sense, for it to be ordered and made comprehensive." All people need explicit practice in moving their bodies, manipulating instruments or tools, and gaining awareness of their kinesthetic and proprioceptive responses. These desiderata provide an unusual justification for sports, dance, and theater programs, mandatory shop classes, and mastery of a musical instrument, especially if part of the training involves a focus on literally feeling one's way into the activities.

Body-thinking exercises can also be made an explicit part of disciplinary and transdisciplinary studies. In some schools "creative movement" is purposefully used to explore many academic subjects. To learn about the physics of sound waves, children may line up in "molecule formations" — the solids are tightly packed, the gases much less so — and experience for themselves how quickly a wave of shoulder taps passes through various materials. Or they may watch and imitate internally the enactments of others. In Okemos, Michigan, members of the Happendance Modern Dance Company model the physical chemistry of molecules. Moving swiftly all over the stage, bouncing balloons quickly between them, the dancers embody the motions

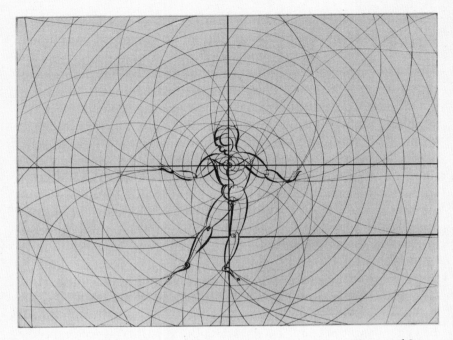

Fig. 9-10. Oskar Schlemmer visualizes proprioceptive extension in *Figure and Space Delineation*, 1924.

of molecules in a hot gas. Then they "cool," condensing into a denser mass, moving in slow motion, the balloons drifting lazily between them. To teach the mathematics of distance, speed, and time, the dancers help children play a movement game called curfew, which allows them to experience these abstract concepts bodily. They learn, for instance, that if they travel a certain distance at a certain speed in eight beats of the drum, to cover the same distance in four beats will require an increase in speed.

Reenactment is also fundamental to understanding a story or a history. When children play out a choreography of movements representing fundamental elements of the narrative, they remember it better. Additionally, students can be encouraged to pay attention to their bodily feelings when a class problem doesn't make sense and use this discomfort as the basis for asking questions. Sensitive teachers can teach them to identify and work with these feelings by "reading" postures and facial expressions, just as we "read" a mime. In all these ways, children learn to identify their knowledge of the world with proprioceptive sensations. They develop a rich lode of sensation memories, which they can draw on to think "out loud" with their bodies.

Body thinking in the classroom can, in fact, be as simple as the exercises suggested by the renowned biologist J. B. S. Haldane for a scientific utopia he once envisioned. "In the shaping class," he wrote, "you have to try to imagine the shape of a . . . railway truck or your mother's face, and then make a picture of it or a model of it. They try to make you imagine yourself running your hands over a shape as well as seeing it. And in the language class they ask you to describe what it feels like to throw something, or walk on stilts, or work on apparatus for gas volumetric analysis. That's called encouraging kinesthetic imagination." Haldane even imagined "kinesthetic explorers" who, like Hindu yogis, would learn with ever-greater clarity how to sense and control every aspect of bodily feeling and function, a skill Haldane believed would be useful for exploring unknown experiences and unsolved problems in the sciences and the arts.

Any or all of these techniques can enrich one's store of body images immeasurably. Indeed, with practice we may all expand our imagination with the sensations of movement, tension, and touch that we experience, imitate, model, and project. "Everything registers *anatomically* somewhere in my brain and through the practice of recalling and reenacting, I am ten times as alert as I was," one student of the proprioceptive and kinesthetic imagination has observed. "I hear and I forget. I see and I remember. I do and I understand," says the ancient Chinese proverb. Doing and remembering how it feels to have done is inseparable from learning to think with the body. So don't just sit there. Monkey around, and you just might find yourself solving problems only your body knows how to answer.

10

Empathizing

WILLA CATHER ONCE wrote that novelists, actors, and physicians have the "unique and marvelous [experience] of entering into the very skin of another human being." That many writers have such empathic experiences goes almost without saying. Alphonse Daudet observed much the same thing — and in language identical to Cather's: "You must enter into the person you are describing, *into his very skin,* and see the world through his eyes and feel it through his senses." To merge with another person physically implies a loss or renunciation of "otherness." This is what Daudet meant when he went on to state that in writing, "direct intervention on the part of the writer is an error." For some authors this empathic identification with created characters has meant that *they write as if they were someone else,* as Charles Dickens did. Novelist George Eliot said that in her best writing someone "not herself" took possession of her so that she became totally identified with the feelings of her characters. The French novelist Blaise Cendrars confessed that he was unable to write until he knew everything there was to know about his fictional characters "from the day of their birth to the day of their death," as his notebooks and dossiers demonstrate. This obsessional preoccupation with biographical details, which many writers share with Cendrars, requires more than a simple compilation of facts; it requires the ability to "make them [the characters] evolve in all circumstances possible and imaginable."

Cather pointed out that actors and, by extension, also other performers play-act and empathize. C. P. E. Bach argued, "A musician cannot move others unless he too is moved. He must feel all the emotions that he hopes to arouse in his audience, for the revealing of his own humour will stimulate a like mood in the listener." The key to unlocking these emotions is what Chilean pianist Claudio Arrau calls "a little miracle . . . a sense of communion between you and the composer that springs from the unconscious." For Arrau the musician is an actor, able to play many styles, many roles. "Interpreters," he has said, "must be able to transform themselves, to feel their way into a world that might be foreign to them."

Dancers, too, may seek to understand movements in terms of a character or even a body different from their own. Isadora Duncan understood that dance, like music, must stimulate an empathy within the bodies of onlookers, creating within them the desire to move. As in acting, this empathy can be created by feeling the role oneself or by emulating the motions that will create the emotions in the onlooker. These techniques sometimes conflict. Ballerina Gelsey Kirkland has chronicled her struggles to bring her own feelings to her dancing against the wishes of choreographer George Balanchine, who wanted her to be just a puppet at his direction. Their conflict emphasizes another aspect of empathizing, which Doris Humphrey discussed. She believed a choreographer must be capable of empathy for his or her *dancers,* who are the raw material from which the dance is made. "In composing for other dancers," Humphrey wrote, the choreographer "must have a high regard for their individuality, remember that they are not like himself and bring all his intelligence to bear on the problem of understanding them, physically, emotionally and psychologically. . . . Many choreographic failures . . . are due to . . . insensitivity to people." Many actors could probably say the same of directorial failures.

Most actors and actresses, of course, create their roles by empathizing with the characters they are to portray. For some, this skill is learned by role-playing as children. Tom Hanks says that as a child he was fascinated with space flight and would walk on the bottom of his pool, breathing through a hose, pretending to be training for weightlessness. Little did he know that he would one day star in *Apollo 13* or direct *From the Earth to the Moon.* Such identification can be taken purposefully further. Daniel Day-Lewis, the British film star, is said to make a point of living his characters off-screen, learning their skills (as in the case of Hawkeye in *The Last of the Mohicans*) or incarnating their behaviors (in the case of the Irish writer Christy Brown in *My Left Foot*). Dustin Hoffman is said to work in the same immersive way, "being" rather than "acting like" or "imitating" a character.

One of the foremost proponents of this kind of "inner truth" in acting was Konstantin Stanislavsky, who told students, "You can understand a part, sympathize with the person portrayed, and put yourself in his place, so that you will act as he would. That will arouse feelings in the actor that are analogous to those required for the part." He himself used empathy when he created the role of an idealistic character in an Ibsen play:

> I understood and liked the play the very first time I read it, and saw how I should play the role at the very first rehearsal. . . . I had only to think of Stockman's thoughts and cares . . . together with the forward stoop of the body, the quick step . . . the index and the middle fingers of the hand stretched forward. . . . I only had to assume Stockman's manners and habits, even off the stage, and in my soul there were born the feelings and perceptions that had given them birth. And during this process I felt the greatest joy an actor can feel, the right to speak on the stage the thoughts of another, to surrender myself to the passions of another, to perform another's actions, as if they were my own.

As Cather mentioned, many physicians also use empathy to understand and treat their patients. Poet William Carlos Williams, himself a working physician, said in his *Autobiography*, "I lost myself in the very properties of their [my patients'] minds. For the moment at least I actually became them, whoever they should be, so that when I detached myself from them . . . it was as though I were re-awakening from a sleep." Oliver Sacks's explorations of neurological conditions in books such as *Awakenings* and *The Man Who Mistook His Wife for a Hat* allow his readers to appreciate, if just momentarily, what it is like to be unable to speak, to feel your body, to control your language, to remember.

Indeed, many medical educators assert that the ability to become, transiently, one's patient is a skill that differentiates the best clinicians from the rest. Empathizing is "a key skill for the practice of any helping relationship," asserts E. A. Vastyan, a medical educator at Pennsylvania State University. The empathic caregiver recognizes the patient's unspoken fear when an unfamiliar test or procedure is ordered. He or she responds to patients with such sympathy and understanding that they are willing to reveal their medical symptoms and secrets to a stranger, willing to cooperate in procedures that may give them pain or a prognosis they would rather not hear, willing to unveil bodies or minds they would prefer to remain hidden. This ability to enter into the "very skin" of another person is so much a part of psychiatry that Alfred Margulies has written a book on the uses of psychiatric empathy entitled, appropriately, *The Empathic Imagination*.

Interestingly, the empathic worlds of the writer, actor, and physician have recently been integrated. In 1981 the Mayo Clinic in Rochester, Minnesota, pioneered the use of theater to help medical students and physicians understand and empathize with their patients, bringing in Jason Robards and several other actors to perform a series of plays in a program called Insight. The actors performed Eugene O'Neill's *Long Day's Journey into Night* to explore narcotics addiction, O'Neill's *The Iceman Cometh* to get inside alcoholism, and Laurence Houseman's *Victoria Regina* to understand aging. Mary Adams Martin, then the director of the series and after-care director of Mayo's chemical-dependency treatment program, explained, "Physicians don't need any more facts, and the time they can spend on human problems, their own and others', is very limited. The theater can move into that gap." New York's Mount Sinai Hospital has taken this approach a step further. Actors assume the roles of patients with various ailments such as terminal cancer or AIDS. Medical students then review the medical charts, make diagnoses, and communicate the prognoses to the patients. These are not games. The students become emotionally involved with their patients, realizing for the first time that they are not just technicians but caregivers who must *care*.

If communal reenactment of medical situations can stimulate empathy in physicians, so too can the private play of emotion involved in reading fiction. Pulitzer Prize–winning psychiatrist Robert Coles urges his students at Harvard Medical School to read George Eliot's *Middlemarch* and Walker Percy's *The Moviegoer*. Unlike standard textbooks, these novels explore in human terms many of the ethical issues that physicians face. Cardiologist John Stone of Emory University School of Medicine recommends Leo Tolstoy's *The Death of Ivan Ilyich* and Albert Camus's *The Plague* for their insights into death and dying, and Jorge Luis Borges's story "The Immortals" for its examination of the psychological effects of bioengineering organ transplants and artificial limbs. "Literature," Stone says, "will help lead a young doctor, if the physician permits, to proper sensitivity; it will help to find the proper words for the proper moment; even to place the doctor, vicariously, in the patient's hospital bed." As E. A. Vastyan explains, "Empathy is not simply a psychological concept. Every fictional character who has the ring of authenticity was created by an author who could, through his imagination, so deeply live that character's experience that he could bring it to life also for the reader. Literature, we have repeatedly found, provides a rich resource for freeing a student's imagination, a necessary accomplishment if the skill of empathy is to be mastered."

In short, Willa Cather's comment reveals an important way in which writers, actors, and physicians work. They learn to understand other people not only objectively from the outside but subjectively from the inside. It is this aspect of "becoming other," of play-acting, that distinguishes empathizing so clearly from imaging or proprioceptive thinking. The key to empathizing is learning to perceive the world through someone else's mind and body.

For all of Cather's perspicacity, however, she was remiss in suggesting that *only* novelists, actors, and physicians empathize. Their experience is far from unique. The entire philosophy of Zen Buddhism is inextricably bound up with the idea that a person must become one with the objects of meditation, to lose his or her sense of self in order to comprehend the otherness of things as if they were not other. Thus all of the arts associated with Zen — the land-scapes, rock gardens, paintings, drawings, architecture, tea ceremonies, and other rituals — require the ability to empathize with nature. One finds the same approach advocated in Shinichi Suzuki's program of Talent Education, which has been bastardized in Western countries as the "Suzuki method" for training children in music. Suzuki's actual goal was to train whole people. Music was simply a way to teach them how to understand how to learn, and the key was *kan,* a difficult-to-translate Japanese term meaning something akin to a combination of empathizing and kinesthetic thinking — becoming one with the music and the instrument producing it. A well-known western-ized and modernized version of this philosophy can be found in Robert M. Pirsig's *Zen and the Art of Motorcycle Maintenance,* a guide to understanding not just people but things through an empathic approach.

An appreciation for the power of empathic understanding is not limited to Eastern philosophies. Seventy-five years ago the German philosopher Martin Buber wrote, "Empathy means to glide with one's own feeling into the dynamic structure of an object, a pillar or a crystal or the branch of a tree, or even of an animal or a man, and as it were to trace it from within, un-derstanding the formation and motoriality *(Bewegtheit)* of the object with perceptions of one's own muscles: it means to 'transpose' oneself over there and in there." About the same time the French philosopher Henri Bergson argued that the most important insights can arise only in this way: "It fol-lows that an absolute can be reached only by an *intuition,* whereas the rest [of our knowledge] arises out of analysis. We here call intuition the *sympathy* by which one transports oneself to the interior of an object in order to coin-cide with its unique and therefore ineffable quality." In 1958 physicist/philos-opher Michael Polanyi's book *Personal Knowledge: Towards a Post-Critical Philosophy* examined how understanding comes from internalizing knowl-edge in such a way that one becomes, in Einstein's words, "a little piece of nature," reflecting in oneself what is external to oneself. The eminent philosopher Sir Karl Popper went so far as to say, "I think the most helpful suggestion that can be made . . . as to how one may get new ideas in general [is] . . . 'sympathetic intuition' or 'empathy.' . . . You should enter into your problem situation in such a way that you almost become part of it."

Indeed, we have found that practitioners of every art, science, and humanistic profession use empathy as a primary tool, for it permits a kind of understanding that is not attainable by any other means. Consider some examples.

For historians, empathizing means being able to see the world through other people's eyes. Take Thor Heyerdahl's voyages in *Kon Tiki* and *Ra,* his attempts to recreate what it might have been like for ancient Polynesians and Egyptians to sail their worlds. These reenactments, despite their controversial elements, strike us forcefully because in a very real sense they took Heyerdahl "there." And, like any good actor, in his books he takes his audience with him. Historian Anthony Michael Cohen, described as the "Underground Houdini," has captured the popular imagination for similar reasons. To understand the experiences of slaves using the Underground Railroad to reach freedom in the northern United States and Canada, Cohen has lived as they did, walking in their shoes, eating their food, sleeping as they did. For instance, in 1848 Henry "Box" Brown escaped from slavery by having himself shipped by train from Richmond to Philadelphia in a wooden box measuring 30 by 28 by 24 inches. Cohen had himself shipped in a box of the same dimensions, and during the seven-hour trip he became severely depressed, claustrophobic, dehydrated, and overheated, losing consciousness several times. Of the fears and deprivations runaway slaves had to endure, he said subsequently, "I think I came very close to understanding how that felt." Those feelings have become the stuff of his historical writing. Princeton classics professor John Ma goes a step further, asking his students to help him recreate Greek battles on the fields of the university so that they, as well as he, can learn directly how ancient war was waged. "Madcap enthusiasm and reenactment also have their place in history," he says.

These are not mere stunts; this kind of play-acting informs a great deal of superb historiography. As historian Dixon Wechter has noted:

> Some of our best professionals have been the least sedentary. A zest
> for field work adds freshness, originality, and vigor to the sinews
> of writing — as instanced by Francis Parkman's journey over the
> Oregon Trail and sojourn among the Sioux; Douglas S. Freeman's

patient exploration of every crater in the battlefields of northern Virginia; Samuel Eliot Morison's sailing with the Navy in the Second World War. Before writing *Admiral of the Ocean Sea* Morison navigated the Atlantic in a sailing boat comparable to the *Santa Maria* — in fact doing almost everything Columbus did except discover America. The feel of an ax or a rifle butt or fishing rod in the hand, a pack at the back, wind upon the face, salt air in the nostrils, are all good disciplines for the writing of history.

The past is a foreign country that can be experienced only by being relived.

The best biographers also use empathy to facilitate emotional and intellectual understanding. They "get into the minds of the subjects — their thoughts, emotions, and even body feelings," as Thomas Söderqvist has put it, "and try to view both the social world and the phenomena in the [workplace] the way they did." Thomas Kuhn, preeminent historian of science in this century, taught his students to *penetrate* a scientist's work by recreating his or her life step by step. Read the existing documents in chronological order, he advised, and when you can predict accurately the subject of the next letter or paper that scientist writes, you are beginning to understand your subject. If you are wrong you must start again from some other perspective, because you have not yet grasped the essence of the life you study. You are not yet thinking and acting like the scientist.

So far, our examples of empathizing and play-acting have involved human subjects, but as both Zen and Western philosophers have suggested, one can acquire "personal knowledge" of anything from animals and trees to inanimate objects. Indeed, human empathy with animals has a long history. In the caves of Trois Frères in France there is a famous Paleolithic drawing called the *Sorcerer*. From the shoulders down, the figure looks distinctly like a man crouching forward, as if sneaking up on someone or something. But from the shoulders up, it is that of a male reindeer or elk. This figure is variously interpreted as a man in some sort of ceremonial costume befitting a "sorcerer or horned god" or as a mythical chimeric creature, literally half man, half beast — the figment of some fevered Paleolithic imagination. Such interpretations ring false to us, however, because they seem to assume that the people who painted this image were simple and superstitious. They do not explain what the sorcerer was doing, or why his image was painted on the cave wall. They do not have the feel of "being there."

We interpret the cave art differently. We believe that the illustrator was an intelligent and thoughtful teacher attempting to open up an important way

Fig. 10-1. *Sorcerer,* Paleolithic painting, Les Trois Frères, France.

of knowing to his or her viewers. We believe that the sorcerer is a man hunting. One of the oldest and best-preserved tricks in the hunter's repertoire is to throw the skin of an animal he has caught over his own form to blend in with his prey. To do this successfully he must learn to act and think like an animal. What better way to learn to hunt than to take on the role of the hunted, to imagine how the creature will respond? Such educational play-acting is still used by people in hunter-gatherer cultures around the world today. Children begin their training by mimicking the behavior of the animal prey. There is a wonderful photograph of a group of aboriginal children following an adult in the Australian bush (see Fig. 10-2). All of them, including the adult, have their bodies painted, their arms outstretched, mimicking the wings-outspread rush of the brolga, a native bird. Eventually, with practice, the children learn to *think* like these birds, thus understand how best to hunt them.

The notion that animals *think* is, in fact, basic to all hunting cultures, past and present. Oren Lyons, a chief of the Onondaga nation of the Six Nation Iroquois Confederacy, has explained that an intense identification with animals, which was absolutely essential to successful hunting and survival, fostered a sense of respect for them. "Our people," he has said, "have never doubted the ability of animals to think. Hunting is a battle of wits, and more often than not, you get defeated. . . . We feel that animals are people. You've

Fig. 10-2. Aborigines mimicking the brolga bird.

got to see them not as animals but as individuals. And beyond thinking of them as individuals, you begin wondering about a soul in the animal. The more you look at animal eyes, the more you begin to perceive them not as animal eyes but as the eyes of other people. . . . That is why we call animals 'our people.'"

While the idea that animals think may bother some people, even the most technologically sophisticated hunters and fishermen must learn to think like their prey to be successful. Those who have read Norman MacLean's novel *A River Runs Through It,* the story of two brothers dedicated to fly fishing, will recognize the hunter's identification with his prey. The older brother, the narrator, intermittently achieves a strong sense of the river, the eddies and currents within which the fish move, the rocks behind which they hide. He knows the fish's environment. He is a good fisherman. But his younger brother, Paul, is a master fisherman. He knows how a fish sees his fly, knows how to make the fly dance on the water like a true insect, how to lure the fish with his understanding of its behavior and instincts. Paul says at one point,

"I'm pretty good with a rod, but I need three more years before I can think like a fish." His older brother replies, "You already know how to think like a dead stone fly."

Temple Grandin understands cows and sheep in the same deep way. She is the single most successful designer of humane and efficient animal restraint systems for veterinarians, livestock-handling facilities, and slaughter plants for the meat industry. Although these animals are farmed rather than hunted, their responses to restraint or mishandling are those of prey animals. Fear can cause panic, and panic can spread chaos within a herd, disrupting the care or processing of the animals. Restraint systems must be designed to reassure the animals, not scare them. The secret to her success, Grandin wrote in her 1995 book, *Thinking in Pictures and Other Reports from My Life with Autism,* is that she becomes the animal who needs to be restrained. "When I put myself in a cow's place, I really have to be that cow and not a person in a cow costume. I use my visual thinking skills to simulate what an animal would see and hear in a given situation. I place myself inside its body and imagine what it experiences. . . . I have to imagine what experiencing the world through the cow's sensory system is like." Grandin's identification is strengthened by the similarities she draws between the sensory responses of animals and her own. She has autism, a bewildering neurological disability that involves overly acute perceptions and easily triggered fears. Like many autists, she is hypersensitive to certain sights and sounds and therefore empathizes with cattle who balk at the reflection of light off the floor, the unexpected hissing of a pneumatically powered gate, the loss of footing on a slippery surface. She then designs handling facilities that eliminate features that can elicit startle or flight responses. Cattle and other animals move through her curved chutes and conveyer systems without fear or confusion, which means they move through efficiently and economically and humanely.

Buck Brannaman, the trainer who inspired the novel and movie *The Horse Whisperer,* employs the same sort of empathic understanding. Brannaman speaks of "thinking harmony with horses" and achieving "true unity" between man and animal. He therefore "starts" rather than "breaks" horses by imaginatively perceiving the world from their point of view. The concept of hunting is again a critical aspect of this view. "The way a person sits on a horse is exactly the way a mountain lion would, climbing on its back with your legs reaching down over it," he says. "So it's easy to understand why a horse wouldn't be that interested in a person crawling up on top of him. . . .

He's scared. And he should be scared. That's how he survives on the range. What you're dealing with is thousands of years of self-preservation that you're asking the horse to just ignore, and allow you to be there." Amazingly, Brannaman "asks" the horse to do just that, and he uses the horse's own language of subtle body movements and gestures. In essence, he pretends to be a dominant herd stallion, moving, responding, and accepting obedience like one. "There's no secret to this," Brannaman says. "I just know what we need to do in order for both of us to speak the same language and dance the same dance."

Empathy is also a key to success in another sort of modern-day hunting expedition, one that only occasionally concerns animals. Many sophisticated thinkers of the modern technological age have consciously appropriated the play-acting and empathic techniques of the hunter in their quest for new facts, ideas, and theories in the sciences. The physicist Ernst Mach (for whom the speed of sound is named) says explicitly in his book on scientific method that scientists are hunters, if only hunters after knowledge, and that "the [scientific] hunter imagines the way of life of the prey he has just sighted, in order to choose his own behavior accordingly." Claude Bernard also compared research to hunting, as did Albert Szent-Györgyi, who wrote, "One wanders more or less aimlessly, till here and there game flies up or one picks up a scent."

The implications of this hunting analogy for scientific research are surprising. In the first place, empathy is certainly not the objective approach most of us are taught to expect of the scientist. On the contrary, identifying with one's prey is as subjective a way of doing research as can be imagined. Yet, as we shall see, many famous scientists credit some of their most important insights to getting into the roles of their "quarry," which might be single-cell organisms, biological processes, physical phenomena — anything from subatomic particles to insects to stars!

Trying to imagine what it is like to be a rock or a quark may be a little too difficult to begin with, so we'll start with something more accessible, the scientific study of animals. Ethologists — scientists who study animal behavior — are among the most forthcoming about the use of empathizing as a research strategy. They use the same basic approach as Australian bushmen, native Americans, Temple Grandin, and horse whisperers. After long years of observing chimpanzees in the wild, Jane Goodall found that empathizing came naturally to her and her assistants and that when used judiciously it was a critical scientific tool. "Because chimpanzees exhibit behavior so remarkably similar to some of our own," she has written, "many of us

Fig. 10-3. *Left:* Frankie Reynolds demonstrating chimpanzee tree drumming; *right:* Dian Fossey pretending to be a gorilla.

who have worked at Gombe over the years have developed a degree of empathy with the individuals studied. In itself, this is not a bad thing. Subtle
communication cues denoting slight changes in 'mood' or attitude toward
other chimpanzees are more readily detected once empathy of this kind has
been established, and this can aid us in understanding complex social processes. . . . Intuitive interpretations which may be based on an understanding
stemming directly from empathy with the subject, can be tested afterward
against the facts set out in the data."

Shirley G. Strum, who is renowned for her study of baboons in the wild,
has also said, in her 1987 book *Almost Human,* that emotion-based empathy
played an important role in learning to understand baboon behavior. She
had difficulty understanding the animals on their own terms until her intense interest in one individual, whom she called Peggy, eventually gave her
access to their lives. The insights she gained reassured Strum that empathy

belonged to science as much as any dispassionate collection of facts. "Peggy taught me that you can have strong emotions, such as the special attachment I felt for her, and still do good science. The two were not, as I had once thought, mutually exclusive. . . . Emotions need not overwhelm science. Techniques could still be put on a firm quantitative footing. Best of all, feeling strongly about the baboons made the science more rewarding." Knowing came through feeling, not despite it.

Lest one suspect that women ethologists are particularly prone to "indulging" in intuitional understanding, it is worth noting that Donald Griffin, an expert on animal thinking, considers empathizing a vastly underrated scientific tool. So does Iain Douglas-Hamilton, an expert on elephant behavior. "Despite the strict training I had been given at Oxford not to give human interpretation to animal behavior," he writes in *Among the Elephants*, "it was quite impossible not to anthropomorphize." Anthropomorphizing — interpreting nonhuman actions in human terms — is explicitly taboo in science. In fact, Desmond Morris, whose best-known work, *The Naked Ape*, is an interpretation of man as animal, argues that truly empathizing with animals does not result in anthropomorphizing at all but represents a method for freeing oneself of human preconceptions. As a teenager, Morris's interest in animals became so intense that he began to dream about them not as the humanized characters of a Disney cartoon but as if he had become an animal himself:

It was a strange little scenario. Not only was I surrounded by animals, but I changed into one myself. In essence, this was what was going to happen to me in my future research, when I became a full-time student of animal behavior. With each animal I studied I *became* that animal. I tried to think like it, to feel like it. Instead of viewing the animal from a human standpoint — and making serious anthropomorphic errors in the process — I attempted, as a research ethologist, to put myself in the animal's place, so that *its* problems became *my* problems, and I read nothing into its lifestyle that was alien to its particular species. And the dream said it all.

Thomas Eisner, who has pioneered the study of the chemical defense and communication systems of insects, has had similar play-acting dreams. Born in Uruguay, he became so familiar with the local insects that he would dream of talking to the ants in Spanish. "Once I [even] dreamed that I was an insect

Fig. 10-4. *The Entomologist,* by
Desmond Morris, 1951.

talking to insects and telling them I dreamed I was human." He says this kind
of familiarity with his subjects gives him many of his research insights.

If a scientist can empathize with an insect, why not with a plant, a cell, or a
chromosome? Without a doubt the scientist who has described this kind of
empathy most clearly is Barbara McClintock, who worked on the genetics of
corn and various other living things. She spent so much time with her plants
and the preparations of their genetic material that she knew them intimately,
as individuals. She quite literally took the time to "make friends" with them
and to "see" them in their own terms, just as Georgia O'Keeffe did in creating
her paintings of flowers (Chapter 3). In the end McClintock says she developed "a feeling for the organism" so profound that she actually felt that she
became a gene or a chromosome herself.

McClintock's experience has been shared by innumerable colleagues. Rita
Levi-Montalcini, a physician who empathized so strongly with her patients
that she had to leave active practice to save herself from the mental anguish
this caused, transferred her ability to the study of cellular growth and the
factors that control it. "I was in the initial and exciting phase of my research
on how grafts from a malignant mouse tumor affect the sensory and sympa-

thetic nervous cells of chick embryos. Such was my enthusiasm that day and night my every thought was concentrated on the phenomenon. I felt as if I, too, was a carrier of the tumor and subject to its prodigious effect." According to neurobiologist Charles Sherrington, the same enthusiasm characterized Santiago Ramón y Cajal, who treated "the microscopic scene as though it were alive and were inhabited by beings which felt and did and hoped and tried even as we do. . . . A nerve cell by its emergent fibre 'groped to find another.'" Sherrington continued, "He would envisage the sperm cells as activated by a sort of passionate urge in their rivalry for penetration into the ovum-cell. Listening to him I asked myself how far this capacity for anthropomorphizing might not contribute to his success as an investigator." Many would say quite far. Molecular biologist Jacques Monod says that in his studies he had "to identify myself with a molecule of protein" to understand its functions. Joshua Lederburg, too, has a high regard for "the ability to imagine oneself *inside* a biological situation; I literally had to be able to think, for example, 'What would it be like if I were one of the chemical pieces in a bacterial chromosome?' and try to understand what my environment was, try to know *where* I was, try to know when I was supposed to function in a certain way, and so forth."

Physical scientists also rely on play-acting and empathizing for insights. Organic chemist Peter Debye explains: "You had to use your feelings — what does the carbon atom *want* to do?" Einstein, as we mentioned in Chapter 1, would view the universe from the perspective of a photon. For Ernest Rutherford, "Atoms and alpha particles were as real . . . as his friends," and he became angry when a colleague suggested they were just theoretical constructs. Subrahmanyan Chandrasekhar made many of his discoveries in astrophysics by imagining the universe "from the point of view of the star," and Richard Feynman revolutionized quantum physics by asking himself questions such as "If I were an electron, what would I do?" Hannes Alfven, another astrophysicist, has written that many of his insights have come by imagining what it is like to be a charged particle: "Instead of treating hydromagnetic equations I prefer to sit and ride on each electron and ion and try to imagine what the world is like from its point of view and what forces push to the left or to the right." Every one of these individuals, from McClintock through Alfven, has won a Nobel Prize, an indication of the power inherent in this method of "hunting."

Not surprisingly, what is true of scientists is also true of inventors. Charles F. Kettering, director of research at General Motors for many decades, would often reprimand engineers who got carried away with complex calculations and models by saying something like, "Yes, but do you know what it *feels* like to be a piston in an engine?" Alexander Graham Bell also employed this approach. His work absorbed him so totally that he *became* the systems he studied. While he was working on new ways to educate the deaf, mute, and blind (an issue of great importance to him since both his mother and his wife were deaf), Bell "disappeared" — not physically but mentally — for so long that his wife gently complained of his inattention to herself and their children. Bell apologized: "My deaf-mute researches have taken me away — far away — from you all. I don't think your thoughts — or feel your feelings — nothing but deaf-mute — deaf-mute — and solitude in my mind. While my thoughts run in the deaf-mute line I am practically vanished from the family." Just as an actor might, he became a deaf-mute in order to understand and address their problems. In other cases he became part of the machine he designed. Feynman similarly described thinking his way into electronic devices to understand their workings. And many computer programmers and chip designers have told us that they walk around inside their microchips and programs somewhat like the characters who are sucked into the world of electronic circuits in the movie *Tron*. These people not only know their subjects objectively, they know the objects of their work subjectively.

Artists also draw upon a "feeling for the organism." Virginia Woolf often found "herself sitting and looking, sitting and looking, with her work in her hands, until she became the thing she looked at." Joan Mitchell has said, "A painting is not part of me. Because when I do paint, I am not aware of myself. As I said before, I am 'no hands'; the painting is telling me what to do." The modern painter who goes by the name WOLS (Alfred O. W. Schulze) describes the same process differently when he says, "Perfect concentration is possible only when you are not." His Zenlike statement expresses the state of insight the artist achieves by becoming one with his subject. Chinese and Japanese artists have purposefully cultivated an empathic intuition for thousands of years. Su Tung-P'o, for example, said some nine hundred years ago, "Before painting a bamboo, you must make it grow inside you, then with a brush in your hand, and with the concentration of your eyes, the vision appears in front of you. You must then catch it as quickly as you can, as it will vanish as fast as the hare when the hunter appears." And Matisse once said, "After I have identified myself with a tree, I create an object which resembles a tree, the sign of a tree." This is also the way Noguchi thought. He once cored a two-meter-high block of orange and black basalt, placing head-sized holes at the top and about halfway up one side (see Fig. 10-5). "Go ahead," he

Fig. 10-5. *Core (Cored Sculpture)* by Isamu Noguchi, 1978.

told visitors to his studio, "put your head into it. Then you will know what the inside of a stone feels like."

We conclude that empathizing and play-acting are common to creative thinking of all sorts. But how can we learn to empathize? The answer is simple enough: just remember Shakespeare's famous line "The play's the thing." Many creative individuals argue that theatrical experience encourages and promotes the empathic imagination. Astrophysicist Jacob Shaham has written that he learned to interpret mathematical equations in living terms by learning to act in the theater. As a teenager, he was cast as a beggar in a community production, but after a few rehearsals, he realized that he had no idea how to be a beggar. So he spent many hours over the next few weeks following some around the streets of Jerusalem, studying their interactions with other people, their gestures, their facial expressions, the way they talked, the way they thought. Although he had very few lines, he finally felt able to convey to the audience the presence of a real beggar. Shaham never forgot this experience or the creative insights to be gained from empathy, even as he worked, in later years, on problems far removed from the stage. He realized that physical equations are exactly like the scripts of plays and must be brought to life by studying the "actors" — energy, mass, light, and so on — in the context of the "action" mathematically described. "For every equation, statement or idea I would study or come by," Shaham writes, "I would always try to look around it, see what follows, what may be related to it, what is missing. . . . It is something that some of my science teachers did their best to give us a feel for, but only now after having been doing science for 20 years, do I realize how close to it I actually was from the start because of that dramatic role."

Must one therefore take acting lessons to become a first-class empathizer? Of course not. But many of the techniques designed by Stanislavsky and other "method actors" are widely applicable. Stanislavsky recommends, for example, that you:

✦ Practice "inner attention, which centers on things we see, hear, touch, and feel" in real and imaginary circumstances. This means observing your own responses to the world and also remembering physical and emotional memories of your responses. How does it feel to open a door? How is this related to the "script" by which the physicist describes the door opening? Actors in any field may exercise this inner attention by remembering and reenacting the feelings of their daily lives.

✦ Practice "external attention" to people and things outside yourself. Actors study other people and things closely. Stanislavsky made his students recall as many details as possible of objects seen once and then hidden. He himself learned to imitate exactly the physical habits he found interesting in others. This approach is beneficial whether one is describing or imitating the behavior of chimpanzees, clocks, or quarks. How would they respond to a particular situation or stimulus?

✦ Imagine what the object of your external attention is sensing and feeling; get close to it. Pretend that its world is your world, its sense organs or physical attributes yours. How would you feel, behave, respond if you were it? Find connections to sensations and emotions that exist in yourself. Even as this approach made Stanislavsky "feel akin to the character in the play and indeed made me one with him," so can it allow you to "feel" what the cell, the virus, or the carbon atom "*wants* to do."

Literature, as physicians have discovered, provides another route to empathizing and play-acting. Nor are its insights limited to the psyches of people. Some of the best literature invites us to explore what it is like to be nonhuman. Primo Levi's *Periodic Table* introduces us to the "desires" of elements, and T. H. White, in *The Once and Future King,* repeatedly has the young King Arthur transformed into an ant, a falcon, an owl, a fish, and many other creatures.

Of course, actually trying to burrow like a mole (though our fingernails aren't up to it) or to swim like a fish would be even more instructive. Emulation is always a useful way to empathize. This is certainly the educational approach used by the PBS television program *Kratt's Creatures.* The hosts of this excellent series roll in the mud to protect themselves against flies the way rhinos and hippos do; they taste the foods that chimpanzees eat; they build a beaver dam from sticks and logs. Enacting these behaviors reveals aspects of the inner life of the animal that are accessible in no other way. The hosts of *Kratt's Creatures* also employ "Creature Vision Goggles" to show viewers what the world looks like to a particular animal, because different types of eyes produce different images of the world. The fish-eye lens used by photographers was, in fact, invented by physicist Robert W. Wood when he decided he wanted to know what the world looked like through the eyes of a fish and discovered that no existing camera could do the job. Many zoos have devices that allow people to recreate the sight or even the hearing of various species, and a number of Web sites display such images. Or one can be clever and invent a novel camera, as the daughter of one of our friends did: she replaced the lens of a cheap plastic camera with an inexpensive plastic-faceted lens to produce photographs that record the world as if perceived by the compound eyes of a fly or a bee.

This approach can be taken yet a step further. At Stanford University dur-

Fig. 10-6. One of the first "fish-eye" photographs ever taken by the inventor of the fish-eye lens, Robert W. Wood.

ing the late 1960s, biologists staged a massive recreation of the entire process by which a cell decodes a genetic message into a protein. Biology students were assigned roles as a base in a DNA or RNA sequence, an amino acid, part of a ribosome, or another molecule necessary for the process. Then, to the beat of rock music played over the loudspeakers of the football stadium, the students performed their assigned functions, and the whole extravaganza was filmed from a helicopter. This classic exercise has been simplified for classroom use by Catherine Bristow of the Entomology Department of Michigan State University. Zafrah Lehrmann in Chicago and Susan Griss in Accord, New York, have designed similar sorts of exercises involving the dancing of chemical reactions or the interactions of various species in ecological systems.

All of these examples show us that understanding is most complete when you are not you but the thing you wish to understand. Acting a part in a system really does build understanding. In fact, when it comes to empathizing, the whole world is a stage for the imagination.

11

Dimensional Thinking

ANCER AGNES DE MILLE was fascinated with moving through space. Even when she was a young child, a hilltop view would fill her "with a passion to run, to roll in delirium, to wreck my body on the earth. Space means this to a dancer — or to a child!" It meant, as well, that in a world of three dimensions, gravity worked constantly to restrict her movements to two. Even the best dancers break away from the floor for only seconds at a time. They move, not between planes, but across a single plane. There is no escape from what de Mille called "the embracing and struggle with the fundamental ground." The limitation can be frustrating, as Oskar Schlemmer found. He came to dance from painting and sculpture, moving "from the geometry of the one-dimensional surface to the half-plastic [relief] and thence to the fully plastic art of the human body." Yet the ironical limitation imposed by gravity did not escape him. "The paradox may be," he conceded parenthetically, "that the more plastic the figure, the flatter it is."

Imagine, then, what the weightlessness of space travel may someday allow dancers to do. No longer imprisoned on a surface by gravity, they will truly be free to move in three dimensions. However, they will have to contend with spatial inertia — a completely different physical problem, as astronauts and cosmonauts have already discovered. Twist a wrench and it twists back. Newton's principle that every action has an equal but opposite reaction reigns supreme, unmitigated by the gravity and friction that govern us here on Earth. If you move your hand one way in space, your body wants to go the other way to keep the center of gravity where it was. No floor to counteract the movement. No up, no down. The spatial implications for dance, sports, arts, games, and sciences are almost unimaginable. Simple games like billiards, when translated from two to three dimensions, may become so esoteric that only the best mathematicians can play it.

Does that sound crazy? Consider this. A standard "trick shot" in the two-dimensional (2-D) billiards we play on earth is to hit the cue ball so that it strikes every side of the table and returns to the place from which it started. This shot is very easy to set up: start at the center of any side of the table and aim for the center of any adjacent side of the table. The same strategy works for any regularly shaped flat surface, whether it is triangular or twelve-sided. But in three-dimensional (3-D) outer space, we aren't limited to one plane. We can try such a shot inside a cubic room, for example. But look out! If you set the cue ball at the center of one face of the cube, and shoot for the center of an adjacent face in the same plane, the ball will return to the original position — but only after striking four of the six faces. You lose! It took a world-class geometrician, Hugo Steinhaus, to figure out how to hit all six faces of that cube, and it took two of the best geometricians of recent decades, John Conway and Roger Hayward, to solve the problem for a simple four-sided tetrahedron. More recently, Matthew Huddleson required the aid of a computer to determine whether such trick shots could be made within other Platonic solids such as the octahedron (eight sides) and dodecahedron (twelve sides).

Of course, we don't have to leave Earth to encounter dimensional puzzles. Here's a classic: you are given eight matchsticks arranged to form four contiguous triangles. The challenge is to take away two matchsticks and still form four contiguous triangles. A similar problem involves nineteen matchsticks forming six contiguous squares. Take away seven and still form six

Fig. 11-1. Matchstick puzzle.

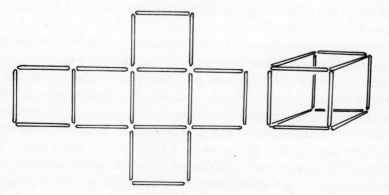

contiguous squares of the same size. Since the problems are given in two dimensions, most people assume the answers must be in two dimensions. The solutions, however, are three-dimensional.

Dimensional thinking involves *moving from 2-D to 3-D* or vice versa; *mapping,* or transforming information provided in one set of dimensions to another set; *scaling,* or altering the proportions of an object or process within one set of dimensions; and *conceptualizing dimensions* beyond space and time as we know them. Every time we make a paper airplane from a flat piece of paper and send it flying or draw a map of the neighborhood with directions to our house we are using dimensional thinking. We scale things when we convert a recipe for two into a recipe for twenty or when we picture Gulliver in Lilliput or watch the miniaturized children in the film *Honey, I Shrunk the Kids.* We play with dimensional thinking, too, when we read science fiction and try to imagine time warps, wormholes, and alternate universes. Dimensional thinking pervades our lives.

To prove the point, let's begin by visiting a perfectly flat 2-D world such as that invented by Edwin A. Abbott in his classic geometric fantasy, *Flatland,* and then we'll consider how frequently we visit this 2-D world without thinking about it. The planar inhabitants of Flatland know our 3-D world only by the tracks and shadows we cast upon their plane. Is it possible for them to get a sense of what we look like? Not really. Our 2-D friends can experience us directly only as shadows or slices. If we stand above their world, they may perceive our shadows. But their view will be distorted by the angle of the sun and by our position relative to their world, for a single object may cast many different shadows, as the wall sculpture in Figure 11-2 demonstrates. Movement will be confusing, too. When we lift a foot vertically to take a step, our shadow jumps horizontally. If we turn, our features and limbs will suddenly appear or disappear. We suspect, as Abbott conjectured in *Flatland,* that their view of us will certainly be different from our own.

Our 2-D friends might learn more about us if they could experience us in slices, just as we might reconstruct the nature of a green pepper from a series of consecutive slices. They could view us this way if we passed through their world from head to toe or lay down and slowly sank through it (see Fig. 11-3). Bear in mind that our 2-D friends will get to "see" our insides as well as our outsides — a view that we do not get of each other. Yet even with all of this information, their minds still operate in 2-D. Can a 2-D mind conceive of 3-D objects? Or will our Flatland friends persist in seeing each of us as a series of independent 2-D slices? Might they even think that they are "seeing" not

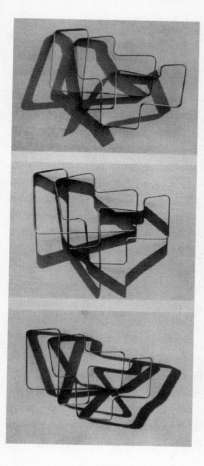

Fig. 11-2. The changing nature of projected form is demonstrated by Ernest Mundt's shadow sculpture for San Miguel School, 1953 (bronze). *Top to bottom:* morning light, noon light, afternoon light. Photographed by Ira Latour.

one individual, but rather a class of many related individuals, each defined as a similar but nonidentical slice? This inability to integrate images is not as far-fetched as it may sound. Oliver Sacks tells the story of one patient of his who could not recognize his dog or his friends from one moment to the next because his view of them kept changing. Writer Jorge Luis Borges explored the same theme in his story "Funes the Memorious," noting that there is no a priori reason that "a dog at three-fourteen (seen in profile) should have the same name as the dog at three-fifteen (seen from the front)." You can get some sense of the problem yourself from the collage of magnetic resonance images in Figure 11-4 or by viewing on the Internet the Visible Human Project of the National Library of Medicine.

Flatland may be imaginary, but it has many counterparts in the real

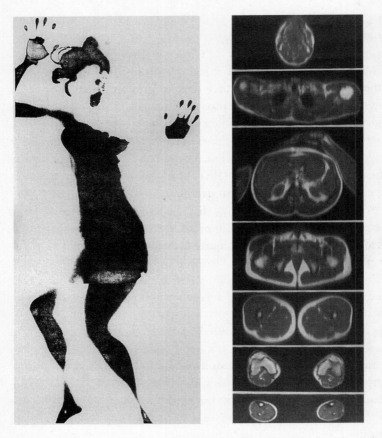

Fig. 11-3. *Prelude to 1,000 Temporary Objects of Our Time,* etching by Colin Self, 1971, suggests what Flatlanders might experience if we lay on their universe.

Fig. 11-4. *Sliced Man,* a collage by Robert Root-Bernstein of magnetic resonance imaging photos, shows how Flatlanders might see us in slices..

world. We have all seen footprints in mud, snow, or concrete and inferred what person or creature left them there. We have all noticed how our shadow follows us around like some misshapen ghost. These phenomena are all projections, or maps, of some or all of a body onto a relatively flat plane, representations of a 3-D object in 2-D. Such representations are of major importance to a number of professions. Archeologists and forensics experts must reconstruct the size, weight, and height of an individual from footprints or other indentations left by bodies in the ground. Intelligence analysts for the armed forces must draw three-dimensional inferences from two-dimensional photographs taken by reconnaissance aircraft and "spy satellites." Physicians analyzing x-ray photographs, CAT (computerized axial tomography) scans, or MRI (magnetic resonance imaging) results see only static slices through their patients' bodies, but they have to interpret what they see in terms of dynamic living beings. The medical literature is now full of articles discussing three-, four-, five-, and even six-dimensional analyses of techniques ranging from calculation of the proper corrections for visual defects such as myopia to facial reconstruction during plastic surgery. Sonograms and positron emission tomography (PET) scans allow us to view the body and its functions not only in space but over time.

Other professions also make use of dimensional transformations. Some are quite esoteric, such as the invention of periodic tables of *compounds* that, unlike periodic tables of elements, require four or more dimensions to display their patterns. Others are so common that they are often overlooked. How does one take a globe and squish it into a map? Anyone who has experimented with peeling the rind of an orange and flattening it out knows how many possibilities there are. The fact is, there is no single right way to do this, either for an orange or for a globe. The result in cartography has been a plethora of mapping systems, as any good atlas will show: the familiar Mercator and gore projections; Gall, Mollweide, and Hammer-Aitoff projections; orthographic, stereographic, azimuthal, and polar projections; cylindrical, conical, and planar projections; Buckminster Fuller's geodesic projection (available as the Dymaxion World Puzzle, a map of triangular pieces); and dozens of others. The names and possibilities boggle the mind. What all have in common is the single word projection. The development of methods of projecting or mapping a three-dimensional object onto a two-dimensional surface was one of the greatest accomplishments of the Renaissance.

The process of projection followed directly from the invention of perspective. To make a perspective drawing or painting — that is, to project a scene or object viewed in three dimensions onto a flat canvas or piece of paper — Renaissance artists used a gridded optical device called variously Alberti's veil (after Leon Baptista Alberti, the fifteenth-century artist who first described the process of geometric perspective) or Leonardo's window (after Leonardo da Vinci, who used a modified version of Alberti's device). One grid, held vertically like a paned window, was placed between the artist and the object to be drawn. A second grid was laid flat on the drawing surface on which the artist was going to work. The artist then transferred the visual information observed within each element of the vertical grid to the grid on

Fig. 11-5. Albrecht Dürer's demonstration of a perspective device, 1525.

the drawing surface. The artist could then accurately draw a globe, a woman, or a landscape. A convenient model of such devices can be found in *The Art Pack,* a sophisticated pop-up book about the history of art.

Westerners take the now-familiar rules of perspective drawing for granted. We all can see straight lines receding to a common point on the horizon in the background, and we interpret this formalism as "real" even though perspective drawings are often grossly distorted or foreshortened in the same way shadows are. There is, however, nothing intrinsically obvious about perspective. Anthropologists have found that many aboriginal peoples have difficulty parsing our 2-D depictions of 3-D objects, and artists, too, must learn the conventions. Bridget Riley notes that "you have to find ways of converging things such as weight and space convincingly, without relying upon the mere representation of the model to do these things for you. It is not sufficient to depict." Indeed, much modern abstract art, including that of Riley, Ellsworth Kelly, Gene Davis, Barnett Newman, and Agnes Martin, explores the issues of working within an explicitly planar world, emphasizing the ways in which masses, colors, and shapes interact differently than they do in our 3-D sensory world. Cubist art also explored the contrasts between a multitude of complementary views of a 3-D object and the limitations of 2-D depiction.

As wonderful as perspective drawing is, it is only one rather simple form of mapping. You can actually map any object of any shape or dimension onto any other object using a modification of perspective drawing called anamorphosis, meaning "altered shape." If, for example, one holds Alberti's veil or Leonardo's window at a very acute angle to an object instead of keeping it vertical, then the image transferred to the grid on the drawing surface will be tremendously elongated. A simple example will illustrate the process. At the very top of a piece of writing paper, in normal-sized printing, write the word SHORT in capital letters. Now, using the rest of the paper, write the same word, SHORT, under the first version, printing the letters the *same width* as before but using the *entire length of the paper* for the height. Chances are that when you show this altered word to someone else, they will not be able to read it. In essence, you have projected the word SHORT at an extremely acute angle onto the paper. To read it, you need to view it from the same very acute angle, as you do every day when you read the painted words on roads as you drive. Painted commands such as STOP AHEAD, or RIGHT TURN ONLY, look fine to a driver sitting in a car, but are extraordinarily elongated if viewed from directly above or from the side.

Dürer, Leonardo, and other artists soon realized that they could also use

Fig. 11-6. Cylinder anamorphosis of the King of Sweden, artist unknown. Swedish National Portrait Collection, Gripsholm.

distorted or warped grids. Such grids alter the appearance of the drawn object just as carnival mirrors make a thin person fat or a fat person thin. The resulting image then needed a complementary grid or mirror — an anamorphic mirror — to reverse the anamorphic mapping process. Almost as soon as artists began to draw and paint in perspective, they also began experimenting with images that could be viewed properly only by means of mirrors in the shapes of spheres, cones, cylinders, and other geometric objects. A seventeenth-century portrait of the king of Sweden (see Fig. 11-6) provides an excellent example; many others (along with directions for making them) can be found in Martin Gardner's column in the December 1974 issue of *Scientific American*. These anamorphic projections are exact analogues of the processes used to make map projections of the globe.

Although "morphing" began as artistic experimentation, it eventually found important uses in many sciences. Gaspard Monge, a late-eighteenth-century draftsman and mathematician, worked out the principles for sur-

Fig. 11-7. D'Arcy Thompson's anamorphic comparison of two species of fish.

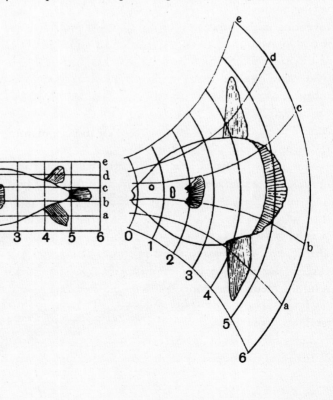

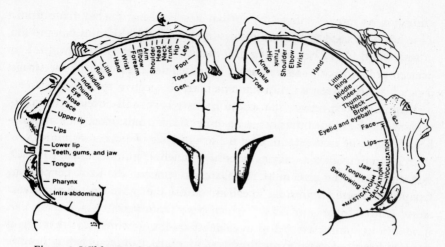

Fig. 11-8. Wilder Penfield's "motor homunculus," showing the anamorphic projection of our tactile sense onto the brain.

veying landscapes and buildings and mapping them accurately onto plans, inventing in the processes the discipline of projective geometry, one of the foundations of modern engineering and architecture. A century later, biologist D'Arcy Thompson, whose book *On Growth and Form* is a classic in the field, demonstrated that the structural forms of organisms evolve by anamorphic changes. All species of fish are related to one another not only historically and genetically but in their shapes. Each is an anamorphic distortion of another. And the same is true for insects, mammals, trees and their leaves, and all other living things.

Neurologists, too, have found uses for anamorphic analysis. Studies of the brain show that mapping the sensory inputs of our body onto the convoluted surfaces of our brain yields a distinctly distorted image. The amount of the brain dedicated to each body part turns out to be proportional to the sensory innervation, so that huge amounts of the brain are taken up with the tongue, lips, and fingers, while relatively little space is given to such huge parts of our anatomy as the stomach, back, and buttocks. The shape of the resulting mental "homunculus" is quite surprising — and notably similar to the human body as drawn by blind people, who cannot see the body but often draw how they feel it.

The entertainment industry has benefited from anamorphic technologies in the form of wide-screen cinema. Wide-screen movies are shot with the same film as movies shown on normal-sized screens, but an anamorphic lens has been used to squeeze images of greater width than usual onto the normal-sized film. The resulting film images must then be shown through projectors fitted with compensating anamorphic lenses that fit the image properly to the screen — hidden movie magic.

Mapping, perspective, and anamorphosis have well-developed mathematical theories, but other types of dimensional transformations are only beginning to be understood. One is the existence of *fractional dimensions.* We tend to think of dimensions as existing in whole number units: 1-D, 2-D, 3-D, and so on. But remember Sierpinski's carpet and the Koch curve from Chapter 7? These are *fractals,* so called because they have fractional dimensions. Unlike squares or circles, which have finite perimeters, fractals can have infinite perimeters. Yet as in Zeno's paradox — which says that if you proceed from one place to another in steps, each of which is half as long as the preceding, you will never quite arrive — some infinite series converges to a calculable answer. Consider the Koch curve. Each time you construct a new set of triangles on the previous set, you increase the length of the perimeter by four-thirds of the previous increase. This process is performed an infinite number of times, creating an infinite series that converges to 1.2618 — the fractional dimension of a Koch curve. Every fractal figure is defined by a unique fractional dimension. These figures exist between our usual dimensions in the same way that fractions exist between integers on a number line. The implications of finding such fractal structures in trees, the branchings of our lungs and capillaries, and other biological systems are still mysterious.

The mathematical properties of other mundane objects are also yielding dimensional surprises. Noguchi once defined sculpture as "something not reproducible in a book," that is, on the flat surface of the page. In fact, some of his last works were made from single sheets of aluminum folded without welding, using a "technique . . . [adapted] from origami, from folding paper in Japan as a child." Origami, it turns out, is actually an art of complex multidimensional thinking. As Brian Hayes has noted, "A sculptor who carves stone or models clay begins with a medium that is already three-dimensional, but the paper folder must envision the solid object in the flat and formless sheet. This calls for strong geometric intuition." Indeed, mathematicians have discovered that origami embodies a precise dimensional logic that can be described as a set of algorithms, or rules, that determine what can and cannot be folded and the sequence of folds that must be carried out to attain any given figure. These rules can be written as mathematical statements or, in the case of machines that assemble packages, as a series of mechanical steps. Origami in turn is a subdivision of a new field of mathematics called plication, which looks at the rules governing any sort of folding. Thus, some five hundred years after we discovered that mathematical rules govern perspective and anamorphosis, we are discovering the rules to other ancient arts, such as origami.

The applications of plication are manifold. Virtually all manufacturing processes involve bending, folding, and pressing two-dimensional materials into three-dimensional shapes. Flat sheets of steel are shaped under great pressure into automobiles, airplanes, trains, tin cans, and utensils. And if you look carefully at many forms of packaging, you will find that these useful objects have been cut from a flat piece of material and folded into a 3-D container. To design and engineer these shapes one must be able to perceive how a flat thing can be transformed into one with body. The ability to relate 2-D blueprints, plans, or maps to 3-D reality is a critical part of the job.

Another aspect of moving from plans to reality involves the dimensional skill of *scaling*. Like mapping or making things in 3-D, changing the size and proportions of an object within a single set of dimensions is a skill required in many disciplines. It is, in fact, possible to identify with some accuracy a person's academic discipline by the scale he or she works with. Philip and Phylis Morrison and the office of Charles and Ray Eames produced a wonderful movie and book called *Powers of Ten* that provides a useful scale running from the smallest suspected subatomic wave-particles to the largest structures in the universe, covering a range from 10^{-16} meters to 10^{25} meters. Anyone working with objects more than a million meters in length is surely an astronomer. Geologists, dealing with objects on the order of a thousand to a million meters, come next. The largest architectural and mechanical objects are on the order of a thousand meters or less, not counting railway lines and highways. The scale used by people who work with people runs from about a third of a meter to ten meters. Biologists work with objects that are ten meters to one ten-thousandth of a meter, biochemists work with objects one ten-thousandth to one billionth of a meter, and almost all of chemistry occurs between 10^{-9} and 10^{-12} meters. Below that scale one is dealing with physics. Interestingly, an artist, Tom van Sant, has spanned perhaps the widest range of dimensional scales, producing both the largest and the smallest artistic image, each one of an eye. One image, made by pushing around atoms using an atomic-force microscope, lasted a fraction of a second before thermal vibrations caused it to collapse. The other eye image was formed by reflecting the light of the sun off strategically placed mirrors spread across the desert into the camera of a NASA Landsat satellite. Even so, most of us experience so little of the spatial universe.

We also live in a very small window of time, as becomes apparent when we use time scales to characterize various disciplines. Things that happen in eons are the domain of astronomers and geologists; those that happen in trillionths of seconds are the domain of physicists. Most of us work in a world bounded by seconds on the one hand and years on the other. All our music is measurable in minutes. What these two exercises tell us is that different kinds of things happen in the universe at different scales and that moving between scales, whether temporal or material, lets us encounter very different kinds of phenomena, types of problems, and physical, physiological, and perceptual principles.

Size and time certainly matter. The scale of a sculpture or a car or a building has social, psychological, and political ramifications. Massive buildings, for instance, connote power; small rooms connote intimacy and privacy. A six-inch model of the Eiffel Tower has none of the impact of the original. Hitler's Reichstag, the palace at Versailles, the Great Wall of China, have meanings that are dependent on their size and mass, as well as their purpose. Scaling is equally important in our interpretations of art. Claes Oldenburg and Coosje van Bruggen's *Batcolumn* in Chicago, a ten-story-high rendition of a baseball bat, strikes us very differently than a three-foot Louisville Slugger does. Georgia O'Keeffe's large flower paintings affect us in ways they would not if the images were as small as the flowers themselves, as O'Keeffe was very well aware. "If I could paint the flower exactly as I see it," she wrote, "no one would see what I see because I would paint it small like the flower is small. So I said to myself — I'll paint what I see — what the flower is to me but I'll paint it big and they will be surprised into taking time to look at it — I will make even busy New Yorkers take time to see what I see in flowers."

Larger is not necessarily better, however. Igor Stravinsky wrote the score for his ballet *Apollo Musagetes* (1928) in six parts for a string orchestra. The first time it was performed, there were sixteen first and fourteen second violins, ten violas, four first and four second cellos, and six double basses. Stravinsky was horrified: "I was struck by both the confusion of sound and the excessive resonance. . . . Everything seemed drowned in indistinct buzzing." He pared the orchestra down to eight first and eight second violins, six violas, four first and four second cellos, and four double basses, and "everything became sharp and clear." As Stravinsky found out the hard way, scaling is a major issue in orchestrating music. Maurice Ravel successfully transposed Modest Mussorgsky's *Pictures at an Exhibition* from piano solo to full orchestra, but just imagine *Twinkle, Twinkle Little Star* for full marching band, or Beethoven's Fifth Symphony transposed for solo piccolo! Scaling music up or down involves risks.

Technologists and inventors also face risks when they change scale. Scaling up a model of a building into the real thing leaves no room for miscalculations of material strength and flexibility — as fallen stadium roofs and collapsed hotel balconies have disastrously proven. And chemical engineers know that a reaction that works efficiently in a laboratory test tube may be difficult to transfer to a thousand-gallon vat. Mass action may interfere, or the reaction may take place on the walls of the reaction vessel, or inadequate mixing may become a problem, or the amount of heat generated by the reaction may get out of control. Similar problems make it difficult or impossible to simply enlarge a model airplane to any size. The stress on the points at which the wings attach to the fuselage increases at an ever-greater rate the larger the surface area of the wings. The amount of power needed to attain lift eventually goes beyond reasonable limits.

The same principles apply to living beings. In his essay "On Being the Right Size," J. B. S. Haldane once observed that an ant experiences the surface tension of a drop of water as if it were wading through glue, while we hardly notice the tension at all. On the other hand, the ant may fall from a skyscraper and not get hurt, whereas a much shorter fall will kill us. Scale up a bird to the size of an elephant and it will no longer be able to fly because its volume will increase as the cube of its dimensions, whereas the surface area of its wings, and therefore its lift, will increase only as the square. If you could scale up a single cell to the size of a room, it would die within minutes. Lacking a circulatory system, cells depend on the diffusion of oxygen and sugars to supply their energy needs, and diffusion is far too slow to keep anything bigger than a pin alive.

Scaling things down can be equally problematic. In December 1959, in a talk entitled "There's Plenty of Room at the Bottom," Richard Feynman challenged members of the American Physical Society to develop micromachines smaller than anything ever imagined before. His challenge has yielded motors so small that you need a microscope to see them, including scanning tunneling microscopes with attachments that allow scientists to make images in crystals by moving one atom at a time and electronic chips so small that quantum effects interfere with their functions. Some engineers are therefore turning these dimensional problems into new possibilities by trying to think of ways to harness quantum effects themselves to computing — another Feynman idea.

It's a different world down there at the atomic and subatomic scale. As particle physicist Carlo Rubbia says, you have to learn to think differently: "When you dive inside matter, it's as exciting as making an infinitely long interplanetary journey. You can see things happening not on a large scale, but on smaller and smaller scales. You get more and more details, and new pictures come in your mind one after the other. . . . There is no *image,* so to speak, of these things that are infinitely small; our image is so primitive that many of our ideas of vision are no longer valid. . . . So it's a genuine trip you're taking inside matter, inside yourself." You have to be prepared to think about things differently.

We may need to think differently about time itself, depending on the scale and the perspective we take. Einstein showed that the passage of time, or what is sometimes called the fourth dimension, is not absolute but relative to the motion of observer and observed. A person moving near the speed of light could travel to another star and return a few years older, only to find all of her children long dead. But we need not rocket to the far corners of the universe to experience the elasticity of time. All of us have had the experience of getting very involved in some project, looking up at a clock, and wondering where the time went. We have all been so bored that every second seemed like a minute and every minute like an hour. (As a soldier keeping watch on enemy movements once reported, "I lay there for four hours and looked at my watch to find that fifteen minutes had passed.") When we sleep or meditate, time seems not to exist at all. Is chronological time the only way to measure the passage of time? Can experiential time be as valid a coordinate as Greenwich mean time? Is a month the same to a one-year-old who experiences that unit of time as one twelfth of his life as it is to a centenarian, for whom it is a mere one twelve-hundredth? Is time, then, a single dimension or a set of dimensions?

Some musicians believe that time is as plastic as clay. Composer/architect Iannis Xenakis describes music as inherently multidimensional, and according to Philip Glass, one of the purposes of music is to play with this dimensionality in time:

> My feeling is that composers have always had a different sense of time, isn't that so? That's true of Monteverdi, that's true of Palestrina . . . of Stravinsky — if you were listening to a Beethoven symphony

and someone asked you how long a movement was, you might have an awfully hard time to figure it out. Music time and colloquial time are obviously very different. My music sets up its own kind of extreme in a way [by means of continuous repetition], but I think music structures itself in time as to create independent coordinates of its own. . . . What happens is that one has an authentic experience of time that is different from the time we normally live in.

Physical time, physiological time, and mental time appear to be different — and that fact is cause for speculation: perhaps there are dimensions of time as unexpected and surprising as fractal dimensions in space.

One thing is certain: our use and control of the dimension of time are still evolving. As we saw in Chapter 5, painters began exploring the problem of displaying movement on canvas around 1910, after Muybridge began taking multiple photographs of running horses and jumping men. Cinematography, the rapid viewing of a succession of images, was a direct development of his photographic invention, which takes advantage of our mind's inability to process separate images that appear in rapid succession. Cinematography has, in turn, led to time-lapse photography, in which very slow events are photographed not thirty times per second, as they are for most movies, but once an hour or once a week or once a year, then viewed at thirty frames per second. The result is a mapping of long periods of time onto short ones — a sort of temporal anamorphosis similar to viewing the very long letters in SHORT at a very acute angle. We can also do the obverse kind of mapping by photographing action at thousands of frames per second and then showing it in "slow motion" to observe events that are normally too rapid for our minds to register.

Time mappings may be only a beginning. Some aspects of the dimension of time are still incompletely harnessed to the other dimensions. Only in this century has 3-D artwork become free to move through time and space. It took the genius of Alexander Calder to bring sculptures to life, first as hand-driven, then motor-driven objects by the end of the 1920s and finally as free-floating mobiles during the 1930s. The position of each part of a sculpture was no longer determined but relative and ever-changing, carving out a new dimension of perception. Not surprisingly, contemporaries compared Calder with Einstein, who was becoming famous at the same time for his work on relativity theory and space-time dimensionality in physics. When one interviewer made the comparison on film, Calder just laughed and replied, "What would Einstein think of that?" Actually, Einstein did visit a Calder exhibition and stood entranced for over forty minutes by a single motorized sculpture — no small praise from a man who disliked most "modern art."

Surely Calder's invention has technological applications. If the ability to describe and harness movement in painting and photography has led to whole industries such as cinematography, what does the mobile portend? Holographic experiences? Robotically controlled 3-D experiences? And what new dimensional worlds may remain to be discovered? Haldane suggested that "multidimensional kinesthetic thinking" might be possible, just as multidimensional visualizing is. Noguchi thought that something he called "emotional space" might exist on stage and around sculpture but not in a television tube. For example, two individuals saying "I love you" as they face away from each other at opposite ends of a room are saying something totally different from two individuals saying "I love you" entwined on a bed. Space itself contains part of the emotional message.

It's fair to say that moving real and imaginary things between dimensions in time and space plays an important role in a wide range of endeavors, from mundane manufacturing to modern arts and, in science, from astronomy to biology. Yet despite its widespread utility, the practice of dimensional thinking has been almost completely absent from education. In the late nineteenth century Francis Galton complained that the mental manipulation of objects in space "is starved by lazy disuse, instead of being cultivated judiciously in such a way as will on the whole bring best return." One hundred years later, our continued disregard for the teaching and exercise of dimensional thinking means that many people are unable to integrate information given in one set of dimensions into a model or image in another set of dimensions. "I find that I cannot work from a blueprint," writer and editor James R. Petersen has confessed. "A sketch on the thin blue lines of graph paper has no meaning for me." He is not alone. Two-dimensional plans and visual instructions plague practically everyone who makes a plastic model, a kit-assembled bicycle, or a dollhouse. Even packing the trunk of the car for a trip is a 3-D problem that can be frustrating.

Henry Moore believed that most people do not fully perceive three-dimensional objects and therefore cannot appreciate sculpture and architecture, let alone contribute to them. Sculpture, he wrote, "depends upon the ability to respond to form in three dimensions. That is, perhaps, why sculpture has been described as the most difficult of all arts; certainly it is more difficult than the arts which involve appreciation of flat forms, shape in only two dimensions. Many more people are 'form-blind' than colour-blind."

Form-blindness has consequences. Flat visual images, as Piet Mondrian once noted, need be "effective from *one* viewing point only . . . [and are] intended for only one person," whereas plastic arts and designs must have "the right effect regardless of where we stand . . . [and are] for many people at the same time." But the importance of being able to perceive multidimensionally goes beyond art, Mondrian maintained, for "as soon as we cease to rely exclusively on our temporary position and view things from all possible positions, in short, as soon as we begin to see universally, then we no longer view things from a unique viewpoint." And vice versa. A reliance on still or moving 2-D visual images in preference to 3-D objects can stunt our ability to think from multiple points of view, both literally and figuratively, limiting the number of people with the ability to become sculptors, architects, designers, and inventors and blinding us to the ways in which single-perspective arts and media bias our understanding.

The problem is not limited to visual designers and the general public. Harvard astrophysicist Margaret Geller believes that form-blindness is just as common among scientists. Geller turned the astrophysics world upside down twenty years ago by demonstrating that galaxies are not uniformly distributed throughout the universe, as contemporary dogma and available evidence had led everyone to believe. The problem was that many scientists were misled by the flat, 2-D photographs of the universe taken through telescopes and, like Flatlanders, failed to reconstruct the 3-D reality correctly. "Three-dimensional thinking . . . ," Geller has said, is "related to what I do. In fact, I think one of the reasons I was able to recognize what we had [in the data revealing the bubble structure of the distribution of galaxies] was . . . early training [in 3-D visualizing]." Geller is able to "visualize in 3-D. And I realize now — I've talked to lots of people in science — that very few people have that ability."

According to geologist David Davies, something must be done to address that lack:

> I can only speak from the physical scientist's side, but there were subjects that I wish I had been better taught, as they lead, I think, to originality in thinking. Two of these I could mention specifically: one is dimensional analysis. I think that to the physicist, dimensional analysis is a major aid to research thinking because it is the way in which you can rapidly come to the point. And the other one is projections, displaying data in imaginative ways. The experience that I have of seeing people being creative in the Earth Sciences (which was my specialisation) is that they often have been most suc-

cessful when they have been able to make a new type of diagram, a new sort of projection, a map that is completely different from those gone before. And both of these, dimensional analysis and map projection, are things that can be taught at university and very often are not because they are considered to be sterile and unimportant.

Granted the need for dimensional-thinking skills, not only in science but in the arts, engineering, manufacturing, and daily life, how might they be taught? To make a start, we can model for ourselves and for our classrooms the training of individuals well versed in this imaginative skill.

One method is to play with geometric shapes and connect them to objects in the real world. Geller learned her 3-D skills from her father, a crystallographer at Bell Labs, who bought "any kind of toy that had anything to do with geometry."

> He'd explain to me the relationship between things that I built and things in the world. For example, I'd make a cube, and he'd explain to me the relationship between that and the structure of table salt. And I'd make an icosahedron, and he'd explain how you see that in the real world. He would talk about filling space and which figures could fill space and which couldn't. . . . He would say things — this structure was this or that — and he'd show me the beautiful models of the crystal structures, and I wouldn't be able to see it. But he would say it again and again and again. And finally, I *would* be able to see those spatial relations.

Geller's experience suggests that playing with any type of 3-D puzzle can be useful. You need not buy them, however. Turn your world (or yourself!) upside down and imagine negotiating your house if the ceiling were the floor — what do the stairways look like and how do you get to the second (now the first) floor? Paul Gallico's 1969 novel *The Poseidon Adventure,* about people trying to escape from a capsized ocean liner, provides a nice model for this game.

Henry Moore would probably have recommended taking up sculpture or some related 3-D art form such as origami. Making things from clay or beeswax, pipe cleaners, or balsa wood provides experience with dimensional thinking that drawing can never do. So do carving in wood and stone. Alexander Calder would probably have recommended engineering toys, since

Fig. 11–9. *Left:* a reconstruction of *Cube Composition,* by Else Mögelin, 1921; *right: Compound of Five Tetrahedra,* by M. C. Escher.

that is where he learned his skills. Legos, K'NEX, Erector sets, Lincoln Logs, the Tensegritoy, Dome Kits, architectural modeling kits — the possibilities are endless. Or you can design your own mobiles, in honor of Calder himself.

The artists and designers of the Bauhaus, recognizing that their art students were uniformly form-blind, developed another set of intriguing exercises. "In order to let students experience primary geometric forms in a three-dimensional manner," Johannes Itten had his students make intersecting geometric forms in plaster to learn how shapes interact with one another, as in the cube composition by Else Mögelin shown in Figure 11-8. M. C. Escher independently explored similar compositions in other mediums. *M. C. Escher Kaleidocycles* by mathematician Doris Schattschneider and artist Wallace Walker provides additional dimensional exercises. Kaleidocycles (see Fig. 6-10) transform paper prints of Escher tilings into polygons, demonstrating the ways in which the tiling symmetries are preserved even as one moves from 2-D to 3-D surfaces, and thereby teaching the art and the mathematics of dimensionality simultaneously.

Another unusual Bauhaus exercise was invented by Josef Albers. Students were asked to design an object on a flat piece of cardboard that could be cut and bent into a 3-D object. Arieh Sharon's solution is particularly unusual. Designs can also be cut into paper or thin, flexible plastic to create space-filling spirals, stars, and other, more intricate objects. Designing your own paper or cardboard containers from flat materials exercises similar skills. Pop-up books are also related to these Bauhaus exercises, and learning how to copy (and eventually invent) your own pop-up figures is excellent dimensional training. You may have to take apart a few pop-up books first, though.

Combinations of blocks can also be used, like tangram pieces, to create unlimited 3-D objects. Frank Lloyd Wright credited the set of Froebel blocks he was given when he was nine with the development of his architectural thinking. Friedrich Froebel was an educational reformer who advocated modeling and three-dimensional thinking as critical aspects of education. Buckminster Fuller and Wassily Kandinsky are also known to have developed a fondness for playing with Froebel blocks. Not only are these blocks still available today, but so are blocks specifically designed for modeling Wright's architectural forms, medieval castles, and many other architectural styles. Some Bauhaus teachers, such as Alma Siedhoff-Buscher, devised their own blocks, recognizing that different shapes make possible different ag-

Fig. 11-10. Reconstruction of *Three-Dimensional Exercise* (1926) by Arieh Sharon.

Fig. 11-11. *Left:* building-block game designed by Alma Siedhoff-Buscher, 1923; *right:* boy building with Tree Blocks.

gregate forms. A comparison between Siedhoff-Buscher's blocks and Tree Blocks makes these differences evident.

Mapping from 3-D to 2-D can be practiced by learning to read animal tracks, by making shadow pictures on the wall, or by making images on solar paper or photographic paper by direct exposure. Make up your own tracks and shadows by dipping common household objects in ink and "printing" them. Experiment with mapping movement as well as shape. Then have others identify your object. (These images are often much harder to identify than you would think.)

Finally, you can learn to think beyond three dimensions, a skill Richard Feynman learned as a teenager. His sister, physicist Joan Feynman, recalls, "When I was little, we used to walk along the beach by the waterside, and you know the way people imagine things in three dimensions? You picture a doughnut in your mind? Well, Richard was imagining things in four dimensions — he was practicing this, to sort of imagine things and manipulate

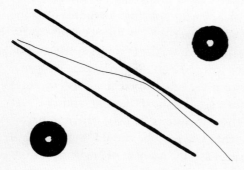

Fig. 11–12. An object has been dipped in ink and printed. As it rolls, it seems to be dragging a tail. What is it? ˙pɐǝɹɥʇ ɟo ʅoods ∀

them in four dimensions." This fourth dimension was not time, as many people may think, but a fourth *spatial* dimension that we can experience only indirectly. And we need not be a Feynman to experience it. Constance Reid, one of the consummate mathematics popularizers of this century, outlined one approach in her 1963 book, *A Long Way from Euclid*, which she used with high school teachers and education students. Philip Davis and Reuben Hersh also introduce the subject in their book, *The Mathematical Experience*. Space does not permit us to describe their techniques in detail, but we can at least introduce their methods.

Oddly enough, we find ourselves back at Flatland, where we began this chapter, and the same lessons apply. Begin by imagining a point: no dimensions. Move the point to form a line: one dimension. Move the line at right angles to its length to form a square planar surface: two dimensions. Move the planar surface at right angles to its surface to form a cube: three dimensions. Now move the cube through space at right angles to its surfaces to form a hypercube: four dimensions. Unfortunately, we can't construct such a figure in reality. We can only perceive the 3-D shadows of 4-D objects. Just as a 3-D object can cast many 2-D shadows, so does a 4-D hypercube cast many 3-D shadows. The best we can do is to construct in our minds what the "real" hypercube might look like from these multiple shadows.

So we have to work backward: What does the shadow of a cube look like in two dimensions? A series of odd-shaped polygons. Similarly, the projections of a four-dimensional cube will be a series of unusual but related three-dimensional objects. The fact that the hypercube must have multiple 3-D manifestations explains why Roger Penrose, a physicist who has made fundamental contributions to geometry, metallurgy, and cosmology, says that when he needs "to visualize something 4-dimensional — and I often have to try to do that . . . I might use lots of different descriptions, each of which would be only a partial description."

Reid goes on to show that although we can see only shadows of our hypercube, we can still "know" its properties by extrapolating. A point has no angles, edges, or faces and one vertex (the point itself). A line segment has no angle, no faces, one edge (1-D form), and two vertices (points at the ends of the segment). A square has four vertices (points), four edges (1-D forms), four angles, and a single face (2-D form). A cube has eight vertices (points) and angles, twelve edges (1-D forms), six faces (2-D forms), and one 3-D form. There are *patterns* here. As the dimensions increase, the number of vertices increases: one, two, four, eight. A hypercube should therefore have sixteen vertices. As the dimensions increase, the number of angles goes from

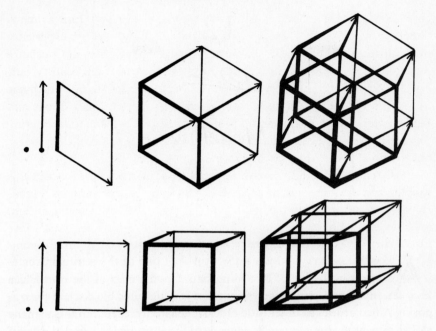

Fig. 11-13. Two of the many 3-D shadows of a 4-D hypercube.

zero to zero to four, to eight, so a hypercube should have sixteen angles. A point has no lower-dimensional objects; a line is defined by two zero-dimensional vertices; a square is defined by four one-dimensional line segments; a cube is defined by six two-dimensional sides. We may therefore extrapolate that a hypercube is defined by eight three-dimensional cubes. If we wanted to extrapolate further, we could even describe the characteristics of a 5-D or a 6-D cube without ever being able to visualize it. Such is the power of dimensional imagination.

12

Modeling

A WORLD WAR I NEWS FILM provoked one of the seminal experiences in the life of Piet Mondrian. Upon a map of the world "the invading German forces appeared as little cubic blocks, and the opposing Allied armies as other little blocks," he later recalled. "In this way the global cataclysm was *plastically represented* in its immensity, not in diverse details or fragments as a naturalistic representation would have done." The blocks stood not only for human armies but for the political and economic forces at work as countries mobilized for war. Because these forces were so vast, they had to be modeled — that is, rendered immediately perceivable in abstract, dimensionally altered terms, and the power of that model was something Mondrian never forgot.

Modeling the movements of armies is a recent historical development. Although miniature soldiers have been found in gravesites from ancient times all over the world, the first use of such models to teach strategy and maneuvers apparently dates back no further than the French kings Louis XIII and Louis XIV, both of whom had huge armies of toy figures and miniature fortresses for this purpose. The modern modeling of war itself, in which two armies act out battles against each other, is even younger, dating from around 1820, when a civilian by the name of von Reiswitz, in collaboration with his son, a Prussian artillery officer, presented the Prussian military authorities with a full-fledged "game" that could be used to recreate battles and test possible battle plans.

The von Reiswitz game was played in three rooms on three identical maps, with markers representing each regiment to be employed in the battle and rules governing movement, engagement, and the outcome of each military action. Umpires occupied the center room, while the two warring parties occupied the rooms to either side. The two war groups each made their moves in secret, with the umpires keeping track on their central map and reporting to each side the commencement and outcome of the maneuvers. Anyone who has played the popular game Battleship will have an idea of the nature of the play. The Prussian and German military authorities used such *kriegspiel* (German for war games) to plan their strategies in the Franco-Prussian war of 1871 and the invasions of France in 1914 and again in 1940. The movie that Mondrian saw was undoubtedly a simplified version of the maps and markers used in these games.

War-gaming would probably have remained a largely esoteric if not secret activity if it were not for H. G. Wells, the famous science-fiction writer. Wells's sons were the proud owners of a spring-loaded model cannon capable of firing a small wooden cylinder or matchstick about ten yards. One day, quite by happenstance, Wells brought his friend Jerome K. Jerome home to lunch at a table littered with tin soldiers. Jerome loaded the cannon, aimed, and knocked one down. Wells, not to be one-upped, engaged him in a target-shooting match that ended with Jerome's wistful remark: "But suppose, suppose somehow one could move the men!" And why not? Soon Wells was discussing the possibility in earnest. "I believe," he told yet another friend, "that if one set up a few obstacles on the floor, volumes of the British Encyclopaedia and so forth, to make a Country, and moved these soldiers and guns about, one could have rather a good game, a kind of kriegspiel."

Before long, Wells had invented his own version of the professional war game to play at home for pleasure. Foot soldiers could move six inches, horsemen twelve. When men came in contact with each other, they engaged in battle, and the outcome was decided by the flip of a coin. At each turn, artillery could be either moved or fired, but not both, as long as there were at least six men on the field to handle the guns. The outcome of an artillery barrage was determined by skill in shooting the model cannon. Soon the encyclopedia volumes gave way to model trees, houses, and castles. Games moved outdoors to more realistic terrain (see Fig. 12-1). Wells then wrote up his invention in two books, *Floor Games* (1912) and *Little Wars* (1913). The interest they created in war-gaming not only stimulated the imaginations of generations of players, including Winston Churchill, it initiated the war-games industry that exists today.

Those who frequent model shops or who recognize the name of the game manufacturer Avalon-Hill may know how far the war game has come from Wells's day. Amateurs can now replay, on a tabletop or a computer screen, al-

Fig. 12-1. H. G. Wells playing with his model soldiers, circa 1912. The politician Charles Masterman, who was present at Wells's early games, has written, "Moves were limited by time on each side and everything depended on rapidity. So that I have seen harmless guests, entering for tea, greeted ferociously with the injunction: 'Sit down and keep your mouth shut.'"

most any famous land, sea, or air battle of the past. Terrain, weather, supply lines, even events on the home front, can affect the recreated combat. Modeling Napoleon at Waterloo, Lee at Gettysburg, or Eisenhower at Normandy provides insights into military and political strategy that reading history can't duplicate. Imaginary situations can even be set up involving hypothetical world crises. Tom Clancy's best-selling novels, such as *Red Storm Rising* or his Op-Center series, are based on such gaming.

Professional strategists and military units the world over play versions of these games — sometimes with supercomputers in defense installations, sometimes with miniature radio-controlled tanks and other movable models wielding laser "weapons" and photoelectric sensors that score hits. The purpose of such games is to test decision-making and strategizing capabilities, as well as military organization and innovation, in advance of the real situation — to make mistakes, find weaknesses, and explore possibilities under conditions in which no one dies and no nations fall. "Game" is clearly the wrong word for such a serious activity. As General Von Meuffling, chief of staff of the Prussian Army, said in 1824 of von Reiswitz's original game, "It's not a game at all, it's training for war; I shall recommend it most emphatically to the whole army." And as British Brigadier General P. Young and Lieutenant Colonel J. P. Lawford wrote much more recently, in 1970, " 'Kids' stuff . . . ,' the scornful teenager cries. His parent nods a dubious assent. But how wrong. . . . War gaming has now in fact developed into an instrument of scientific research."

War games really are practical tools, *simulations* created, as the U.S. Department of Defense puts it, to mimic "military operations involving two or more opposing forces and using rules, data, and procedures designed to depict an actual or hypothetical real-life situation." This definition, with minor modifications, could be used to define modeling in any discipline. The result may be a *representational or physical* model, displaying the physical characteristics of a real object; a *functional* model, capturing the essential operations of an object or mechanism; a *theoretical* model, embodying the basic concepts governing the operation of some process; or an *imaginary* model, invented to display the features of something we can't observe directly. The most sophisticated models are often combinations of all four types. All models are distillations of the elements considered to be the most critical determinants of structure and function. They always embody both abstractions and analogies and, usually, dimensional alterations.

Models can be smaller than life, life-sized, or bigger; physical or mathematical; realistic or not, depending on their intended uses. In almost all cases, the point of a model is to make accessible something that is difficult to experience easily. Harvard University's Botanical Museum, for example, has a collection of stunningly realistic flowers from around the world modeled in unwilting glass that can be studied at any season. The Art Institute of Chicago houses the Mrs. James Ward Thorne collection of model room interiors, which allow visitors to look inside 1/12-scale recreations of some two hundred rooms and their furnishings from every period of Western history. It is a condensation of time and place that would be impossible to encompass in any other way.

Modeling an atom or a cell at a scale millions of times its real size can integrate information from hundreds or thousands of experiments and thus represent sophisticated theoretical constructs. Even a human head or heart can be expanded to fill a museum room so that people can experience what it would be like to explore the insides of their own mouth, sinuses, or ears or to follow the path of the blood as it circulates. The huge size of the model allows them to play-act the part of something much smaller — a red blood cell, perhaps, or a microbe, or a molecule or air.

Models of large objects, such as buildings, airplanes, ships, tanks, and cars, are almost invariably scaled down to make them amenable to manipulation and control by individuals with limited budgets and space. Mountaineers plan their climbs on models; soldiers plan raids. When LucasFilms builds sets for the Star Wars movies, they are producing imaginary models of an entire universe. On a more pedestrian scale, we want to see what the architect's design will look like before we have the new house built, so we look at a physical model or a representational one on the computer screen. Models of other large things, such as whales and dinosaurs, may be scaled down for play in a bathtub or sandbox, or they may be rendered life-sized so that museum visitors can experience the grandeur of these immense mammals. The size of a model, like the dimensional scale of a sculpture, has meaning. Crawling through a true-scale model of a claustrophobic slave ship, entering a frightening reconstruction of a concentration camp, or squeezing into a mock-up of the incredibly cramped *Mercury* space capsule gives one a palpable sense of what it is like to go beyond the pale of normal human existence.

As may already be apparent, modeling requires and therefore teaches many imaginative skills. Models can be formulated only after a real system or situation has been intensively observed, simplified by abstracting critical features, rescaled for human manipulation, and embodied physically or expressed in some verbal, mathematical, or artistic form. Its actual construction, whether the model is a physical or an intellectual one, requires experience with different mediums and careful analysis of their relative strengths and weaknesses. Once the model has been made, experimenting or playing with it determines whether the properties modeled are accurate abstractions of real situations or systems. Models that render imperceptible phenomena accessible to direct cognition require strong imaging skills. Models that "stand in" for the "real thing" depend upon analogizing and abstracting. Nearly all models utilize dimensional-thinking skills as well. Clearly, modeling is a higher-order thinking tool dependent upon the skilled use of many of the tools discussed in this book.

Perhaps the most important thing that modeling does is to provide the modeler with complete control of a situation, object, or idea — or, conversely, to reveal explicitly where control or understanding is lacking. As Picasso said, "To model an object is to possess it." Thus, when the philosopher and novelist Johann Wolfgang von Goethe visited Rome in the 1780s to study various figures of antiquity, he made models of them "so as to make them really my own." Auguste Rodin modeled sculptures from the past to "quickly grasp" their essential principles. Psychologist Carl Gustav Jung took up building model castles as a depressed teenager to create "another time and another world . . . [in which] I would be grown up and able to arrange my life as I wished." And for sculptor Henry Moore, modeling conferred a creative omnipotence: "I prefer to do a sketch-model, hand-size that you can turn around and control, as though you were God." Each of these men realized that modeling conferred an unparalleled understanding of a craft or discipline. The engineer who models car designs for a manufacturer, the biochemist who models drug designs for a pharmaceutical company, the social scientist who models theories of human behavior, and the amateur who builds a miniature house from scratch all acquire a depth of knowledge that requires lengthy study and attention to detail. If the model works, if it leads to a new artistic idea, a new car, a new drug, a new prediction about human events, a new appreciation of architectural style and design, the modeler has mastered the material. When it doesn't work, it elucidates unforeseen problems, which can then be addressed with a better understanding of what has to be accomplished.

As these examples suggest, modeling of various sorts is used in every discipline. Writers find representational and even functional models for fictional characters and events in people they know and situations they experience directly or indirectly. They find theoretical models for the structure of their work in the works of their predecessors. Novelist Christopher Isherwood once complained to Igor Stravinsky that he was having grave difficulties resolving a technical problem of narration. Stravinsky "advised him to find a model." That anecdote, in turn, caused music critic Robert Craft to ask Stravinsky, "How do you model in music?" Put on the spot, Stravinsky replied that he had upon occasion used interesting rhythmic devices from the past to pattern his own compositions — "so that I could 'construct in orderly fashion.' . . . I attempted to build a new music on eighteenth-century classics . . . , using the constructive principles of that classicism (which I cannot define here) and even evoking it stylistically." When Stravinsky advised Isherwood to find a model to resolve his writing problem, he was suggesting that the novelist do what he had done: find a predecessor who had already solved his type of narrative problem, then modify the solution to his own ends.

According to composer Roger Sessions, the use of theoretical and functional models in composing has illustrious precedent. "I have in my possession," he has written, "photostatic copies of several pages of Beethoven's sketches for the last movement of his 'Hammerklavier Sonata'; the sketches show him carefully modelling, then testing in systematic and apparently cold-blooded fashion, the theme of the fugue." Sessions goes on to ask where the inspiration is in this case. The answer is in turning old models, such as the fugue, to new uses or, as Philip Glass has done, adapting both Indian and Western music and ancient forms of chanting to his own needs. Indeed, Glass's avant-garde compositions build upon ground bass (a continually repeating bass line set against a changing melody and harmony), antiphonal effects, melodic repetition, and close, overlapping harmonies, all of which are hundreds, if not thousands, of years old. A good deal of Glass's originality comes not from intrinsic novelty, not from ignoring the models of the past, but from discovering his own voice through them. "As the composer continues to work exercises in imitation of his models," writes Harold Shapero, "he will be surprised to find that along with the thousand subtleties of technique he will absorb from his masters, he will discover the personal materials of his own art."

Iannis Xenakis makes clear that the musician, like the writer, may also make use of representational models. Much of Xenakis's music involves the production of unusual sounds on standard orchestral instruments. He has asked stringed-instrument players to play hand-stretching chords or difficult glissandos — sustained, continuous movements of pitch from one note to another — across the entire range of a string. He has asked harpsichordists and organists to play two manual keyboards simultaneously with a single hand. He has required musicians of every sort to generate various percussive sounds between notes or simultaneously with them. On first looking at his scores, musicians often comment that their parts are impossible to play. But Xenakis knows better, for he tries out hand positions and fingerings in advance on instrumental models of his own making. His "harpsichord," for example, is a "piece of cardboard, rectangular in shape, folded in a 'terraced' manner, on the horizontal surfaces of which [are] painted the keyboards of the harpsichord." He also has a "string orchestra" consisting of a stick somewhat thicker and longer than a meter rod, on three sides of which are drawn the fingerboards of a viola, a cello, and a violin. He says, "It's all a question of fingers — where we place them, how to produce a special effect."

Artists use a similar range of representational models. The most common form of modeling in the visual arts is the preliminary sketch. Very few painters work directly on the canvas; most begin by sketching. At the Art Institute of Chicago, near Georges Seurat's masterpiece *Sunday Afternoon on La Grande Jatte* — a wall-sized painting measuring 6 feet 9 inches by 10 feet — hangs a tiny plan of the painting in much less detail, completed earlier by Seurat. Sketches of his painting *The Circus* are displayed in the Musée d'Orsay in Paris. The purpose of such sketches was clearly to allow Seurat to scale down his ideas to a size that would permit him to evaluate the overall design and to foresee execution problems before committing himself to the painstaking work of applying hundreds of thousands of dots of color to the full-sized canvas.

Sculptors and architects employ maquettes for similar purposes. The word maquette is French, from the Italian *macchia,* "a sketch," but artists and architects use the term to mean a three-dimensional model. Architects, of course, often build small physical models of their design plans to give clients a better notion of what the building will look like than can be gleaned from blueprints or drawings, or to envision some of the construction problems they may encounter. These models vary from fairly simple cardboard and

Fig. 12-2. Isamu Noguchi at Crescent Iron Works, fabricators of *Bolt of Lightning . . . A Memorial to Benjamin Franklin,* 1984.

paper constructions to incredibly detailed wood and metal constructions. The maquettes of sculptors also vary greatly. Louise Bourgois says she moves "from sketch to cardboard model to corrugated cardboard model to wood to stone" as she plans and develops her sculptures. Isamu Noguchi said he made "drawings and then models — in [some] cases paper models" from which metal or other maquettes were fabricated. In his later years, Henry Moore actually had three studios to carry out the different stages of modeling: a maquette studio, where hand-sized models were made; a transitional studio, where issues of scaling and materials were addressed; and his "garden" studio, where the huge final pieces were built. His working style matched the physical layout of his grounds. "I prefer," he once said, "to do perhaps ten or eleven little maquettes, only one of which may ever get carried out as a large, full-scale sculpture. . . . I'll try out a working-model size in which alterations will take place. And then alterations will take place again as one does the big one, because the size of something — well, one sees it in perspective in a different way from what one does as a small thing. . . . So it's a mixture of building up, of modelling, and of carving."

Many artists, of course, also use living people and inanimate objects as models. They ask models to assume certain poses for long periods of time; they arrange still lifes, which they then interpret in painting or sculpture. But sculptors George Segal and Duane Hanson actually take plaster casts of their models, using the same techniques as a physician fixing a broken arm or leg. Leonardo da Vinci used a similar technique during the Renaissance, adding a small amount of gesso (a plaster of Paris preparation) to his models' clothing to stiffen and preserve the folds and creases from one sitting to the next. Leonardo's contemporary, Luca Cambiaso, solved this problem by modeling the models: he made his preliminary drawings from arrangements of geometric wooden dolls, which could retain their poses indefinitely. Posable dolls are still available from most artists' supply houses.

Models of human models have a lengthy and diverse history. In the eighteenth century, the French fashion industry exported its wares throughout Europe by means of exquisitely dressed dolls. Madame Alexander dolls, Barbie and Ken, GI Joe, and a plethora of action figures model today's dress styles as well as social norms and values. On a more lifelike scale, the display-window or museum mannequin performs similar functions without moving an inch for weeks, months, or even years. The tailor's dummy mimics the human form day after day, putting up with pins, needles, and tedium that no person would tolerate. And crash dummies provide safety information in situations to which no human being could be exposed purposefully. In a

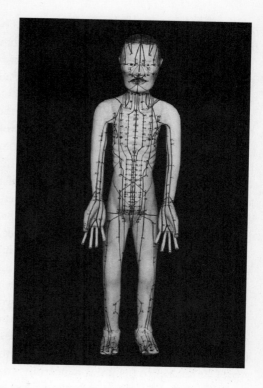

Fig. 12-3. Japanese papier-maché acupuncture figure, showing the proper places to insert needles.

sense, every robot, whether in a factory, a laboratory, or in outer space, is also a model. Functionally, these models outperform their originals within a very limited sphere of operations precisely because they are not human.

The field of medicine may have the widest range of representational and functional human models. In many cases, the models are also works of art. This is certainly true of the small, naked ivory dolls traditionally carried to doctors' offices by upper-class Chinese women in centuries past. Forbidden by cultural taboos and modesty to disrobe for male doctors, women used the dolls to indicate the nature and location of their symptoms. Asian physicians also marked human figurines with the locations of acupuncture points or other relevant information. Western use of anatomical models has been somewhat different. Religious and secular disapproval of the use of bodies for dissection made detailed anatomical information difficult to obtain during and after the Renaissance. Some physicians resorted to creating fantastically detailed, full-sized wax models of human beings in various stages of dissection. Their detail puts even the wax works of Madame Tussaud to shame, yet the models could not provide the interactive opportunities subsequently provided by cadavers. Today computerized models of everything from frog dissections to human anatomy have entered biological and medical classrooms. But, like the wax models of old, these visualizations provide no training in the proper manipulation of a scalpel or the emergency suture of an artery suddenly and uncontrollably bleeding in the wound. In medicine, as in many of the arts and sciences, models that can be seen but not felt and handled have definite teaching limitations.

Many modern medical models attempt to remedy the need for hands-on experience. Current catalogues contain an amazing range of representational models that are also functional. Some realistically mimic the feel of a breast with a tiny tumor inside so that medical personnel can learn to do breast examinations without embarrassing a real patient. Others realistically represent the size and feel of a patient's arm or leg so that medical personnel or diabetic patients, say, who must administer injections can learn the procedure before experimenting on a live human being. Model vaginas allow obstetricians to learn how to do a vaginal exam, to place a diaphragm or pessary, or to show a patient how to do so. And anyone who has taken a cardiopulmonary resuscitation (CPR) course has, of course, met the infant and adult dolls used to teach the lifesaving procedure.

Models for human medical problems need not be human, however, and this fact returns to the point concerning mannequins and robots: they need not be "realistic" to be useful. All models are abstractions to one degree or another, sometimes to a surprising degree. Gregor Mendel, for example, was

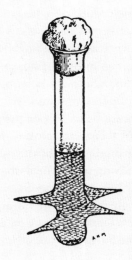

Fig. 12-4. Alexander Fleming's spiky test tube for testing the resistance of microbes to antiseptic solutions.

able to shed light on the principles of human genetics by studying peas, just as scientists today learn about human genetics from intensive genetic study of microorganisms, worms, and fruitflies. The principles of genetics, it turns out, are basically the same in every organism, so in this case at least, animal models reasonably simulate human functions. Similarly, the behavior of cells in a test tube may often model what is happening inside our bodies. During World War I Alexander Fleming made a test tube with spiky points to investigate why the irregular wounds caused by compound fractures or shrapnel were unresponsive to antibiotic treatment. He learned that bacteria isolated in the points of the spikes could "hide" from antiseptic treatment. The model convinced him that the only effective way to treat most contaminated wounds would be from inside the body itself, an insight that prepared his mind for the discovery of penicillin in 1928. Fleming then researched the effect of his new drug *in vitro*, in cell cultures grown in petri dishes and test tubes, to learn how it worked *in vivo*, in the body.

New drugs today are still tested for both beneficial and unwanted effects in just this way. But because all such models are abstractions, they have limitations. Human organs such as the intestines and liver, which don't exist in cell cultures, can modify the effects of drugs. Some drugs won't pass through the intestines and therefore can't be taken orally. The liver modifies many chemicals, turning beneficial compounds into useless ones or safe ones into lethal ones. Guinea pigs are allergic to penicillin, but rats are not: which animal is the appropriate model for human beings in any particular instance? Knowing the limitations of a model is as important as knowing its valid uses.

Medicine also depends on theoretical models, like the ones pioneered by Jean Gimpel to teach concepts of public health. Gimpel, a historian of technology, developed a professional interest in modeling during his attempts to reconstruct how medieval machines were invented and used. He built small-scale working models. Subsequently, he began developing "appropriate technologies" for rural societies, technologies that utilize available materials and skills rather than large-scale industrialized infrastructures. Gimpel found that the best way to teach poorly educated, often illiterate people was by showing them small, functional models of these technologies in the same way he modeled historical ones. It was a short step to adapting such models to teach public health as well. Trying to explain to a farmer why he should not let his cattle urinate and defecate beside his well can be difficult when the farmer has no understanding of ground-water movement or germs, but a model showing how ground water contaminated by the urine and feces is pulled into the well and then drunk by the farmer is very effective. So is a model showing the solution: put a fence around the well to keep the cattle away. Doctors who treat patients in rural communities as well as those treating the urban homeless are increasingly adopting Gimpel's models to prevent the transmission of diseases such as tuberculosis. Actively experiencing a complex chain of events by manipulating a working model is always more effective as a means of learning than merely being told. Models, in short, can allow us to reify — make concrete — ideas and concepts that are otherwise difficult to understand.

In science, modeling is inextricably bound to the generation of new ideas, the development of theories, and their experimental verification or falsification. Linus Pauling, one of the greatest scientific modelers of recent times, described modeling as a unique way of thinking. "The greatest value of models is their contribution to the process of originating new ideas," he wrote. "I would say that models constitute a language." Pauling spent decades studying protein molecules and using models to explore their possible structures, eventually earning a Nobel Prize for his efforts. Precise models represent precise thinking.

Modeling also played a role in determining one of Pauling's most celebrated failures: his incorrect structure of DNA, the molecule that contains our genes. "If you have a model," he wrote, "you know what the permissible structures are. . . . The models themselves permit you to throw out a large number of structures that might otherwise be thought possible." And that is precisely what happened. During 1951 and 1952, Pauling and several other scientists, including James Watson and Francis Crick, were attempting to elucidate the structure of DNA by building models, which they then compared with the scant data then available. Comparisons between the predictions

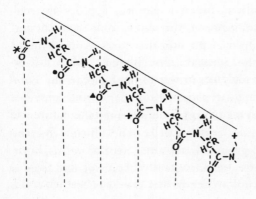

Fig. 12-5. A reconstruction of Linus Pauling's paper model of his alpha helix, which he folded into a tube. "In Oxford, in bed with a cold, I got bored . . . I thought, Why don't I think about the structure of proteins? So I took a sheet of paper and constructed, carefully, a drawing of a polypeptide chain, the bond lengths and angles correctly shown."

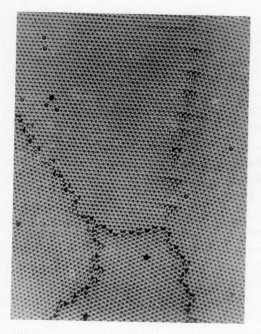

Fig. 12-6. Cyril Stanley Smith's bubble model of the structure of a metal.

made by the different models quickly revealed that Pauling's contained fatal flaws. Watson and Crick's initial model-building attempts, made with carefully cut-out pieces of cardboard, also failed, but, learning from their mistakes, they produced what has now become the standard textbook model of the DNA double helix. Their model incorporated not only the structural details of DNA revealed by experiment but, equally important, the manner in which genetic information is encoded and transmitted from generation to generation. Thus, the double-helical model elegantly combined representational, functional, and theoretical elements.

Unlike most scientific models, however, the double helix is often portrayed as being representationally real, a physical embodiment of something that is simply too small to see. Most scientific models are not taken so literally. They are like maquettes for sculptors or war games for generals: useful tools for building ideas but not literal representations. Cyril Smith provided a good example from his work in metallurgy. To understand the nature and effects of structural flaws in alloys, he created a tray full of bubbles, then carefully popped a few in strategic places. This procedure allowed him to observe the ways in which the bubble-atoms reorganized in response to the disturbance, revealing interesting effects relevant to the alloys. Neither Smith nor his colleagues regarded these bubble models as "real," but they were extremely useful for exploring their theories.

The role of scientific models can be compared to that of the scaffolds and cranes erected around large buildings as they are being built. There is no way to construct the building without these scaffolds and cranes, but once the building is completed, they need to be removed. Thus, in his classic book *The Character of Physical Law*, Richard Feynman argued that theory should always try to wean itself from the models upon which it was built. "It always turns out that the greatest discoveries abstract away from the model and the model never does any good," he wrote. "Maxwell's discovery of electrodynamics was first made with a lot of imaginary wheels and idlers in space. But when you get rid of all the idlers and things in space the thing is O.K." Models help us gain mastery of concepts, Feynman went on to say, but should not be confused with the concepts themselves.

To achieve conceptually pure models, many scientists have turned to mathematics. Like war-gaming, the mathematization of models is relatively recent, dating back no further than Galileo's mathematical descriptions of falling bodies. The notion that every equation or mathematical concept can be represented physically or visually and that every such representation can be expressed as an equation came much later. Mathematician, historian, and photographer Gerd Fischer suggests that the first clear indication of an interest in mathematical model-building as a conceptual tool within mathematics itself appeared only in the 1860s, when the German mathematician Ernst

Fig. 12-7. Kummer's quartic model with 12 A double points is derived from the intersection of a surface of degree four with a sphere given by the equation $(x^2 + y^2 + z^2 - \mu k^2)^2 = \lambda[(z - k)^2 - 2x^2] \cdot [(z + k)^2 - 2y^2]$.

Kummer published a series of wire and plaster models of complex algebraic functions. Fischer notes, "The construction of these models went hand in hand with work at the furthest frontiers of research in the area of algebraic surfaces," some of which are now known as "Kummer surfaces." The effectiveness of Kummer's approach was appreciated by other mathematicians. During the 1850s August Ferdinand Möbius used models to invent the figure called the Möbius strip, a one-sided two-dimensional twist that is often used as a symbol for infinity. Felix Klein, one of the greatest mathematicians of his age, produced an extensive array of models using cardboard, thread, wire, plaster, and modeling clay. Among many other things, he invented the so-called Klein bottle — a three-dimensional equivalent of the Möbius strip that appears to be one continuous surface without an identifiable inside or an outside. Simple paper, wire, clay, Plasticine, and even tin-foil models are still sometimes used today to help students understand concepts in geometry, topology, and knot theory (the mathematics of objects that cannot be unraveled without breaking them).

Until recently, the only major collections of mathematical models were in European institutes and in the Mathematica exhibit designed around 1970 by Ray and Charles Eames for a half-dozen American science museums. The advent of computer-aided design (CAD) systems and general problem-solving programs such as Mathematica have now made mathematical modeling available to almost anyone with a desktop computer. It is important to emphasize, however, that computer and physical models are not equivalent in terms of the thinking tools they embody. Computer graphics are 2-D, even with displays that allow 3-D vision. Merely perceiving 3-D visually in one's mind is not the same as experiencing 3-D kinesthetically and tactilely. The difference is important, says computer-graphics expert Michael Bailey of the San Diego Supercomputer Center. For years he touted the computer as the be all and end all of modeling, but new technology has changed his mind. Computers can be linked to machines that produce 3-D models made of plastic, paper, resin, or metal by stereolithography or casting. One of these techniques, invented by a blind chemist named William Skawinski for his own use, has led to the development of "chemical model libraries" for teaching both blind and sighted students. "It's embarrassing," Bailey now admits, "but graphics are just not as good as having an object to touch and hold."

One reason that graphic models are not as good as physical ones is that abstract "maps" do not always correspond to real "terrain." It is possible to produce a visual image in 2-D of an object that cannot exist physically in

3-D, as M. C. Escher, L. S. and Roger Penrose, and other designers of impossible objects have known for ages. Anyone who has assembled self-designed objects, whether as architect, carpenter, modeler, or builder, undoubtedly has imagined something on paper that he or she has not been able to construct. Working in time and space is not the same as working in equations, in graphics, or on paper. Dimensional issues become important.

Even when visual models are accurate, they may be less than candid, as John Johnson, a biologist at the Scripps Research Institute who studies virus structures, learned. For years he and his colleagues have relied on computer-generated graphic images to see into those structures, though only incompletely. In 1997 Johnson had Michael Bailey construct polymer-based models of the protein building blocks that made up one of his viruses. Almost as soon as he got his hands on the models, Johnson realized that there was a hole at the interface between proteins that was not visually discernible in the graphic images. This was an exciting discovery, because drugs could be designed to fit into the hole, preventing the virus from assembling, and so curing the infection it causes. "I was running around like a crazy man," Johnson recalls, "showing everyone how stupid we had been. I think that is going to be a fairly universal experience when it comes to looking at the assembly of subunits with these models."

To give Johnson his due, he was not really stupid, he had just shortchanged himself. As many inventors and engineers could have told him, there is no substitute for hands-on modeling. Indeed, Arthur C. Clarke, who created the idea of the stationary orbiting satellite, worries that people trained today "are only used to looking at images on their computer screens and never touch any real metal, and so are creating disasters for the future." Clarke's words have been echoed by a number of engineers, including Eugene Ferguson, Samuel Florman, and Henry Petroski, all of whom attribute the major engineering failures of the past two decades (bridges, buildings, rockets, planes) to ever-increasing reliance on computer graphics in place of the hands-on experience gained by having to create working models.

The lesson is obvious. If we are to understand the world around us, we need to create useful, often multiple, models. With encouragement and training, the task should be as easy and natural as playing. Indeed, children spontaneously make models when they play with the kinds of toys discussed in Chapters 8 and 11. Simple blocks, all-purpose dolls, craft and building materials of all sorts become representations of other things. What is important is not the quality of the fort children build in the backyard, the zoo in the basement, or the dollhouse in their room, nor its realism or permanence or practicality, but the act of modeling itself. For out of modeling come under-standing and control.

Many creative individuals remember their deep immersion in modeling activities and its effect on their adult interests. Georgia O'Keeffe recalled playing with a dollhouse she made herself from two thin boards. She sawed a slit in each board and fitted them together, creating four "rooms" that satis-fied her — though nothing more existed than the partitions between those rooms. This may have been the beginning of her understanding of abstraction. Sculptor Claes Oldenburg invented his own private world, too, making homemade books, newspapers, maps, and charts. In adolescence he turned to model airplanes, "sometimes changing the design so that they looked more the way I wanted them to." For both artists, modeling was the begin-ning of a lifelong habit of inventing their own constructions of the world.

Many scientists and engineers report that modeling provided them with formative experiences as well. Jung wrote that his teenage hobby of modeling was the beginning of his interest in scientific things in general. "I began to build castles and artfully fortified emplacements out of small stones, using mud as mortar," he commented. "I studied all the available fortification plans of Vauban, and was soon familiar with all the technicalities. From Vauban I turned to modern methods of fortification, and tried with my lim-ited means to build models of all the different types. This preoccupied me in my leisure hours for more than two years, during which time my leanings to-ward scientific study and concrete things steadily increased." A member of the American National Academy of Sciences who took part in an anony-mous interview attributed his interest and success in science to similar expe-riences: "I was always interested in things to make. I used to make model air-planes and things like that. When I was old enough to go to the library, I used to go and get books that described things that kids could make . . . and that was extremely significant in my education because essentially what I [came] across in college courses . . . was not entirely new to me." Similarly, an emi-nent mathematician in another anonymous study said, "This may not seem related to mathematical development, but in my mind it is: I began building model airplanes of balsa wood when I was very young. By five, I was already building them by myself. I used to see in my mind what they would look like and how the struts would go in and turn the designs over in my head." By building models, all of these inventive people learned early the imaging, ab-stracting, analogizing, and dimensional skills necessary to their adult cre-ative endeavors.

Beginning is easy. In any library or bookstore one can find books on how

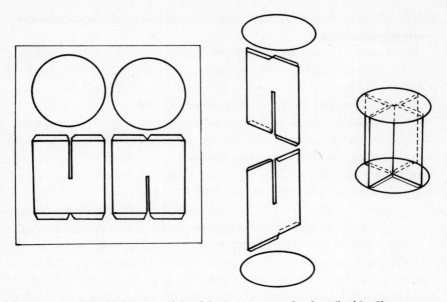

Fig. 12-8. Steps for building models of the imaging puzzles described in Chapter 4.

to build models using anything from corrugated cardboard to balsa wood, from wire and plastics to cloth and paper. These simple materials are not to be scoffed at. Recall that Wells's original war game used books for hills and buildings; Xenakis's "orchestra" was made of cardboard and sticks; Pauling's protein structure consisted of penciled markings and a tube of paper. Augusto Odone, whose effort to discover the cause of his son's disease is featured in the movie *Lorenzo's Oil,* made models of fat molecules out of paper clips. If starting from scratch is too daunting, model kits with preformed plastic and wood parts exist for anything you can imagine, from dinosaurs to dollhouses, from stage coaches to *Star Wars* spaceships. Paper models range from the classic paper dolls and airplanes to castles and clocks. Many model shops and scientific catalogues carry working models of steam engines, trains, race cars, airplanes, and rockets. The important thing in a model is not the materials from which it is made, but the ideas or functions it embodies and the effort made by the modeler to understand every detail of the recreation. The model is nothing until endowed with "life" by the efforts of imagination.

In school modeling can also be directed toward mastery of various subjects. Making models in math class, for instance, reifies the concepts. The earlier a student learns that every equation has its physical manifestation and every physical phenomenon its mathematical model, the better equipped he or she is to be inventive. Visual thinking can also be improved by modeling, because there is a direct connection between the kinesthetic sense and vision. Modeling simple visual things like the forms we asked you to imagine in Chapter 4 can therefore be valuable to students of all ages.

Develop spatial skills by modeling your school, house, or neighborhood. Learn engineering and design skills by making structural models of Buckminster Fuller's tetrahedron-based geodesic domes, Snelson's tensegrity sculptures, and other architectural forms. Teacher Brenda Jackson particularly recommends the modeling of bridges for its multidisciplinary aspects: "In [a] bridge design project," she says, "a variety of disciplines is involved. Drawing the proposed design, coping with the practical problem of tension, and using calculations and manual skill in making the model, are all parts of the problem. Testing the bridge to destruction, although somewhat noisy, involves learning in a practical way, and the results are often so spectacular that they are unlikely to be quickly forgotten."

In grade school, high school, and even college, teachers of arts, design, sculpture, crafts, engineering, mathematics, and science can collaborate to create an integrated experience for students that itself models the types of interactions that take place in many workplaces. Politics, history, and anthropology can be learned in unique ways by modeling physically, functionally, or theoretically the course of battles, the evolution of architectural styles, the efficacy of traditional medical treatments, the outcome of competing economic activities, or the purposes of religious ceremonies. Because it requires figuring out how things work, modeling is a great way to learn, no matter your age. Make modeling a lifelong habit, and you hold a key to a lifetime of fun and learning.

13

Playing

I N 1936 A RELATIVELY OBSCURE medical researcher named Alexander Fleming gave two demonstrations at the Second International Congress of Microbiology in London. In the first he presented his discovery of an odd mold called *Penicillium,* which produced a compound that inhibited the growth of various infectious bacteria. In the second he discussed his odd invention of microbe painting, in which variously pigmented bacteria were carefully brushed with a wire loop onto agar plates, producing a pleasing picture. The scientific world ignored both presentations. Fleming did not make a convincing case for *Penicillium,* nor had he worked any miracle cures with it. And Queen Mary had summed up the response to bacterial paintings a short time before, when she was shown a moldy Union Jack that Fleming had prepared for her visit to the hospital where he worked. "Yes, but what *good* is it?" she had asked. She might as well have asked, "What good is play?"

Everyone who knew Fleming knew he liked to play. He was a brilliant student, a hard-working scientist, and one of the first to adopt Paul Ehrlich's "magic bullet," Salvarsan — the first totally synthetic drug — for treating syphilis. But Fleming always made time for sports and games of all sorts: rifle shooting, golf, billiards, croquet, penny pitching, checkers, bridge, poker, quiz games, table tennis, water polo . . . He did not always play by the usual rules, either. He found delight, according to one friend, in "making difficulties for himself, just for the fun of overcoming them." He would play a round of golf with only one club or, lying on the ground, use the club like a billiard cue to putt. He devised various indoor golf games for the amusement of children. He thought nothing, one biographer has written, of interrupting an evening conversation with distinguished bacteriologists to organize a game

Fig. 13-1. Bacterial paintings by Alexander Fleming. The one on the right reads: "This is not written with ink but with bacteria which develop colour as they grow. (1) B. violaceus (2) B. prodigiosus (3) Staphylococcus (4) A. bacillus (5) Sarcina."

of shove-ha'penny. Nor did Fleming confine his playful spirit to after-hours only. He played at work — or, more accurately, he played *with* his work. "You treat research like a game," his boss, Sir Almroth Wright, once said to him. "You find it all great fun."

Wright may have been criticizing Fleming, or perhaps he was jealous. In any event, Fleming agreed wholeheartedly. Play was his style. He made up games within the game of science. "I play with microbes," he said whenever anyone asked what he did. "There are, of course, many rules to this play . . . but when you have acquired knowledge and experience it is very pleasant to break the rules and to be able to find something nobody had thought of." In this he was very much like ethologist Konrad Lorenz and Max Delbrück, one of the founders of molecular biology. Lorenz once told Desmond Morris, "Contrary to your Shakespeare, there is madness to my method!" His book *King Solomon's Ring* (1952) recounts truly outrageous situations — such as allowing his geese and ravens full run of his house — resulting in observations that no careful scientist would ever encourage, let alone report. Delbrück is famous for his "principle of limited sloppiness": be sloppy enough that something unexpected may happen but not so sloppy that you can't tell what it was. For Fleming, bacterial play was a way of courting serendipity, that uncanny knack of finding valuable things *not sought for.*

Most scientists don't understand such playful "methods." Fleming's lab partner, V. D. Allison, for example, was somewhat shocked when Fleming pulled "my leg about my excessive tidiness. Each evening I put my 'bench' in order and threw away anything I had no further use for. Fleming told me I was a great deal too careful. He, for his part, kept his cultures sometimes for two or three weeks and before getting rid of them, looked very carefully to see whether by chance any unexpected or interesting phenomena had appeared. The sequel was to prove how right he was."

The sequel, of course, was penicillin, and Fleming's microbe paintings were arguably the stimulus for his discovery. Each painting was a technical tour de force, requiring just the right conditions of acidity, nutrients, temperature, moisture, and timing to develop as pictures. They also required the association of microbes that would never be found together under normal circumstances. The microbe paintings were experiments, excuses to see what else might happen. The need for colored bacteria for his paintings also gave Fleming reason to accumulate all kinds of cultures higgledy piggledy just to see what "odd and interesting things" might turn up. One of the things that might turn up was a new and interesting "color" to add to his palette of microbe pigments. One of the things that *did* turn up was the bluish green mold *Penicillium notatum,* from which Fleming isolated the first antibiotic.

No one knew what this mold meant at first, not even Fleming, because play has no direct or directing purpose outside of itself. Play is simply for the fun of it, for the enjoyment of doing and making without responsibility. There is no success or failure in play, no holding to account, no mandatory achievement. Play breaks the rules of serious activity and establishes its own. Play is frivolous, wandering according to the whims of curiosity and interest. It involves what anthropologist Stephen Miller has called "galumphing" — awkward, exaggerated, even subversive action and the deliberate complication or elaboration of activity for its own sake, whether this involves body movements, hand-held objects, symbolically expressed ideas, golf, or microbes. However, to say that play has no inherent goal does not mean that its results cannot *afterward* be put to good purposes beyond motivating enjoyment.

Play can be useful because, as psychologist Jean Piaget suggested, it strengthens various mental skills in one or more of three ways. First, *practice play* can exercise and develop any thinking tool by enhancing skill through practice. The teenage Richard Feynman play-practiced the visualization of four-dimensional figures simply for the fun of mastering such problems.

Fleming enhanced his technical skill and knowledge through his bacterial paintings. M. C. Escher mastered his pattern recognition and pattern forming skills by finding images in wallpaper. Second, *symbolic play* fosters tools such as analogizing, modeling, play-acting, and empathizing by invoking a make-believe world where one thing stands for another. Georgia O'Keeffe played symbolically when, as a child, she imagined that two interlocking boards represented a dollhouse; Fleming used bacteria symbolically as pigments. Third, *game playing* teaches the making of rules within externally bounded situations that define how we may behave or think, as well as the breaking of those rules. H. G. Wells played games when he modeled wars in miniature. So did Fleming, discovering and inventing new rules for the "game" of bacteriology. Playing is therefore more than just exercising other tools for thinking; it is a tool in and of itself. Galumphing around with the materials, techniques, and rules of any endeavor generates novel behaviors, observations, and ideas, especially when, as in Fleming's case, all three elements of play are in play.

Considering the sheer joy of fooling around, not to mention its potential rewards, it is not surprising that many scientists have galumphed with their subjects. Richard Feynman's exuberantly playful style has, in fact, made him something of a household name. Tales of his scientific (as well as personal) exploits fascinate the layman, for whom physics is normally a dry-as-dust subject. Why? The title of one of his books, *Surely You're Joking, Mr. Feynman*, tells it all. Feynman liked to tell jokes and to play practical jokes on others; he played at his hobbies and at his work. Fresh out of graduate school, working on the team at Los Alamos that developed the first atomic bomb, Feynman pulled pranks on his colleagues and pilfered their safes (for fun, not profit). Later, as a professor at Caltech, he frequented a dancing bar to ogle the girls and fiddle with equations. Sometimes his looking and his thinking merged, and he doodled faces and figures over and between his calculations. He played at becoming an artist, taking drawing lessons and entering fine sketches in local art shows under the pseudonym "Ofey" — itself a play on his name and on the word "fey," which can mean crazy or unusually high-spirited. He also fooled around with music and gained near-professional mastery of the bongo drums.

Feynman's combination of play mixed with serious work was, like Fleming's, a deliberate strategy. He achieved such a great reputation so early in his career that the accompanying expectations threatened to stifle him. At an age when most people are just finishing their Ph.D.s, he contemplated leaving physics. At the critical moment, however, he saw the light: "Then I had another thought: Physics disgusts me a little bit now, but I used to enjoy doing physics. Why did I enjoy it? I used to play with it. I used to do whatever I felt like doing — it didn't have to do with whether it was important for the development of nuclear physics, but whether it was interesting and amusing for me to play with. . . . So I got this new attitude. . . . I'm going to play with physics whenever I want to, without worrying about any importance whatsoever."

Feynman could not have foreseen how quickly his determination to play would lead to something interesting. "Within a week," he later recalled, "I was in the cafeteria and some guy, fooling around, throws a plate in the air. As the plate went up in the air I saw it wobble, and I noticed the red medallion of Cornell on the plate going around. . . . I had nothing to do, so I start to figure out the motion of the rotating plate." For fun, Feynman worked out equations for the wobbles, and, delving into relativity, electrodynamics, and quantum electrodynamics, he thought about how electron orbits are supposed to move.

> And before I knew it (it was a very short time), I was "playing" — working, really — with the same old problem that I loved so much, that I had stopped working on when I went to Los Alamos . . .
>
> It was effortless. It was easy to play with these things. It was like uncorking a bottle. Everything flowed off effortlessly. I almost tried to resist it! There was no importance to what I was doing, but ultimately there was. The diagrams and the whole business that I got the Nobel Prize for came from that piddling around with the wobbling plate.

Feynman's experience, like Fleming's, is typical of inventors in general. As Arthur Molella, director of the Smithsonian Institution's Lemelson Center for the Study of Invention and Innovation, has said, "The sense of play is the essence of inventive activity. Invention begins in the joyful, free association of the mind." Even engineers, who in general are known for their pocket protectors and nerdlike seriousness, play. Elmer Sperry provides a case in point. Anyone who has flown in a plane on autopilot, sailed in a ship with antiroll stabilizers, or roared into space on a rocket owes much to the man — and his sense of fun. He invented the gyrocompass and gyrostabilizers, used to maintain attitude control, and he did it by ignoring the textbooks in favor of playing with his children's toys:

First I had somewhat of a library on the gyroscope. Almost without exception these books and pamphlets were terrifying in the profuse use (I have often thought rather in the line of abuse) of higher mathematics. These did not serve me very far, but our family was blessed with three boys and I tried to keep these youngsters supplied with gyroscopic toys of various varieties, some of which I imported. I got more out of these toys than the boys did, inasmuch as they served the very useful purpose of putting me wise as to the magnitudes involved in the gyroscopic reactions that I knew about. These latter were more or less familiar to me, but the former in some respects astonished me. I never would have realized the possibilities had I not been able thus to visualize them while they were actually taking place.

Toys also played an important and early role in Jerome Lemelson's development as an inventor. Lemelson was one of the most prolific inventors since Edison, eventually taking out more than five hundred patents relating to robotics, computer vision, the VCR, the camcorder, fax machine, and cordless telephone. But, mixed in with these inventions, his notebooks show a continuous fascination with toys. In fact, his first two patents were for toys: a variation of the child's propeller beanie cap activated by blowing into a tube; and a jet-propelled toy using a balloon for propulsion. These amusing inventions may seem obvious today, but they were novel enough to merit patents in the 1950s. Moreover, the proceeds kept Lemelson financially secure enough to play with his other, more "serious" inventions. More important, they provided experience with the process of invention itself in a fun and relatively risk-free way. Walter Rudolf Hess, a Nobel laureate in medicine and one of the most prolific inventors of medical devices ever to grace this earth, similarly laid his abilities at the feet of practice play: "During my free time I used to make toys such as bows and arrows, sail boats, and airplanes from improvised materials to be found in and around the house. This did much to develop not only manual skills, but a certain practical sense and inventiveness."

And, of course, toys themselves are inventions of play. One of the most popular toys of the last few years is the Super Soaker, a high-pressure, oversized squirt gun. In this case, it was not the toy that led to the invention, but the invention that led to the toy. Engineer Lonnie Johnson has patents for thermostats, hair-drying rollers, wet-diaper detectors, a flow-actuated pulsator — forty-nine patents in all. He's been designing robots since he was in high school and worked for the National Aeronautics and Space Administration's Jet Propulsion Laboratory for many years as a space probe specialist. While trying to invent a heat pump that would use water instead of Freon, he made a prototype that he played with in his bathroom sink. (Some engineers can play anywhere.) The spray from the pump was "so powerful that the curtains were swirling in the breeze it sent out. I thought, 'This would make a great water gun.'" It did. Current estimates are that four Super Soakers have been sold for every child in the United States. The heat pump worked, too.

Sometimes the engineer's playful approach emerges in even more unusual forms. A large number of kinetic sculptors, from George Rickey and Jean Tinguely to the late automotive wizard of MIT, Charles Fayette (Fay) Taylor, have all had engineering backgrounds. This was also true of Alexander Calder, who segued from an abortive career as an engineer to the invention of mobile sculptures. Calder, like Fleming and Feynman, was known for his almost childlike sense of humor and playful attitude toward both life and art. He used his dry Yankee wit on everyone, and his dancing partners complained of his exuberant style. Friends report that his hands were never still. He unceasingly painted, carved wood, and made constructions out of corks, old tin cans, balls, and almost anything else he could manipulate. Wire was his favorite material, "something to twist, or tear, or bend." He always had a roll of it along with pliers in his pocket, for, as he put it, wire was "an easier medium . . . to think in" than any other.

Calder invented things because it was fun, not to impress anyone. He refused to label anything he ever created, including his mobiles, as "art." He saw no shame in designing a line of movable toys for children, and he called his wire sculptures "toys," albeit for adults. Like Fleming, Calder not only played with his toys, he played while making them. In fact, his artistic reputation first took root in an activity that he did simply for fun. While in Paris as a young man, he became enchanted with the circus and built himself a working model out of wood and wire. Eventually this toy circus grew to have hundreds of individual pieces, including animals, props, and entertainers with movable parts, a trapeze with a net, and a tent. On more than one occasion Calder invited a veritable who's who of the Parisian art world to his tiny apartment and gave them a show. A film recording of one such event shows Calder playing with his miniature big top just as any child would. While the audience sat on makeshift bleachers constructed of champagne crates, Calder knelt on the floor, activating his acrobats and animals, providing the dialogue and announcements, blowing whistles, sending in the clowns, bringing on the ambulance crew to carry off a trapeze artist who accidentally fell or a knife thrower nicked by her partner. It was fun to perform and fun to watch, and Calder never claimed anything more for its meaning than that.

It was more, however, just as Fleming's bacterial paintings were more. Calder's circus has been called a "laboratory" for his subsequent work. "Most of all," he once said, "I loved the space of the circus, the spatial relations and the vastness of space." Exploring that space and the ways objects moved through it as he played directly fed the kinetic ideas with which he later revolutionized sculptural art. In fact, his studios, cluttered with works in progress as well as works abandoned, functioned suggestively like Fleming's messy lab bench. If he left things sitting around long enough, surprising things happened, so Calder never threw out or destroyed anything. "I find that if I keep [something] long enough," he once said, "and change something here or there, it becomes a satisfactory piece of work."

One innovative change to Calder's conception of the mobile sculpture was made by a young art student who also briefly tried his hand at engineering. Kenneth Snelson spent two summers at Black Mountain College in

Fig. 13-2. Alexander Calder and his circus, 1929.

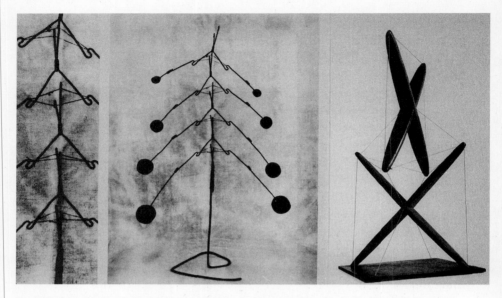

Fig. 13-3. Kenneth Snelson's steps to inventing tensegrity. *Left:* detail of sculpture combining the principles of Calder's mobiles with Buckminster Fuller's tetrahedral structures; *center:* the entire sculpture; *right:* the first "X" sculpture, in which two rigid Xs are suspended relative to one another by means of cables under tension.

North Carolina studying with Bauhaus master Josef Albers and with Buckminster Fuller. As Fuller's assistant, Snelson developed the idea of tensegrity (mentioned in Chapter 8), an idea that has had biological, architectural, engineering, and even outer-space applications. Yet Snelson had none of these goals in mind. "As many ideas do, the 'tensegrity' discovery resulted in a way from play; in this case, play aimed at making mobile sculptures." What would happen, Snelson wondered, if one were to combine "variations on Calder mobiles" with Fuller's tetrahedral principle of stability? The first trial produced a mysteriously swaying sculpture made of tetrahedral units connected by almost invisible wires. "One step leading to the next, I saw that I could make the structure even more mysterious by tying off the movement altogether, replacing the clay weights with additional tension lines to stabilize the modules one to another, which I did. . . . Forfeiting mobility, I managed to gain something even more exotic, solid elements fixed in space, one-to-another, held together only by tension members. I was quite amazed at what I had done."

The art of invention and the invention of art really do find common ground in playing — a point that anyone will appreciate who has ever enjoyed the fascinating "useless" machines of Jean Tinguely or Rube Goldberg, constructed the Mousetrap in the children's board game of that name, or assembled a Chaos construction system. In fact, engineer Jim Rothbart, the inventor of Chaos systems, says he was inspired by artist George Rhoads to think of the toys he created as "kinetic sculptures." He's quick to add, however, that learning how to manipulate Chaos systems also "teaches kids about physics." Playing, as Calder's, Snelson's, and Rothbart's inventions demonstrate, does not acknowledge disciplinary boundaries. In play, things are whatever we want them to be.

Playing with distinctions, boundaries, unassailable truths, and the limits of utility is, in fact, what many of the most innovative people in all disciplines do. When the rules of grammar are systematically broken, logic overturned, or perceptions puzzled, we know that a "game's afoot" and something interesting will happen. No better examples exist than in the topsy-turvy worlds of those masters of play, Edward Lear, Lewis Carroll, and M. C. Escher.

Consider Lear, who worked without inspiration as a painter of landscapes but played brilliantly with words. "Lear [is] a delightful companion, full of *nonsense*, puns, riddles, everything in the shape of fun," wrote one friend. His games were endless. He played with rebuses, writing his own name as an L followed by a sketch of an ear, the word "fortitude" as "42de", and addressing his friend Fortescue as "40scue." He collected ridiculous-sounding words like "absquatulate," "fuliginous," "granulosely," and "squamulose" (go ahead, look them up). He invented new spoonerisms, those humorous turns of phrase named for an Oxford don who had a habit — much magnified by Oxford undergraduates — of transposing the first syllables of consecutive words. Spooner is supposed, for example, to have dismissed a student with the words, "Sir, you have hissed my mystery lectures; you have tasted a whole worm," and sent him packing on the "town drain" to London. Lear, for his part, referred to Mary Squeen of Cotts. He also inverted syllables within words, creating "ozbervations," "buplishers," and similar confusions. He punned endlessly, even in dignified company. An artist became "a nartist" who made "vorx of *hart*" — works/vortexes of heart/art (remember that some Britons drop their *h*'s when speaking) that were dear/deer (hart) to the viewer. At one formal party, he suggested that a classical reference involving the Latin word *sequax* might be remembered by thinking of ducks — "sea-quacks." A dignified nobleman responded frostily that he abominated "the forcible introduction of ridiculous images calculated to distract the mind from what it is contemplating." Pleased by the reproof, Lear "chuckled inwardly" and put the lord in his category of "glumy" persons.

Wordplay and invention came naturally to Lear, and his "boshblobberbosh" (meaning particularly foolish foolishness) was well enough appreciated to make his *Book of Nonsense* and *Laughable Lyrics* enduring bestsellers. One reason that these books have appealed to generations of children and adults alike is that they break all the boundaries of word use, exploring connotations, combinations, and sounds as few have done before or since. When Lear writes that he needed to "epopsimate the fangropunxious feelings of my buzzim," we think we know what he means. In his use of terms such as "melloobius mumbians" (a kind of melody that mimics the sound of a rolling river) and "ombliferous scribbledbibble" (dark and murky epistles), he just skriggles (but only just) to make himself understood and thereby extends what is possible in the English language. Such wordplay tells us that the dictionary is not the limit of possible words and that existing words need not limit the nature of thought, as Immanuel Kant once suggested. We *can* think what cannot be said, and we can invent new ways of saying previously unsayable things — if we do it as a game.

What Lear did for words, his near-contemporary Charles Dodgson, also known as Lewis Carroll, did for logical concepts. An obscure Oxford don in mathematics, Dodgson was as pedantic and conventional in his professional work as Lear was as a painter or Leslie Stephen was as a writer. Somehow he found it impossible to play with his work as Feynman and Fleming did. Dodgson the scholar was consequently too serious and staid to accept the non-Euclidean geometries that invaded his professional world. But away from work, he was a different man, who played at nonsense poems and whimsical stories for children, at photography and at logical games and puzzles that reached the heights in *Alice in Wonderland*.

Even in his guise as Carroll, however, Dodgson adhered to a strict regard for internal consistency, and this is typical of productive play in general. Where rules are broken, new ones are invented to replace them. A strong sense of his own invented rules of discourse and narrative was necessary to Dodgson's creative capacities. As one scholar expressed it, "the rules place limits on what may be done, but more importantly, they provide guides to improvisation and innovation." Humpty-Dumpty gives Alice a very logical explanation for nonsense words such as "slithy." They mean two things at once, in this case "lithe" and "slimy" — a conceptual elision of meaning and sound. And it may seem absurd that the Mad Hatter has a watch that tells the day of the month rather than the hour of the day, but Alice has fallen to the center of the earth, where the sun would always appear to be in the same place (if it could be seen) and therefore would always tell the same time. Only the phases of the moon would mark the passage of time, so only the days of the month would be relevant. The Mad Hatter's watch is not only surprisingly logical, it is logically innovated. By the same token, Alice's adventures are all games, but as Martin Gardner's annotated version of the story demonstrates, these games are never meaningless or arbitrary. For instance, making Alice immensely big or immensely small explores in human terms, much as Jonathan Swift did in *Gulliver's Travels,* the problems of scaling described scientifically by Galileo and subsequent scientists. Dodgson/Carroll's amusing tale for children actually rests upon very sophisticated play with the logic of language and the laws of mathematics and physics.

Like Carroll, M. C. Escher also played games with reality.

> My subjects are often . . . playful. I can't keep from fooling around with our irrefutable certainties. It is, for example, a pleasure knowingly to mix up two- and three-dimensionalities, flat and spatial, and to make fun of gravity.
>
> Are you really sure that a floor can't be a ceiling?
>
> Are you definitely convinced that you will be on a higher plane when you walk up a staircase?
>
> Is it a fact as far as you are concerned that half an egg isn't also half an empty shell?

Among the people with whom Escher shared his reality-bending games were L. S. Penrose and his son, Roger. The senior Penrose was a biologist who greatly enjoyed making puzzles and games of various sorts. His son, a mathematician, acquired a taste for the same pleasures, and one day, while attending a mathematics conference in Amsterdam, was invited to view an Escher exhibit. "I remember I was absolutely spellbound by his work, which I was seeing for the first time," Roger Penrose later recalled.

> On my journey back to England, I determined to make something "impossible" myself. I experimented with various designs of bars lying behind and in front of each other in different combinations, and finally arrived at the impossible triangle (later known as the impossible tri-bar) which, it seemed to me, represented the impossibility which I sought in its purest form. . . . I showed my father the above-

mentioned triangle at the next possible opportunity. He immediately sketched a number of variants and eventually came up with the drawing of an impossible flight of stairs leading continuously downwards (or upwards).

The Penroses published their work in the *British Journal of Psychology* in 1958 and sent a copy to Escher in appreciation for his stimulus. Escher, in turn, found new ways to play with their impossible ideas, noting, in a retrospective of his prints, "Above all I take pleasure in the contacts and friendships with mathematicians that I owe to this. They have often provided me with new ideas, and sometimes an interaction between them and myself even develops. How playful they can be, those learned ladies and gentlemen!"

Indeed, the game had not yet come to an end. Roger Penrose soon mastered the art of designing Escher-like tessellations himself and began to play with the idea of creating irregular ones. Was it possible, he wondered, to produce patterns that never repeated, using a limited number of regularly shaped tile pieces? It was, and the patterns Penrose invented are among a class now known as aperiodic tilings (see Fig. 13-5). Being a mathematician, he wrote rules for his new tilings, which were popularized by Martin Gardner in his famous "Mathematical Recreations" column in *Scientific American,* where they stimulated play in many other minds.

We have said that Lear's verbal nonsense, Carroll's logical conundrums, Escher's perceptual puzzles, and Penrose's aperiodic tilings challenge our conceptions of nature and reality. But as play of the most creative sort, they do more than that. The games they invented have practical applications. Lear's nonsense rhymes and words, or ones very similar, are used in psychological and linguistic research to determine how we acquire language and whether older people can learn new "words" as quickly as younger people. Linguists examine how we recognize syntax and accurately identify the noun, verb, and adjective in nonsense sentences like, "ou priffed xe nork stimmulously," even though we cannot understand any of the words. Dodgson's games are similarly useful for exploring the limits of reason. Physicists, for example, use the "Carroll group" to explore an imaginary universe modeled on Carroll's Red Queen who has to run continuously just to stay where she is. Escher's ceilings-that-are-also-floors and up-down staircases are no longer fictions: the zero gravity of outer space has made such architectures viable. Others of his impossible figures have become a staple of perceptual

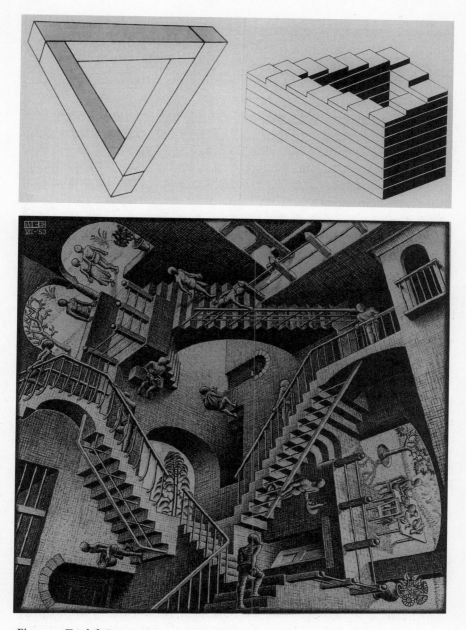

Fig. 13-4. *Top left:* Roger Penrose's impossible tribar; *top right:* L. S. Penrose's impossible stairs; *bottom: Relativity* by M. C. Escher, showing how he developed the Penroses' visual games into an art form.

Fig. 13-5. *Left:* Roger Penrose's aperiodic chicken tessellation; *right:* an aperiodic tiling with Roger Penrose's rhombuses.

psychologists, because their existence in our minds but not in nature begs for understanding. And Penrose's aperiodic tilings turn out to have an unexpected pseudo-fivefold symmetry that just happens to explain the structure of many previously uncharacterized metal alloys.

The power of play is that it reveals the nature of worlds that might be and sometimes are, testing the limits of conventional practice by inventing alternatives. This is as true in music as in any other discipline. The playful investigations of Charles Ives and his father, George, provide exemplars. The senior Ives, a professional composer, bandleader, and music teacher, had the utmost respect for his children's play and the utmost disregard for musical convention. Charles remembered that his father "never disturbed our mental processes when we [Charles and his brother] were at play. He always entered into it seriously." When the boys were playing train, George often showed up with his violin to provide the noise of the wheels as they sped along the tracks. We guess that he played with the hard part of the bow rather than the hairs or rasped his fingers on the wood rather than playing some recognizable tune, for George Ives enjoyed reproducing "nonmusical" sounds. Charles remembered the time his father raced out into the garden during a severe thunderstorm to listen to the church bells ringing an alarm and then raced back inside to find the same sounds on his piano. The sounds seemed impossible to recreate, so in and out he went, as his wife yelled for him to stop his foolishness. What a commotion that must have been!

There was, however, method to such madness. In trying to recreate natural sounds on his piano, the senior Ives became intensely interested in "the cracks between the piano keys," the microtones between the standard notes of modern Western music. (For a fuller explanation of these cracks see the Appendix at the end of this chapter.) And he passed his intense curiosity about these microtones and his dissatisfaction with the conventional musical scale on to his son. Charles began learning the drums and piano around the age of five, later adding a number of other instruments, and his father allowed him a "boy's fooling" at his practice as long as "there was some sense behind it." The young Ives learned his standard chords and then made up new ones as he tried to imitate drum sounds — and, like his father, bell sounds — on the piano. Following his father's example, he played around with homemade and "found" instruments, such as cowbells, whistles, sticks, rasps, boxes, and reeds; he toyed with microtones and tone clusters in place of chords; and eventually he composed music based on percussive rather than tonal harmonies. The boy who had been trained to hear thunder, rain, a neighbor whistling, crickets buzzing, alarm bells, and sirens, among many other sounds, as forms of music became the man whose mature and highly idiosyncratic compositions have provided inspiration for generations of modern musicians. His acceptance as a composer did not come easily, but his "harmonic discoveries" and "musical naturalism" are now an important part of modern twentieth-century music.

There are lessons here for parents and teachers who confine the practice of musical instruments to the playing of notes in a piece. There is more to the study of piano or violin than just reproducing tones, and more to making music than musical conventions or contemporary taste might suggest. By the same token, there may be more to playing with music than musical play. Play with patterns of all kinds can improve skills in composition and improvisation. A famous collaborative piece for piano by Aleksandr Borodin, Nikolay Rimsky-Korsakov, Anatoly Liyadov, Ceśar Cui, and Franz Liszt had just this sort of playful origin. Those who have heard "Paraphrases" will recognize it as being based on the same type of simplistic theme as the two-fingered "Chopsticks," which even the musically naive can learn. "The origin of the work," Borodin wrote to a friend in 1886, "is very funny. One day,

Gania (one of my adopted daughters) asked me to play a duet with her. 'Well, but you do not know how to play, my child.' 'Yes, indeed, I can play this.' " Using the first finger of each hand, Gania played alternating notes, as follows:

Fig. 13-6. Gania Borodin's "chopsticks" pattern, which her father turned into the piece "Paraphrases."

The notes she played actually describe a numerical pattern: 4,5; 4,5; 3,6; 3,6; 2,7; 2,7; 1,8; 1,8, and so forth, with the intervals between each pair increasing by odd numbers; 1,1; 3,3; 5,5; 7,7, and so on. It is one of the simplest patterns imaginable and thus a challenge to make interesting. Borodin was intrigued. He improvised a simple polka and played it for his musical colleagues, and they, too, eagerly tried their hands, becoming joint authors of "Paraphrases." "We amused ourselves by performing these things with people who could not play the piano. Finally we were requested to publish this work," Borodin recalled. The joke was well received by the composers' friends, but music critics were horrified. Apparently the idea of serious musicians having fun — and helping nonmusicians have fun with music, too — was beyond their comprehension. Either that or they were abysmally ignorant of the fact that all composers play with simple patterns, as one can easily verify by listening to any composition with the word "Variations" in the title. Mozart's Variations in C for Piano on the theme of "Twinkle, Twinkle, Little Star" and Johan Halvorsen's Passacaglia on a theme from Handel are two excellent examples.

Such pattern play, like all other kinds of play, transcends disciplines. Mozart and Bach both played games with their music that mimicked pattern games played with words. Reference to the *Oxford Guide to Word Games* shows that such amusements come in a huge variety. Perhaps the most popular is the making of anagrams, taking a word and seeing how many other words can be made from its letters: OWN, NOW, WON; ADOBE, ABODE; READ, DEAR, DARE. Anagrammatic phrases and sentences are also possible. "The Morse Code" converts to "Here Come the Dots"; the command "Question!" becomes the inspiration for "I quest on!" Lewis Carroll once converted the politician William Ewart Gladstone's name into three different anagrammatic sentences: "Wilt thou tear down all images?" "A wild man will go at trees," and "Wild agitator! Means well." A subset of anagrams involves words that when read backward form a different word: TROT/TORT; LIVE/ EVIL; NOW/WON; REED/DEER. (If there is a specific name for such reversible words, we have not been able to find it. Perhaps duograms — double words — or antigrams — opposite words — would do.) A few words (especially if printed in an appropriate typeface) can even yield another word when read upside down: mom/wow. Such words represent a special case of inversions or "ambigrams." Inversions are a game pioneered by Scott Kim in a 1981 book of that title and by John Langdon in his 1992 book *Wordplay*. Words are written so that they read the same way from left to right and when rotated 180 degrees. MOW is a good example, as is the word designed in the figure below.

Fig. 13-7. Thought. Turn it over and see what happens.

It is also possible to form words that read the same forward and backward as a mirror image without turning the word upside down. These are called palindromes: NOON; DAD; TOT; BOB. Like anagrams, palindromes can be made with sentences as well as words. "Madam, I'm Adam" and "'Tis Ivan, on a visit" are palindromic sentences.

Most of these word games have direct analogues in music. Anagrams have often provided the basis for musical compositions. Bach, for example, based one of the arrangements in *The Art of the Fugue* on anagrams of his own name: B, A, C, H (in the German notation of the period, B would be our B flat and H would be our B). The piece is a tour de force of playing with a theme. Another example can be found in the finale of Mozart's string quartet in F, K.V. 590, in which he takes as his theme the three notes A, G, and F#. Mozart's game is very clever. He repeats these three notes in exactly the same order, over and over, but because he is doing so in 2/4 time with four notes per bar, what one hears are not the repeated triplets but various orders of *four* notes. Mozart, in short, produced all of the anagrams of A, G, F#, A without varying their basic triplet sequence.

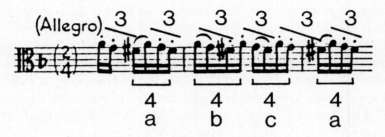

Fig. 13-8. A musical anagram by Mozart.

Mozart also made frequent use of cancrizans, which is the musical term for playing a musical sequence in reverse — a form of mirror-image play similiar to verbal duograms or antigrams. In fact, he may very well have been musically inspired by word games. Musicologist Emanuel Winternitz has pointed out that Mozart indulged with abandon in puns, anagrams, nonsense rhymes, inversions, and just about any other transposition that one can think of. He regularly signed his letters Trazom or Romatz instead of Mozart. He loved bawdy rhymes and improper jokes. In fact, his three-voice canon, K.V. 559, contains a nonsensical Latin text, which when sung can be heard as bawdy German — a very clever multilingual word game indeed. Winternitz believes, and we concur, that such word games not only expressed Mozart's need to play with patterns but also honed his composing skills.

Many of the pattern games that can be played with words and notes can be played with images and structures, too, once again demonstrating that games can reveal general principles applicable to a wide range of creative and natural phenomena. Consider two more word games that can be played with simple words such as "MOW" and "bid." Rotating "MOW" by 180 degrees results in the word becoming an inversion of itself. It therefore has rotational symmetry. The word "bid," on the other hand, can be read in a mirror to yield the same word and so represents an example of mirror-image symmetry. All geometric tilings, such as those executed by Escher, involve figures with either rotational or mirror-image symmetry, and much of the science of crystallography is built upon these bases; in fact, it is often taught with reference to Moorish or Escher tilings. Many natural and fabricated objects have these same properties. Rotate most flowers, a starfish, the nut on a bolt, through some part of a circle and their appearance will not change. They, like the word "MOW," have rotational symmetry. Many other objects have mirror-image symmetry: your right and left hands or feet, a spoon, the basic body plan of a human being or a car.

Fig. 13-9. Enantiomorphs: mirror-image figures occur in nature and in art.

Objects in nature that can exist in two nonsuperimposable mirror-image forms are called enantiomorphs, and these include most of the important molecules that make up our bodies. If one were to synthesize these molecules in a laboratory, one would end up with equal proportions of right- and left-handed forms, but, interestingly, only one form is synthesized by our cells. All of our sugars are right-handed; all of the amino acids that make up our proteins are left-handed. One of the great mysteries of evolution, first described by Louis Pasteur, is why living things generally employ only one form of an enantiomorph. No one has yet explained it. Perhaps more pattern play is called for!

There's no doubt about it. Word games, board games, musical games, visual games, puzzles, toys, and almost any other intellectual amusement imaginable all develop some skill, knowledge, or concept that can be turned to good account — and often in more than one discipline or endeavor. What we learn about word games can inform music and crystallography; about card games, statistics and evolutionary theory; about visual games, architecture, psychology, and biochemistry. What we do for fun rewards us many times over in unexpected ways when we apply it to some real-world problem or use it as an analogy for some mysterious phenomenon. The only difficulty with playing — and it's a big one — is being able to remain enough of a child to do it. What charms us about a Fleming or a Feynman or a Calder or a Mozart is the fact that, in some way, they never grew up. They continued to "face nature like a child," to use T. H. Huxley's phrase. Everyday things remained as exciting and fresh to these men as if they had just seen them for the first time. Conventions of behavior, thought, and action were not taken too seriously. Each man cultivated, in Feynman's term, a sort of "creative irresponsibility." We can learn from that.

Indeed, we must learn from that. Playing has become so rare in our society that some people, such as engineer Henry Petroski and neurobiologist Arthur Yuwiler, worry that the art of it will be lost. Both men have noted that many of their professional skills were developed by taking apart clocks and watches, fixing old bicycles and radios, and generally making things just for the fun of it when they were young. Kids don't do that anymore. When something breaks, we replace it. Obsolescence is planned, not fixed. Electronic gadgets don't reveal their inner workings even when taken apart. As a result, many universities have had to institute what Petroski calls "remedial play courses" for engineers and scientists, in which students, for the first time in their life, take apart and reassemble a bike, a laser printer, a fishing reel, or some other common object to find out how it works. The need for such courses is a sad commentary on the failure of both our home environments and our schools to foster basic curiosity.

So play! When an appliance or machine breaks, take it apart just to see what makes it tick, even if you can't put it back together. See what else you can make with the pieces. Or, more radical still, give yourself permission once in a while to do some things that you have been "trained" not to do: fiddle with your food; stomp in the mud. You can take this advice literally or figuratively. It doesn't matter. Either way, you are bound to break normal habits of action, thought, and perception.

To see what we mean, take a look at the book *Play with Your Food,* by Joost Elffers. The clever photographs invite us to look with fresh eyes at sweet potatoes, radishes, peppers, pears, oranges, artichokes, and a host of other vegetables and fruits. What was once a squash suddenly becomes a duck, stretching its neck to the sun. What was once a bunch of leeks becomes, with the addition of bean "eyes" and food-coloring "lips," a bunch of wild-haired guys. The secret is to search for a likeness between any particular vegetable and something in the larger world of animals, insects, and imaginary beings — and then to play it out. You will certainly never look at food the same way again.

If you're the outdoor type, splash in the rain, play in the mud, indulge

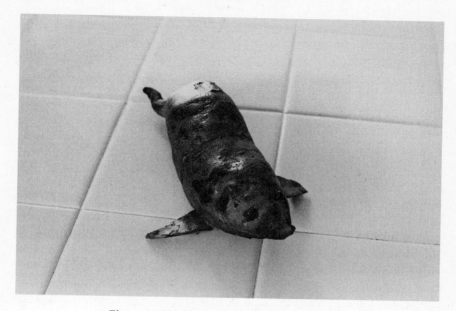

Fig. 13-10. Food play can turn a yam into a seal.

your primitive urges and senses. That's what a young dance company called Pilobolus did one muggy day in 1981 with surprising results. After working for hours at composing a new dance in a "steamy rehearsal barn," the group had gotten nowhere. Then the atmosphere suddenly changed — in more ways than one. First it rained and then the sun appeared, offering instant relief to body and mind. The dancers abruptly stopped working and started playing. They went outside, according to one of the dancers, to "slog in the mud and romp on the rooftop." And before they knew it, they were playing with movement images of sun and mud and rain and thunder. Rather than dismiss such fooling around as childish, they took what chance had offered them, and for the next fifteen hours they improvised nonstop, creating a new choreography. "Day Two," as they called it, became the company's signature dance.

Play returns us to the presymbolic drives of gut feelings, emotions, intuition, and fun from which creative insights stem, thereby making us inventors. When rule-bound work does not yield the insights or results we want to achieve, when conventional thought, behavior, and disciplinary knowledge become barriers to our goals, play provides a fun and risk-free means of seeing from a fresh perspective, learning without constraint, exploring without fear. Play transforms knowledge and builds understanding as we create our own worlds, personas, games, rules, toys, and puzzles — and through them new sciences and new arts.

APPENDIX

The Cracks Between the Keys of the Piano

George Ives recognized that there are many more notes than can actually be played on a piano. The piano's production of sound is governed by physics. If you take a vibrating string and halve its length, you double the frequency of its vibration and get the exact pitch an octave higher. Divide the string into thirds and you get a new note one fifth higher than the octave. Divide it into fifths and you get a note one third higher than the octave. The standard major triad of Western music (C, G, E) is based on these divisions. Continue to divide and subdivide the string by whole-number divisions, and you get a huge number of additional overtones. The piano, however, does not include them all. The tones that fall between B flat and A, for instance, cannot be produced by that instrument for reasons of functional necessity. Each of the standard twelve keys (C major, C minor, and so on) requires a different set of divisions of the string. While it is a simple matter to provide all of the overtones for any given key, if you want to modulate between complete keys within a single piece or play several pieces in a row written in different complete keys without retuning the instrument each time, you would require seventy-seven notes within each octave rather than the standard twelve. This would make the piano impossibly unwieldy. Obviously, only some of these overtones can be incorporated into a manageable instrument. So some overtones are left out, while others are tampered with, or "tempered," so that they can perform a reasonable, if not exact, function in several keys.

Interestingly, violinists, cellists, and other instrumentalists are trained to "temper" their strings or slides by ear. Theoretically, however, any of the intervening microtones are available to them, since the finger can be placed anywhere on the string or the slide moved to any position. Oddly, only a few modern composers such as Iannis Xenakis have taken advantage of the continuous scale of such instruments, inventing new notations in the process — and forcing players to retrain their ears and hands.

14

Transforming

IN THE DESERT OF LAETOLI, Tanzania, in 1978, Mary Leakey and her colleagues made one of the most famous discoveries in modern paleontology, uncovering an eighty-foot-long series of hominid footsteps preserved in 3.5-million-year-old volcanic ash. The discovery and interpretation of these prints, which eventually proved that our hominid ancestors walked upright, involved a complex creative process that integrated many imaginative tools. Leakey's experience shows both how and why the integrated use of many different tools for thinking is typical of creative work.

In her autobiography, *Disclosing the Past,* Leakey tells us that serendipity played a role in her team's discovery, as it does in so much of science. She assembled her team not to find hominid remains but to characterize prehistoric flora and fauna. Moreover, the three team members who made the initial discovery, of some animal footprints, were not even working. They were playing. On their way back to camp one day in 1976, Jonah Western, Kaye Behrensmayer, and Andrew Hill "for some reason . . . amused themselves by throwing lumps of dried elephant dung at each other and there was certainly plenty of it around in the flat open space where they were. Andrew fell down in the process and noted that he was lying on a hard surface which appeared to contain ancient animal footprints, including those of rhinoceros. He was right." Hill's serendipitous observation of a telltale pattern led the team to focus attention on what turned out to be some of the best-preserved and most extensive beds of animal footprints in the world.

The next year, 1977, when the team began excavating the animal tracks they discovered four unusual prints that resembled those of human feet. Leakey's experts never agreed whether these particular prints matched the

Fig. 14-1. Trail of hominid footprints at Laetoli.

pattern typical of human feet, but the possibility that hominids may have been present in Laetoli millions of years ago primed the team's expectations. These were fulfilled in 1978 when geochemist Paul I. Abell "came upon what he thought was the heel part of a hominid print; erosion had removed the front part." Once again the experts disputed the idea that a hominid had made the track, but Leakey instructed her most skilled worker, the Kenyan Ndibo Mbuika, to excavate the site further. Mbuika's meticulous work soon revealed a significant trail of very well preserved hominid footprints. Leakey and her team had hit the jackpot.

The team's work had, however, just begun. All they had were the remains of a static, abstract, two-dimensional mapping of three-dimensional bodies in movement every bit as abstruse as a painting by Jackson Pollock or the trail of a subatomic particle in a cloud chamber. What kinetic process did it represent? What had happened those 3.5 million years ago? The stride length,

Fig. 14-2. One reconstruction of the origins of the Laetoli footprints, at the American Museum of Natural History. Most scientists now believe this reconstruction to be inaccurate.

the size of the prints, and their depth seemed to show that two hominids, one small, probably a child, and one larger one, had walked through rain-spattered mud just prior to a large volcanic explosion that covered their footprints with ash. This reconstruction presented problems, though. Mbuika observed almost immediately that the footprints of the larger individual were more than twelve inches long — huge even by modern standards and almost inconceivable for primitive hominids, whose bones suggest small stature. Moreover, the larger footprints were much less well defined than the smaller footprints, an observation that could not, at first, be explained. These anomalies added up to a broken pattern that had Leakey and her colleagues stumped. They spent considerable time in 1978 consulting their own sense of the body in search of some way a normal-sized individual could create super-sized footprints. Would slipping do the trick? What about sliding one's feet as one walked? Their experimental play-acting failed to give an answer. No matter how they moved their feet, they could not form footprint patterns with the right characteristics. The tracks just didn't make sense.

The matter rested unresolved until the nature photographer and film-maker Alan Root came to the site in 1979 and had, in Leakey's words, a "brilliant piece of insight that had simply never occurred to any of us." Root remembered seeing young chimpanzees play follow the leader by stepping directly into the footprints of the chimpanzee in front. Might an analogy between chimp behavior and hominid behavior hold the answer to Leakey's mysterious footprints? It did. Modeling the same kind of follow-the-leader game resulted in just the type of supersized, poorly defined footprints that had left the team puzzled. Leakey now realized there had been three, not two, individuals walking through the mud of Laetoli those millions of years ago. She imagined two adults, perhaps a mother and a father, walking in single file, the individual in back placing his or her feet in the prints left by the individual in front and enlarging them. One of the adults may have been holding the hand of the child, who trailed somewhat to the side. Were they frightened by the rumbling volcano about to erupt? Were they seeking shelter from the rain? Did some other drive, such as hunger, motivate their movements? These things the abstract record of footprints could not reveal, though they played a part in subsequent pictorial renditions of the scene created for museum displays.

The discovery and interpretation of the Laetoli footprints illustrates one of the most important aspects of creative imagination. Leakey and her team played, observed, recognized patterns and anomalies, engaged in dimensional thinking, imagined body movements, play-acted, formed patterns, analogized, and modeled, ultimately transforming the fossil abstractions into kinesthetic, visual, and empathic images of the hominids who left their footprints at Laetoli. Even while the puzzle was being worked out, these imaginative insights were translated into photographs, paintings, models, words, and reenactments to test ideas and communicate with other people. Clearly, no single tool for thinking would have sufficed. Creative work in the real world requires the ability to define a problem using one set of tools, to investigate it using others, and to express the solution using yet a third set.

We call the serial or simultaneous use of multiple imaginative tools in such a way that one (set of) tool(s) acts upon another (set) *transforming* or *transformational thinking*. Many people may work together in different ways on a single shared problem, as in the case of the Laetoli research, or one person may feel and think her or his way through a problem with various imaginative tools. At the very least, the way in which a person thinks about things will require transformations in order to express his or her insights in communicable form. In Chapter 1 we discussed scientists Barbara McClintock, Albert Einstein, and Richard Feynman, for whom visual and kinesthetic images and empathic feelings had to be translated into words and equations; writers Isabelle Allende and Stephen Spender, for whom inspiration arrived as indefinable bodily feelings, emotions, and visual images that grew, after considerable struggle, into verbal life; and artists Pablo Picasso and Bridget Riley, for whom everything from emotions to mathematical patterns were necessarily mediated by the kinesthetic and visual demands of their media.

Take a close look at any creative endeavor and you will invariably find ideas and insights transformed through many tools for thinking and translated into one or more expressive languages. The transformational thinking displayed by Leakey and her colleagues is typical of the creative process in every field. Consider, for example, the invention by MIT professor Harold Edgerton of the strobe light for ultrafast flash photography. Edgerton wanted to take pictures of processes and events that occurred so quickly they could not be seen. Ordinary photographs captured only a blur of movement. But Edgerton realized that if he could produce an extremely bright light that flashed many times within an extremely short period of time, the visual blur of objects in motion could be broken down into discrete, observable steps. Like Marey and Muybridge before him, he wanted to extend human visualizing and observing capabilities. Right from the start, his observational problem became one of inventing the proper tool.

The solution lay in electronics. Edgerton visualized a new electronic de-

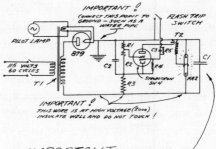

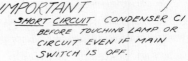

Fig. 14-3. Harold Edgerton's
abstract drawing of his Stroblite
Flash Unit, circa 1940.

Fig. 14-4. Edgerton with some of his strobe units, 1944.

vice that would perform the functions he desired and then translated his vision into an abstract diagram detailing the parts of such a device and the
connections between them. Then he transformed the diagram into a working model capable of making repeated flashes of light. This was the strobe.
Edgerton devised hundreds of versions of the strobe as he played around
with one factor after another in the electronic equipment, the setup of the
shoot, and the conditions governing the super-fast movement of a wide
range of objects. In each instance he had to imagine how all the relevant
components — film, camera, strobe, subject — would interact. Finally, after

Fig. 14-5. Edgerton and Bobby Jones set up for a stroboscopic photograph of a golf shot in the lab at MIT, 1948.

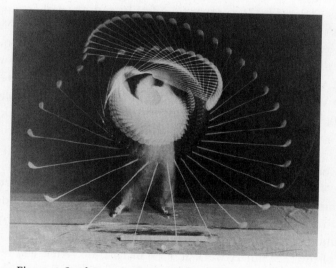

Fig. 14-6. Stroboscopic photo of Bobby Jones at MIT, 1948.

weeks of experimental search for the most aesthetically satisfying result, he would produce one of his memorable photographs.

Edgerton's process of invention cannot be distinguished from that used by artists. The collaboration between Claes Oldenburg and Coosje van Bruggen on *Torn Notebook*, a large outdoor sculpture at the University of Nebraska, provides one example. The idea for the sculpture originated in the fact that both Oldenburg, an artist, and van Bruggen, a writer, liked to jot down ideas in small spiral-bound notebooks. When they no longer needed a notebook, they would tear the pages in two, leaving the halves still joined by the twisted metal spiral. For Oldenburg and van Bruggen, the torn pages seemed to represent a visual image of the two halves of their collaboration, the metal spiral an analogy for the spiral of marriage and artistry that bound their work together. The metaphor had additional reverberations in the twisting tornados that sweep the plains of Nebraska and the whirlwinds of creative activity that integrate image, word, and process.

Beginning with drawings, they proceeded to watercolor sketches, paper and cloth models, and finally metal maquettes of their conception. After playing around with many versions of the sculpture, they turned the final maquette over to their longtime collaborator, engineer Bob Jennings. He abstracted the maquette back into drawings — this time detailed engineering and fabrication plans — then abstracted the plans into mathematical calculations of stress loads, construction details, and materials requirements. Jennings's plans were forwarded to the Tallix Foundry in upstate New York, where a team of construction experts turned the plans back into a new set of small-scale models using the same materials the final sculpture would be made of, to assure the team that each piece could be fabricated as designed and the whole assembled without unexpected problems. The plans were scaled up using a computer, and the foundry machines milled, turned, curved, soldered, and finished the pieces into a sculpture. Van Bruggen researched and oversaw the types of paint and other finishes used to color and protect the piece and to ensure its aesthetic quality.

Even with the sculpture finished, many steps remained. A soil expert had to be employed to determine the best footing for the sculpture; landscape architects had to design its setting; lighting experts were called in to create the right atmosphere at night; and a large team of construction workers carried out all of the preliminary work and the installation. What had begun as a vague idea had passed through various stages of analogizing, visualizing, modeling, playing, abstracting (in the form of plans and engineering calculations), and dimensional thinking before its final translation into a finished piece of sculpture. While neither Oldenburg nor van Bruggen could have carried out all of these steps themselves, they obviously had to understand and be able to control the process through which the transformations occurred. Their experience, like that of the Leakey team or Harold Edgerton, can be considered a model for the production of almost any kind of object, product, or idea in any field. No single imaginative skill will suffice, whether the work is scientific, technological, or artistic. In fact, Leakey's, Edgerton's, and Oldenburg/Van Bruggen's work contained elements from all three areas, a point to which we will return.

Most creative people handle complex transformational thinking with ease. This thinking tool is really no more sophisticated than any of the others we have discussed. Most of us probably engage in a little transforming every day. If you have ever used a mnemonic device to try to remember something, you've engaged in a transformation. For example, the rhyme "Thirty days hath September / April, June, and November / All the rest have thirty-one / Save February . . ." converts arithmetical information into an easily recalled verbal pattern. Similarly, in the musician's mnemonic "Every **good** **boy** **de**serves **f**udge" the first letters of each word represent the notes on the lines of the treble clef, from lowest to highest. And chemistry students employ the acronym OIL RIG to stand for "Oxidation Is Loss [of electrons]; Reduction Is Gain." Nineteenth-century French students made up a more complex rhyme to remember the numerical value of pi, 3.14159 . . . The number of letters in each word represents the value of one digit in pi — : "*Que* (3) *j* (1) '*aime* (4) à (1) *faire* (5) *apprendre* (9) *un* (2) *nombre* (6) *utile* (5) *aux* (3) *sages* (5)*!*" and so on. ("How I love to teach a number useful to the wise!") An even more sophisticated undertaking is Harold Baum's *The Biochemists' Songbook* (1982), a classic melding of rigorous biochemistry and amusing lyrics set to well-known tunes. Once you've heard it, who can forget the respiratory pathway set to "The Battle Hymn of the Republic": "Mine eyes have seen the glory of respiratory chains / In every mitochondrion, intrinsic to membranes." All of these examples are playful transformations of detailed information into known patterns that are easily remembered.

Some mnemonic devices render abstractions concrete by superimposing them on the body. Some people, for instance, use a kinesthetic mneme instead of saying the old jingle about the number of days in the months. Make both your hands into fists and place them in front of you, thumb touching thumb in such a way that the knuckles of both first fingers lie side by side. Now look at the knuckle of one of your little fingers and say "January." January, a long month, is represented by your knuckle sticking up. Now proceed to the trough between that knuckle and the knuckle of your ring finger and say "February." February is a short month, represented by the dip between your knuckles. The knuckle of your ring finger is now March, a long month; April is the next trough; and so forth. Notice that when you go from the first-finger knuckle of one hand to the first-finger knuckle of the other there is no

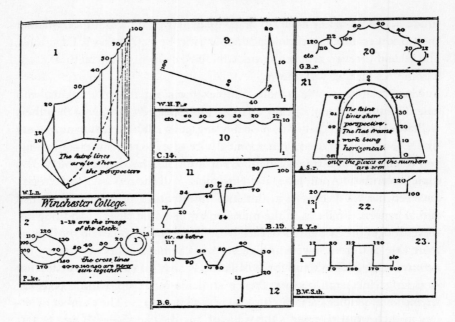

Fig. 14-7. Some of the number forms documented by Francis Galton.

trough; July and August are two long months in a row. Your body has now become the repository of the months and their relative lengths. In a similarly handy system invented by Guido d'Arezzo, an eleventh-century monk, to help members of the choir remember music, each finger joint and fingertip represented a note. Some natives of New Guinea remember numbers by imagining them not only on their fingers and toes but on other parts of their bodies, such as their elbows, shoulders, ears, eyes, nose, and so forth. Sir Francis Galton, one of the founders of modern psychology, documented in his classic *Inquiries into Human Faculty and Its Development* (1883) that such mnemonic devices are extremely common: "Persons who are imaginative almost invariably think of *numerals* in some form of visual imagery."

Sometimes people collaborate on a mnemonic transformation that integrates concepts from many disciplines. For centuries, students of music and poetry in India have memorized a nonsense word in order to learn and remember all of the basic patterns of sound rhythm. The word is *yamatarajabhanasalagam,* which when written according to its spoken rhythm of stresses looks like this: yaMATARAjaBHAnasalaGAM. As composer George Perle has explained it, "There is a lot in those ten syllables. As you pronounce the word you sweep out all possible triplets of short and long beats. The first three syllables, *ya MA TA,* have the rhythm short, long, long. The second through the fourth are *MA TA RA:* long, long, long. Then you have *TA RA ja:* long, long, short. Next there are *RA ja BHA:* long, short, long. And so on." Thus a simple word, when pronounced properly, condenses a huge amount of pattern information that can be applied to many of the arts.

Perle's friend, the mathematician Sherman Stein, took the transformation another step. He pointed out that the basic pattern in the Indian word is digital: syllables are either long (stressed) or short (unstressed). To preserve the triplet information, however, we do not need all of the different sounds that make up the word, just their rhythm. In fact, we need only two symbols, one to represent long and one to represent short beats. We can therefore abstract from the original spoken syllables and assign each short beat a value of 0 and each long beat a value of 1. Then we can rewrite the word ya°MA¹TA¹RA¹ja°BHA¹na°sa°la°GAM¹ as 0111010001. 011 now represents short, long, long; 111 is long, long, long; and so on. This sequence may now be considered to be a number in base two that can be transformed into its base-ten equivalent for ease of recall: $0111010001 = (256 + 128 + 64 + 16 + 1) = 465$. (See Appendix 1 to this chapter if you have forgotten your bases.) Or, since there are ten digits in the number, the number may be turned into a physical mneme with the thumb and little finger of the left hand bent and the three middle fingers of the right hand bent. The bent digits represent zeros; unbent, ones. All of these mnemes are logically equivalent to the original Hindu word.

Significantly, however, the digital numerical sequence presents possibilities that the original Hindu word does not. Imagine, Stein suggests, a kinetic analogy in which this string of numbers is a snake that grabs itself by the tail. Visualizing this "snake" shows that the first 01 (its "mouth") will overlap the last 01 (its tail) and a continuous circle of numbers will be formed. Although the number sequence has now lost two digits, the circle still has all

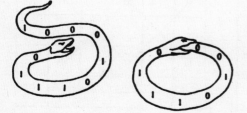

Fig. 14-8. Imagine the number pattern 0111010001 as a snake that eats its own tail. The result is a memory wheel.

of the possible combinations of three pairs of elements — whether they are musical beats, syllabic accents in words, numbers, the results of flipping three pennies, ways of grouping three people of either sex, or a great many other things. This numerical snake is therefore the most concise description of such information that is possible. Notably, it has the same pattern as entities known to mathematicians since the 1880s as "memory wheels," which can store all the possible pairs of things, triplets of things, quadruplets of things, and so on, in the most condensed forms. They can encode everything from telegraph messages to servomechanism instructions and decode everything from encryptions to the sequences of genes. The power of transformational thinking is that it can reveal meta-patterns connecting music, genes, telegraphy, poetry, and math or any other set of disciplines.

Transformational thinking has, in fact, blurred the lines between fields, including that between mathematics and the fine arts. "It must always be emphasized," artist Max Bill has written, "that rational thought is one of the chief intrinsic characteristics of man. It is by means of rational thinking that we are able to arrange the sensorial values in such a way as to produce works of art. . . . Thus, even as mathematics is . . . intrinsically a science of the relationship of object to object, group to group, and movement to movement . . . it is natural that these relationships themselves should also be captured and given form." One of the most accessible transformations Bill has made in-

Fig. 14-9. *Left:* the structural schema of Max Bill's *1–8*, 1955; *right:* notice that similar elements of the painting are always laid out symmetrically. What other symmetries can you find?

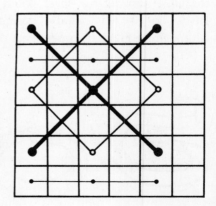

volves the arithmetic fact that $1 + 2 + 3 + 4 + 5 + 6 + 7 + 8 = 36$ and so does 6×6. He transformed this numerical pattern into a checkerboard of thirty-six squares, six on a side, and colored one square red, two dark pink, three light purplish pink, four blue, five light blue, six pale green, seven pastel green, and eight pale yellowish green. The different colors group the squares into the numbers of the original equation. Bill placed his colors with careful forethought: the four blue squares form a square; the five light blue squares form a cross; the six pale green ones form a pair of parallel lines. Every group of colors is symmetrical — a lovely piece of puzzle solving.

Sculptor Naum Gabo, who was trained as an engineer, was another important figure in the disciplinary blurring between mathematics and the arts. "I am convinced of the possibility of developing art wherein the mathematical approach is fundamental," he wrote. Among his many sculptures that have a mathematical basis is his 1937 series *Construction in Space,* based on a model of the oscillating development of a cubic ellipse. Gabo's lead has been followed by mathematician-artist Hellaman Ferguson, who interprets equations in stone and bronze; artists Brent Collins and Carlo Sequin, who work their topological intuitions in wood and metal; and mathematician Nat Friedman, who works in many media. In a series of marble prints Fried-

Fig. 14-10. *Mother and Child Relationship,* by Nathaniel A. Friedman, 1993, a print made from a broken marble block, contrasting the fractal nature of the broken edges with the geometric perfection of the cut edges.

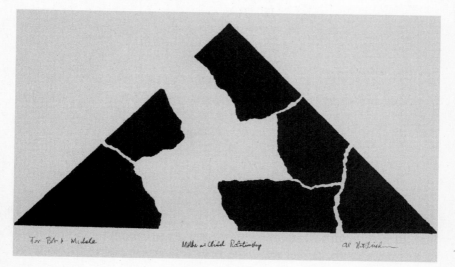

man compares the finite length of smooth edge and the infinite fractal dimensions of jagged break.

Friedman's *Mother and Child Relationship* suggested to one of us (Michèle) further verbal transformations:

> *(to enter within)*
>
> *he cracked a solid*
> *block of marble*
> *into pieces*
>
> *and loving the math*
> *of smooth plane*
> *and fractal edge*
>
> *he arranged each*
> *separate face*
> *as part of the whole*
>
> *removing the core*
>
> *(to render the way)*
>
> *he laid paper*
> *on the inked rock*
> *and ironed it*
>
> *drawing a sign*
> *from one geometry*
> *to another*
>
> *and he found unknown*
> *in the prism of stone*
> *a mother and child*
>
> *shaping infinite place*

Like the graphic visualizations of and written papers about our hominid ancestors made by the Leakey team, the analytical, visual, and verbal transformations of Friedman's work reveal complementary perspectives that are synergistic.

Such transformations are often commutative, too. That is to say, if A can be transformed into B, then B can be transformed back into A. Problems expressed as words can be converted into equations — "If John can paint a house in four days and Jim can do it in five, then how long will it take John and Jim working together?" — and equations have meanings that can be stated in words: $dx/dt = k(d^2x/dy^2)$ could be translated colorfully as "it oozes." As we explored in Chapter 12, every mathematical formula has a visual or physical counterpart. Thus Richard Feynman described "a scheme" he developed for solving mathematical problems by visual modeling: "I keep making up examples. For instance, the mathematicians would come in with a terrific theorem, and they're all excited. As they're telling me the conditions of the theorem, I construct something which fits all the conditions. You know, you have a set (one ball) — disjoint (two balls). Then the balls turn colors, grow hairs, or whatever, in my head as they put more conditions on. Finally they state the theorem, which is some dumb thing about the ball which isn't true for my hairy green ball thing, so I say 'False!'"

Milton Halem, former chief of space data and computing at NASA's Goddard Space Flight Center, took such transformations a step further, employing professional artists such as Sara Tweedie of the Corcoran School of Art to analyze the artistic means best suited to translating data from satellite measurements into maps and images that would convey the most meaning. A similar approach is used by mathematician George Francis at the National Center for Supercomputing Applications, where he directs a group of mathematicians, artists, and programmers who work together to create and study visualizations of complex equations. Indeed, such transformations have become commonplace. As Yale political science professor Edward Tufte has pointed out in a series of stunningly beautiful books, including *The Visual Display of Quantitative Information* (1983) and *Envisioning Information* (1990), data in every field are converted into graphs and visual images of one sort or another. It is impossible to open a newspaper or magazine or watch a news report without being bombarded with transformed data. Tufte's books focus on the principles by which such transformations can best be accomplished.

Nor are transformations limited to mathematics, words, and images. Feynman translated many equations into sounds. Arithmetic progressions (1, 2, 3, 4, 5 . . .) became a steadily ascending, continuous musical scale. Geometric progressions (1, 2, 4, 8, 16 . . .) became accelerating *whoops*. He hummed, tapped, and moved about, correlating ideas about the physical world with physical sensations he could perceive and manipulate.

The kinds of transformations Feynman performed to increase his personal understanding of physics have also been carried out by collaborative groups of professionals. One of the most intriguing data-sound transformations has been made by a team of biochemists, musicians, and computer programmers at Michigan State University to improve urinalysis. In the standard procedure, a machine measures the different amounts of each wavelength of light that passes through the urine. The amount of light tells how much of each type of chemical is present. But herein lay a problem. The team found that many different urine samples give visual traces so similar to one another that the human eye has difficulty distinguishing among them. To find out if the ear could do better, they sent the output of the chromatograph to a computer instead of a chart recorder. The computer implemented various rules regarding signal intensity, time, and other parameters to transform the data into a form readable by a sound synthesizer. The computer also converted the sound signals into musical notation, which could be turned into a musical score. The results were spectacular. People could hear differences between one urinalysis and another that their eyes could not see. The transformation of numerical data into information observed aurally produced a significant and useful increase in pattern discrimination.

Musical urinalysis might seem laughable except for two points: first, this type of technology allows visually impaired individuals to participate in forms of research that would otherwise be beyond their ken, and, equally important, aural observation turns out to be more acute than visual observa-

Fig. 14-11. The two chromatograms of urine *(left)* look virtually identical, but when converted into music *(right)* by a computer, their differences become immediately apparent.

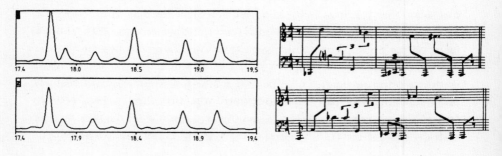

tion for a wide range of phenomena. Researchers such as Susumo Ohno at the Beckman Research Institute at the University of Illinois and Phil Ortiz at Skidmore College find that by transforming genetic sequences into music they can hear similar sequences faster than when they scan for them visually. What's more, the ears can observe complexity that the eyes cannot. Eyes can follow only a single line, one pattern at a time. When we listen to a musical ensemble, however, we hear each individual instrument even as we hear the harmony that results from their interaction. Thus Ortiz's DNA music embeds not only the gene sequence but characteristics of the resulting protein structures as well, all of which can be heard simultaneously. This multiplicity of levels of meaning is what makes the "computer between our ears" so much better than the "computer behind our eyes." In consequence, major corporations, such as Xerox and Lucent Technologies (formerly Bell Labs), and many universities are experimenting with transformations of complex databases — for instance, economic indicators — into a music that allows analysts to hear the synthetic patterns while simultaneously following individual trends. It is also worth noting that an ever-increasing number of musicians, ranging from Iannis Xenakis, who uses statistical databases, to Susan Alexjander, whose CD *Sequenzia* interprets DNA, are also exploring data-music transformations.

The point here is that different transformations of an idea or a set of data will have different characteristics and uses. The more unexpected the transformation, the greater the likelihood that a surprising insight will result. Thus people in fields as distinct as neurology and physics have found that transforming data into dance and dance notation yields simultaneously beautiful and useful results.

While graphic illustrations of dance steps have been traced back to prehistory, the invention of notations for the description of complex bodies in motion is a recent development. The three notations most commonly used today are Labanotation, invented by Rudolf Laban in 1928; Benesh Movement Notation, invented by mathematician-inventor-artist Rudolf Benesh and his ballet-dancer wife, Joan, in 1955; and Eshkol-Wachmann notation (1958). In 1979 two neurologists, Ilan Golani of the Weizmann Institute in Israel and his American colleague Philip Teitelbaum, made a major advance in the analysis and recording of movement defects associated with neurological disorders by applying Eshkol-Wachmann notation to the study of animals and human patients. Their analysis revealed what they call a "natural geometry" of the recovery of movement following neurological damage. Subsequently, physiotherapists and exercise physiologists have adapted Benesh

Movement Notation and Labanotation to understand, characterize, and communicate new developments in patient care as well.

Physicist Marvin Cohen of the University of California at Berkeley is another pioneer in the use of dance in scientific exploration. Cohen is an expert on theories of superconductivity, the physics of electrical currents moving through extremely cold metal alloys without resistance. During the late 1980s, Cohen turned to choreographer David Wood in search of insight. Using dancers to represent moving electrons, Wood and Cohen explored the various states — paired and unpaired, symmetrical and asymmetrical — that electrons may take as they move within an atom. Cohen considers the resulting dance, called "Currents," an excellent translation of mathematical theory into a kinesthetic model that is accessible to many people. But he also sees the dance as a form of physical research. "I told David Wood that if he or the dancers came up with some new ordered state or some new motions I'd appreciate hearing about them," he has said. "We're hoping that perhaps he can give us some new ideas." After all, if physicists can imagine themselves as electrons, why not learn to move like them, too? Cohen, in fact, is not the only physicist to have had this idea: a group of French physicists who were themselves dancers also produced a dance about superconductivity as part of their research around 1990. It is just as natural, it seems, to dance equations as it is to graph them, sculpt them, or write them, and it improves the physical intuition of the scientist.

Transforming concepts from one form into another can yield discoveries in any field. Many people have addressed the interconvertibility of music and art, as Paul Klee did in his music-image transformations. With the exceptions of Klee and Joseph Schillinger, most have connected music with color, as we discuss in Chapter 15 with regard to the phenomenon of synesthesia. But our brains perceive color and sound very differently. As noted above, the computer between our ears is able to keep track of individual instruments playing at the same time, so we hear the synthesis of sound as a whole. This ability to perceive parts and wholes simultaneously does not exist in most visual art, especially that based on color, because colors blend. If we juxtapose dots of yellow and blue in a painting, the observer sees green, even if the colors are put down as distinct points or pixels. This is the basis of color printing, color television, and pointillist art, such as that of Seurat. To prevent such mixing, colors must be presented in large, perceptually distinct areas, but then our focus on the distinct parts prevents us from seeing the whole. Klee wanted to create a visual form in which the viewer perceives parts and wholes simultaneously, as the listener does in music.

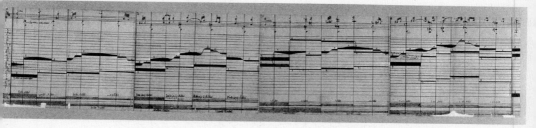

Fig. 14-12. Paul Klee transformed some of Bach's music into a novel visual form for his Bauhaus lectures.

Klee recorded his experiments in notebooks for lectures to students at the Bauhaus. He began with a simple graphic representation of musical notes, showing the duration and intensity of the tones. These ideas were then abstracted to yield images of notes as lines of tone, still in an implied (but absent) clef, that could be sung or played but that are clearly meant to stand as images in their own right. In a final step, Klee abstracted the line-notes into pure lines devoid of any reference to musical notation at all. By employing lines rather than colors, Klee found that he was able to "mix" the visual elements of his compositions to create complex patterns in a manner strictly analogous to that used to create polyphonic music. In *Five-Part Polyphony*, for example, he drew five types of lines, each at a different angle, representing the five "voices" (see Fig. 14-14). These then intersect to form patterns without losing their individual character. We can see the whole pattern at the same time that we can see the constituents of each part. A particularly strik-

Fig. 14-13. A more abstract transformation of music by Klee.

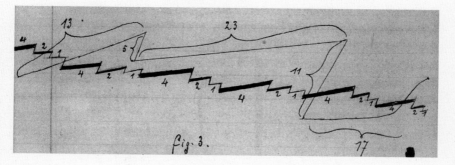

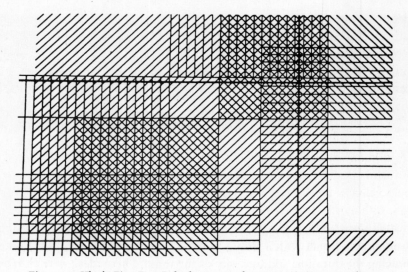

Fig. 14-14. Klee's *Five-Part Polyphony* transforms music into pure line.

ing aspect of Klee's solution to the image-music transformation is that the image acquires a new property not found in music. Music can be heard only unidirectionally through time, but visual polyphony can be scanned in any direction or combination of directions and at any rate, thereby creating relationships that do not exist in music.

Because transformations of emotions, ideas, and data are not absolutely equivalent, the transformational process can yield unexpected discoveries like Klee's. In consequence, transformational thinking is a conscious strategy used by many creative individuals. Physicist/novelist Alan Lightman noted in a review of Richard Feynman's *Character of Physical Law* that the author placed "great value on seeking different formulations of the same physical law, even if they are exactly the equivalent mathematically, because different versions bring to mind different mental pictures and thus help in making discoveries. [As Feynman said,] 'Psychologically they are different because they are completely unequivalent when you are trying to guess new laws.'" Robert Burns Woodward, a Nobel Prize–winner in chemistry, made a similar point in one of his notebooks: "Write formula in as many ways as possible. Each way may suggest different possibilities." Linus Pauling advocated the same technique in a lecture called "The Genesis of Ideas." Most people ask, he said, "What conclusion . . . are we forced to accept by these results of experiment and observation?" Instead, Pauling said he asked himself, "What ideas" — note the plural — "about this question, as general and aesthetically satisfying as possible, can we have that are not eliminated by these results of experiment and observation?" The best scientists do not look for *the* answer but, like Klee, look for multiple *answers*. (We provide a simple mathematical example of how multiple answers can be generated in Appendix 2 to this chapter.)

Transformational thinking produces other benefits, too. A century of educational research has demonstrated that skills and concepts learned in a multimodal way are more likely to be used broadly than are ideas learned in problem-specific contexts. Thus, transformational thinking is more likely to yield valuable insights than is domain-specific thinking. And since people have different talents and abilities, a variety of transformations on a single idea will create meaningful connections to more people than will a single formulation. Robert W. Wood, although a mathematically trained physicist, preferred to work with pictures, which, his biographer notes, "he felt he (and many others) could understand better than mathematical equations." Similarly, James Clerk Maxwell, the playful Scot who revolutionized nineteenth-century physics with his laws of electromagnetism, recommended that "for the sake of persons of different types, scientific truth should be presented in different forms and should be regarded as equally scientific, whether it appears in the robust form and vivid coloring of a physical illustration, or in the . . . paleness of a symbolic expression."

We would do well to take the words and actions of these eminent thinkers seriously in our own educational endeavors. Too often today we advocate one method, one approach, and expect only one answer to questions in every field. In reality, the first method and the first answer are only the beginning of understanding, not its end. This was a lesson no one taught our friend John (Chapter 1), for whom a torque equation remained a torque equation and a door just a door. It is a lesson the Gymnasium never taught Einstein's son Hans, for whom physics and sailing remained separate experiences. It is a lesson Virginia Woolf's father, Leslie Stephen, never learned about emotions, experiences, and words. We cannot attain true understanding except through transformational thinking that links as many ways of knowing to as many forms of communication as possible.

Because transforming involves any combination of imaginative tools and disciplinary expressions, any exercise that fosters their interaction can be beneficial. One relevant program is Odyssey of the Mind, an international competition that challenges students to solve problems and to express their solutions in as many ways as possible — for example, to portray through a musical play the process by which they design an award-winning model bridge or to present through artwork the solution to a mechanics problem. Another educational program with transformational merit is River of Words, a yearly poetry and art contest developed by Robert Hass, former poet laureate of the United States, and a number of environmental and other groups in an effort to foster an understanding of nature. Students from kindergarten to twelfth grade submit writing and artwork on the theme of their geographical watershed. The term "watershed" refers to the area drained by a river, but it can also mean the dividing line between phases of a process. Thus River of Words asks students to explore not only the nature of their environment but also the watershed between scientific and technological knowledge of that environment and direct, experiential understanding by focusing on the intersections in personal, literary, artistic, economic, or social terms.

The regular curricula of public schools can include many transforming activities. Theater or video productions require many imaginative tools and many transformations: a series of words on paper must be interpreted emotionally, kinesthetically, empathically; costumes must be visualized, designed, and sewn; characters must be placed in an abstract, dimensionally conceived setting, a working model of a real or imagined world; light and sound effects must be observed naturally, imagined dramatically, and manipulated technologically to enhance the stage experience; and all of this — people, props, sets, lighting, sound, and recording equipment — must be integrated in a functional, aesthetic manner. To discover all that in a script and make it work is a magical transformation indeed. At the other end of the curricular spectrum, computer programming provides another excellent way to develop transforming skills. Whether a programmer is developing a new computer game, generating pictures or sounds, or recording and calculating the results of a science project, the process is one of transformation into and out of an abstract language.

Many types of building projects can be designed to emphasize transformational thinking. At the Israel Academy for Arts and Sciences in Jerusalem, students design, construct, and fly kites. They learn the aerodynamic theory behind kite flying as well as the basic engineering requirements. The actual design of a kite, however, opens up a whole range of collaborative and artistic possibilities. Learning to imagine an idea, sketch the design, translate the design into a series of parts to be assembled, master the proprioceptive skills and feelings associated with flying the kite, and then take that knowledge back to the mental "drawing board" — all of this is practice in the kind of serial tool use that any project requires. Then there are specific challenges. What is the biggest kite you can design? What is the smallest that will still fly? How much weight can you lift? Can you design a flying-saucer kite or one based on a tetrahedral structure, as Alexander Graham Bell did? How about a "Jacob's ladder"? Tom van Sant invented a series of kites attached so that each multiplies the lift of the others, creating a "stairway" of kites that theoretically could ascend miles into the sky. Kite building and flying touch upon and transform many areas of knowledge that students in this day and age must master.

Although many transformational exercises are naturally collaborative, some can be quite personal, relying upon paying attention to one's synthetic experience of the world. For example, California artist Ruth Armer painted very realistic works directly from nature until an accident kept her confined to her house. Listening to music to pass the time, she suddenly realized that the sounds suggested visual images, and she began to paint what she heard. She transformed Wagner, Mozart, and Schoenberg "in my own medium of line and color. Later, to my surprise, a musician actually named the composers whose work had suggested the paintings." The same process fascinated Georgia O'Keeffe, who translated music "into something for the eye" in a series of paintings such as *Music, Pink and Blue I* in 1919. A 1998 exhibit at the Smithsonian Institution called *Seeing Jazz* provides evidence of similar experiments by many other artists. Their lead can be followed with simple transforming exercises in school and at home that specifically address these questions: What do I see when I hear things? What do I hear when I see things? What does op art sound like? What would cubist or pointillist music be? The very young can try Morton Subotnik's CD-ROM *Making Music,* which allows children to "paint" or "draw" images like those designed by Klee, which are then transformed into music by the computer.

Don't stop with the visual and aural senses. We remember with great fondness "painting" with spices when we were young. Each area of the paper was carefully prepared with glue and then a spice was dusted or pressed onto it. Since different spices have different colors and textures, the visual palette they offer is large, but the greatest pleasure is olfactory. Each spice painting is an experiment in fragrance. Not only can one recreate the artistic style typical of a particular culture, one can, by choosing to use its spices, recreate simultaneously a sense of its culinary traditions. Or try making collages with dried plants and flowers while learning to identify them, their habitats, their smells, their textures, and their aesthetic possibilities.

And finally, think about how to transform ideas from one language of communication into another, such as words into images. Concrete poetry, for example, uses words — or musical notes — arranged on the page to make a visual image.

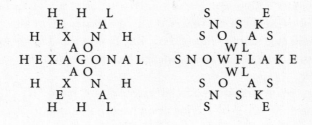

```
        H   H   L                    S           E
          E     A                    N   S   K
      H   X   N   H                  S  O     A  S
          A O                             W L
      H E X A G O N A L          S N O W F L A K E
          A O                             W L
      H   X   N   H                  S  O     A  S
          E     A                    N   S   K
        H   H   L                    S           E
```

Another challenging transformational game that was popular in the 1920s (and seems to have been forgotten) was called nomagrams. We have reinvented the game as "pictonyms." Both words mean word images. The object in devising a pictonym is to use the letters of a word to make an image of the thing symbolized. The limits imposed by the number of letters and their shapes create interesting design problems that alter your perception — and communication — of words.

Finally, rebuses, representations of words by pictures, sounds, or symbols, are perhaps the most developed type of puzzle that builds word-number-image transforming skills. A medieval knight named Cockcroft might, for example, have used a crowing rooster for his heraldic coats of arms. We have neighbors who have put a capital letter D followed by a red heart on their

Fig. 14-15. Pictonyms. Can you see how the letters of each word (love, pen, gorilla) form its image?

Fig. 14-16. Puzzles from one of Sam Loyd's classic puzzle books. (Answers: bear and dog.)

mailbox to signify their name: D'Valentine. Playing with rebuses can be as simple as decoding I8AP and O!G!ICAB! and deciphering vanity license plates on cars. Or it can be as challenging as figuring out the classic set of Sam Loyd's puzzles in Figure 14-16.

The real trick, of course, is to perceive in all this fun an analogy to imaginative thinking itself. When we become aware of the transformations our ideas undergo, we are well on the road to an awareness of creative imagining as a process we can play with and control.

APPENDIX 1

Number Bases

Most arithmetic is done in base ten, meaning that we have ten digits, 0 through 9, with which we count. Numbers are written in columns: the ones column, tens column, hundreds column, and so on. The values in each column are ten times larger than the values in the column immediately to the right. Therefore the number 111 in base ten is made up of a single one, one ten, and one hundred. Arithmetic can, however, be done in any base. In base two, which is used by most computers, there are only two digits, 0 and 1. Numbers are written the same way as in base ten, but the columns have different values, each increasing by a factor of two. The first column is still ones, but since there are only two digits, 0 and 1, the only possible values are zero and one. The second column is the twos. The third column is two squared, or the fours. The fourth column is two cubed, or the eights. Thus, 111 in base two is made up of a single one, one two, and one four, and equals seven in base ten. Any number in any base can be converted into a number in another base. As the memory wheel example earlier demonstrates, sometimes one base is more useful for a particular application than another. Transforming between bases therefore can promote insight.

APPENDIX 2

Multiple Transformations of a Single Problem

Mathematicians Philip Davis and Reuben Hersh provide a concrete example of multiple transformations and their importance in their 1981 book, *The Mathematical Experience.* We have modified and simplified the problem here.

Suppose you are given the following verbal directions: Enter a house from the outside (O) by way of the door, A. Door A leads to two halls, B and C. Both B and C meet at another doorway, D, which in turn provides entrance to two more halls, E and F. Halls E and F meet at doorway G, which leads to the innermost room, I. To begin with, what does the inside of the house look like, and, once you are inside, what is the quickest way to reach the innermost room, I?

If one converts the verbal description into a visual image, it turns out to be a simple maze (Fig. 14-17a). This particular maze is simple enough that you can see immediately that you will reach the innermost room just as fast if you turn left on entering as if you turn right. This would not be true for more complex mazes, for which one might have to search visually, by trial and error, for an optimal solution. When many possibilities exist, it is often convenient to use a computer to search through them. But computers can't handle visual mazes or their verbal descriptions. Another transformation is

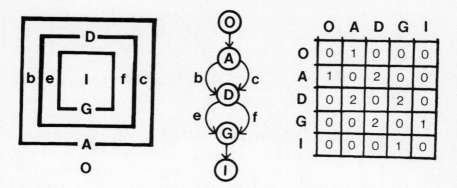

Fig. 14-17. Three equivalent representations of the maze described in the text. *Left to right: a,* a diagram; *b,* a directed graph; and *c,* a Poincaré table or matrix.

needed. In this case, each doorway can be considered a point at which a decision must be made, and each hallway a line linking one decision point to another. You can therefore redraw the maze as what is known as a directed graph (Fig. 14-17b). Directed graphs are logically and visually related to the flow charts used to design computer programs. In consequence, such "decision-tree" graphs are often used in critical-path methods of industrial and military modeling. Alternatively, another type of mathematics, called matrix algebra, can be used to describe a series of choices. By creating what is known as a Poincaré table, a matrix of the number of choices that are possible at each point in the graph can be generated (Fig. 14-17c). Such tables can be used to determine the number of possible paths that must be searched to find the fastest one. Each representation — verbal, visual, graphic, and matrix — is logically equivalent, but each transformation makes possible a way of solving the problem that is amenable to different tools and different minds.

15

Synthesizing

THE INEVITABLE RESULT of transformational thinking is synthetic understanding, in which sensory impressions, feelings, knowledge, and memories come together in a multimodal, unified way. Vladimir Nabokov wrote lovingly about such interactions in his extraordinary memoir, *Speak, Memory* (1947). "I may be inordinately fond of my earliest impressions, but then I have reason to be grateful to them. They led the way to a veritable Eden of visual and tactile sensations," he wrote. By way of example, he recounted what he felt when, as a young boy, he ran into the village schoolmaster in a wooded lane. Exchanging pleasantries, Nabokov noticed "simultaneously and with equal clarity" the flowers the man held, his tie, his sweaty face, the call of a bird, a butterfly fluttering in the road, a mental image of pictures hanging in the village school, the recollection of a lost pedometer, the taste of the grass stalk he himself was chewing. "And all the while," he concluded, "I was richly, serenely aware of my own manifold awareness."

Nabokov also described his manifold awareness as a "cosmic synchronization." When his senses and his sensibility suddenly intermeshed, he was flooded with a feeling of communion between self and universe. At such moments, he believed, "the scientist sees everything that happens in one point of space, the poet feels everything that happens in one point of time." All sensations, all perceptions became all knowing, and the synthesis of sensing, feeling, and knowing became the wellspring of his imaginative achievements. As someone with formal training in science, art, and poetry, Nabokov could not do without "the capacity of thinking of several things at a time." His memories and thoughts were always multisensory, emotional, and intellectual, and this synthetic approach to experience was also the style in which he wrote.

Scientists also experience the world in this synthetic sensual-intellectual way. Sir James Lighthill provides a wonderful example. As an applied mathematician and provost of University College, London, he has, by his own count, made forays into some sixty disciplines, ranging from physics and engineering (his major areas) to history, psychology, and many languages. He confesses, however, to having a special fondness for fluids. "I have a general pleasurable feel about fluids and, of course, I'm very interested in flight . . . and my hobby is swimming; I have a great deal of interest in the ocean — ocean waves, ocean currents, ocean tides — and I so enjoy observing all when I swim. . . . I do a three mile swim every weekend to keep fit." He also takes "adventure swims," extremely long outings on the open sea in rough weather, around and between islands. These outings are motivated not only by his desire to experience nature directly and to commune with seals and fish along the way but to prove to himself that he understands the math and physics of fluids. When he modeled aerodynamic conditions for pilots as a young man, it occurred to him that fliers were "stak[ing] their lives on the correctness of the science." Like Einstein, who considered sailing a form of applied physics, Lighthill realized that swimming could also be a test of his understanding of aerodynamics and fluid dynamics. He could share the pilots' risk, experimenting, as it were, on himself. "I've done a lot of work on ocean waves and tides and currents, and I feel I understand them well enough to be quite prepared to swim in them, because with my theoretical knowledge, supplemented by an immense amount of experience in swimming in these conditions, I can swim safely and have an exciting adventure in the process. . . . [I] actually use [my] knowledge of waves and tides in order to do it. . . . I constantly [have] to sort of add up vectorially my swimming velocity and the current velocity, and the wave drift due to these very powerful waves." For Lighthill, the equations he writes, the fluids they model, and the physical observations and sensual experience of the ocean that he shares with other animals all coalesce into one of Nabokov's "cosmic synchronizations."

The synthetic thinking that Nabokov and Lighthill describe clearly involves a transcendence of the normal boundaries of experience — we feel what we know and know what we feel. This kind of understanding depends upon an integrated use of thinking tools such that, first, we synthesize sensory impressions and feelings and, second, we fuse our sensory synthesis with the abstract knowledge that exists in our memories as patterns, models, analogies, and other higher-order mental constructs. Many gifted individuals thus work toward synthetic understanding by purposefully cultivating a multiple-sensing of the world.

Some, like Lighthill, actively immerse themselves in experience, learning to connect its many aspects with information acquired through education. Others, such as Nabokov, seem born with this proclivity for multiple-sensing or learn it very young. Nabokov's encounter with his teacher in the woods evoked a plethora of real and imagined sensations, and in his autobiography he deliberately recalled each perception to express the sensory fusion of the scene. We say deliberately, for writing is always deliberate, but in Nabokov's case one sense often provoked another willy-nilly; he frequently *saw* sounds at the same time that he heard them. When saying or visualizing the letters of the alphabet, he experienced the sensation of color. "The long *a* of the English alphabet . . . has for me the tint of weathered wood, but a French *a* evokes polished ebony. . . . The yellows comprise various *e*'s and *i*'s, creamy *d*, bright-golden *y*, and *u*, whose alphabetical value I can express only by 'brassy with an olive sheen.' "

In his synthetic perception of letters and colors, Nabokov may have been a rare bird, but he was not unique. Nabokov's mother saw colors, too, when she spoke the alphabet, as did Nabokov's wife and their son. So, for that matter, did the poet Arthur Rimbaud, who described his color-letter associations in a poem called "Vowels": "Black A, white E, red I, green U, blue O — vowels / I'll tell, some day, your secret origins." Other creative people also experience uncontrolled intersections of senses. Richard Feynman reported seeing the letters used as mathematical symbols in various colors: "When I see equations," he once said, "I see the letters in colors — I don't know why. As I'm talking, I see vague pictures of Bessel functions from Jahnke and Emde's book, with light-tan *j*'s, slightly violet-bluish *n*'s, and dark brown *x*'s flying around. And I wonder what the hell it must look like to the students." François Jacob, winner of a Nobel Prize in molecular biology, experiences an elaborate sight-sound-motor response to whole words. "There is an abyss between a *porc* (pig) and a *port* (port)," he has written. "*Porc* is extended by the c which bends it into round shapes; *port* is tightened by the t which stands erect like a crane on a dock. . . . If someone says *perroquet* [parrot], if I think *perroquet,* I immediately see the letters parade by: the p pops, the r's roll, the q clicks. Only later does the parrot itself come to mind."

In susceptible individuals, sights, sounds, and all sorts of other sensations get mixed up. For Wassily Kandinsky, colors evoked sounds, kinesthetic feelings, and many empathic emotions:

When I was thirteen or fourteen, I bought a paintbox with oil paints from money slowly saved up. The feeling I had at the time — or better: the experience of the color coming out of the tube — is with me to this day. A pressure of the fingers and jubilant, joyous, thoughtful, dreamy, self-absorbed, . . . came one after another these unique beings we call colors — each alive in and for itself. . . . It sometimes seemed to me that the brush, which with unyielding will tore pieces from this living color creation, evoked a musical sound in this tearing process. Sometimes I heard the hissing of the colors as they were blending.

Elsewhere he described hearing specific types of music associated with different colors: azure — flute, blue — cello, black — bass.

The German artist Ernst Barlach experienced a similar range of intersecting sensations: "I paint as I walk along the street; I taste, see, and feel color." Georgia O'Keeffe also had a taste and feel for color. In her autobiography she recalled that as a little girl, "I remember arriving at the road [leading to our house] with great pleasure. The color of the dust was bright in the sunlight. It looked so soft I wanted to get down into it quickly. It was warm, full of smooth little ridges made by buggy wheels. I was sitting in it, enjoying it very much — probably eating it . . . the same feeling I have had later when I've wanted to eat a fine pile of paint just squeezed out of the tube." A violinist, O'Keeffe also heard music in what she saw, writing to one friend, "I imagine I could tell about the sky tonight if I could only get the noises I want to out of [my violin]. . . . I'm going to try to tell you — about tonight — another way — I'm going to try to tell you about the music of it — with charcoal — a miserable medium — for things that seem alive — and sing." Interestingly, May Sarton found the "key" to each novel and poem she wrote in a piece of music, and playwright Harold Pinter says, "I *feel* a sense of music continually in writing." Mathematician Rolf Nevanlinna has written, "Music has been a constant companion throughout my life. In a mysterious way, which I find hard to analyse, it has been a continual accompaniment to my research." Philip Davis and Reuben Hersh even report hearing "musical themes" attached to particular equations.

More commonly, music is linked to and stimulates color. Artist David Hockney perceives color when he hears music, which is useful when he designs sets for musical productions. "In Ravel," he has said, "certain passages seem to me all blue and green." Hockney sees music by Stravinsky, on the other hand, as transparent color. "It's the blueness and this sense of transparency that made me think of the very refined, beautiful china of the 17th century." Franz Liszt also heard in color. He was known to tell his orchestra, "Please, gentlemen, a little bluer if you please. This key demands it." Composer Aleksandr Scriabin expressed his sound-color evocations in his music, as did Olivier Messiaen. When Messiaen heard or read music of any kind, he "saw" with an interior eye "the corresponding colors that turn, move and mix like the sounds turn, move and mix, and simultaneously with them." So vivid were these colors, and so consistent in their evocations, that he developed as part of his own musical language a precise correspondence between the harmonic resonances he heard and their associated hues.

In addition to sight- or sound-triggered associations, perceptual fusions may also originate in other sensations such as touch or taste. Artist Carol J. Steen has said that "when touched in specific ways, I see colors. I always have. Often, the colors are seen bright and luminous: azures, greens, and blues against a black background as dark and rich as silk velvet." Recently Steen exhibited paintings in a show entitled *Seen Shapes,* based upon her visual response to acupuncture, which causes "colors and shapes to appear and float and move around." In his book *The Man Who Tasted Shapes* (1993), Richard Cytowic describes a friend who tasted a spoonful of sauce from the meat dish he had prepared and cried out in dismay, "The chicken has no points!" Taste, for this man, was invariably accompanied by tactile sensations somewhere on his body or face, most often sweeping down his arms into a "space" where his hands could sense their weight, texture, temperature, and shape. "How can I explain? . . . Flavors have shape. I wanted the taste of this chicken to be a pointed shape, but it came out all round. . . . Well, I mean it's nearly spherical. I can't serve it if it doesn't have points." Intrigued, Cytowic documented and studied many other unusual sensory interfusions as well: a young boy for whom the sounds of words provoked different body postures and movements; a person in whom taste produced color; one for whom sight produced smell; and so on.

All of these varied and idiosyncratic manifestations of interfused sensations are forms of *synesthesia,* from the Greek root words *syn* (union, together) and *aisthesis* (sensation), a "feeling-together" or union of the senses. The kind of conscious sensory fusion and the intensity with which it occurs clearly differ from individual to individual. People who cannot control the nature or degree of sensory fusion are rare. Cytowic and other neurologists consider such involuntary, invariable fusions to be a neurological condition called true synesthesia, which appears to be inherited and seems to affect fewer than one in one hundred thousand people. Associational or learned synesthesia, in which people are consciously sensitized to the simultaneity of sense impressions, their harmony, and ultimately their fusion, is far more common.

One might consider Marcel Proust's famous description of the sudden, intense memories that accompanied the first bite of a madeleine dipped in tea as an archetype of associational synesthesia. For the protagonist in *Remembrance of Things Past,* the smell and taste of the tea-soaked cake brought back in vivid sensory detail every aspect of an experience and a time long forgotten. For Nabokov, a sure memory trigger was afternoon tea with chocolate. He could recall the long table on which it was laid one day in his childhood: "And then, suddenly, just when the colors and outlines settle . . . some knob is touched and a torrent of sounds comes to life." For Virginia Woolf an early memory of a beautiful day "still makes me feel warm as if everything were ripe; humming, sunny; smelling so many smells at once; and all making a whole that even now makes me stop — a complete rapture of pleasure that I stopped, smelt, looked." Everyone has similar memories of specific sounds, smells, tastes, or actions that trigger particularly pleasant or unpleasant synesthetic experiences. This is natural because, as we have discussed in previous chapters, we store memories and ideas as kinesthetic, visual, auditory, and other sensory forms or patterns. When we remember or think about them, they return in the multimodal form in which we experienced them.

Associational synesthesia occurs in about half of all young children and from 5 to 15 percent of the adult population. The huge difference between the number of synesthetic children and adults clearly suggests that the typical educational focus on unisensory experiences and expression stifles an early and natural association of perceptions. "Synesthetic perception is the rule," the French philosopher Maurice Merleau-Ponty has written, ruing the fact that "we unlearn how to see, hear, and generally speaking, feel." Psychologist Lawrence Marks and his colleagues are more positive, suggesting that because so many children have synesthetic experiences, "the potential to experience synesthetically may lie latent within everyone." Neurobiologist Cytowic agrees: "I believe that synesthesia is actually a normal brain function in every one of us, but that its workings reach conscious awareness in only a handful. . . . We know more than we think we know."

If thinking *is* naturally synesthetic, it should be possible to maintain and develop associational synesthesia with practice. The arts and rituals of non-Western cultures suggest that it is. Philosopher Steve Odin points to Japan, where artists and philosophers have long considered synesthesia to be the highest form of aesthetic experience and where it is explicitly cultivated. Traditional rituals such as the *chanoyu,* or tea ceremony, combine culinary art with the arts of pottery, interior design, landscaping, and gesture choreography. The ceremony purposefully stimulates taste, touch, smell, sight, hearing, and proprioception in such a way that, in Odin's words, "the boundaries of the senses actually merge, and the multivariate sense qualities — colors, sounds, flavors, scents, tactile and thermal sensations — all seem to melt into a continuum of feeling." The tea hut is designed to suggest a natural setting, and the landscaping is an abstraction of nature designed to enhance contemplation by eliminating clues to scale. The "tea kettle sings well, for pieces of iron are so arranged in the bottom as to produce a peculiar melody in which one may hear the echoes of a cataract muffled by clouds, of a distant sea breaking among the rocks, a rainstorm sweeping through a bamboo forest, or of the soughing of the pines on some faraway hill." The green tea represents the living things of nature, and drinking it infuses the celebrant with the aroma, taste, color, and feel of this nature. Every sensation is orchestrated to produce a oneness. "True practice of Tea," according to one Japanese tea master, "brings all senses to function simultaneously and in accord."

Anthropologist Margaret Mead made the same point about the synesthetic nature of the arts of cultures present and past. Rituals in Indonesia or Africa appeal "to all of the senses, just as also a medieval high mass involved all the senses, through the eye and ear to the smell of incense, the kinaestheticism of genuflection and kneeling or swaying to the passing procession, to the cool touch of holy water on the forehead. For Art to be Reality, the whole sensuous being must be caught up in the experience." Mead contrasted such rituals and ceremonies with the unimodal arts that dominate the Western world today.

Mead underestimated the synesthetic basis of modern art, however. In the West the social cultivation of the synesthetic experience is simply less explicit, requiring a greater effort of imagination, but it is no less important than in other places or times. Stravinsky believed that the physical sensations of making music are part and parcel of the experience of listening to it. He praised Bach's works because "you can smell the resin in his violin parts, taste the reeds in the oboes." And Merleau-Ponty has written, "Cezanne declared that a picture contains within itself even the smell of a landscape," meaning "that one could see the velvetiness, the hardness, the softness, and even the odor of objects," as well as their shape or color. "My perception," Merleau-Ponty explains, must be "therefore not a sum of visual, tactile, and audible givens: I perceive in a total way with my whole being which speaks to all my senses at once."

To achieve such sensual syntheses, many artists have purposefully combined expressive forms. Poet-artist E. E. Cummings made copious notes on analogies between the arts, translating many "an image of one of the senses in terms of another of the senses," as he did in the last lines of *somewhere i have never travelled:* "the voice of your eyes is deeper than all roses / nobody, not even the rain, has such small hands." Photographer Ansel Adams and writer Nancy Newhall mixed images and words to create *This Is the American Earth,* a 1955 exhibit and book assembled for the Sierra Club. In that project, "photographs and text maintain a synergistic relationship; the pictures do not illustrate the text," wrote Adams in his autobiography, "nor does the text describe the pictures. I prefer the term 'synaesthetic,' as two creative elements join to produce a third form of communication." Martha Graham used Calder mobiles for her 1935 dance "Horizons" for a similar reason: "The dances do not interpret the 'mobiles' nor do the 'mobiles' intepret the dances," she explained. "They are employed to enlarge the sense of horizon . . . a new conscious use of space."

In addition, the common synesthetic association of music and color has led to formal attempts at expressive fusion. During the seventeenth century Matteo Zaccolini created a type of color music to be used medically to help people heal more quickly. During the 1890s, A. Wallace Remington invented a keyboard instrument that projected colors on a screen in time to the music it played. Scriabin attempted to communicate his synesthetic experience in his 1922 work *Prometheus, the Poem of Fire,* which was scored for orchestra, choir, and an organ that controlled a panoply of colored lights. And around 1925, Laszló Moholy-Nagy invented a mechanical stage designed to combine not just color and sound but actors, movement, and even smell for his *Score for a Mechanical Eccentric.* Such multi-modal compositions are the direct predecessors of high-art video productions such as the 1983 Philip Glass–Godfrey Reggio collaboration *Koyaanisqatsi* or the 1998 documentary series *Inspired by Bach,* in which Yo-Yo Ma reinterpreted the Bach cello suites by interacting with other arts, including the dancing of choreographer Mark Morris, the ice skating of Jayne Torvill and Christopher Dean, and the Kabuki artistry of Tamasaburo Bando.

Perhaps the most explicit innovator in synthetic art was the pioneering film director Sergey Eisenstein. He intensively studied traditional Japanese aesthetic theory, particularly Kabuki theater, for inspiration. As he said in an essay on *Chushingura,* one of the most famous Kabuki dramas, "In experiencing Kabuki, one involuntarily recalls an American novel about a man in whom are transposed the hearing and seeing nerves, so that he perceives light vibrations as sounds, and tremors of the air as colors: he hears *light* and *sees* sound. This is also what happens in Kabuki. . . . Sound-movement-space-voice here do not accompany each other, but function as elements of equal significance . . . a monism of ensemble." Eisenstein's description applies equally to great theater or great motion pictures from any culture. Only when an experience is synesthetic do we really lose ourselves and become one with it, a fact that explains not only the enduring value of theater, opera, and art film today but the worldwide popularity of rock concerts, MTV, and commercial movies.

But there is so much more to synthesizing than just a sensual or aesthetic component. Both Nabokov and Lighthill suggest that synesthesia is the key not only to experiencing but to *understanding* things at a much deeper level than is possible using single modes of perception. In using the word "understanding," we are employing Aldous Huxley's definition. To know, he wrote, is passive; to understand is to be able to act on one's knowledge. Our friend John and Einstein's son Hans knew physics but did not understand it. Leslie Stephens knew literature but he did not understand it. One must actively integrate sensual experience with what one knows intellectually to achieve understanding.

Solo percussionist Evelyn Glennie makes this point in no uncertain terms. Glennie is clearly synesthetic, describing sounds in terms of proprioceptive and tactile sensation. "You're dealing with sounds that can be high or tingly," she says. "You're dealing with sounds that can be hard and sharp and short. You can be dealing with sounds that can be low and bold and fat or sounds that are so mellow it's like sitting on a cushion." She even describes acoustic characteristics of a music hall "in terms of how thick the air feels." For Glennie, synesthesia is not an aesthetic frill, it is the way in which she — literally — comprehends her world. Though she became profoundly, though not totally, deaf as a young girl, she learned to understand music and to hear with her other senses. As she and her husband, Greg Malcangi, have written, "Even someone who is totally deaf can still hear/feel sounds." In Glennie's case, she has become highly sensitive to the proprioceptive effects of sound: "The low sounds she feels mainly in her legs and feet and high sounds might be particular places on her face, neck and chest." If you have been to a rock concert or have a subwoofer on your stereo system, you have experienced these feelings. For her part, Glennie admits no difference between feeling sound and hearing sound, nor does she differentiate between the visual observation of lips moving and the spoken words she hears. Indeed, she insists that "hear" *is* the correct word: "I see something, I hear it. If you dropped your pencil or whatever on the floor, I'm assuming that's making a noise; therefore I'm using my imagination; therefore I hear it. And that's basically how my sound world is made up. It's entirely through my imagination; entirely through touch, entirely through feel, and what I see. It's all using every sense you have." The percussionist actively creates her perceptual world using her mind.

Glennie's melding of sense and thought is at least as common among creative people as associative synesthesia. Recall from our chapter on imaging that biologist Geerat Vermeij says that he sees with his hearing, smell, touch, and sense of movement. Similarly, Matthew Botvinick's psychological experiments on tactile ventriloquism (see Chapter 9) show that a person with an artificial limb feels it when he or she sees it touched. Helen Keller, too, argued that she heard and saw primarily with her senses of touch and smell. In one poem she wrote, "My hands evoke sight and sound out of feeling, / Intershifting the senses endlessly; / Linking motion with sight, odor with sound." Moreover, Keller stood her ground against those who disbelieved her. "If the mental consciousness of the deaf-blind person were absolutely dissimilar to that of his fellows," she wrote, "he would have no means of imagining what they think . . . [but the mind supplies] some sort of equivalent for missing physical sensations. It must perceive a likeness between things outward and things inward, a correspondence between the seen and the unseen."

What Keller, Glennie, Vermeij, and amputees who master the "feel" of their prostheses are telling us is that thinking — *all thinking* — involves, or at least *should* involve, a synergistic interaction between our sensations and abstract knowledge. Glennie is explicit on this point: "I think people are still separating all our senses, which is wrong," she says, frustration palpable in her voice. "It's wrong. I mean, all our senses — of course we have to give names to things, we categorize things — but at the end of the day if I'm blind, I hear something, so I see it. If I see something but I don't hear it, I see it, so my eyes will tell me what it is, therefore I hear. So I don't, perhaps like you or the majority of people, split our senses up, and just because you lose one you assume you simply cannot hear anything at all. That's simply not the case."

We agree. Whether or not people cultivate a conscious awareness of sensory fusion, thinking depends upon the associations and connections made between sense and knowledge. Although we are used to believing that each of our senses perceives the world differently and discretely, they must, in fact, be coordinated for us to be able to think and act reasonably. Aristotle understood this when he wrote in *De Anima* that although our ability to discriminate sweet from salty or white from red must exist within defined senses, our ability to distinguish sweet from white or salty from red can exist only if the senses are unified. Similarly, our ability to link the red color of an apple with its sweetness must also lie in the unity of senses. We hear the word "apple," and by an act of synesthetic imagination most of us can simultaneously see an apple in our mind's eye, hold it in our mind's hand, feel its smooth skin and water-wet weight, taste its tart sweetness in our mind's mouth, smell its unique aroma in our mind's nose, and hear the crunch of biting it in our mind's ear. Contrary to popular myth, we are all whole-brain thinkers. An accurate understanding of apple taste relies as much on the eyes, the nose, and the hand as it does on the tongue. Anyone who has taken the schoolroom taste test, in which apple and potato slices are served up unseen, unsmelled, and untouched, can vouch for that: most people readily confuse one with the other. In everyday life, all our senses work in tandem within the mind, just as the body and mind cooperate to move us in a coordinated and balanced manner. Disconnecting the experiences of the senses, as the potato-apple experiment does, or as sometimes happens with a stroke or inner-ear infection, confuses and confounds the intellect. Conversely, misleading the mind by combining a visual image of pizza with a smell image of chocolate actively disturbs sensation. Mind and body are not distinct but one. Sense and sensibility cannot be separated.

Grant, then, that we sense and make sense of the world in multiple, concurrent, and intersensory or "cross-modal" ways. But we do even more than that. We can spell the word "apple" or say it, we can paint or draw the object. If we are botanists or farmers, we can reel off its Latin name, list its evolutionary cousins (such as the wild rose), identify its pests, describe its nutrient requirements and its preferred environment, estimate its worth per pound, and a million other things — all from the association with a word or the taste on our tongue. This is more than a mere combining of senses. This is *synthetic knowing* — a combining of sensation, feeling, memory, and rational thought. All creative work is based upon this. As biologist Agnes Arber has written, "New hypotheses come into the mind most freely when discursive reasoning (including its visual component) has been raised by intense effort to a level at which it finds itself united indissolubly with feeling and emotion. When reason and intuition attain this collaboration, the unity into which they merge appears to possess a creative power which is denied to either singly." More simply, Immanuel Kant wrote in his *Critique of Pure Reason*, "The intellect can intuit nothing, the senses can think nothing. Only through their union can knowledge arise."

Recognition of the synthetic nature of creative understanding is apparently so rare that there is no word for it, so we suggest *synosia,* derived from the Greek words *syn* (union), as in synthesis, the combining of ideas, and *gnosis* (knowledge) or *noesis* (exercise of reason or cognition). Put these together and the new compound, *synosis,* or synosia, sounds in English like its meaning: the union of different forms of knowledge, or *syn*thetic *know*ing. But it is more than that. In previous chapters we said that to feel is to think and to think is to feel, a message aptly conveyed by Nabokov and Lighthill. A chance meeting with a teacher is not just the sense impressions gained at the time; it involves the memories and thoughts that arise simultaneously. Fluids are not just substances to be drunk or swum in but mathematical expressions and engineering problems. Hearing and seeing are not passive experiences; they require active intelligence, whether or not we are blind or deaf. Eating an apple is not just a sensual experience but a physical embodiment of all the agricultural, botanical, chemical, physical, and economic understanding that delivered it into our hands. Synosia is therefore the intellectual extension of synesthesia. Just as synesthesia is considered the highest form of aesthetic sensibility, so synosia denotes the highest integration of multimodal feeling with multiple ways of knowing to create an ultimate form of understanding. Thus the word *synosia* may also be derived from the union of *synesthesia* with *gnosis* or *noesis.*

Synosia is the natural and necessary result of imaging, analogizing, modeling, playing, and transforming. Although an individual or group must work step by step through a series of transformations to define and create something new, when the process of invention is completed, the individual or group understands the creation *as a whole.* More, the inventors carry within themselves the processes by which they invented and the proprioceptive and emotional senses of excitement, frustration, and eventual validation that occur during the course of creating. By the time Mary Leakey figured out how the Laetoli footprints had been made, she understood them both objectively and subjectively, analytically and synthetically, as scientific evidence and archeological treasures. By the time Feynman converted his equations into green and purple fuzzy balls and into acoustic patterns that he could see or drum, had sung their vocal equivalent, had proven his conjectures in some mathematical formalism, and then looked for all the analogous cases he could imagine, he experienced his stuff in as many ways as possible. By the time Oskar Schlemmer could dance, sculpt, paint, and write about his idea of the human body in space, combining "internal anatomy, physiology, and especially psychology, not to forget philosophy in general,"

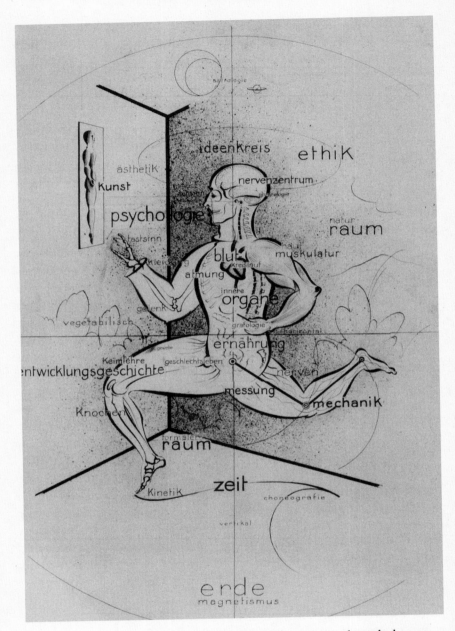

Fig. 15-1. *Man in the Sphere of Ideas*, by Oskar Schlemmer, 1928, places the human being at the intersection of space, time, stars, earth, science, art, choreography, and ideas, all synthesized by the body's muscles, mechanics, organs, senses, and psychology. To be creative, said Schlemmer, one must understand how all these elements work together.

he clearly sensed it and knew it in every conceivable manner. By the time Isabelle Allende brought her novel from inside her belly through her mind into the world, or Stephen Spender thought through the logic of his emotions and images, they were so much more than words on paper; they were a clarion of feelings and ideas resonating within writer and reader both.

Clearly, despite the novelty of the term synosia, there is nothing new about the concept. Creative people have always combined many ways of feeling and knowing simultaneously, often describing in detail personal "tea ceremony" equivalents melding sensual and intellectual concerns. Albert Michelson, who first measured the speed of light, was not only a physicist but a well-trained painter and a collector of insects, especially brightly colored beetles. The common denominator in all of his endeavors was a fascination with light and color: "If a poet could at the same time be a physicist," he wrote, "he might convey to others the pleasure, the satisfaction, almost the reverence, which the subject inspires. The aesthetic side of the subject is, I confess, by no means the least attractive to me. Especially is its fascination felt in the branch which deals with light." Organic chemist Robert Woodward provided another evocative example. Described by his daughter as an "artist of chemistry" for the way he designed and built his molecular structures, Woodward wrote that it was "the *sensuous* elements" that "play so large a role in my attraction to chemistry. I love crystals, the beauty of their form — and their formation; liquids, dormant, distilling, sloshing!; swirling, the fumes; the odors — good and bad; the rainbow of colors; the gleaming vessels of every size, shape and purpose. Much as I might *think* about chemistry, it would not exist for me without these physical, visual, tangible, sensuous things."

Desmond Morris provides the most complete personal description of this synosic approach to understanding. To begin with, as noted in Chapter 10, he becomes the animal he studies: "I think like the species I am studying, whatever it is. If I am watching a lizard, I become the lizard. Gazing down at the water at a pike, I become a pike." He also analyzes and responds to the animal visually, studying its characteristics simultaneously as an artist and a scientist:

> When I see a red spot on a bird's beak I know that it is an important visual sign. As a scientist I learn about its potency as a sign stimulus. I study it and I analyse its function. While this is happening, I am also developing a subjective feeling for the dramatic qualities of "redness" and "spottedness." Unconscious ambiguities set in — red,

Fig. 15-2. *The Blind Watchmaker,* by Desmond Morris, 1986, which was used as the cover for Richard Dawkins's book by that name on evolution, shows Morris exploring nature simultaneously as artist and scientist.

fire, danger, blood, dramatic, fixating, conspicuous, attention spot, eye, sun, hole, orifice, point, full stop. Visual echoes, symbolic equivalents, substitutions all start to come into operation, but I am never conscious of what has been happening until after I have completed the painting. I paint as if I am in a dream, as if I am hallucinating. The actual moment of creation is like watching a dream unfold.

Although Morris is a surrealist painter, drawing automatically from the internal images of his mind, his artistic explorations are not divorced from his understanding of biology. "There is little or nothing in my paintings that can be identified as belonging to a particular species in the external world, but the underlying principles active in natural forms are all there. Cephalization, for example, which is a process by which the extremity of an organism becomes differentiated into a head; or segmentation, by which a body becomes subdivided into repeated units; or allometric growth, or cell division, or bifurcation, or polymorphism. I am aware of all these biological processes." Morris is able to explore the consequences of these processes within the imaginary world of his art and so develop an even more complete and diversified understanding of them than he would by studying a few real-world examples. "In portraying an imaginary organism I can manipulate emphasis by exaggerating some elements and suppressing others. A similar process occurs in nature — the anteater's nose and the porcupine's quills become exaggerated during evolution, while the limbs of the snake and the tail of the ape become suppressed. As a painter, I can follow this same general trend, while making my own special rules in each case. In this way I can evolve my own fauna."

Put another way, Morris carries out thought experiments with imaginary organisms he calls biomorphs. While many people may question the utility of such fantasizing, especially for a scientist, it is worth remembering the words of François Jacob, who says science "is a game . . . of continually inventing a possible world, or a piece of a possible world, and then comparing it with the real world." Morris's artistic dreams describe universes that *could be,* which he can then compare with what actually *is.* The result is a form of knowledge that Morris says transcends any particular discipline: "The imaginative and the analytical — artist and scientist . . . to be both at once." This is synosic thinking at its best.

Indeed, this synthetic way of knowing is what all creative people strive for in their work and look for in the work of others. Igor Stravinsky clearly understood the concept of synosia when he said, "I cannot begin to take an interest in the phenomenon of music except insofar as it emanates from the integral man. I mean from a man armed with the resources of his senses, his psychological faculties, and his intellectual equipment." He even refused to listen to recordings, asserting that seeing the kinesthetic performance of music is as important as hearing it. And artist Otto Piene felt strongly that "mind, which is really body, and body, which really exists in the mind, do not wish to allow us to treat them as separate entities. . . . The man who uses his body to enclose his mind and his mind to lift up his body, who lives this timeless moment, this heavenly reality, in order to stride free through space, this man has paradise within him." George Bellows agreed: "The ideal artist is he who knows everything, feels everything, experiences everything, and retains his experience in a spirit of wonder and feeds upon it with creative lust. . . . He uses every possible power, spirit, emotion, conscious or unconcious, to arrive at his ends."

When we look at how creative individuals characterize the highest forms of their art or science, we often find them expanding on such ideas. Loie Fuller wrote that dance is "light, colour, motion, and music. / Observation, intuition, and finally comprehension." Aaron Copland felt that to compose a piece of music or to appreciate a composition completely, an individual must be aware simultaneously on three planes: "(1) the sensuous plane, (2) the expressive [emotional] plane, (3) the sheerly musical [intellectual] plane." Poet T. R. Henn of Cambridge University believed that the same three things were necessary to understand or to create literature. All literature and poetry, he said, "seeks to express a peculiar fusion of ideas and emotions which are normally on the edge of consciousness, or even beyond it." And Richard Feynman waxed poetic about physics, chiding those who experience the world as less than whole:

> Poets say science takes away from the beauty of the stars — mere globs of gas atoms. I too can see the stars on a desert night, and feel them. But do I see less or more? The vastness of the heavens stretches my imagination — stuck on this carousel my little eye can catch one-million-year-old light. A vast pattern — of which I am a part. . . . What is the pattern, or the meaning, or the *why*? It does not do harm to the mystery to know a little about it. For far more marvelous is the truth than any artists of the past imagined it. Why do the poets of the present not speak of it? What men are poets who can speak of Jupiter if he were a man, but if he is an immense spinning sphere of methane and ammonia must be silent?

For Feynman, the desire to penetrate and understand the mysteries of the universe could be satisfied only by unifying all that we sense and feel with all that we know. Walter Gropius, multifaceted architect, engineer, and educator, founded the Bauhaus with this sort of synthesizing in mind. "In a work of art," he wrote, "the laws of the physical world and the intellectual world and the world of the spirit function and are expressed simultaneously." The only real schooling, he believed, trains the mind, the body, and the spirit to strive for synthesis. The challenge in modern life and education still remains to reintegrate poetry and physics, art and chemistry, music and biology, dance and sociology, and every other possible combination of aesthetic and analytical knowledge, to foster people who feel that they want to know and know that they want to feel. Feynman realized that no scientist worth his or her salt just thinks about the world, he or she senses it; Gropius realized that no true artist merely feels the world, but knows it, too. What both are after is the active understanding that is at the heart of creativity. Those who wish, in turn, to understand and teach science and art need to recreate that totality.

The need for a synesthetic and synosic education is best summarized by the simple image with which we close this chapter, one of the most telling "cosmic synchronizations" of modern times. This image is not a piece of art, although it looks like one. Or rather it *is* a piece of art, but only unintentionally. It is a pattern, a series of visually designed logical relationships, a mathematical calculation. It is a picture of an electronic computer chip. That it has

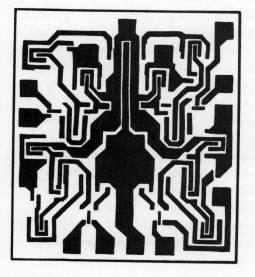

Fig. 15-3. Art, logic, or both?
The design of a computer chip.

the form of a piece of artwork is not by chance. As we have noted throughout this book, every logical relationship has its visual equivalent, and every topological object or puzzle has its electronic and logical conversions. But here the story has an unexpected connection: electronic chips are made by a process derived from the techniques of etching and silk-screen printing and adapted to coating silicon components with copper and gold. Chips are literally designed as patterns on huge pieces of paper, photographically reduced, and made into the masks used to etch or to plate materials onto silicon wafers.

This is where the course of civilization has taken us. Logic is an image that must be printed, just like an art print. The purpose and the materials may be different, but the links between art and science and technology are as strong today as they were in the Renaissance. To comprehend the advances of this century, one must be able to perceive the connections between mathematical calculations, logical constructions, patterns, visual images, and the technical processes of manipulating artistic media to produce electronic inventions — or to make similarly unexpected concatenations of thinking tools. Only those who become excited by such inspirations will have the desire to create the next synthesis.

We desperately need synthetic minds. No major problem facing the world today can be boxed neatly within a single discipline or approached effectively by analysis, emotion, or tradition alone. Innovation is always transdisciplinary and multimodal. The future will therefore depend upon our ability to create synthetic understanding by integrating all ways of knowing. Recognizing this, Piet Mondrian called for the "new man" who could meld the external world of perception and analysis with the internal world of feelings and emotions: "He will be distinguished precisely by the complete attention to everything external [and] will not rest until the external becomes pure expression of the *inner* and *outer* in one." Oliver Sacks has called for a new medicine that joins inner and outer, the "I" and the "It," in a similarly synosic way:

> It is the function of medication, or surgery, or appropriate physiological procedures, to rectify the mechanisms which are so deranged in . . . patients. It is the function of scientific medicine to rectify the "It." It is the function of art, of living contact, of existential medicine, to call upon the latent will, the agent, the "I," to call out its commanding and coordinating powers, so that it may regain its hegemony and rule once again — for the final rule, the ruler, is not a

measuring rod or clock, but the rule and measure of the personal "I."
These two forms of medicine must be joined, must co-inhere, as
body and soul.

What applies to art and medicine applies to all people working in every
area, argued biologist, philosopher, artist, and art historian C. H. Waddington. In 1972 he wrote in his far-sighted book *Biology and the History of the
Future,* "The acute problems of the world can be solved only by whole men
[and women], not by people who refuse to be, publicly, anything more than
a technologist, or a pure scientist, or an artist. In the world of today, you have
got to be everything or you are going to be nothing." Buckminster Fuller
concurred. In his essay "Emergent Humanity," he warned that in evolution
"overspecialization leads to extinction. We need the philosopher-scientist-
artist — the comprehensivist, not merely more deluxe quality technician-
mechanics."

With so many eminent people in so many different disciplines proclaim-
ing the same need, it is incumbent that we listen. Synosia is not an ideal or a
dream; it is a necessity.

16

Synthesizing Education

WE HAVE NOW TEASED APART the threads of creative thinking and rewoven them into a synthetic understanding of innovation that, in turn, requires a new kind of transdisciplinary, synthetic education.

Our foray into the hearts and minds of inventive individuals demonstrates that imagination can be encouraged and trained through the exercise of thinking tools and a desire for synosic understanding. Clearly these elements are lacking in most curricula today. Implementing thinking tools and synosic lessons in our schools will not, however, require major alterations in curricula. We need not change *what* we teach. A synthetic education requires only that we change *how* we teach, bearing eight basic goals in mind.

First, we must emphasize the teaching of universal processes of invention in addition to the acquisition of disciplinary products of knowledge. The purpose of education should be understanding rather than simply knowing; its focus should be the active process of learning and creating rather than the passive acquisition of facts. As we pointed out in Chapter 2, it is possible to know about principles of literature or physics without being able to use them. However, it is not possible to use them without also understanding how they function in nature and human affairs. Active understanding subsumes passive knowledge and builds upon it. Students must not only analyze the products of creative understanding, such as novels, poems, experiments, theories, paintings, dances, and songs, they must copy and imitate them, thereby learning the sensual and synosic processes of their invention.

Second, it follows that we must teach the intuitive and imaginative skills necessary to inventive processes. As we have shown, creative thinking in every field begins in nonlogical, nonverbal forms. To think is to feel and to feel is to think. Everyone should receive early and continuing stimulation of visual, aural, and other body senses and learn how to imaginatively recreate sense images. Everyone should be schooled in the mixing and melding of synesthetic imageries. Everyone should explore the feelings and emotions of the body. Everyone should learn to abstract, analogize, and empathize; to transform one to the other; and to translate intuitive forms of knowing into words, numbers, plastic images, movement, sound. In some cases, sensing and feeling are most naturally communicated as visual, literary, or musical expressions. Indeed, the arts in a liberal arts education are important because they provide the *best* and in some cases the *only* exercise of many thinking tools, both in imagination and in expression. This leads to our next point.

Third, we must implement a multidisciplinary education that places the arts on an equal footing with the sciences. Arts and sciences constantly interact in very fruitful ways that are often overlooked. Beginning with kindergarten and progressing through college, *every* student should study the arts as thoroughly as the sciences, the humanities, and mathematics. This means reversing the marginalization of the arts in colleges and secondary schools across the country and making the a**R**ts the "fourth **R**" of everyone's education. The arts are not merely for self-expression or entertainment. They are, as we have shown, disciplines as rigorous as medicine or mathematics, with their own bodies of knowledge, techniques, tools, skills, and philosophies. Moreover, because the imaginative tools used in the arts are critical to the humanities and the sciences, they deserve support not just for their own sake but for the sake of education as a whole. Math, science, and technology have flourished in the past only when and where all the arts have flourished. They will flourish or fail together in the future.

Fourth, we must integrate the curriculum by using a common descriptive language for innovation. There is no point in teaching a liberal arts and sciences curriculum that continues to fragment knowledge and creates specialists who cannot communicate across disciplinary lines. Education must focus on the trunk of the tree of knowledge, revealing the ways in which the branches, twigs, and leaves all emerge from a common core. Tools for thinking stem from this core, providing a common language with which practitioners in different fields may share their experience of the process of innovation and discover links between their creative activities. When the same terms are employed across the curriculum, students begin to link different subjects and classes. If they practice abstracting in writing class, if they work on abstracting in painting or drawing class, if they abstract relevant information from a history text or a biology experiment, and if, in all cases, they call it abstracting, they begin to understand how to think beyond disciplinary boundaries. They see how to transform their thoughts from one mode of conception and expression to another. Linking the disciplines comes naturally when the terms and tools are presented as part of a universal imagination.

Fifth, we must emphasize the transdisciplinary lessons of disciplinary learning. A common creative language is not enough. A century of educational studies has shown that students are far more likely to remember and apply what they have learned if information and skills are taught as generally useful rather than as unique solutions to unique problems. Teachers should downplay tags such as "art," "music," or "science" that place knowledge in insular boxes and focus instead on how the same material can be used flexibly in many disciplines. The object is to help everyone think simultaneously as artist *and* scientist, musician *and* mathematician, dancer *and* engineer. An education that trains the mind to imagine creatively in one field prepares the mind for creative application in any other, for thinking tools as well as flexible knowledge are transferable.

Sixth, we must use the experiences of people who have successfully bridged disciplines as exemplars of creative activity within our curricula. The best way to learn is to watch others and then model their techniques, insights, and processes. This book is filled with examples of people who have integrated knowledge in new ways, with descriptions of how they learned their imaginative skills and how they created. Such examples should be used in every class in every subject at every curricular level as spurs to inventive imitation and innovation. Until students see the human face of the creative process that underlies the disembodied products of their world, they cannot realize that they, too, may participate in creating their own vision of the future. And when they see that so many innovators in every discipline have been innovative precisely *because* they melded tools and concepts from numerous fields, they will understand and desire a synthesizing education.

Seventh, to reach the widest range of minds, ideas in every discipline should be presented in many forms. There is no one single imaginative skill or creative technique that is adequate for all thinking needs. The intuitive approach is as valuable as the logical one; the analytical, algebraic mind is no better than the geometric, visual mind or the kinesthetic, empathic one. Every idea can and should be transformed into several equivalent forms, each of which has a different formal expression and emphasizes a different set of thinking tools. The more ways students can imagine an idea, the better their chances of insight. The more ways they can express that insight, the better their chances that others will understand and appreciate it.

Finally, we must forge a pioneering education, whose purpose is to produce the imaginative generalists who can take us into the uncharted future. Every novel idea takes us into new territory, and creative people are, by necessity, pioneers. The tools and skills that pioneers take to the frontiers are not specialized or narrow. They are basic, general-purpose tools that can be adapted to the need at hand. Pioneers of the creative imagination must have adaptable minds, too, and all-purpose toolboxes of inventive skills that enable them to make new knowledge.

What this new knowledge may be, we can only guess, but much remains to be known and invented. As Aldous Huxley noted shortly before his death, what we know now is a small part of what we can and will know in the future. "The purified language of science, or even the richer purified language of literature," he asserted, "[will] never be adequate to the givenness of the world." To expand our conceptions in keeping with this givenness will require manifold acts of the creative imagination, as biologist John Rader Platt cogently speculates: "Our verbal and musical symbols scarcely represent the whole field of possible sound; painting, sculpture and architecture scarcely scratch the surface of the organization of visual space; and I am not sure that mathematical symbols represent all the forms of biological logic. What new kinds of symbols," he asks, "are we preparing to manipulate, color organs, Labanotation for the ballet, or a dozen others, calling for new talents and developing new types of youthful genius?" What kinds indeed? One thing is certain. The new symbols will be unexpected and surprising, and in Huxley's view they will emerge only when the humanities and the sciences, the arts and technologies, "advance together."

To advance together means, said C. H. Waddington, whose book *Tools for Thought* inspired this one, "a very much more profound generalism than is usually considered." It means, as Waddington's colleague, biologist Chandler M. Brooks has written, that "in our educational endeavors, we may be compelled to think of specialization in breadth rather than specialization in minutiae." We must resist the pedagogical tracking of different kinds of learners. We must reverse the trend toward early and narrow specialization of student interest and activity. For when we look closely at the formative years of productive artists, scientists, and inventors we find that although the strong enthusiasms of youth shaped their future contributions, *they did not lead to them in any direct, disciplinary fashion.* Consider the following four people, who showed strong early proclivities but whose adult achievements would have been crippled by early specialization and constriction of interests and activities.

In 1894 a young man climbed to the top of Scotland's highest peak, Ben Nevis. It was the kind of misty, translucent day when rainbows form in perfect circles around the sun and the shadows it casts. The young man thought these sights were the most beautiful he had ever experienced. "The wonderful optical phenomena shown when the sun shone on the clouds surrounding the hill top," he later wrote, "and especially the coloured rings surrounding the sun (coronas) or surrounding the shadow cast by the hill top or observer on mist or cloud (glories) greatly excited my interest, and made me wish to imitate them." Later, he did.

In 1895 another highly sensitive individual explained her creative aspirations. From a very young age, she recalled, "I loved poetry with a passion. Its very form, its very rhythm delighted me. I greedily devoured every excerpt from Russian poets that caught my eye and, I have to confess, the more highflown the poetry the better I liked it. . . . The very beat of poetry enchanted me so much that I began composing at the age of five. . . . By the age of twelve, I was unshakably convinced I was going to become a great poet." Indeed, nothing seemed more divine to her than to create new worlds with poetic imagination.

At about the same time, another young man discovered that geometry was "the process that sets the truth before us. We start from a brilliantly-lighted spot and gradually get deeper and deeper into the darkness, which, in its turn, becomes self-illuminated by kindling new lights for a higher ascent. . . . It is assuredly a majestic enterprise, commensurate with man's immense ambitions, to seek to pour the universe into the mould of a formula and submit every reality to the standard of reason. . . . It is superb. You feel as if you were witnessing the creation of a world." Moved by the immense beauty of reason, he, too, aspired to illuminate new worlds.

Finally, listen to the words of a contemporary of these young people, whose love was the social sciences. "Different studies gave me practice in 'abstract' thinking, in learning to penetrate into fundamental questions," he wrote. "Aside from my chosen specialty (economics . . .), I was powerfully attracted, sometimes successively, sometimes simultaneously, to other different fields: Roman law . . . criminal law . . . the history of Russian law and peasant law . . . ethnology . . . all these claimed my attention and helped me to think in an abstract manner." This young man's goal was to alter fundamentally the conditions of humanity.

Who were these people? One might expect the young man who wanted to capture the coronas and glories of Ben Nevis to have become a painter; the young girl who loved poetry to have become a poet; the schoolboy who loved geometry to have become a mathematician; and the youth who loved the social sciences to have become an economist or politician. In our modern schools, they might have been pushed in these directions. None of these identifications is accurate, however. Each of the four used his or her unique blend of talents, training, and passion in unexpected ways.

"He who has once seen the intimate beauty of nature," Konrad Lorenz once said, ". . . must become either a poet or a naturalist and, if his eyes are good and his powers of observation sharp enough, he may well become both." C. T. R. Wilson, the young man so inspired by glories and coronas in the Scottish highlands, returned to his Cambridge laboratory and invented the cloud chamber with the poetry of physics in mind. Cloud chambers, as we discussed in Chapter 5, allowed scientists to visualize subatomic particles for the first time. But as Wilson revealed in his Nobel Prize lecture many years after the fact, his first concern had been a purely visceral and aesthetic one. His cloud chamber truly embodied both art and science, not only for himself, but for future generations, too. "I have seen the glory effect, and have made a Wilson cloud chamber when I was a youth," wrote chemist William Lipscomb some eighty years later. "Both effects are beautiful indeed."

The woman who was sure she would become a poet did so, and became an internationally recognized playwright as well — but only in her spare time. Sofya Kovalevskaya is remembered mainly for her outstanding contributions to mathematics. "You are surprised at my working simultaneously in literature and in mathematics," she wrote in her autobiography. "Many people who have never had occasion to learn what mathematics is confuse it with arithmetic and consider it a dry and arid science. In actual fact, it is the science which demands the utmost imagination. One of the foremost mathematicians of our century says very justly that it is impossible to be a mathematician without also being a poet in spirit. . . . The poet must see what others do not see, must see more deeply than other people. And the mathematician must do the same." Indeed, one of Kovalevskaya's teachers, Karl Weierstrass, proclaimed that "a mathematician who is not somewhat of a poet, will never be a perfect mathematician." Kovalevskaya took these words to heart, writing the poetry of numbers.

The schoolboy who loved geometry did not become a mathematician or a physicist or even an engineer. Rather, Henri Fabre earned for himself the sobriquets "poet and prophet of the insect world" and "prose Homer of the wasps and spiders." His writings inspired thousands of young people to become entomologists in the first half of this century and gave pleasure to millions of readers. Nevertheless, geometry was never far from Fabre's creative imagination. "If it has ever fallen to my lot to write a page or two which the reader has run over without excessive fatigue," he once wrote, "I owe it, in great part, to geometry, that wonderful teacher of the art of directing one's thought. . . . It arranges what is confused, thins out the dense, calms the tumultuous, filters the muddy and gives lucidity, a superior product to all the tropes of rhetoric." Fabre would undoubtedly have agreed with Edna St. Vincent Millay, had he known of her then unpublished poetry, that "Euclid alone has seen beauty bare," for to him geometry was beautiful, in the same way that a poem or narrative was beautiful when its words, rhythms, and structure led toward illumination.

Finally, the young social scientist was Wassily Kandinsky, considered to be the first artist to paint nonrepresentational pictures. His love of abstract concepts and his desire to reform the conditions of mankind did not lead him into economics but into painting, where he reinvented perception and representation itself. To say, however, that Kandinsky "changed fields" is to miss the unity of his vision. "Painting is a thundering collision of different worlds," he wrote, "intended to create a new world in, and from the struggle with one another, a new world which is the work of art. . . . The trunk of the tree does not become superfluous because of a new branch: it makes the branch possible." Someone like Charles Ives understood this, too. He worked in the insurance industry his whole life and not only was proud of his business experience but felt that it contributed in fundamental ways to his music: "You cannot set art off in a corner and hope for it to have vitality, reality, and substance. The fabric weaves itself whole. My work in music helped my business and my work in business helped my music." Out of youthful enthusiasms and mature interests, the creative individual interleaves vocations and avocations that together stimulate imagination and innovation.

The point of these examples is simply put: these were whole people, not specialists. They made contributions to particular disciplines because of, not in spite of, their broad interests. They were pioneers, generalists, who bridged areas of expertise and pulled together disparate areas of knowledge. They met the challenges of their time and place and expanded the human imagination by being polymaths. And it is polymaths such as these to whom we will owe the great synthetic breakthroughs of the future.

The word *polymath*, derived from the Greek words meaning "to know much" or "very knowing," has come to mean in common parlance a person of encyclopedic learning. Polymaths are not to be confused with dilettantes, who take up new subjects for amusement or pleasure. Polymaths master their activities to a significant degree and perceive the fundamental connections between them. The greatest polymaths of all, like the "Renaissance men" Leonardo da Vinci, Vesalius, and Michelangelo, seem capable of encompassing all that is known. Of course, no one has ever had truly encyclopedic knowledge, and that is not what we are calling for here. But it has long been observed by psychologists that people who are innovative tend to participate in a wider range of activities and develop a higher degree of skill in those activities than other people. Certainly that has been the case for virtually every artist, scientist, inventor, and humanist discussed in these pages, nearly all of whom can be called polymaths.

One need not be a genius to be a polymath. Everyone can develop hobbies, arts, crafts, intellectual interests, and challenging physical pastimes. Everyone can draw connections between an amateur avocation and a professional vocation. And everyone should, for the practical payoff is tremendous. Recent studies have found that the best predictor of career success in any field is not IQ, grades, or standardized test scores but participation in one or more mentally intensive leisuretime activities or hobbies — anything from painting, composing music, or writing poetry to programming computers, creating videos, or playing around with scientific ideas or mathematics. This is true for professionals of all kinds; it is true for business entrepreneurs and CEOs; it is true for artists, academics, and entertainers.

Some polymaths develop their multiple interests and activities so thoroughly that they achieve dual careers, for example, mathematician-poet Kovalevskaya, composer-chemist Aleksandr Borodin, poet-physician William Carlos Williams, and painter-biologist Desmond Morris. Others simply adapt the tools and knowledge of their avocational interest to their vocational field in the various ways we have discussed throughout this book. They conceptually integrate their many interests into "activity sets" or "networks of enterprise" that focus energy and nurture imagination by concentrating on the common skills and ideas that transcend any single avocation. As composer Robert Schumann stated, "The cultivated musician may study a Madonna by Raphael, the painter a symphony by Mozart, with equal advantage. Yet more: in sculpture, the actor's art becomes fixed; the actor in turn transforms the sculptor's works into living forms; the painter turns a poem into a painting; the musician sets a picture to music."

E. E. Cummings provides another exemplar. He thought of himself as primarily a painter and wished to make a name for himself in that field. Yet it was not in visual art but in poetry that he made his most important contributions — not in spite of his love of painting but *because* of it. Cummings tackled the transformation from painting to poetry quite literally. As a painter he used chiaroscuro, contrasting shades to highlight and give depth to images, and explored cubism, which contributed to what he called "seeing around" things. By direct imitation, in poetry he invented the concept of "knowing around" ideas, which he achieved by pairing words with their opposites, as in "big little," "glad sorry," "foolishwise" or "proudhumble." His innovation could not have come through training in literature courses; it could come only from sources manifestly outside that discipline.

Nobel laureate Georg von Békésy also believed in the cross-fertilization of knowledge and skills. When he wanted to understand how to do the best biology, he turned to art, where by diligent study he learned that the elements that characterize the greatest art — imagination, surprise, consistency, skill — also characterize the greatest science. As painter and Pulitzer Prize–winning novelist Paul Horgan has written, "Profoundly to understand one art is to be able to articulate principles — though not necessarily techniques — applicable to all arts. Form in one art can never convincingly be imitated in another; but analogies are possible — and not only from one art to another, but from science to art, and *vice versa*."

Some creative people take this cultivation of transdisciplinary, transferable skills to extremes. Poet Gary Snyder, for instance, has argued that an excellent mechanic or chef has as much to teach about the making of poetry as a master poet. "You learn how to use your mind in the act of handling parts and working," he has said. "You learn how things go together. . . . It's a *true* analogy. A master is a master. . . . Say you wanted to be a poet, and you saw a man that you recognized as a master mechanic or a great cook — you would do better, for yourself as a poet, to study under that man than to study under another poet who was not a master." Kurt Vonnegut also values mastery of the creative process over mastery of specific material. He has argued that it is pointless to look for the next generation of innovative writers in English and creative writing classes. They will, he believes, be found in the sciences and medicine, for mastery of those crafts will provide not only the basis for writing great fiction but the unusual experiences needed to enrich it.

Polymath- and imagination go hand in hand. Multiply trained individuals transform experience, synthesize knowledge, and lead us toward synosia, the understanding that, in the words of physiologist Claude Bernard, "everything in nature is connected with everything else." Some part of this synosic understanding is within everyone's grasp. The same impulse that motivates the best art, the best literature, the best science can be harnessed to provide the best schooling, as innovators and their teachers have been doing for centuries. In Japan, people who perform the tea ceremony have always been trained synthetically. The method, based on the teachings of Zen Buddhism, reached its peak when Kobori Enshū built the Bosen (final attainment) tearoom in the seventeenth century. Enshū was a painter, poet, architect, gardener, and tea master. The room he designed for his tea ceremony integrated all that he knew into one harmonious whole. Tea masters today are expected to attain an equivalent synthesis of talent and experience. Shinichi Suzuki imbued his Talent Education program with a similar philosophy, based on personal observations of Einstein and other musically talented scientific friends. "I believe sensitivity and love toward music and art are very important things to all people whether they are politicians, scientists, businessmen or laborers," Suzuki wrote. "We are not teaching . . . children to make them professional musicians. . . . Talent education is life education." Education is meant to open many doors, leading to many rooms.

Many Western teachers have also striven for integration of sense and reason, emotion and analysis, the widest range of knowledge and understanding. Pestalozzi, Montessori, and other educators have insisted on using visual and proprioceptive modes of thinking to teach analytical material. At the Bauhaus in the 1930s, teachers strove to integrate daily life, art, and technology by ranging over an enormous number of disciplines. For a single painting course on human form, Oskar Schlemmer covered biology, ethics, anthropology, and theater as well as nude and figural drawing. His fellow teacher Paul Klee presented his classes with a chart of fields relevant to painting that included natural history, philology, literature, philosophy, and mathematics. Elsewhere, Merce Cunningham's dance and choreography teacher, Nellie Cornish, of Seattle's Cornish College of the Arts, also had her students study all of the arts. By the same token, poet Amy Lowell wrote that no subject should be "alien" to the poet, "and the profounder his knowledge in any direction, the more depth there will be to his poetry." For composer-architect-engineer Iannis Xenakis, "The artist-conceptor will have to be knowledgeable and inventive in such varied domains as mathematics, logic, physics, chemistry, biology, genetics, paleontology (for the evolution of forms), the human sciences and history; in short, a sort of universality, but one based upon, guided by and oriented towards forms and architectures." Charles Steinmetz encouraged his engineering students at Union College in Schenectady, New York, "to study Greek, Latin, history, philosophy, and other subjects offered in the Liberal Arts College. The classics open the world of art and literature to the student. A neglect of them is one of the most serious mistakes. Technical training alone is not enough to fit a man for an interesting and useful life."

This advice is certainly as valid today as it was in Steinmetz's day. We need polymaths and pioneers who know that imagination thrives when sensual experience joins with reason, when Illusions link to Reality, when intuition couples with intellect, when the passions of the heart unite with those of the mind, when knowledge gained in one discipline opens doors to all the rest.

Everything in your life ends up in your act.

Addressing a conference on art, science, and creativity, comedian Aaron Freeman recently boiled it all down to that single punch line. We couldn't agree more. Every example in this book demonstrates Freeman's conclusion. You are all that you can do, and all that you can do is mirrored in what you create. The wider your range of knowledge and feeling, the greater your range of imaginative possibilities and the more synthetic and important your work will be.

The point of education must be to create whole people who, through their wholeness, can focus the accumulated wisdom of human experience into illuminated patches of splendor.

> *I live to buy in every mart;*
> *To try the hand at every art;*
> *In every science take a part;*
> *With every passion prove the heart. . . .*

So wrote the young Sir Ronald Ross, physician, scientist, musician, composer, and poet many years before he was honored with a Nobel Prize for his discovery of the mode of transmission of malaria. His aspirations could not be more worthy in our fragmented world. For, as Robert Frost said so eloquently in "Two Tramps in Mud Time," to fuse emotion, intellect, and purpose into one universal imagination is the greatest joy and greatest resource of the individual and of humankind:

But yield who will to their separation,
My object in living is to unite
My avocation and my vocation
As my two eyes make one in sight.
Only where love and need are one,
And the work is play for mortal stakes,
Is the deed ever really done
For Heaven and the future's sakes.

A synthesizing education strives for nothing less.

NOTES

BIBLIOGRAPHY

MINDS-ON
RESOURCES

ILLUSTRATION
CREDITS

INDEX

NOTES

1. Rethinking Thinking

On feeling in creative process: McClintock in E. F. Keller 1983, 103–4; Gauss in Arber 1964, 47; Bernard in Bernard 1927, 43; Picasso in Ashton 1972, 28; Stravinsky in Stravinsky 1970, 67; Allende in Epel 1993, 8.

Einstein on thinking in Hadamard 1945, 142–143; and Wertheimer 1959, 228, n.7. McClintock in E. F. Keller 1983, 117. Emotional thinking: Bernard in Bernard 1927, 43; Pauli in Chandrasekhar 1987, 146. Emotion/logic connection: Einstein in Hadamard 1945, 142–43; Ulam in Ulam 1976, 183; Lipscomb in Curtin 1982, 1–4.

Clarke on creative process in Clarke and Lee 1989, 320. Einstein on secondary step in Hadamard 1945, 142–143; Infeld, 1941, 312; and Wertheimer 1959, 228, n.7; McClintock in E. F. Keller 1983, 203; Smith in C. S. Smith 1981, 353–54; Heisenberg in Heisenberg 1974, 146; and Feynman in Gleick 1992, 244–45.

Rothenberg, Truitt, and Riley in Stiles and Selz 1996, 102, 112, 264. Picasso in Ashton 1972, 131–32. Translation in art: Albers, Bourgeois, and Bill in Stiles and Selz 1996, 107, 40, and 74; O'Keeffe in O'Keeffe 1976, n.p.

Feeling in writing: cummings in M. A. Cohen 1987, 73; Snyder in Snyder 1980, 32; Spender in Ghiselin 1952, 120–21; Frost in *Writers at Work,* ser. 2, 31–33; Fisher in Ghiselin 1952, 175; Allende in Epel 1993, 8; Translation in writing: Fisher 1952, 175; Eliot in *Writers at Work,* ser. 2, 104; Snyder in Snyder 1980, 32; Goyen in *Writers at Work* ser. 6, 203; LeGuin in LeGuin 1976, introduction; Spender in Ghiselin 1952, 119.

Intuition in creative process: Einstein in E. F. Keller 1983, 201; Poincaré in Poincaré 1913, 129; Planck in Planck 1949. Universality of creative process: Curtin 1982, 139, and passim on Nobel Conference; Gell-Mann in Judson 1980, 20–21. "Absolute similarities" in Curtin 1982, 142; confirmed by Nicolle and Trousseau in L'Echevin 1981, 192 and 9; Gabo in Herbert 1964, 112; Stravinsky in Stravinsky and Craft 1959, 17; Koestler 1976, passim. See also R. Root-Bernstein 1984a, b, 1985, 1987a, b, 1989b.

Imagination in education: Lipscomb in Curtin 1984, 19; Berg and Burnside in Berg 1983, 51, 65.

2. Schooling the Imagination

Illusions and Reality in Juster 1961, 115–17. Einstein and sailing in Sayen 1985, 132; concern for son in Highfield and Carter 1994, 204. Disconnection between mathematical and physical knowledge: Thomson 1937, 127–30; Poincaré 1946, 138; Eisenberg in Krebs and Shelley 1975, 16–17; Feynman in Feynman 1985b, 36–37.

Woolf on Stephen: Woolf 1976, 125–26; Annan 1984, 133. Stephen as student and tutor: Annan 1984, 39, and passim; Grosskurth 1968, 7. Stephen as philistine: Grosskurth 1968, 16–17, 20–30, and passim; Annan 1984, 37; Stephen 1977, 30, and 1968, 192. Woolf's education: Lee 1996, 57, 145, and passim. Dewey on art training in Dewey 1934, 3.

Fragility of knowledge in Feynman 1985b, 37. Bamberger in Bamberger 1991, 38, 44; F. R. Wilson 1998, 284; Escher in M. C. Escher 1989, 21.

Union of Illusions and Reality: Juster 1961, 118–19; for scientists, Root-Bernstein 1996a, 53; for writers, Chaplin 1964, 291; Horgan 1964, 98; LeGuin in LeGuin 1976, introduction; Gregory in Gregory and Gombrich 1980, 93–94. Generative role of invented fiction: Pasteur 1939, vol. VII, 584, under "Idées préconçus" (see also Ramón y Cajal 1893, 139); Einstein in Clark 1971, 87.

Art as a lie: Picasso in Ashton 1972, 3; photograph anecdote in Nachmanovitch 1990, 117.

Collins on using thinking tools in Collins 1991. Galton on imaginative skills in Galton 1874; 1892; and 1883. Smith on integrating thinking tools in C. S. Smith 1981, ix–x.

3. Observing

Camouflage: Thayer 1909; Stephenson and Stewart-Evison 1955, vii.

Artists observing: Johns in Rosen 1978, 135; O'Keeffe 1976, n.p; Read 1957, 209. Picasso in Salmon 1961, 133. Matisse in J. D. Flam 1978, 54. Delacroix ibid., 163, n.12; van Gogh in Van der Wolk, Pickvance, and Pey 1990, 16.

Writers observing: cummings in Gettings 1976; Dos Passos in Dos Passos 1966, 83; Maugham described in Watkins and Knight 1966, 66, 67; and Morgan 1931, 54. Du Maurier 1977, 80, and passim.

Scientists observing: von Frisch 1967, 20; Lorenz 1952, ix; Simons in Wolpert and Richards 1997, 152; Diamond ibid., 33.

Aural observing: Diamond in Wolpert and Richards 1997, 33; Messiaen 1986, 93; Hughes 1987, 26.

Tactile observing: Fischer and Vermeij in Vermeij 1997, x, 14, 151.

Musical observing: Schumann in Morgenstern 1956; Telemann et al. ibid., 40, and *passim;* Stravinsky in Stravinsky and Craft 1959, 149.

Performing arts observing: Humphrey 1959, 20; Graham 1991, 253; Nikolais in Brown 1979, 116; Boleslavsky 1939, 97, 99; Stanislavsky quoted in Gardner 1983, 227.

Olfactory observing: Cairns in Wolpert and Richards 1998, 93–94; French microbiologist in Jacob 1988, 246; chemistry: Levi and Regge 1989, 62; Eisner 1988, 451; and J. Horgan 1991, 60; physicians in Cox 1999, 2A, and Service, 1998, 1431.

Taste: Root-Bernstein and Root-Bernstein 1997, 112, 123; Beveridge 1950, 96; archeology in Wechter 1985, 43.

Sublimity of mundane: Root-Bernstein 1989a, b; Szent-Györgyi 1966, 116–17; Stravinsky 1970, 71; Cunningham in Cunningham 1968, n.p.; and Klosty 1975, 14; Halprin in Brown 1979, 128; Duchamp in Rosen 1978, 129; Oldenburg, quoted ibid., 120.

Mind controls observing: visual in Arnheim 1969, 13; olfactory in Cassidy, Doherty, and Murphy 1997, 3; Steinbeck and Ricketts 1941, introduction; Pepper in Greenburg and Jordan 1993, 96; Szent-Györgyi 1957, introduction.

Art trains observing: Read 1943; Brown and Korzenik 1993; Johns in Rosen 1978, 138; Lewis and Morgan in Morgan 1931, 46; Nabokov 1947, 90–92; Lowell in *Writers at Work,* ser. 2, 340; general source for artistic writers: Hjerter 1986; Szladits and Simmonds 1969; see also Kelly 1996 for Du Maurier; Dale 1985 for Chesterton; Hammond and Scull 1995 for Tolkein; Thackeray's illustrations in Thackeray 1901.

Arts train scientific observing: Ramón y Cajal 1937, 134–35; Haden in Zigrosser 1976, 14–15; general sources for artistic scientists: Ritterbush 1968 passim; Root-Bernstein 1989b, 312–40. Arts train observing in medicine: Pellegrino in Berg 1983, ix; Stone 1988, 108; Coulehan 1993, 57–59. See also Pasztor 1993.

Medicine as observational training for arts: Maugham in Morgan 1931, 54; Moore in *Writers at Work,* ser. 2, 66; see also Kandinsky in Herbert 1964, 37.

Exercises: Stanislavsky 1936, 87; Schlemmer in Lehmann and Richardson 1986, 80.

4. Imaging

Engineers imaging: Steinmetz anecdote from Seymour 1966, 97; Tesla in Tesla 1977, 13, 18; Sperry in E. S. Ferguson 1992, 51; Lovelock in Wolpert and Richards 1997, 73; Morse and Fulton in Hindle 1981; general sources: Petroski 1996; Stewart 1985.

Role of visual thinking generally: Koestler 1976, 168; Feynman 1988, 54; Arber 1964, 122; Wertheimer 1959.

Scientific imaging: Roe 1953; Root-Bernstein et al. 1995; A. I. Miller 1984; Gilbert and Mulkay 1984, 141–71. Black in Wolpert and Richards 1997, 126; Jacob 1988, passim; Debye in Anon. 1966, 81; Feynman in Gleick 1992, 245; Geller in Lightman and Brawer 1990, 372.

Artists imaging: O'Keeffe in Robinson 1989, 184; Adams 1985, 76–79; Sokolow in John-Steiner 1985, 164; Hodes in Horosko 1991, 116; see also Graham in Horosko 1991, 49, 51, 105.

Writers imaging: Spender in *Writers at Work,* ser. 6, 70; Dryden in Prescott, 1922, 44; Coleridge in Harding 1967, 29; Sassoon ibid., 28; Murray in Duke and Jacobsen 1983, 52; Dickens in Harding 1967, 28; Williams in *Writers at Work,* ser. 6, 84; Nabokov 1947, 39, 187; Thackeray in Harding 1967, 28; Miller in *Writers at Work,* ser. 2, 166; Moore ibid., 66. Writers as artists in Hjerter 1986; and Szladits and Simmonds 1969.

Polysensory imaging: Barlow, Blakemore, and Weston-Smith 1990, ix, *passim.* Taste imagery: Herme in Critchell 1998; Trotter in Critchell 1999; Nabokov in Nabokov 1980, 379. Smell imagery: Vroon 1997.

Aural imaging in musicians: Copland in Ghiselin 1952, 52; Mozart ibid., 45; Beethoven in Morgenstern 1956, 87; Cowell in Jourdain 1997, 161; de Larrocha in Dubal 1984, 140; Bar-Illan ibid., 60; Graham in Graham 1991, 231.

Visual imaging in musicians: Antheil 1945, 124 and passim; Stravinsky 1936, 31–32, 56; Pavarotti 1999; Honegger in Morgenstern 1956, 468; Copland in Ghiselin 1952, 52; Cowell in Jourdain 1997, 161.

Aural imaging in writers: Lowell in Ghiselin 1952, 110; Williams in *Writers at Work,* ser. 6, 89–90.

Aural imaging in scientists: Einstein in Clark 1971, 106; Sayen 1985, 26; Highfield and Carter 1993, 13. Einstein on musical intuition and physics: Curtin 1982, 84; Suzuki 1969, 90. Feynman in Gleick 1992, 244–45; and Root-Bernstein et al. 1995 passim; Geller in Lightman and Brawer 1990, 372; Carruthers in Broad 1984, 58; Dyson 1979, 64–88.

Visual versus nonvisual imagers: Poincaré 1946, 212; Feynman 1985, 23; Hoyle in Lightman and Brawer 1990, 60; Poincaré 1913, 212; Einstein in Holton 1972; Pestallozi in *Encyclopaedia Britannica* 1959; Geller in Lightman and Brawer 1990, 372; Mitchell in Wolpert and Richards 1997, 84.

Efficacy of imaging training: engineers: Schaer et al., 1985; Stewart 1985; scientists: Bonner in Root-Bernstein et al. 1995, 127; writers: Nabokov 1980, 3–4; Lowell 1930, 11–12; composers: Sessions in Ghiselin 1952, 48; Shapero ibid., 52; mathematics: Wiener 1953, 75–76.

Difficulty in translating images: Einstein in Holton 1972, 26–27nn.; Bill in Stiles and Selz 1996, 76; Ives in Burkholder 1985, 51; Ives 1962, 84; Swafford 1996, 446, n5; Drabble in Barlow, Blakemore, and Weston-Smith 1990, 332; Tesla in Cheney 1981, 11.

5. Abstracting

Abstracting: Heisenberg in Heisenberg 1974, 71; Picasso in Ashton 1972, 10, 131 (ideograms). Abstracting/mathematics/intelligence link: Dirac in Davis and Hersh 1981, 113; Davis and Hersh ibid. Abstracting in writing: Johnson 1899; Cather 1920, 40–41, 102. Abstracting in dance, painting, sculpture: Graham 1991, 231; Schlemmer 1972, 49; Moore in Sylvester 1968, 54.

Effort of abstracting: Robinson in Goodman 1994, 36; Wald in Szent-Györgyi 1971,

2. As scientist's most important talent: M. Wilson 1949, 103; Picasso in Ashton 1972, 68; as "greater generality," Heisenberg 1974, 144; Feynman in Gleick 1992, 217.

Robertson's Stein anecdote in Riley 1995, 81. Origins in reality: Picasso in Ashton 1972, 64, 68. Lichtenstein's bulls in Rosen 1978; Kelly in Greenberg and Jordan 1991, 50. Matisse's snails in Munthe 1983.

Muybridge, Marey, Richer, and Duchamp abstractions: Marey 1895; Richer 1895; Braun 1992; Vitz and Glimcher 1984, 127–31. Cunningham in Kisselgoff 1999, 7.

Abstracting in scientific writing: Szent-Györgyi in Szent-Györgyi 1971, 2; Hinshelwood in Digby and Brier 1977, 210; Hoffman 1987, 1988; Davy 1840, 306–8.

Ramón y Cajal 1937, passim; Matisse's ideal studio in J. D. Flam 1973, 56. Feigenbaum on arts/sciences abstracting in Gleick 1984, 71.

General sources on abstracting: Root-Bernstein 1991; Hale 1972; Kepes 1965.

6. Recognizing Patterns

Biological and psychological pattern recognition in Dodwell 1970, 1–2. Pattern recognition as prediction in Judson 1980, 28. Lehrer on expectancy in jokes in Tauber 1997.

Pattern recognition in random scenes and sounds: George Escher quoted in M. C. Escher exhibit wall label, Kresge Art Museum, Michigan State University, 31 Jan.–15 Mar. 1998; Gallé in Silverman 1989, 238; Max Ernst in Evans 1937, 74; Leonardo in Winternitz 1982, 134.

Rhythm recognition in Padgett 1987, 166. Adams in Adams 1985, 24; commenting on synthesis ibid., 28. Dichter memorizing patterns in Elyse Mach 1980, 65. Bernstein conceptualizing patterns in Bernstein 1976, 7. Schoenberg on musical relationships in Morgenstern 1956, 383. Pattern recognition among dyslexics in Parkinson and Edwards 1977, passim.

Mathematicians extracting structure: Gauss in Salem et al. 1992, 78; Goldbach's conjecture in Davis and Hersh 1981, 172. Nüsslein-Volhard on scientific puzzle solving in Fenzl 1997, 45; Yang in Curtin 1982, 141–42.

Ignorance in science: Weller in Witte et al., 1988; Rabi in M. Wilson 1972, 17; Szent-Györgyi in Root-Bernstein 1989b, 407. Curriculum on medical ignorance: Witte et al. 1989; see also Edwards 1990. Learning from absence: Hearst 1991.

Feynman playing with patterns in Sykes 1994, 20. Nabokov in Nabokov 1947, 85.

7. Forming Patterns

Artistic pattern forming: Gene Davis in Wall 1975, 30–31; Riley in Riley 1995, 23–24; Stuart Davis, San Francisco Museum of Modern Art exhibit, wall label.

Musical pattern forming: African tribal music in Arom 1991, esp. 210–15, 287–90; Schillinger in F. Schillinger 1949; J. Schillinger 1948, 109*ff.*; Glass and Reich in Kostalanetz and Flemming 1997, passim; quote, 107; Stomp in performance and on video; Bach in Schillinger 1948; *Mr. Bach,* audiocassette; Milhaud in Morgenstern 1956, 473–74.

Art-science pattern forming: moiré patterns: Oster and Nishishima 1963; Parola 1969; *Encyclopaedia Brittannica* 1959 under "Moiré." Fourier transforms: Davis and Hersh 198, 255–63; and *Encyclopaedia Britannica* 1959 under "Fourier." Fractals in Gleick 1987, 98–103.

Pattern forming with words: Woolf 1976, 72; Nabokov 1980, 379; de Jong in Quennel 1980, 59–72; Gould in E. Mach 1980, 94; and Girard 1995 (Gould video); Fleischman 1988.

Combinatorial patterns in dance: Cunningham 1968, n.p.

Multiple patterns: art-science similarities: Root-Bernstein 1984a, b, 1996; human evolution in Wood and Collard 1999; periodic tables in Mazurs 1974. Other examples from biology and chemistry in Root-Bernstein 1989b, 77–79, 118–19, 199–202, 213, 273–75, 288–90, 293–98, 356.

Learning pattern forming: words: Hoberman in Hall 1985, 275; visual patterns: Parola 1969; building toys: Resnick in Wallach 1998; Grey and Glickman in Jana 1998.

8. Analogizing

Atom–musical instrument analogy: Gamow 1966, 6–80; Kuhn 1979. Einstein in Schilpp 1969, vol. 1, 45; de Broglie in Gamow 1966, 81–97; MRI in Kleinfeld 1985, passim.

Resonant ideas: Diderot 1966, 156.

Keller on analogizing in H. Keller 1920, 14, 105–6, 128–30.

Analogy as measure of intelligence: Heath 1947, 51; *Encyclopaedia Britannica* 1959 under "Analogy."

Analogies as imperfect correspondences: Laënnec in Moulton and Schifferes 1960, 300; Arber 1964, 44; Heath 1947, 54.

Universality of analogizing: Holyoak and Thagard 1995, introduction.

Biomimicry: leeches, etc., in Root-Bernstein and Root-Bernstein, 1997a, 181–83 and 198–211; Velcro, etc., in Benyus 1997; Pearce 1978; bridge in Petroski 1997.

Literary analogies: Bronowski 1956, 30–31; Wordsworth 1800, xxxii; Frost in Watkins and Knight 1966, 157; Spender in Ghiselin 1952, 119–24; Valéry ibid., 105; Snyder discussed by Haas 1997 (video).

Artistic analogies: *akari* in Noguchi 1994, 103; Moore in Sylvester 1968, 530; Chillida in Schwartz 1969, 69.

Sciences/arts analogies: tensegrity–cell structure in Heidemann 1993 and Ingber 1998. Tosney on chick-origami analogy, personal communication; Gilbert on music-embryology analogy, personal communication.

Music/arts analogies: Escher 1989, 20–21; J. Schillinger 1948, passim; see also Klee in Kagan 1983, passim.

Learning to analogize: Brooks 1998, 108; Ruef 1992; Leonardo da Vinci in Winternitz 1982, see index under "analogies"; Siler 1990, 1997; Khayyam 1941, 98.

9. Body Thinking

Kohler/chimp anecdote in M. Gardner 1978, vi.

Proprioception: Sacks 1987, 43, 72; Critchley 1953 passim; Shreeve 1993, 42. Mozart's body thinking in Harding 1967, 37. Keller feeling music in H. Keller 1902, 288. Keller and dancers in Graham 1991, 148. Cocteau on Nijinsky in *Writers at Work*, ser. 3, 63. Graham on logic in H. Gardner 1983, 224. Feld composing with body in John-Steiner 1985, 20. Keller on pump in H. Keller 1902, 23, 316; on ice cream in H. Keller 1920, 115; on wordless thoughts in H. Keller 1902, 23. Hutchinson on body imaging in Hutchinson 1959, 142.

Artists on body thinking: Cannon 1945, passim. Mandelbrojt in Mandelbrojt 1994, 186; Itten in Droste 1993, 31; Noguchi in Noguchi 1994, 37; Ghiberti in H. Keller 1920, 84; Oldenburg in Greenburg and Jordan 1993, 99; Simonds ibid., 73; Rodin in Pinet 1992, 89; on how *Thinker* thinks in Silverman 1989, 261; Moore on feeling bones in Sylvester 1968, 128; on feeling positions in Packer and Levine, 1985, 116; Matisse in J. D. Flam 1978, 43; Graham in Horosko 1991, 39, 111; Menuhin 1972, 87; Ozawa in Weisgall 1997–98, 14–15; Antheil in Antheil 1945, 67–68; Laredo in Dubal 1984, 242; Gould ibid., 182–83.

Scientists using body thinking: Root-Bernstein 1989b, passim; Waddington 1969, 158; C. S. Smith 1981, 353; M. Wilson 1949, 71; E. S. Ferguson 1992, 58; Jansons in Weiskrantz 1988, 503; blind feeling space in J. F. Wilson 1948, 221; Ulam 1976, 17, 147; Wiener 1956, 85–86; Nabokov on body thinking in illness in Nabokov 1947, 24, 36–37.

To think is to feel: Nabokov 1947, 291; Russell in Hutchinson 1959, 19; Bensley in *Encyclopaedia Britannica* 1959, 884D. Sympathetic body imaging: Martin 1939, 53, also 47–52; Stanislavsky 1961, 220.

Phantom limb: Sacks 1987, 66–67; Shreeve 1993, 36 and passim. Limb phantoms: Botvinick in Anon. 1998, 21; "Pole Dance" in Lehmann and Richardson 1986, 155; Nikolais in Brown 1979, 114; Menuhin 1997, 311, 315, 320–21; F. Wilson 1998, 63, 92; TeSS in Ritter 1998; machine operators in F. Wilson 1998, 63.

Training body thinking: Humphrey in Brown 1979, 61; creative movement in Griss 1994, 78. Haldane in Haldane 1976, 69; "everything registers" in Boleslavsky 1939, 101.

10. Empathizing

Empathic writers: Cather in Jefferson 1995, 7; Cendrars in *Writers at Work*, ser. 3, 45; Daudet in Harding 1967, 45; Dickens ibid.; Eliot 1885, vol. 3, 421–24.

Empathic performers: Bach in Morgenstern 1956, 60; Arrau in Dubal 1984, 20;

Duncan in Highwater 1978, 101; Kirkland 1987, 92 and passim; Humphrey 1959, 21; Stanislavsky 1936, 1925, 292; Hanks, media interviews, 1998.

Empathic physicians: general sources: Berg 1983; Morrison 1993. Williams in *Writers at Work,* ser. 6, 84–90; Sacks 1967; Vastyan in Berg 1983, 128; Margulies 1989; IAMA Newsletter 1985; Coles in Stone 1988, 108–9; Stone in Stone, ibid.

Empathy as understanding: general sources: E. F. Keller 1983. Zen in Arber 1964, 68; Suzuki in S. Suzuki 1969, passim; and Hermann 1981, passim. Buber 1920, 34; Bergson in E. F. Keller 1983; Polanyi 1958; Popper in Krebs and Shelley 1975, 18.

Empathic historians: Cohen in Suhr 1998; Wu in Anon. 1999, 11; Wechter 1985, 43; Soderqvist in Soderqvist 1996, 1681; Kuhn: personal experience as his student.

Empathic hunting: "sorcerer" in Pfeiffer 1982, 108; bushmen ibid., 165; Lyons in Gucwa and Ehmann 1985, 207–8; fly fishing MacLean 1992, 110; thinking like cow: Grandin 1995, 142; Brannaman in Trachtman 1998, 60.

Scientific hunting: Mach 1926, 1; Bernard 1927; Szent-Györgyi 1971, 2.

Scientific empathizing: Goodall 1986, 58; Strum 1987, vii, 203; Griffin 1984; Douglas-Hamilton in Gucwa and Ehmann 1985, 197; Morris 1980, 58; Eisner in Wolkomir and Wolkomir 1990, 44; McClintock in E. F. Keller 1983, 117; Levi-Montalcini 1988, 172; Sherrington on Ramón y Cajal in Knudtson 1986; Monod 1970, 170; Lederburg in Judson 1980, 6; Debye in Anon., 1966, 81; Rutherford in G. P. Thomson 1961, 69–70; Chandrasekhar 1987, 67; Feynman in Gleick 1992, 142, 394; Alfvèn 1988, 250.

Inventors empathizing: Kettering in Levine 1960, 114; Bell in Eber 1982, 67; Feynman 1985b, passim.

Artists empathizing: Woolf 1927, 100–101; Mitchell in Stiles and Selz 1996, 34; WOLS ibid., 45; Tung-P'o in Mandelbrojt 1994, 186; Matisse in J. D. Flam 1973, 171; Noguchi in Greenburg and Jordan 1993, 84.

Learning to empathize: Shaham, personal communication, partly published in Root-Bernstein 1990, 13; Stanislavsky 1936, 75–83, and 1961, 223; Wood in Seabrook 1941, 128, 98–99 (photos).

11. Dimensional Thinking

Dancers on dimensionality: De Mille 1951, 18; T. Schlemmer 1972, 82.

3-D billiards: Cipra 1997, 1070.

Flatland: Abbott 1952; Visible Human Project Web site. Maps: *Times Atlas of the World,* 8th ed., 1990.

Multidimensional periodic tables: Thomsen 1987; F. Flam 1991; Rouvray 1994.

Dimensional seeing: Sacks and Borges in Sacks 1995, 129 and note.

Perspective and anamorphosis: Frayling, Frayling, and van der Meer 1992; Leeman, Elffers, and Shuyte 1976; Kemp 1990; M. Gardner 1974. Riley in Riley 1995, 64; other abstract artists in Auping 1989.

Scientific anamorphosis: mathematics of in Gardner 1974; Monge in *Encyclopaedia Britannica* 1959 under "Monge." In evolution, D. Thompson 1942; Huxley 1932. In neurology, A. Miller 1982, 14–22; Blakemore 1977, 77–81; Woolsey 1978. In cinematography, Gardner 1974.

Mathematical dimensions: fractals in Gleick 1987; origami in Noguchi 1994, 39, 151; math and origami in Cipra 1998; plication in Hayes 1995, 504.

Scaling: Morrison, Morrison, and Eames 1982; O'Keeffe 1976, n.p.; Stravinsky 1970, 142, 173–74; Haldane 1928, 20–28; Feynman in Sykes 1994, 167–68; Rubbia in Wolpert and Richards 1997, 198–99.

Musical time: Xenakis in Bois 1967, 13; Glass in Kostalanetz and Flemming 1997, 164.

Calder on spatial relativity: Calder video, PBS, 1998. Haldane on multidimensional kinesthetic thinking: Haldane 1976, 101. Noguchi on "emotional space" in Noguchi 1994, 80.

Dimensional "blindness": general: Galton 1883, 113–14; architectural plans: Peterson 1998, 132; sculptural: Moore in Ghiselin 1952, 73; perceptual: Mondrian 1995, 56, 108–9. Geller in Lightman and Brawer 1990, 361; Davies in Krebs and Shelley 1975, 16.

Learning dimensional thinking: Geller's 3-D puzzles in Lightman and Brawer 1990, 361. Bauhaus 3-D exercises in Droste 1990, 28, 93; Whitford 1993, 226; Moholy-Nagy 1947, passim. Kaleidocycles in Schattschneider and Walker 1987. Wright, Fuller, Kandinsky, and Froebel blocks: Brosterman 1997. Pop-up books: e.g., Miller and Pelham 1983; reconstructing animal tracks: Ennion and Tinbergen 1967.

4-D thinking: Feynman in Sykes 1994, 25; Penrose in Lightman and Brawer 1990, 426. Methods for: Reid, 1963, 401*ff;* Davis and Hersh 1981, 400–405.

12. Modeling

Modeling war: Mondrian 1995, 54; Featherstone 1962; Brewer and Shubik 1979; Wells in Wells 1913, 12; MacKenzie and MacKenzie 1973, 231; Von Meuffling, Young, and Lawford in Brewer and Shubik 1979, 45; U.S. Dept. of Defense ibid., 8.

Modeling for control: Goethe in King 1996, 193–94; Rodin ibid., 193; Jung in Jung 1963, 80–81; Moore in Sylvester 1968, 55.

Musical modeling: Isherwood and Stravinsky in Stravinsky and Craft 1959, 18; Sessions in Ghiselin 1952, 47; Glass discussed in Kostalanetz and Flemming 1997, 88; Shapero in Ghiselin 1952, 52; Xenakis in Varga 1996, 65.

Artistic modeling: Seurat's *The Can-Can* in Anfam et al. 1985, 266–69; Bourgeois in Stiles and Selz 1996, 38–39; Noguchi 1994, 133; Moore in Schwartz 1969, 205–15; Packer and Levine 1985, passim; Segal and Hanson in Greenburg and Jordan 1993, 28, 43; Leonardo da Vinci in Vasari 1978, 180; Cambiaso: Michigan State University exhibit material.

Medical modeling: Chinese dolls: Lyons and Petrucelli 1978, 129; acupuncture: ibid., 148; wax dissections: ibid., 470; Welcome Medical Rooms, Science Museum, London.

Modern medical models: Health Education Company catalogue, Anatomical Products catalogue; Fleming's spiky test tube in Colebrook 1954; and Root-Bernstein 1989, 152; Gimpel's models in P. Brown 1993, 47–48.

Scientific modeling: Pauling in Judson 1980, 121–24; DNA model in Watson 1968; Smith's bubbles in C. S. Smith 1981, frontispiece; Feynman on Maxwell in Feynman 1985a, 57. See also Freudenthal 1961 (general science); Macmillan 1989 (geography).

Mathematical models: Kummer in Fischer 1986, v and passim; Freudenthal 1961.

Computer versus 3-D models: Skawinski in Holden 1998, 37; Johnson and Bailey in Svitil 1998, 81–83; Davis and Hersh 1981, 375–79; Clarke in Anon. 1997, 78; Florman 1982; Petroski 1985; E. Ferguson 1992.

Learning modeling: O'Keeffe 1976, n.p.; Oldenburg in Greenburg and Jordan 1993, 99; Jung 1963, 82; anonymous scientist in Root-Bernstein et al. 1995, 127; anonymous mathematician no. 7 in Gustin 1985. Bridge design and testing in Jackson 1972, 102.

13. Playing

Fleming sources: Maurois 1959, 32–33, 74, 82, 95, 109, 124, 152; Macfarlane 1984, 252–53, 286; Root-Bernstein, 1989a passim, 1989b, 129–91.

Lorenz in Morris 1980, 60; Delbruck in Judson 1979, 41.

Functions of play: S. Miller 1973, 89–93; Piaget 1951, 110–13.

Feynman sources: Feynman 1985b, 173–74; Feynman 1988; Gleick 1992; Sykes 1994.

Engineering play: Molella 1998; Sperry in Ferguson 1992, 50; Lemelson in Molella 1998, 1; Hess in Hess 1963, 43; Johnson in Mays 1999.

Sculptors' play: Rickey in Anon. 1956; Tinguely in Schwarz 1969; Taylor in MIT Archives. Calder sources: Calder video 1998; Mancewicz 1969, 7–11, 37; Evans 1939, 63; Marter 1991, 62–64, 231. Snelson: personal communication; also Snelson Web site. Rothbart in Jana 1998, 50.

Lear sources: Lear 1975; Byrom 1977, 9; Alderson 1975, 208; Strachey 1907, vol. 1, xxv, 253; Hark 1982, 20.

Carroll sources: Blake 1972, 187; Weaver 1956, 118; Nyman 1974, 16; Lehmann 1972, 17–18. Applications to physics: Levi and Regge 1989, 59.

Escher and Penrose sources: Escher 1989, 21–22; R. Penrose in Ernst 1992, 71–72; Gardner 1977. Applications to alloys: Peterson 1985; Nelson and Halperin 1985; Peterson 1999.

Musical play: Ives in Swafford 1996, 46 and passim; Nyman 1974, 34–36. Borodin in Morgenstern 1956, 218–19. Bach in *Mr. Bach* CD; Mozart in Winternitz 1958.

Word play: Augarde 1984, 75; Kim 1981; Langdon 1992.

Music play: Bach in Schillinger 1948; Mozart in Winternitz 1958.

Learning to play: mechanical play: Petroski 1999; Yuwiler, personal communication. University courses: Petroski 1999; Stewart 1985. Engineering of play: Gordon 1961, 119–44; visual play: Stewart 1985; food play: Elffers 1998. Dance play: Pilobolus from Belans's Web site.

Appendix: Bernstein 1976, 25.

14. *Transforming*

On Leakey's discovery: Leakey 1984, 170–80; Agnew and Demas 1998, 44–57. Edgerton: MIT Archives. Oldenburg and van Bruggen process described in "Torn Notebook," video documentary.

French mnemonic device for pi: Rothstein 1995, 147; Baum: *Biochemists' Songbook* 1982; Guido's system in Rowley 1978, 58, 174; counting in New Guinea in Ifrah 1985, 10–14; number images in Galton 1928, 79, plates 2, 3. Hindu mnemonic device and memory wheels in S. Stein 1963, 110*ff.*

Bill images and quote in Waddington 1969, 208. Gabo ibid., 206. Gabo's math-art transformations are illustrated in Nash and Merkert 1985. Ferguson's work in C. Ferguson 1994; Cipra 1992. Collins's and Sequin's work is illustrated in Peterson 1998. A general source for art-math transformations is Cipra 1992 and the newsletter *Art & Mathematics,* edited by Nat Friedman.

Scientists performing math-image transformations: Feynman in Feynman 1985a, 85; and Gleick 1992, passim; Halem, personal communication; NCSA in Peterson 1987; Tufte 1983, 1990.

Musical urinalysis transformation: Sweeley et al. 1987. Musical DNA: Ohno and Ohno 1986; Ohno 1993; Hayashi and Munakata 1984; Ortiz Web site. General music-data transformations: Levarie 1980; Peterson 1985b, 1994. Musicians transforming data: Xenakis transformations in Bois 1967; Varga 1996; Alexjander and Deamer, *Sequencia* CD.

Science-dance transformations are illustrated in Golani, Wolgin, and Teitelbaum 1979; Cohen in "Race for the Superconductor," *Nova,* 1988.

Music-art transformations by Klee: Kagan 1983, 44, 81; similar experiments in J. Schillinger 1948, passim.

Transformational thinking as creative strategy: Lightman 1992, 34; Woodward 1989, 250; Pauling 1963, 46; Wood in Truesdell 1984, 409; Maxwell in Rukeyser 1942, 439.

Bell's kite designing: Eber 1982, passim.

Music-art transformation exercises: Armer in Anon., 1956, 1–2; O'Keeffe in O'Keeffe 1976; Subotnik, *Making Music,* CD-ROM (Voyager Co.).

Good sources of concrete poetry are: Augarde 1984, 151–59; Padgett 1987, 52–56; Kennedy 1978, 187–96. No compendium of pictonyms seems to exist, but we have designed hundreds. Rebuses: Loyd 1912 and other Loyd books; and Augarde 1984, 84–91.

Multiple transformations adapted from Davis and Hersh 1981, 130–33.

15. Synthesizing

Nabokov in Nabokov 1947, 24, 218, 219. Lighthill interviewed in Wolpert and Richards 1997, 60–64.

Sensory mixing: Nabokov 1947, 34–35; Rimbaud in Koch and Farrell 1985, 98; Feynman 1988, 59; Jacob 1988, 38; Kandinsky in Herbert 1964, 34; and Cole 1993, 52. Barlach in Anon., 1956, 11; O'Keeffe 1976, n.p.; Robinson 1989, 122; Sarton in Sarton 1968, 58; Pinter in *Writers at Work,* ser. 3, 354. Nevanlinna in Lehto 1980; Davis and Hersh 1981, 310–11. Hockney in Anon. 1989, 70–71; Liszt in Jourdain 1997, 326. Messiaen 1986, 39, 65–66. Steen at International Synaesthesia Association Web site.

Sensory fusion: general: Wolpin et al. 1986, 34; Harrison and Baron-Cohen 1995. Cytowic 1993, 5, 53–54.

Associational synesthesia examples: Nabokov 1947, 171; Woolf 1976, 66.

Commonness of synesthesia: Wolpin et al. 1986, 33–36; Marks et al. 1987, 2–4. Merleau-Ponty in Odin 1986, 271. Cytowic 1993, 166–67.

Synesthesia in culture: tea ceremony: Odin 1986, 256–58. Mead 1974, pt. 2, 386; Stravinsky in Stravinsky and Craft 1959, 3; Merleau-Ponty on Cezanne in Odin 1986, 273; cummings in Cohen 1987, 225; Adams and Newhall in Adams 1985, 215; Graham and Calder in Graham 1991, 166; Zaccolini, Remington et al. in Cole 1993, 52; Moholy-Nagy in Poling 1975, 41; Eisenstein 1949, 21–22.

Knowing versus understanding: Huxley 1963.

Glennie: Glennie video and Web site. H. Keller 1920, 125, 194.

Synosia: Arber 1964, 21; Kant quoted ibid., 124. Schlemmer 1972, 233. Michelson 1903, introduction; Woodward 1989, 137. Morris material: Morris 1987, 12; in Remy 1991, 12; Morris 1971, 22; and R. Root-Bernstein, 1997a. Other: Stravinsky 1970, 35; Piene in Stiles and Selz 1996, 408–9; Bellows in Herbert 1964, 461; Gropius in Harrison and Wood 1992, 340; Fuller in Brown 1979, 17; Humphrey ibid., 62–63; Copland 1957, 18–22; Henn 1966, ix, 5. Feynman in Gleick 1992, 373.

Need for synthetic thinkers: Mondrian 1995, 110; Sacks 1967, introduction; Waddington 1972, 360; Fuller 1979, 104.

16. Synthesizing Education

Previous statements of our educational position: R. Root-Bernstein 1984a, 1987a, 1989b, 1991, 1997a, b, c; R. Root-Bernstein et al. 1995; M. Root-Bernstein 1997.

Inadequacy of present knowledge: Huxley 1963, 118; Platt 1962, 108.

Need for generalists: Huxley 1963, passim; Waddington 1972, 52; Brooks 1966, 13.

Transdisciplinary innovators: Wilson in Rayleigh 1942, 99; Kovalevskaya 1978, 102–3; Fabre in Simons 1939, 4, 12–13; Kandinsky in Herbert 1964, 24–25; Lorenz 1952, 12; Lipscomb in Curtin 1982, 20–21; Weierstrass in D. Smith 1934, 1; Xenakis in Bois 1967, 15; Ives in Moore in *Writers at Work,* ser. 2, 68, 86.

On polymaths and success: Harding 1967, 3; Galton 1874; van't Hoff 1878; Ramón y Cajal 1893, 170*ff;* White 1931, 482; Simonton 1984, 47; Hadamard 1945; Roe 1953; Root-Bernstein 1987a, b, 1989a, b, esp. 312*ff;* Root-Bernstein 1991; Root-Bernstein et al. 1995.

Avocations as predictors of career success: Hong et al. 1993; Milgram and Hong 1993; Root-Bernstein et al. 1995; Branscomb 1986; Simonton 1984, passim. See also Ramón y Cajal 1937; E. Ferguson 1992, 23–26; Hjerter 1986; Papert in Wechsler 1978, 104; Root-Bernstein 1996a; golfing and business in Bryant 1998, 1.

Integrative activity sets and networks of enterprise: Dewey 1934, passim; King 1996, 6–8, 52, 228–29, 259; Gruber 1984, 1988, 1989; Root-Bernstein et al. 1995, 131–32.

Learning from other disciplines: Schumann in Morgenstern 1956, 149; Békésy in Ratliff 1974, 15–16; Horgan 1973, 157; Snyder 1980, 60*ff;* Vonnegut in *Writers at Work,* ser. 6, 226; Bernard 1927, 223.

Polymathic teaching programs: Zen: Odin 1986; Suzuki 1969, 96–97; and Hermann 1981, 73. Bauhaus: Schlemmer 1972, 229; Klee in Kagan 1983, 163 n.28; Cunningham in Kisselgoff 1999, 7; Lowell in Ghiselin 1952, 112; Xenakis 1985, 3; Steinmetz in Seymour 1966, 119.

Freeman at Art, Science and Creativity conference, Chicago Academy of Sciences, 1994; Ross 1928, 23; Frost 1969.

BIBLIOGRAPHY

In the writing of this book we delved into archives, museums, and libraries; we interviewed people, read interviews of them, and watched them on video and film; we read autobiographies, biographies, and academic studies; we looked at, listened to, touched, moved around, and otherwise sensed their works; and, most important, we tried to recreate their insights ourselves. The bibliography that follows is therefore only one source for the information used in this book. See, too, Minds-On Resources, page 365.

Abbott, Edwin A. 1952. *Flatland: A Romance of Many Dimensions.* New York: Dover.

Adams, Ansel, with Mary Street Alinder. 1985. *Ansel Adams: An Autobiography.* Boston: Little, Brown.

Agnew, Neville, and Martha Demas. 1998. "Preserving the Laetoli Footprints." *Scientific American* 279 (Sept.): 44–57.

Alfvèn, Hannes. 1988. "Memoirs of a Dissident Scientist." *American Scientist* 76: 250.

American Heritage. 1985. *A Sense of History: The Best Writing from the Pages of American Heritage.* New York: American Heritage.

Anfam, David A., et al. 1986. *Techniques of the Great Masters of Art.* London: QED.

Annan, Noel. 1984. *Leslie Stephen: The Godless Victorian.* New York: Random House.

Anonymous, eds. 1956. *Art and Artist.* Berkeley: University of California Press.

———. 1966. *The Way of the Scientist.* New York: Simon and Schuster.

———. 1989. "David Hockney's Melodic Palette." *U.S. News and World Report,* 13 Nov.: 70–71.

———. 1997. "Scientists at Play." *Discover,* Dec.: 78–81.

———. 1998. "There's the Rub." *Discover,* June: 21.

———. 1999. "Greek Warfare Comes to Campus." *Princeton Alumni Weekly,* 19 May: 11.

Antheil, George. 1945. *Bad Boy of Music.* Garden City, N.Y.: Doubleday, Doran.

Arias, Enrique Alberto. 1989. "Music as Projection of the Kinetic Sense." *Music Review* 50: 1–33.

Arber, Agnes. 1964. *The Mind and the Eye.* Cambridge: Cambridge University Press.

Arnheim, Rudolf. 1969. *Visual Thinking.* Berkeley: University of California Press.

Arom, Simha. 1991. *African Polyphony and Polyrhythm.* Trans. Martin Thom, Barbara Tuckett, and Raymond Boyd. Cambridge: Cambridge University Press.

Ashton, Dore, ed. 1972. *Picasso on Art: A Selection of Views.* New York: DaCapo.

Augarde, Tony. 1984. *The Oxford Guide to Word Games.* New York: Oxford University Press.

Auping, Michael, ed. 1989. *Abstraction Geometry Painting: Selected Geometric Abstract Painting in America Since 1945.* New York: Harry N. Abrams.

Bamberger, Jeanne. 1991. "The Laboratory for Making Things." In D. Schon, ed., *The Reflective Turn: Case Studies in and on Educational Practice.* New York: Teachers College Press.

Barlow, Horace, C. Blakemore, and M. Weston-Smith, eds. 1990. *Images and Understanding: Thoughts about Images, Ideas and Understanding.* Cambridge: Cambridge University Press.

Baum, Harold. 1982. *The Biochemists' Songbook.* Oxford: Pergamon Press.

Benyus, Janine M. 1997. *Biomimicry: Innovation Inspired by Nature.* New York: William Morrow.

Berg, Geri, ed. 1983. *The Visual Arts and Medical Education.* Carbondale, Ill.: Southern Illinois University Press.

Bernard, Claude. 1927. *An Introduction to Experimental Medicine.* Trans. H. C. Greene. New York: Macmillan.

Bernstein, Leonard. 1976. *The Unanswered Question: Six Talks at Harvard.* Cambridge, Mass.: Harvard University Press.

Beveridge, W. I. B. 1950. *The Art of Scientific Investigation.* New York: W. W. Norton/ Vintage Books.

Blakemore, Colin. 1977. *Mechanics of the Mind.* Cambridge: Cambridge University Press.

Bois, Mario, ed. 1967. *Iannis Xenakis: The Man and His Music.* London: Boosey & Hawkes.

Boleslavsky, Richard. 1939. *Acting: The First Six Lessons.* New York: Theatre Arts.

Bower, Bruce. 1998. "Seeing Through Expert Eyes." *Science News* 154, no. 3: 44–46.

Boxer, S. 1987. "Play the Right Bases and You'll Hear Bach." *Discover,* Mar.: 10–12.

Branscomb, Lewis M. 1986. "The Unity of Science." *American Scientist* 74: 4.

Braun, Marta. 1992. *Picturing Time: The Work of Etienne-Jules Marey (1830–1904).* Chicago: University of Chicago Press.

Brewer, S., and T. Shubik. 1979. *The War Game: A Critique of Military Problem Solving.* Cambridge, Mass.: Harvard University Press.

Broad, William J. 1984. "Tracing the Skeins of Matter" (interview with Peter A. Carruthers). *New York Times Magazine*, 6 May: 54–62.

Bronowski, Jacob. 1956. *Science and Human Values*. New York: Harper and Row.

———. 1978. *The Origins of Knowledge and Imagination*. New Haven: Yale University Press.

Brooks, Chandler M. 1966. "Trends in Physiological Thought." In C. M. Brooks, ed., *The Future of Biology*. New York: New York University Press.

Brooks, Geraldine. 1998. "The Quarter-Acre Universe." *New York Times Magazine*, 27 Sept.: 108.

Brosterman, Norman. 1997. *Inventing Kindergarten*. New York: Abrams.

Brown, Jean Morrison, ed. 1979. *The Vision of Modern Dance*. Princeton: Princeton Book Co.

Brown, Maurice, and Diana Korzenik. 1993. *Art Making and Education*. Urbana: University of Illinois Press.

Brown, Phillida. 1993. "A Model Approach to TB." *New Scientist*, 4 Sept.: 47–48.

Bryant, Adam. 1998. "Duffers Need Not Apply." *New York Times*, 31 May, sec. 3: 1, 9.

Buber, Martin. 1920. *Die Rede, die Lehre, und das Lied*. Leipzig: Vieweg.

Burkholder, J. Peter. 1985. *Charles Ives: The Ideas Behind the Music*. New Haven: Yale University Press.

Byrom, Thomas. 1977. *Nonsense and Wonder: The Poems and Cartoons of Edward Lear*. New York: E. P. Dutton.

Cannon, Walter. 1945. *The Way of the Investigator*. New York: Hafner.

Cassidy, John, Paul Doherty, and Pat Murphy. 1997. *Zap Science*. Palo Alto, Calif.: Klutz Books.

Cather, Willa. 1920. *On Writing: Critical Studies on Writing as an Art*. Reprint, 1968: New York: Alfred A. Knopf.

Chandrasekhar, Subrahmanyan. 1987. *Truth and Beauty: Aesthetics and Motivations in Science*. Chicago: University of Chicago Press.

Chaplin, Charles. 1964. *My Autobiography*. New York: Simon and Schuster.

Cheney, Margaret. 1981. *Tesla: Man Out of Time*. New York: Dorset.

Cipra, Barry. 1992. "Cross-Disciplinary Artists Know Good Math When They See It." *Science* 257: 748–49.

———. 1997. "How to Play Platonic Billiards." *Science* 275: 1070.

———. 1998. "Proving a Link between Logic and Origami." *Science* 279: 804–5.

Clark, Ronald W. 1971. *Einstein: The Life and Times*. New York: World.

Clarke, Arthur C., and Gentry Lee. 1989. *RAMA II*. New York: Bantam.

Cohen, Milton A. 1987. *PoetandPainter: The Aesthetics of E. E. Cummings's Early Work*. Detroit: Wayne State University Press.

Cohen, Morton N., ed. 1989. *Lewis Carroll: Interviews and Recollections*. London: Macmillan.

Cole, Allison. 1993. *Color: An Eyewitness Book*. London: Dorling Kindersley.

Cole, K. C. 1985. *Sympathetic Vibrations: Reflections on Physics as a Way of Life*. New York: Bantam.

Colebrook, Leonard. 1954. *Almroth Wright: Provocative Doctor and Thinker*. London: Heinemann.

Collins, Brent. 1991. "Wood Sculpture and Topological Allegories." Exhibit brochure, AAAS Art of Science and Technology Program, Washington, D.C., 9 Apr.–7 June.

Connelly, Robert, and Allen Back. 1998. "Mathematics and Tensegrity." *American Scientist* 86: 142–51.

Copland, Aaron. 1957. *What to Listen For in Music*. New York: McGraw-Hill.

Coulehan, Jack. 1993. "Physician as Poet, Poem as Patient." *Poets & Writers Magazine*, Mar./Apr.: 57–59.

Cox, Meki. 1999. "Researchers Have Nose for Diagnosis." *Lansing State Journal*, 8 June: 2A.

Critchell, Samantha. 1998. "Dessert Master Shares." *Lansing State Journal*, 21 Dec.: 8D.

———. 1999. "Chicago Restaurateur Maestro in the Kitchen." *Lansing State Journal*, 11 Jan.: 5D.

Critchley, Macdonald. 1953. "Tactile Thought, with Special Reference to the Blind." *Brain* 76: 19–35.

cummings, e. e. 1925. "The Adult, the Artist and the Circus." *Vanity Fair*, Oct.: 57, 98.

———. 1962. *73 poems*. New York: Harcourt, Brace Jovanovich.

Cunningham, Merce. 1968. *Changes: Notes on Choreography*. New York: Something Else Press.

Curtin, Deane, ed. 1982. *The Aesthetic Dimension of Science*. The Sixteenth Nobel Conference, 1980. New York: Philosophical Library.

Cytowic, Richard E. 1989. *Synesthesia: A Union of the Senses*. New York: Springer-Verlag.

———. 1993. *The Man Who Tasted Shapes*. New York: G. P. Putnam's Sons.

Dale, Alzina Stone. 1985. *The Art of G. K. Chesterton*. Chicago: Loyola University Press.

Damasio, Antonio R. 1994. *Descartes's Error: Emotion, Reason, and the Human Brain*. New York: G. P. Putnam's Sons.

Davies, Graham, Haydn Ellis, and John Shepherd, eds. 1981. *Perceiving and Remembering Faces*. New York: Academic Press.

Davis, Philip J., and Reuben Hersh. 1981. *The Mathematical Experience*. Boston: Houghton Mifflin.

Davy, Humphry. 1840. "Parallels Between Art and Science." *The Collected Works of Sir Humphry Davy*. Vol. 8. Ed. John Davy. London: Smith and Cornhill.

De Mille, Agnes. 1951. *Dance to the Piper*. London: Hamilton.

———. 1973. *Speak to Me, Dance with Me*. Boston: Little, Brown.

———. 1978. *Where the Wings Grow*. Garden City, N.Y.: Doubleday.

Deregowski, J. B. 1980. *Illusions, Patterns and Pictures: A Cross-Cultural Perspective*. New York: Academic Press.

Dewey, John. 1934. *Art as Experience*. New York: Minton, Balch.

Diderot, Denis. 1966. "Conversation Between D'Alembert and Diderot." In *Rameau's Nephew and D'Alembert's Dream.* Trans. L. W. Tancock. Pp. 149–64. London: Penguin.

Digby, Joan, and Bob Brier, eds. 1977. *Permutations: Readings in Science and Literature.* New York: William Morrow.

Dodwell, P. C. 1970. *Visual Pattern Recognition.* New York: Holt, Rinehart and Winston.

Dos Passos, John. 1966. *Best Times: An Informal Memoir.* New York: New American Library.

Droste, Magdelena. 1990. *Bauhaus: 1919–1933.* Berlin: Taschen.

Dubal, David. 1984. *Reflections from the Keyboard: The World of the Concert Pianist.* New York: Summit Books.

Duke, Charles R., and Sally A. Jacobsen, eds. 1983. *Reading and Writing Poetry.* Phoenix, Ariz.: Oryx Press.

Du Maurier, Daphne. 1977. *Myself When Young: The Shaping of a Writer.* Garden City, N.Y.: Doubleday.

Dyson, Freeman. 1979. "The World of the Scientist — Part II." *The New Yorker,* 13 Aug.: 64–88.

Eber, Dorothy. 1982. *Genius at Work: Images of Alexander Graham Bell.* New York: Viking.

Edelglass, Stephen, Georg Maier, Hans Gebert, and John Davy. 1997. *The Marriage of Sense and Thought: Imaginative Participation in Science.* Hudson, N.Y.: Lindisfarne Books.

Edwards, John. 1990. "Rediscovering Ignorance." *Research in Science Education* 20: 1–7.

Eisenstein, Sergei. 1949. *Film Form: Essays in Film Theory.* Trans. Jay Leyda. New York: Harcourt, Brace and World.

Eisner, Thomas, et al. 1988. "Seventy-Five Reasons to Become a Scientist." *American Scientist* 76: 451.

Eliot, George. 1885. *George Eliot's Life.* 3 vols. Boston: Dana Estes.

Ennion, E. A. R., and N. Tinbergon. 1967. *Tracks.* Oxford: Clarendon Press.

Epel, Naomi, ed. 1993. *Writers Dreaming.* New York: Vintage Press.

Ernst, Bruno. 1992. *Optical Illusions.* Cologne: Taschen.

Escher, M. C. 1989. *Escher on Escher: Exploring the Infinite.* Trans. Karin Ford. New York: Harry N. Abrams.

Evans, Myfanwy. 1939. *The Painter's Object.* London: Gerald Howe.

Featherstone, Donald F. 1962. *War Games.* London: Stanley Paul.

Fenzl, Christine. 1997. "Journey to the Center of the Egg" (on Christiane Nüsslein-Volhard). *New York Times Magazine,* 12 Oct.: 42–45.

Ferguson, Claire. 1994. *Helaman Ferguson: Mathematics in Stone and Bronze.* Erie, Pa: Meridian Creative Group.

Ferguson, Eugene S. 1992. *Engineering and the Mind's Eye.* Cambridge, Mass.: MIT Press.

Feynman, Richard. 1985a. *The Character of Physical Law*. Cambridge, Mass.: MIT Press.

———. 1985b. *Surely You're Joking, Mr. Feynman!* New York: W. W. Norton.

———. 1988. *What Do You Care What Other People Think?* New York: W. W. Norton.

Fischer, Gerd. 1986. *Mathematische Modelle. Mathematical Models*. 2 vols. Braunschweig/Wiesbaden, Germany: Vieweg und Sohn.

Flam, Faye. 1991. "Move Over, Mendeleyev." *Science* 252: 648–50.

Flam, Jack D. 1973. *Matisse on Art*. Reprint, 1978: New York: Dutton.

Fleischman, Paul. 1988. *Joyful Noise: Poems for Two Voices*. New York: Harper and Row.

Florman, Samuel C. 1982. *Blaming Technology*. New York: St. Martin's Press.

Frayling, Christopher, Helen Frayling, and Ron Van der Meer. 1992. *The Art Pack*. New York: Alfred A. Knopf.

Freudenthal, Hans, ed. 1961. *The Concept and the Role of the Model in Mathematics and Natural and Social Sciences*. Dordrecht, Netherlands: Reidel.

Frost, Robert. 1969. *The Poetry of Robert Frost*. Ed. Edward C. Lathem. New York: Henry Holt.

Fuller, Loie. 1913. *Fifteen Years of a Dancer's Life*. London: Herbert Jenkins.

Fuller, R. Buckminster. 1979. *R. Buckminster Fuller on Education*. Ed. P. H. Wagschall and R. D. Kahn. Amherst: University of Massachusetts Press.

Fusell, Paul, Jr. 1965. *Poetic Meter and Poetic Form*. New York: Random House.

Galton, Francis. 1874. *English Men of Science: Their Nature and Nurture*. London: Macmillan.

———. 1883. *Inquiries into Human Faculty and Its Development*. Reprint, 1928: New York: E. P. Dutton.

———. 1892. *Hereditary Genius*. Reprint, 1972: Gloucester, Mass.: Peter Smith.

Gamow, George. 1966. *Thirty Years That Shook Physics: The Story of Quantum Theory*. Garden City, N.Y.: Doubleday.

Gardiner, Martin F., Alan Fox, Faith Knowles, and Donna Jeffrey. 1996. "Learning Improved by Arts Training." *Nature* 381: 284.

Gardner, Howard. 1983. *Frames of Mind: The Theory of Multiple Intelligences*. New York: Basic Books.

———. 1993. *Creating Minds: An Anatomy of Creativity*. New York: Basic Books.

Gardner, Martin. 1963. "On 'Rep-tiles,' Polygons That Can Make Larger and Smaller Copies of Themselves." *Scientific American* 208 (May): 154–64.

———. 1974. "The Curious Magic of Anamorphic Art." *Scientific American* 232: 110–16.

———. 1977. "Extraordinary Nonperiodic Tiling That Enriches the Theory of Tiles." *Scientific American* 233: 110–14.

———. 1978. *Aha! Insight*. San Francisco: W. H. Freeman.

George, William Herbert. 1936. *The Scientist in Action: A Scientific Study of His Methods*. London: Williams and Norgate.

Gettings, Frank. 1976. *E. E. Cummings: The Poet and Artist.* Exhibition catalogue, Hirshhorn Museum and Sculpture Garden, Smithsonian Institution, Washington, D.C.

Ghiselin, Brewster, ed. 1952. *The Creative Process.* Berkeley: University of California Press.

Gilbert, G. Nigel, and Michael Mulkay. 1984. *Opening Pandora's Box: A Sociological Analysis of Scientists' Discourse.* Cambridge: Cambridge University Press.

Girard, François. 1995. *Thirty-Two Short Films about Glenn Gould.* Columbia Tristar Home Video.

Gleick, James. 1984. "Solving the Mathematical Riddle of Chaos." *New York Times Magazine,* 10 June: 31–71.

———. 1987. *Chaos: Making a New Science.* New York: Viking.

———. 1992. *Genius: The Life and Science of Richard Feynman.* New York: Pantheon.

Golani, I., D. L. Wolgin, and P. Teitelbaum. 1979. "A Proposed Natural Geometry of Recovery from Akinesia in the Lateral Hypothalamic Rat." *Brain Research* 164: 237–67.

Goodall, Jane. 1986. *The Chimpanzees of Gombe: Patterns of Behavior.* Cambridge, Mass.: Belknap Press of Harvard University Press.

Goodman, Michael E. 1994. *Edwin Arlington Robinson.* Mankato, Minn.: Creative Education.

Goossen, E. C. 1973. *Ellsworth Kelly.* New York: Museum of Modern Art.

Gordon, William J. J. 1961. *Synectics: The Development of Creative Capacity.* New York: Harper and Row.

Graham, Martha. 1991. *Blood Memory.* New York: Doubleday.

Grandin, Temple. 1995. *Thinking in Pictures and Other Reports from My Life with Autism.* New York: Doubleday.

Greenburg, Jan, and Sandra Jordan. 1993. *The Sculptor's Eye: Looking at Contemporary American Art.* New York: Delacorte Press.

Gregory, Richard, and E. H. Gombrich, eds. 1980. *Illusion in Nature and Art.* New York: Charles Scribner's Sons.

Griffin, Donald. 1984. *Animal Thinking.* Cambridge, Mass.: Harvard University Press.

Griss, Susan. 1994. "Creative Movement: A Language for Learning." *Educational Leadership* 51, no. 5: 78–80.

Grosskurth, Phyllis. 1968. *Leslie Stephen.* London: Longmans, Green.

Gruber, Howard E. 1984. *Darwin on Man: A Psychological Study of Scientific Creativity.* 2nd ed. Chicago: University of Chicago Press.

———. 1988. "The Evolving Systems Approach to Creative Work." *Creativity Research Journal* 1: 27–51. Also in D. B. Wallace and H. E. Gruber, eds. 1989. *Creative People at Work.* Pp. 3–24. New York: Oxford University Press.

Gucwa, David, and James Ehmann. 1985. *To Whom It May Concern: An Investigation of the Art of Elephants.* New York: W. W. Norton.

Gustin, W. 1985. "The Development of Exceptional Research Mathematicians." In

Benjamin Bloom, ed. *Developing Talent in Young People.* New York: Ballantine Books.

Hadamard, Jacques. 1945. *The Psychology of Invention in the Mathematical Field.* Princeton: Princeton University Press.

Halberg, Franz, and Julia, Francine, and Erna Halberg. 1973. "Reading, 'Riting, 'Rithmetic, and Rhythms: A New 'Relevant' 'R' in the Educative Process." *Perspectives in Biology and Medicine* 17: 128–41.

Haldane, J. B. S. 1928. *Possible Worlds.* New York: Harper.

———. 1976. *The Man with Two Memories.* London: Merlin Press.

Hale, Cabot Nathan. 1972. *Abstraction in Art and Nature: A Program of Study for Artists, Teachers, and Students.* New York: Watson-Guptill.

Hall, Donald, ed. 1985. *The Oxford Book of Children's Verse in America.* New York: Oxford University Press.

Hammond, Wayne G., and Christina Scull. 1995. *J. R. R. Tolkien, Artist and Illustrator.* Boston: Houghton Mifflin.

Harding, Rosamond E. M. 1967. *An Anatomy of Inspiration.* 2nd ed. London: Frank Cass.

Hark, Ina Rae. 1982. *Edward Lear.* Boston: Twayne.

Harrison, Charles, and Paul Wood, eds. 1992. *Art in Theory, 1900–1990.* Oxford: Blackwell.

Harrison, J., and S. Baron-Cohen. 1995. "Synaesthesia: Reconciling the Subjective with the Objective." *Endeavour* 19, no. 4: 157–60.

Hassler, M., N. Birbaumer, and A. Feil. 1985. "Musical Talent and Visual-Spatial Abilities: A Longitudinal Study." *Psychology of Music* 14: 99–113.

Hayashi, K., and N. Munakata. 1984. "Basically Musical." *Nature* 310: 96.

Hayes, Brian. 1995. "Pleasures of Plication." *American Scientist* 83: 504–8.

Hearst, Eliot. 1991. "Psychology and Nothing." *American Scientist* 79: 432–43.

Heath, A. E. 1947. "Analogy as a Scientific Tool." *Rationalist Annual:* 51–58.

Heidemann, Steven R. 1993. "A New Twist on Integrins and the Cytoskeleton." *Science* 260: 1080–81.

Heisenberg, Werner. 1974. *Across the Frontiers.* Trans. Peter Heath. New York: Harper and Row.

Herbert, Robert L., ed. 1964. *Modern Artists on Art: Ten Unabridged Essays.* Englewood Cliffs, N.J.: Prentice-Hall.

Hermann, Evelyn. 1981. *Shinichi Suzuki: The Man and His Philosophy.* Athens, Ohio: Senzay.

Higginson, William J., with Penny Harter. 1985. *The Haiku Handbook: How to Write, Share, and Teach Haiku.* New York: Kodansha International.

Highfield, Robert, and Paul Carter. 1994. *The Private Lives of Albert Einstein.* New York: St. Martin's Press.

Highwater, Jamake. 1978. *Dance: Rituals of Experience.* New York: Alfred van der Marck.

Hindle, Brook. 1981. *Emulation and Invention.* New York: New York University Press.

Hjerter, Kathleen. 1986. *Doubly Gifted: The Author as Visual Artist.* New York: Harry N. Abrams.

Hobbs, Christine. 1985. "A Comparison of the Music Aptitude, Scholastic Aptitude, and Academic Achievement of Young Children." *Psychology of Music* 14: 93–98.

Hoffmann, Roald. 1988. "How I Work As Poet and Scientist." *The Scientist,* 21 Mar.: 10.

———. 1988. *The Metamict State.* Orlando: University of Florida Press.

Holden, Constance. 1998. "Leveling the Playing Field for Scientists with Disabilities." *Science* 282: 36–37.

Holton, Gerald. 1972. *On Trying to Understand Scientific Genius.* New York: Cooper Union School of Art and Architecture. Reprinted in Holton. 1978. *The Scientific Imagination: Case Studies.* Cambridge, Mass.: Harvard University Press.

Holyoak, Keith J., and Thagard, Paul. 1995. *Mental Leaps: Analogy in Creative Thought.* Cambridge, Mass.: MIT Press.

Hong, E., R. M. Milgram, and S. C. Whiston. 1993. "Leisure Activities in Adolescence as a Predictor of Occupational Choice in Young Adults: A Longitudinal Study." *Journal of Career Development* 19: 221–29.

Horgan, John. 1991. "Profile: Thomas Eisner." *Scientific American,* Dec.: 60–61.

Horgan, Paul. 1964. *Things As They Are.* New York: Farrar, Straus and Giroux.

———. 1973. *Approaches to Writing.* New York: Farrar, Straus and Giroux.

Horosko, Marian, ed. 1991. *Martha Graham: The Evolution of Her Dance Theory and Training, 1926–1991.* Chicago: a cappella books (Chicago Review Press).

Humphrey, Doris. 1959. *The Art of Making Dances.* Ed. Barbara Pollock. New York: Grove Press.

Hutchinson, Eliot Dole. 1959. *How to Think Creatively.* New York: Abington-Cokesbury Press.

Huxley, Aldous. 1963. *Literature and Science.* New York: Harper and Row.

Huxley, Julian. 1932. *Problems of Relative Growth.* New York: Dial Press.

Ifrah, Georges. 1985. *From One to Zero: A Universal History of Numbers.* New York: Viking.

Infeld, Leopold. 1941. *Albert Einstein: His Work and Its Influence on the World.* New York: Charles Scribner's Sons.

Ingber, Donald E. 1998. "The Architecture of Life." *Scientific American* 278 (Jan.): 48–57.

Ives, Charles. 1962. *Essays Before a Sonata, the Majority, and Other Writings.* New York: W. W. Norton.

Jackson, Brenda. 1972. *Model Making in Schools.* New York: Van Nostrand Reinhold.

Jacob, François. 1988. *The Statue Within: An Autobiography.* New York: Basic Books.

Jaki, Stanley L. 1988. *The Physicist as Artist: The Landscapes of Pierre Duhem.* Edinburgh: Scottish Academic Press.

Jana, Reena. 1998. "Toying with Science." *New York Times Magazine.* Pt. 2: *Home Design.* Fall: 22, 24, 50, 56.

Jefferson, Margo. 1995. "A Journey to a Mysterious Country: The Mind." *New York Times,* 26 Mar.: Pt. H: 7.

Jennerod, M. 1994. "The Representing Brain: Neural Correlates of Motor Intention and Imagery." *Behavioral and Brain Sciences* 17: 187–245.

Johnson, Samuel. 1899. *Rasselas.* Oxford: Clarendon Press.

John-Steiner, Vera. 1985. *Notebooks of the Mind: Explorations of Thinking.* Albuquerque: University of New Mexico Press.

Jones, Caroline A., and Peter Galison, eds. 1998. *Picturing Science, Producing Art.* New York: Routledge.

Jourdain, Robert. 1997. *Music, the Brain, and Ecstasy: How Music Captures Our Imagination.* New York: William Morrow.

Judson, H. F. 1980. *The Search for Solutions.* New York: Holt, Rinehart, and Winston.

Jung, C. G. 1963. *Memories, Dreams, Reflections.* Ed. Aniela Jaffe, trans. Richard and Clara Winston. New York: Pantheon Books.

———. 1979. *Word and Image.* Ed. Aniela Jaffe. Princeton: Princeton University Press.

Kagan, Andrew. 1983. *Paul Klee/ Art and Music.* Ithaca, N.Y.: Cornell University Press.

Kandinsky, Wassily. 1913. *Reminiscences.* In Herbert, Robert L. 1964. *Modern Artists on Art.* Englewood Cliffs, N.J.: Prentice-Hall.

Keller, Evelyn Fox. 1983. *A Feeling for the Organism: The Life and Work of Barbara McClintock.* San Francisco: W. H. Freeman.

Keller, Helen. 1902. *The Story of My Life, with Her Letters (1887–1901) and a Supplementary Account of Her Education . . . by John Albert Macy.* New York: Grosset and Dunlap.

———. 1920. *The World I Live In.* New York: Century.

Kelly, Richard. 1996. *The Art of George Du Maurier.* Aldershot, Eng.: Scholar Press.

Kemp, Martin. 1990. *The Science of Art.* New Haven: Yale University Press.

Kennedy, X. J. 1978. *An Introduction to Poetry.* 4th ed. Boston: Little, Brown.

Kepes, Gyorgy, ed. 1965. *Education of Vision.* New York: George Braziller.

———. 1965. *Structure in Art and in Science.* New York: George Braziller.

———. 1965. *The Nature and Art of Motion.* New York: George Braziller.

———. 1965. *The Man-Made Object.* New York: George Braziller.

———. 1965. *Module, Proportion, Symmetry, Rhythm.* New York: George Braziller.

———. 1965. *Sign, Image, and Symbol.* New York: George Braziller.

Khayyam, Omar. 1941. *The Rubaiyat of Omar Khayyam.* Trans. E. Fitzgerald. New York: Pocket Books.

Kim, Scott. 1981. *Inversions.* Cambridge, Mass.: MIT Press.

King, James Roy. 1996. *Remaking the World: Modeling in Human Experience.* Chicago: University of Illinois Press.

Kirkland, Gelsey, with Greg Lawrence. 1987. *Dancing on My Grave.* New York: Jove Books.

Kisselgoff, Anna. 1999. "Ceaseless Novelty in a Lifetime of Dance." *New York Times,* 18 July, sec. 2: 1, 7.

Kleinfeld, Sonny. 1985. *A Machine Called Indomitable.* New York: Times Books.

Klosty, James, ed. 1975. *Merce Cunningham.* New York: E. P. Dutton.

Kneller, George F. 1978. *Science as a Human Endeavor.* New York: Columbia University Press.

Knudtson, P. M. S. 1985. "Ramón y Cajal: Painter of Neurons." *Discover* 85: 66–72.

Koch, Kenneth, and Kate Farrell, eds. 1985. *Talking to the Sun.* New York: Metropolitan Museum of Art and Henry Holt.

Kock, Winston. 1978. *The Creative Engineer: The Art of Inventing.* New York: Plenum Press.

Koestler, Arthur. 1976. *The Act of Creation.* London: Hutchinson.

Kostalenetz, Richard, and Robert Flemming, eds. 1997. *Writings on Glass: Essays, Interviews, Criticism.* New York: Schirmer Books.

Kovalevskaya, Sofya. 1978. *A Russian Childhood.* Trans. B. Stillman. New York: Springer-Verlag.

Krebs, Hans A., and Julian H. Shelley, eds. 1975. *The Creative Process in Science and Medicine.* Amsterdam: Excerpta Medica / American Elsevier.

Kuhn, Thomas. 1979. *Black Body Theory.* Chicago: University of Chicago Press.

Langdon, John. 1992. *Wordplay.* New York: Harcourt Brace Jovanovich.

Leakey, Mary. 1984. *Disclosing the Past: An Autobiography.* Garden City, N.Y.: Doubleday.

L'Echevin, Patrick. 1981. *Musique et Médecine.* Paris: Stock-Musique.

Lee, Hermione. 1996. *Virginia Woolf.* London: Chatto and Windus.

Leeman, Fred, Joost Elffers, and Mike Schuyt. 1976. *Hidden Images: Games of Perception, Anamorphic Art, Illusion.* New York: Harry N. Abrams.

LeGuin, Ursula. 1976. Introduction to *The Left Hand of Darkness.* New York: Ace Books.

Lehman, Arnold, and Brenda Richardson, eds. 1986. *Oskar Schlemmer.* Baltimore: Baltimore Museum of Art.

Lehmann, John F. 1972. *Lewis Carroll and the Spirit of Nonsense.* Nottingham: University of Nottingham.

Lehto, Olli. 1980. "Rolf Nevanlinna." *Suomalainen Tiedeakatemia Vuosikiria* / Finnish Academy of Sciences Yearbooks: 108–12.

Lester, James. 1994. *Too Marvelous for Words: The Life and Genius of Art Tatum.* New York: Oxford University Press.

Levarie, S. 1980. "Music as a Structural Model." *Journal of Social and Biological Structures* 3: 237–45.

Levi, Primo, and Tullio Regge. 1989. *Dialogo.* Trans. Raymond Rosenthal. Princeton University Press.

Levi-Montalcini, Rita. 1988. *In Praise of Imperfection: My Life and Work.* Trans. L. Attardi. New York: Basic Books.

Levine, Sigmund A. 1960. *Kettering: Master Inventor.* New York: Dodd, Mead.

Lightman, Alan. 1992. "The One and Only." *New York Times Book Review,* 17 Dec.: 34–36.

Lightman, Alan, and Roberta Brawer. 1990. *Origins: The Lives and Worlds of Modern Cosmologists*. Cambridge, Mass.: Harvard University Press.

Lorenz, Konrad. 1952. *King Solomon's Ring*. New York: Thomas Crowell.

Lowell, Amy. 1930. *Poetry and Poets: Essays*. Boston: Houghton Mifflin.

Loyd, Sam. 1912. *Sam Loyd's Puzzles*. Philadelphia: David McKay.

Lyons, Albert S., and R. Joseph Petrucelli. 1978. *Medicine: An Illustrated History*. New York: Harry N. Abrams.

Macfarlane, Gwyn. 1984. *Alexander Fleming: The Man and the Myth*. Cambridge, Mass.: Harvard University Press.

Mach, Elyse. 1980. *Great Pianists Speak for Themselves*. New York: Dodd, Mead.

Mach, Ernst. 1926. *Knowledge and Error: Sketches on the Psychology of Enquiry*. Ed. T. J. McCormack and P. Foulkes. Reprint, 1976: Dordrecht, Netherlands: Reidel.

MacKenzie, Norman, and Jeanne MacKenzie. 1973. *H. G. Wells*. New York: Simon and Schuster.

MacLean, Norman. 1992. *A River Runs Through It and Other Stories*. New York: Simon and Schuster.

Macmillan, Bill. 1989. *Remodelling Geography: Model Building as a Method of Geographical Enquiry*. London: Blackwell.

Mancewicz, Bernice Winslow. 1969. *Alexander Calder: A Pictorial Essay*. Grand Rapids, Mich.: William B. Eerdman.

Mandelbrojt, Jacques. 1994. "In Search of the Specificity of Art." *Leonardo* 27:185–88.

Marey, Etienne-Jules. 1895. *Movement*. New York: D. Appleton.

Margulies, Alfred. 1989. *The Empathic Imagination*. New York: W. W. Norton.

Marks, Lawrence E., Robin J. Hammeal, and Marc H. Bornstein. 1987. "Perceiving Similarity and Comprehending Metaphor." *Monographs of the Society for Research in Child Development* 52, no. 1: 1–102.

Marter, Joan M. 1991. *Alexander Calder*. Cambridge: Cambridge University Press.

Martin, John. 1939. *Introduction to the Dance*. New York: W. W. Norton.

Maurois, André. 1959. *The Life of Sir Alexander Fleming, Discoverer of Penicillin*. Trans. Gerard Hopkins. London: Jonathan Cape.

Mays, Patricia J. 1999. "Rocket Scientist Invents Squirt Gun." *Lansing State Journal*, 24 Jan.: 5A.

Mazurs, E. G., 1974. *Graphic Representations of the Periodic System During One Hundred Years*. Tuscaloosa: University of Alabama Press.

Mead, Margaret. 1974. "What I Think I Have Learned about Education." *Education* 94, no. 4 (Apr.–May): 291–406.

Meeker, J. W. 1978. "The Imminent Alliance: New Connections among Art, Science, and Technology." *Technology and Cultures* 19: 187–98.

Menuhin, Yehudi. 1972. *Theme and Variations*. New York: Stein and Day.

———. 1997. *Unfinished Journey: Twenty Years Later*. New York: Fromm International.

Mercier, Ann M. 1990. "NASA's Halem Illustrates Need for Info Visualization." *Federal Computer Weekly*, 8 Oct.: 28, 35.

Messiaen, Olivier. 1986. *Musique et Couleur: Nouveaux entretiens avec Claude Samuel.* Paris: Pierre Belfond.

Milgram, Roberta, and E. Hong. 1993. "Creative Thinking and Creative Performance in Adolescents as Predictors of Creative Attainments in Adults: A Follow-up Study after 18 Years." In R. Subotnik and K. Arnold, eds. *Beyond Terman: Longitudinal Studies in Contemporary Gifted Education.* Norwood, N.J.: Ablex.

Miller, Arthur I. 1984. *Imagery in Scientific Thought.* Boston: Birkhauser.

Miller, Stephen. 1973. "Ends, Means, and Galumphing: Some Leitmotifs of Play." *American Anthropologist* 75: 87–98.

Mitchell, Alice L., ed. and trans. 1983. *Carl Czerny: A Systematic Introduction to Improvisation on the Pianoforte.* New York: Longman.

Moholy-Nagy, L. 1947. *Vision in Motion.* Chicago: Paul Theobald.

Molella, Arthur. 1998. "From the Director." *Lemelson Center News* 3, no. 2.

Mondrian, Piet. 1995. *Natural Reality and Abstract Reality.* Trans. Martin S. James. New York: George Braziller.

Monod, Jacques. 1970. *Le Hasard et la necessité.* Paris: Le Seuil.

Moore, Henry. 1934. "The Sculptor's Aims." In Robert L. Herbert, ed. 1964. *Modern Artists on Art.* Englewood Cliffs, N.J.: Prentice-Hall.

Morgan, Louise. 1931. *Writers at Work.* London: Chatto and Windus.

Morgenstern, Sam, ed. 1956. *Composers on Music: An Anthology of Composers' Writings.* London: Faber and Faber.

Morris, Desmond. 1971. "The Naked Artist." *Observer Magazine,* 10 Oct.: 22–25.

———. 1980. *Animal Days.* New York: William Morrow.

———. 1987. *The Secret Surrealist: The Paintings of Desmond Morris.* Oxford: Phaidon.

Morrison, Jim. 1993. "Bedside Matters." *American Way Magazine,* 1 Oct.: 48–51.

Morrison, Philip, Phylis Morrison, and the Office of Charles and Ray Eames. 1982. *Powers of Ten.* New York: Scientific American Library.

Moulton, F. R., and J. J. Schifferes, eds. 1960. *The Autobiography of Science.* 2nd ed. Garden City, N.Y.: Doubleday.

Mukand, Jon. 1990. *Vital Lines: Contemporary Fiction about Medicine.* New York: St. Martin's Press.

Munthe, Nellie. 1983. *Meet Matisse.* Boston: Little, Brown.

Nabokov, Vladimir. 1947. *Speak, Memory: An Autobiography Revisited.* Reprint, 1966: New York: G. P. Putnam's Sons.

———. 1980. *Lectures on Literature.* Ed. Fredson Bowers. New York: Harcourt Brace Jovanovich.

Nachmanovitch, Stephen. 1990. *Free Play: Improvisation in Life and Art.* Los Angeles: Jeremy Tarcher.

Nash, S. A., and J. Merkert, eds. 1985. *Naum Gabo: Sixty Years of Constructivism.* New York: Prestel Verlag.

Nelson, David R., and Bertrand I. Halperin. 1985. "Pentagonal and Icosahedral Order in Rapidly Cooled Metals." *Science* 229: 233–36.

Noguchi, Isamu. 1994. *Isamu Noguchi: Essays and Conversations.* Ed. Diane Apostolos-Cappadona and Bruce Altschuler. New York: Harry N. Abrams and Isamu Noguchi Foundation.

Nyman, Michael. 1974. *Experimental Music: Cage and Beyond.* London: Studio Vista.

Oddleifson, Eric. 1998. *Public Education Rooted in the Arts: Moving from Concept to Practice.* Hingham, Mass.: Center for the Arts in Basic Curriculum.

Odin, Steve. 1986. "Blossom Scents Take Up the Ringing: Synaesthesia in Japanese and Western Aesthetics." *Soundings* 69, no. 3: 256–81.

Ohno, Susumi. 1993. "A Song in Praise of Peptide Palindromes." *Leukemia* 7, suppl. 2: S157–59.

Ohno, Susumi, and Midori Ohno. 1986. "The All Pervasive Principle of Repetitious Recurrence Governs Not Only Coding Sequence Construction but also Human Endeavor in Musical Composition." *Immunogenetics* 24: 71–78.

O'Keeffe, Georgia. 1976. *Georgia O'Keeffe.* New York: Viking Penguin.

Oster, Gerald, and Yasunori Nakashima. 1963. "Moiré Patterns." *Scientific American* 208 (May): 54–63.

Packer, William, and Gemma Levine. 1985. *Henry Moore: An Illustrated Biography.* New York: Grove Press.

Padgett, Ron, ed. 1987. *The Teachers and Writers Handbook of Poetic Forms.* New York: Teachers and Writers Collaborative.

Parkinson, S. E., and J. H. Edwards. 1997. "Innovative Visual-Spatial Powers of Dyslexics: A New Perspective?" Internet Service Dyslexia Paper Archive.

Parola, René. 1996. *Optical Art: Theory and Practice.* New York: Dover Press.

Pasteur, Louis. 1939. *Oeuvres de Pasteur.* 7 vols. Paris: Masson.

Pasztor, E. 1993. "The Role of Humanities and Arts in Medical Education with Special Reference to Neurosurgery." *Acta Neurochirurgica* 124: 176–78.

Pauling, Linus. 1963. "The Genesis of Ideas," in *Proceedings of the Third World Congress of Psychiatry, 1961.* Vol. 1. Toronto: University of Toronto Press.

Pavarotti, Luciano. 1999. Interview, *Morning Edition,* National Public Radio, 7 Jan.

Pearce, Peter. 1978. *Structure in Nature Is a Strategy for Design.* Cambridge, Mass.: MIT Press.

Peterson, Ivars. 1985a. "The Fivefold Way for Crystals." *Science News* 127: 188–89.

———. 1985b. "The Sound of Data." *Science News* 127: 348–50.

———. 1987. "Twists of Space." *Science News* 132: 264–66.

———. 1994. "Bach to Chaos. Chaotic Variations on a Classical Theme." *Science News* 146: 428–29.

———. 1998. "Twists through Space." *Science News* 154: 143.

———. 1999. "A Quasicrystal Construction Kit." *Science News* 155: 60–61.

Petroski, Henry. 1985. *To Engineer Is Human: The Role of Failure in Successful Design.* New York: St. Martin's Press.

———. 1996. *Invention by Design: How Engineers Get from Thought to Thing.* Cambridge, Mass.: Harvard University Press.

———. 1997. "Design Competition." *American Scientist* 85: 511–15.

———. 1999. "Work and Play." *American Scientist* 87: 208–12.

Pfeiffer, John E. 1982. *The Creative Explosion: An Inquiry into the Origins of Art and Religion.* New York: Harper and Row.

Piaget, Jean. 1951. *Play, Dreams and Imitation in Childhood.* New York: W. W. Norton.

Pinet, Helene. 1992. *Rodin: The Hands of Genius.* Trans. Caroline Palmer. New York: Harry N. Abrams.

Planck, Max. 1949. *Scientific Autobiography.* Trans. Frank Gaynor. New York: Philosophical Library.

Platt, John Rader. 1962. *The Excitement of Science.* Boston: Houghton Mifflin.

Poincaré, Henri. 1913. *The Foundations of Science: Science and Hypothesis; The Value of Science; Science and Method.* 3 vols. Trans. G. B. Halsted. Reprint, 1946: Lancaster, Pa.: Science Press.

Polanyi, Michael. 1958. *Personal Knowledge: Towards a Post-Critical Philosophy.* Chicago: University of Chicago Press.

Poling, Clark V. 1975. *Bauhaus Color.* Atlanta, Ga.: High Museum of Art.

Pollock, M., ed. 1983. *Common Denominators in Art and Science.* Aberdeen, Scotland: Aberdeen University Press.

Prescott, Frederick C. 1922. *The Poetic Mind.* Ithaca, N.Y.: Great Seal Books.

Quennell, Peter, ed. 1980. *Vladimir Nabokov: His Life, His Works, His World: A Tribute.* New York: William Morrow.

Ramón y Cajal, Santiago. 1937. *Recollections of My Life.* Trans. E. H. Craigie and J. Cano. Cambridge, Mass.: MIT Press.

———. 1951. *Precepts and Counsels on Scientific Investigation: Stimulations of the Spirit.* Trans. J. M. Sanchez-Perez. Mountain View, Calif.: Pacific Press.

Ratliff, Floyd. 1974. "Georg von Békésy: His Life, His Work, and His 'Friends.'" In J. Wirgin, ed. *The Georg von Békésy Collection.* Pp. 15–16. Malmo, Sweden: Allhems Folag.

Rauscher, Frances H., Gordon L. Shaw, and Katherine N. Ky. 1993. "Music and Spatial Task Performance." *Nature* 365: 611.

Rayleigh, Lord. 1942. *The Life of Sir J. J. Thomson, O. M.* Cambridge: Cambridge University Press.

Read, Herbert. 1943. *Education Through Art.* Reprint, 1957: New York: Pantheon Books.

Reid, Constance. 1973. *A Long Way from Euclid.* New York: T. Y. Crowell.

Remy, Michel. 1991. *The Surrealist World of Desmond Morris.* Trans. Leon Sagaru. London: Jonathan Cape.

Richer, Paul. 1895. *Physiologie artistique l'homme en mouvement.* Paris: Hachette.

Riley, Bridget. 1995. *Bridget Riley: Dialogues on Art.* Ed. Robert Kudielka. London: Zwemmer.

Ritter, Malcolm. 1998. "Doctors from a Distance." *Lansing State Journal,* 8 Apr.: 6D.

Ritterbush, P. C. 1968. *The Art of Organic Forms.* Washington, D.C.: Smithsonian Institution Press.

Robin, Harry. 1992. *The Scientific Image: From Cave to Computer.* New York: Harry N. Abrams.

Robinson, Roxana. 1989. *Georgia O'Keeffe: A Life.* New York: Harper and Row.

Roe, Ann. 1953. *The Making of a Scientist.* New York: Dodd, Mead.

Root-Bernstein, M. M. 1997. "Arts Are the 4th 'R' in Education." *Lansing State Journal,* 2 Dec.: 7A.

Root-Bernstein, R. S. 1984a. "Creative Process as a Unifying Theme of Human Cultures." *Daedalus* 113: 197–219.

———. 1984b. "On Paradigms and Revolutions in Science and Art." *Art Journal* 43: 109–18.

———. 1985. "Visual Thinking: The Art of Imagining Reality." *Transactions of the American Philosophical Society* 75: 50–67.

———. 1987a. "Tools of Thought: Designing an Integrated Curriculum for Lifelong Learners." *Roeper Review* 10: 17–21.

———. 1987b. "Harmony and Beauty in Biomedical Research." *Journal of Molecular and Cellular Cardiology* 19: 1–9.

———. 1989a. "How Do Scientists *Really* Think?" *Perspectives in Biology and Medicine* 32: 472–88.

———. 1989b. *Discovering.* Cambridge, Mass.: Harvard University Press. Reprint, 1999: Replica Press.

———. 1989c. "Beauty, Truth, and Imagination: A Perspective on the Science and Art of Modeling Atoms." In J. Burroughs, ed. *Snelson's Atom.* Catalogue for Novo Presents: Art at the Academy Exhibit, New York Academy of Science. Pp. 15–20.

———. 1990. "Sensual Science." *The Sciences,* Sept.–Oct.: 12–14.

———. 1991. "Exercises for Teaching 'Tools of Thought' in a Multi-disciplinary Setting. I. Abstracting." *Roeper Review* 13: 85–90.

———. 1996a. "The Sciences and Arts Share a Common Creative Aesthetic." In A. I. Tauber, ed. *The Elusive Synthesis: Aesthetics and Science.* Pp. 49–82. Amsterdam: Kluwer.

———. 1996b. "Do We Have the Structure of DNA Right? Aesthetic Assumptions, Visual Conventions, and Unsolved Problems." *Art Journal* 55: 47–55.

———. 1997a. "Art, Imagination and the Scientist." *American Scientist* 85: 6–9.

———. 1997b. "For the Sake of Science, the Arts Deserve Support." *Chronicle of Higher Education* 43 (11 July): 15.

———. 1997c. "Hobbled Arts Limit Our Future." Commentary. *Los Angeles Times,* 2 Sept.: B7.

Root-Bernstein, R. S., and M. M. Root-Bernstein. 1997. *Honey, Mud, Maggots and Other Medical Marvels.* Boston: Houghton Mifflin.

Root-Bernstein, R. S., M. Bernstein, and H. Garnier. 1995. "Correlations Between Avocations, Scientific Style, Work Habits, and Professional Impact of Scientists." *Creativity Research Journal* 8: 115–37.

Rosen, Randy. 1978. *Prints: The Facts and Fun of Collecting.* New York: E. P. Dutton.

Ross, Ronald. 1928. "Ambitions." In *Poems.* London: Elkin, Matthews, and Marrot.

Rothstein, Edward. 1995. *Emblems of Mind: The Inner Life of Music and Mathematics.* New York: Times Books.

Rouvray, Dennis. 1994. "Elementary, My Dear Mendeleyev." *New Scientist,* 12 Feb.: 36–39.

Rowley, Gill, ed. 1978. *The Book of Music.* Englewood Cliffs, N.J.: Prentice-Hall.

Rukeyser, Muriel. 1942. *Willard Gibbs.* Garden City, N.Y.: Doubleday, Doran.

Sacks, Oliver. 1967. *Awakenings.* New York: E. P. Dutton. Reprint, 1983: New York: Summit.

———. 1987. *The Man Who Mistook His Wife for a Hat.* New York: Harper and Row.

———. 1989. *Seeing Voices: A Journey into the World of the Deaf.* Berkeley: University of California Press.

———. 1995. *An Anthropologist on Mars.* New York: Random House.

Salem, Lionel, Frédéric Testard, and Coralie Salem. 1992. *The Most Beautiful Mathematical Formulas.* New York: John Wiley.

Salmon, André, 1961. *Modigliani: A Memoir.* Trans. D. and R. Weaver. New York: Putnam.

Sarton, May. 1968. *Plant Dreaming Deep.* New York: W. W. Norton.

Sayen, Jamie. 1985. *Einstein in America.* New York: Crown.

Schaer, Barbara, L. Trentham, E. Miller, and S. Isom. 1985. "Logical Development Levels and Visual Perception: Relationships in Undergraduate Engineering Graphic Communications." Paper presented at the Mid-South Educational Research Association, 6 Nov. 1985, Biloxi, Miss.

Schattschneider, Doris, and Wallace Walker. 1977. *M. C. Escher Kaleidocycles.* Reprint, 1987: Corte Madera, Calif.: Pomegranate Press.

Schillinger, Frances. 1949. *Joseph Schillinger: A Memoir.* New York: Greenberg.

Schillinger, Joseph. 1948. *The Mathematical Basis of the Arts.* New York: Philosophical Library.

Schilpp, Paul A. 1949. *Albert Einstein: Philosopher-Scientist.* 2 vols. New York: Harper Brothers.

Schlemmer, Tut, ed. 1972. *The Letters and Diaries of Oskar Schlemmer.* Trans. Krishna Winston. Middletown, Conn.: Wesleyan University Press.

Schwartz, Paul Waldo. 1969. *The Hand and Eye of the Sculptor.* New York: Praeger.

Seabrook, William. 1941. *Doctor Wood: Modern Wizard of the Laboratory.* New York: Harcourt, Brace.

Service, R. F. 1998. "Breathalyzer Device Sniffs for Disease." *Science* 281: 1431.

Seymour, Alta. 1966. *Charles Steinmetz.* Chicago: Follett.

Shindell, Steve M. 1986. "History and Frequency of Reported Synesthesia." In Milton Wolpin, Joseph E. Shorr, and Lisa Krueger, eds. *Imagery.* Vol. 4, *Recent Practice and Theory.* New York: Plenum Press.

Shreeve, James. 1993. "Touching the Phantom." *Discover* 14, no. 6: 35–42.

Siler, Todd. 1990. *Breaking the Mind Barrier*. New York: Simon and Schuster.

———. 1996. *Think Like a Genius*. Reprint, 1997: New York: Bantam.

Silverman, Debora L. 1989. *Art Nouveau in Fin-de-Siècle France*. Berkeley: University of California Press.

Simons, Lao Genevra. 1939. *Fabre and Mathematics*. New York: Scripta Mathematica.

Simonton, Dean Keith. 1984. *Genius, Creativity and Leadership*. Cambridge, Mass.: Harvard University Press.

Smith, Cyril S. 1981. *A Search for Structure: Selected Essays on Science, Art, and History*. Cambridge, Mass.: MIT Press.

Smith, David Eugene. 1934. *The Poetry of Mathematics and Other Essays*. New York: Scripta Mathematica.

Snyder, Gary. 1980. *The Real Work: Interviews and Talks 1964–1979*. Ed. W. Scott McLean. New York: New Directions.

———. 1992. *No Nature: New and Selected Poems*. New York: Pantheon.

Soderqvist, Thomas. 1996. "Partners in Physiology." Book review. *Science* 271: 1681–82.

Spender, Stephen. 1955. *The Making of a Poem*. London: Hamish Hamilton.

Stanislavsky, Konstantin. 1925. *My Life in Art*. Trans. G. Ivanov-Mumjiev. Moscow: Foreign Languages Publishing House.

———. 1936. *An Actor Prepares*. Trans. Elizabeth Reynolds Hapgood. Reprint, 1958: New York: Theatre Arts Books.

———. 1961. *Stanislavsky on the Art of the Stage*. Trans. David Magarshack. New York: Hill and Wang.

Stein, Dorothy. 1985. *Ada: A Life and a Legacy*. Cambridge, Mass.: MIT Press.

Stein, Sherman. 1963. *Mathematics: The Man-Made Universe*. San Francisco: W. H. Freeman.

Steinbeck, John, and Edward F. Ricketts. 1941. *Sea of Cortez*. Mamaroneck, N.Y.: Paul P. Appel.

Stephen, Leslie. 1968. *Some Early Impressions*. New York: Burt Franklin.

———. 1977. *Sir Leslie Stephen's Mausoleum Book*. Oxford: Clarendon Press.

Stephenson, E. M., and C. S. Stewart. 1955. *Animal Camouflage*. 2nd ed. London: Adam and Charles Black.

Stewart, Doug. 1985. "Teachers Aim at Turning Loose the Mind's Eyes." *Smithsonian*, Aug.: 44–55.

Stiles, Kristine, and Peter Selz. 1996. *Theories and Documents of Contemporary Art: A Sourcebook of Artists' Writings*. Berkeley: University of California Press.

Stone, John. 1988. "Listening to the Patient." *New York Times Magazine*, 12 June, 108–9.

Strachey, Constance, ed. 1907. *Letters of Edward Lear*. London: T. Fisher Unwin.

Stravinsky, Igor. 1936. *Igor Stravinsky: An Autobiography*. Reprint 1975: London: Calder and Boyars.

———. 1970. *The Poetics of Music*. Trans. Arthur Knodel and Ingolf Dahl. Cambridge, Mass.: Harvard University Press.

Stravinsky, Igor, and Robert Craft. 1959. *Conversations with Igor Stravinsky.* Garden City, N.Y.: Doubleday.

Strum, Shirley. 1987. *Almost Human: A Journey into the World of Baboons.* New York: Random House.

Suhr, Jim. 1998. "'Underground Houdini' Finishes His Journey." *Lansing State Journal,* 30 Nov., 5B.

Suzuki, Daisetz T. 1962. *The Essentials of Zen Buddhism.* New York: E. P. Dutton.

Suzuki, Shinichi. 1969. *Nurtured by Love: A New Approach to Education.* Trans. Waltraud Suzuki. New York: Exposition Press.

Svitil, Kathy A. 1998. "A Touch of Science." *Discover* 19 (June): 81–84.

Swafford, Jan. 1996. *Charles Ives: A Life with Music.* New York: W. W. Norton.

Sweeley, C. C., J. F. Holland, D. S. Towson, and B. A. Chamberlin. 1987. "Interactive and Multi-Sensory Analysis of Complex Mixtures by an Automated Gas Chromatography System." *Journal of Chromatography* 399: 173–81.

Sweeney, James Johnson. 1963. "Alexander Calder: Work and Play." *Art in America* 51: 93–96.

Sykes, Christopher. 1994. *No Ordinary Genius: The Illustrated Richard Feynman.* New York: W. W. Norton.

Sylvester, David. 1968. *Henry Moore.* London: Arts Council of Great Britain.

Szent-Györgyi, Albert. 1957. *Bioenergetics.* New York: Academic Press.

———. 1966. "In Search of Simplicity and Generalizations (50 Years of Poaching in Science)." In N. O. Kaplan and E. P. Kennedy, eds. *Current Aspects of Biochemical Energetics.* Pp. 63–76. New York: Academic Press.

———. 1971. "Looking Back." *Perspectives in Biology and Medicine* 15: 1–6.

Szladits, Lola L., and Harvey Simmonds. 1969. *Pen and Brush: The Author as Artist.* New York: New York Public Library.

Tauber, Peter. 1997. "The Cynic Who Never Soured." *New York Times Magazine,* 2 Nov.: 50.

Tesla, Nikola. 1977. *My Inventions.* Zagreb, Yugoslavia: Skolska Knjiga.

Thackeray, William. 1901. *Pendennis.* London: Macmillan.

Thayer, Gerald. 1909. *Concealing-Coloration in the Animal Kingdom: An Exposition of the Laws of Disguise Through Color and Pattern: Being a Summary of Abbott H. Thayer's Discoveries.* New York: Macmillan.

Thomas, Ann. 1997. *Beauty of Another Order: Photography in Science.* New Haven, Conn.: Yale University Press with the National Gallery of Canada, Ottawa.

Thomsen, D. E. 1987. "A Periodic Table for Molecules." *Science News* 131: 87.

Thomson, G. P. 1961. *The Inspiration of Science.* Oxford: Oxford University Press.

Thomson, J. J. 1937. *Recollections and Reflections.* New York: Macmillan.

Trachtman, Paul. 1998. "The Horse Whisperer." *Smithsonian* 29 (May): 56–66.

Truesdell, Clifford. 1984. *An Idiot's Fugitive Essays on Science.* New York: Springer-Verlag.

Tufte, Edward R. 1983. *The Visual Display of Quantitative Information.* Cheshire, Conn.: Graphics Press.

———. 1990. *Envisioning Information*. Cheshire, Conn.: Graphics Press.

Ulam, Stanislaw. 1976. *Adventures of a Mathematician*. New York: Charles Scribner's Sons.

Van Briessen, Fritz. 1962. *The Way of the Brush: Painting Techniques of China and Japan*. Rutland, Vt.: Charles E. Tuttle.

Van der Wolk, Johannes, Ronald Pickvance, and E. B. F. Pey. 1990. *Vincent Van Gogh: Drawings*. Otterlo, Netherlands: Rijksmuseum Kröller-Müller.

Van't Hoff, J. H. 1878. "Imagination in Science." Inaugural lecture. Trans. G. F. Springer. Reprint, 1967, in *Molecular Biology, Biochemistry, and Biophysics*, vol. 1. New York: Springer-Verlag.

Varga, Balint A. 1996. *Conversations with Iannis Xenakis*. London: Faber and Faber.

Vasari, Giorgio. 1978. *Artists of the Renaissance*. Trans. George Bull. New York: Viking.

Vermeij, Geerat. 1997. *Privileged Hands: A Remarkable Scientific Life*. San Francisco: W. H. Freeman.

Vitz, Paul C., and Arnold B. Glimcher. 1984. *Modern Art and Modern Science: The Parallel Analysis of Vision*. New York: Praeger.

Von Frisch, Karl. 1967. *A Biologist Remembers*. Trans. Lisbeth Gombrich. New York: Oxford University Press.

Vroon, Piet, with Anton van Amerongen and Hans de Vries. 1997. *Smell: The Secret Seducer*. New York: Farrar, Straus and Giroux.

Vygotsky, Lev. 1971. *The Psychology of Art*. Cambridge, Mass.: MIT Press.

Waddington, C. H. 1969. *Behind Appearance: A Study of the Relations between Painting and the Natural Sciences in This Century*. Cambridge, Mass.: MIT Press.

———. 1972. *Biology and the History of the Future*. Edinburgh: Edinburgh University Press.

———. 1977. *Tools for Thought*. London: Jonathan Cape.

Wall, Donald, ed. 1975. *Gene Davis*. New York: Praeger.

Watkins, Floyd C., and Karl F. Knight, eds. 1966. *Writer to Writer: Readings on the Craft of Writing*. Boston: Houghton Mifflin.

Watson, James. 1968. *The Double Helix*. New York: Atheneum.

Weaver, Warren. 1956. "Lewis Carroll: Mathematician." *Scientific American* 194 : 116–28.

Wechsler, Judith, ed. 1978. *On Aesthetics in Science*. Cambridge, Mass.: MIT Press.

Wechter, Dixon. 1985. "How to Write History." In *A Sense of History: The Best Writing from the Pages of American Heritage*. Pp. 38–45. New York: American Heritage.

Weisgall, Deborah. 1997–98. "Bridging Two Cultures." *Guest Informant Boston/Cambridge*.

Weiskrantz, L. ed. 1988. *Thought Without Language*. Oxford: Clarendon Press.

Weiss, Peter. 1998. "Atom-Viewing 101: Make STMs at Home." *Science News* 154: 269.

Wells, H. G. 1913. *Little Wars*. London: Macmillan.

Wertheimer, Max. 1959. *Productive Thinking*. Enlarged ed. New York: Harper and Brothers.

White, R. K. 1931. "The Versatility of Genius." *Journal of Social Psychology* 2: 460–89.

Whitford, Frank, ed. 1993. *The Bauhaus: Masters and Students by Themselves.* Woodstock, N.Y.: Overlook Press.

Wiener, Norbert. 1953. *Ex-Prodigy: My Childhood and Youth.* New York: Simon and Schuster.

———. 1956. *I Am a Mathematician.* London: Gollancz.

Wilson, Frank R. 1998. *The Hand: How Its Use Shapes the Brain, Language, and Human Culture.* New York: Pantheon.

Wilson, J. F. 1948. "Adjustments to Blindness." *British Journal of Psychology, General Section* 39, no. 4: 218–26.

Wilson, Mitchell. 1949. *Live with Lightning.* Boston: Little, Brown.

———. 1972. *Passion to Know.* Garden City, N.Y.: Doubleday.

Winternitz, Emanuel. 1958. "Gnagflow Trazom: An Essay on Mozart's Script, Pastimes, and Nonsense Letters." *Journal of the American Musicological Society* 9: 200–216.

———. 1982. *Leonardo da Vinci as a Musician.* New Haven: Yale University Press.

Witte, Marlys H., A. Kerwin, and C. L. Witte. 1988. "On Ignorance." *Perspectives in Biology and Medicine* 31: 524–25.

Witte, Marlys H., A. Kerwin, C. L. Witte, and A. Scadron. 1989. "A Curriculum on Medical Ignorance." *Medical Education* 23: 24–29.

Wolkomir, Joyce, and Richard Wolkomir. 1990. "Uncovering the Chemistry of Love and War." *National Wildlife,* Aug.–Sept.: 44–51.

Wolpert, Louis, and Allison Richards. 1997. *Passionate Minds.* Oxford: Oxford University Press.

Wolpin, Milton, J. E. Schorr, and Lisa Krouger. 1986. *Imagery.* Vol. 4: *Recent Practice and Theory.* New York: Plenum.

Wood, Bernard, and Mark Collard. 1999. "The Human Genus." *Science* 284: 65–71.

Woodward, C. E. 1989. "Art and Elegance in the Synthesis of Organic Compounds: Robert Burns Woodward." In D. B. Wallace and H. E. Gruber, eds. *Creative People at Work.* New York: Oxford University Press.

Woolf, Virginia. 1927. *To the Lighthouse.* Reprint, 1977: Harcourt Brace.

———. 1976. *Moments of Being: Unpublished Autobiographical Writings.* New York: Harcourt Brace Jovanovich.

Woolsey, Thomas A. 1978. "C. N. Woolsey — Scientist and Artist." *Brain Behavior and Evolution* 15: 307–24.

Wordsworth, William. 1800. *Lyrical Ballads,* vol. 6. 2nd ed. London: Macmillan.

Writers at Work: The Paris Review Interviews, 1963–1984. Series 1–6. New York: Viking Press.

Xenakis, Iannis. 1985. *Arts/Sciences: Alloys.* New York: Pendragon Press.

———. 1992. *Formalized Music: Thought and Mathematics in Composition.* Harmonologia Series, No. 6. New York: Pendragon Press.

Zigrosser, C., ed. 1976. *Ars Medica: A Collection of Medical Prints.* Pp. 14–15. Philadelphia: Philadelphia Museum of Art.

MINDS-ON RESOURCES

THINGS FOR ALL AGES TO PLAY WITH

Art to Zoo: News for Schools from the Smithsonian Institution. Office of Elementary and Secondary Education, Washington, D.C. 20560. An educator's guide to materials, games, and other exercises associated with the Smithsonian's exhibits. Covers every possible tool for thinking in the most multicultural way.

Beeswax for Modeling. Stockmar Wax in many different colors is available from Hearth Song, P.O. Box B, Sebastopol, CA 95473. 1-800-325-2502.

Dymaxion World Puzzle, Buckminster Fuller Institute. 1987. Available from Pacific Puzzle Company, 378 Guemes Island Road, Anacortes, WA 98221. A puzzle-map illustration of one of Fuller's basic structural ideas.

Dimensional Man. (David Pelham, 1999). New York: Simon and Schuster. A life-sized, 3-D cutaway model of the human body with moving parts.

Edmund Scientific Catalog. Edmund Scientific Company, Consumer Science Division, 1101 East Gloucester Pike, Barrington, NJ 08007-1380. 1-800-728-6999. The home source for everything from models, motors, and gears to electronics and cameras you can build yourself. Covers the range of tools for thinking.

Edwards, Betty. 1979. *Drawing on the Right Side of the Brain.* Los Angeles: Tarcher. Imaging, dimensional thinking, empathizing, and other tools, channeled in the direction of visual art.

Ernst, Bruno. 1992. *Optical Illusions.* Cologne, Germany: Taschen. Describes how to make Penrose impossible staircases and tribars. Also covers Escher's geometric impossibilities and cognitive aspects of perception.

Exploratorium Quarterly. The Exploratorium, 3601 Lyon Street, San Francisco, CA 94123-9835, is the premier hands-on museum in the world. Its quarterly magazine and *Exploring* reprints (*Exploring Rhythm; Exploring Patterns; Exploring Transformations*) provide many activities.

Froebel Blocks (Friedrich Froebel, 1831). Museum of Modern Art. Mail Order Department. 11 West 53rd St., New York, NY 10019-5401. 1-800-447-6662. The 3-D building game that stimulated the likes of Frank Lloyd Wright, Buckminster Fuller, and Wassily Kandinsky.

Gardner, Martin. 1978. *Aha! Insight.* San Francisco: W. H. Freeman. Any book by Gardner is great, and this is one of the best. Pattern recognition and forming, 2-D and 3-D puzzles, and much more.

Geodesic Dome Model Kits, Avionics Plastics Corporation, Farmington, NY 11735. Build Buckminster Fuller geodesic domes and much more.

Haab, Sherri, and Torres, Laura. 1994. *The Incredible Clay Book.* Palo Alto, Calif.: Klutz Press. A gem for building 3-D and manipulative skills.

Klutz Catalogue, 455 Portage Avenue, Palo Alto, CA 94306-2213. 1-800-558-8944. The best hands-on books around for building body thinking, imaging, patterning, and related skills.

Kohl, MaryAnn F. 1989. *Mudworks: Creative Clay, Dough, and Modeling Experiences.* Bellingham, Wash.: Bright Ring Publishing. The title says it all.

Long Jump Preceded by a Run: A Chronophotograph by Etiennes-Jules Marey. Optical Toys. P.O. Box 23, Putney, VT 05346. A flipbook recreating Marey's studies of motion.

Making Music. (Morton Subotnik. 1995.) Voyager CD-ROM (www.voyager.com). A visual-pattern approach to composing music on computers.

Mindware. 2720 Patton Road, Roseville, MN 55113. 1-800-999-0398. One of the best general catalogues of 3-D games, puzzles, building toys, tessellations, and much more.

Ninomiya, Yasuaki. 1980. *Whitewings, Excellent Paper Airplanes.* AG Industries, 3832 148th Ave. NE, Redmond, WA 98052. 1-206-885-4599. Some of the best paper airplane designs around. Good for dimensional and modeling skills.

One Milk Drop. (Harold "Doc" Edgerton, 1996.) Optical Toys, P.O. Box 23, Putney, VT 05346. A flipbook recreating Edgerton's stop-motion photography.

Origami. You'll find many good books on origami at your library or bookstore. Refer to the articles by Barry Cipra listed in the Bibliography for the mathematical basis of origami.

Parola, René. 1996. *Optical Art: Theory and Practice.* New York: Dover Publications. Hands-on examples of how to make moiré patterns, optical illusions, Vasarely– and Bridget Riley–style drawings, and more, with examples from pros and teenagers.

Pentagram. 1989. *Puzzlegrams.* New York: Simon and Schuster. Puzzles using many tools for thinking.

Pentagram. 1990. *Pentagames.* New York: Simon and Schuster. Games using many tools for thinking.

Prairie Style Building Blocks and Guggenheim Architecture Blocks. Frank Lloyd Wright Collection. P.O. Box 64412, St. Paul, MN 55164-0412. 1-800-735-2587. Different block styles for building 3-D skills.

Ruef, Kerry. 1992. *The Private Eye: Looking/Thinking by Analogy.* Seattle: Private Eye Project. Exercises for analogical thinking across the curriculum.

Schattschneider, Doris, and Wallace Walker. 1977. *M. C. Escher Kaleidocycles.* Corte Madera, Calif.: Pomegranate Press. Escher prints that you cut and paste to form geometric solids and kaleidocycles, a novel 3-D geometric form invented by the authors, a mathematician and an artist, respectively.

Sculpstone. T&M McCurry, Box 372, Philo, CA 95466. 1-707-895-2291. Sculpting material for learning basic 3-D techniques and manipulative skills.

Set. (Marsha Falco, 1991.) Game of pattern recognition and, equally important, nothingness perception for people of any age. Widely available in retail stores.

Seymour, Dale, and Jill Britton. 1989. *Introduction to Tessellations.* Palo Alto, Calif.: Dale Seymour Publications. Ever wonder how Escher actually made his tessellations? Hands-on exercises show you.

Skwish (1991). Pappa Geppetto's Toys Victoria, Ltd. Box 3567, Blaine, WA 98231-3567. A Kenneth Snelson tensegrity model in the form of a squishable toy for kids of all ages.

Sunprint Kit. Lawrence Hall of Science, University of California, Berkeley, CA 94720. 1-415-642-1016. Available at Natural Wonders stores. Makes photographic prints using sunlight and water as a developer. Great for thinking about how 3-D maps onto 2-D.

Tangrams. The ancient Chinese puzzle is available in many forms in most hobby and toy stores. Teaches pattern recognition and pattern forming.

Tensegritoy. Tensegrity Systems Corporation. Tivoli, NY 12583. 1-800-227-2316. A building system based on Kenneth Snelson's tensegrity principle.

The Magic Mirror: An Antique Optical Toy. 1979. New York: Dover Publications. Anamorphic pictures that use a cylindrical mirror (included).

The Magic Moving Picture Book. 1977. New York: Dover Publications. Recreates the kinds of images Muybridge and Marey made popular.

Tree Blocks. Von Oppen Toy Company, 2022 Cliff Drive, Suite 292, Santa Barbara, CA 93109. 1-818-992-4569; e-mail: elves@treeblocks.com. These, the most unusual blocks we have come across, provide a very different approach to 3-D building than do geometric shapes.

SELECTED VIDEO AND AUDIO SOURCES

"Alexander Calder," *An American Masters Special* (WNET, 1998). WNET, P.O. Box 2284, South Burlington, VT 05407. 1-800-336-1917.

Behind the Scenes. Ten half-hour episodes with Penn and Teller, directed and produced by Ellen Hovde and Muffie Meyer. WNET, P.O. Box 2284, South Burlington, VT, 05407. 1-800-336-1917. This introduction to how creative people work illustrates all of the thinking tools. Particularly good for children and teens.

From the Earth to the Moon. Part 5: Spider (1999). Directed by Tom Hanks. An excellent example of transformational thinking, recreating the development of the lunar lander from sketch through model to functional machine.

"Georgia O'Keeffe," *American Masters* Series. Directed by Perry Adato. WNET, P.O. Box 2284, South Burlington, VT 05407. 1-800-336-1917.

Helen Keller in Her Story. American Foundation for the Blind, 11 Penn Plaza, Suite 300, New York, NY 10001. Original film interviews with Keller, revealing her incredible intelligence.

"Innovation and Imagination." Robert Haas, recorded 26 Feb. 1997 by CSPAN2 for "About Books." Available from the National Association of Independent Schools, 1620 L Street NW, Washington, DC 20036.

Lorenzo's Oil (1992). Directed by George Miller. A factually accurate reconstruction of the Odones' attempt to find a cure for their son's mysterious disease; pattern recognition and modeling play major roles.

"Martin Gardner, Mathemagician." *The Nature of Things* (Canadian Broadcasting Corporation, 1996) (http://www.cbc.ca). Directed by David Suzuki. Mathematical art, magic, game playing, pattern forming, and everything else wonderful that Martin Gardner has always melded.

"People in Motion II." Directed by Vicki Sufian. WNET, P.O. Box 2284, South Burlington, VT 05407. 1-800-336-1917. A look at how Evelyn Glennie makes music and how other handicapped people make art or do other unlikely things. Illustrates many tools in unexpected ways.

The Race for the Double Helix (1993). Directed by Mick Jackson. A factually accurate reconstruction of the Watson-Crick discovery of the DNA double helix, starring Jeff Goldblum and emphasizing the roles of hunches, emotions, modeling, and transformational thinking.

"Race for the Superconductor," *Nova*, 1988 (WNET, Boston). Proprioceptive and transformational thinking that mixes dance with physics.

Sequencia (Susan Alexjander). CD, Logos Series, Science and the Arts, P.O. Box 8162, Berkeley, CA 94707. DNA-based music.

"Special Effects: Titanic and Beyond." *Nova*, 1999. WNET, P.O. Box 2284, South Burlington, VT 05407. 1-800-336-1917. Dimensional thinking, modeling, and an excellent segment on the electronic motion-capture technology that Marey's abstract photography has engendered.

Stomp Out Loud (Stomp, 1998). Pattern forming and proprioceptive thinking through urban primitive dance-music. Try it with a group of your friends!

Thirty-Two Short Films About Glenn Gould (1995). Directed by François Girard. Columbia Tristar Home Video. Everything from pattern forming to transformational thinking. Stunning!

Torn Notebook (University of Nebraska Television). Directed by Gene Bunge. Great Plains National, P.O. Box 80669, Lincoln, NE 68501-0669. 1-800-228-4630. A look at how Claes Oldenburg and Coosje von Bruggen created their sculpture

"Torn Notebook," from idea through models to installation. Great example of transformational thinking.

Yo-Yo Ma Plays Bach's Cello Suites (Rhombus Media with WNET, 1997). WNET, P.O. Box 2284, South Burlington, VT 05407. 1-800-336-1917. Ma collaborates with a wide range of artists, architects, dancers, and filmmakers to produce a truly synesthetic experience.

Note: The Public Broadcasting System, the Canadian Broadcasting System, and the British Broadcasting Corporation put out catalogues of their programs each year. Many valuable documentaries concerning individual dancers, artists, sculptors, and scientists not listed here are available.

INTERNET SOURCES

Because of the incredibly rapid proliferation of Internet sites, any list is out of date before it is printed. The Internet references below are limited to those cited in the text. Many museums are now putting their resources on the Web, and almost every person mentioned in the book is discussed on at least one site. A careful choice of search terms will bring up other useful sites bearing on most of our tools for thinking as well.

Art-Science Collaborations, an organization that does what it says at: http://www. asci.org.

Bee vision (empathizing) can be found at: *http://cvs.anu.edu.au/andy/beye/ beyehome.html* and at *http://www.geocities.com/Athens/Oracle/5410/bee.html.*

"Dance Review: Pilobolus Dance Theatre, Old Tale Just Isn't the Same," by Linda Belans: *www.nando.net.*

DNA music can be found at Phil Ortiz's Web site, Sounds of Science: *http://www. skidmore.edu/foureyes/phil/sos/sos.htm.*

Evelyn Glennie's home page, with interesting documents, is *http://www.evelyn.co.uk/ bodypg.htm.*

The Exploratorium in San Francisco is one of the world's best hands-on museums specializing in science but exploring the arts as well. See their exhibits and other educational materials at: *http://www.exploratorium.edu/ti.*

The golden section as a pattern found in art, architecture, music, poetry, biology, and so on: *http://www.mcs.surrey.ac.uk/Personal/R.Knott/Fibonacci/ fib'nArt.html.*

"Innovative Visual-Spatial Powers in Dyslexics: A New Perspective?" by S. E. Parkinson and J. H. Edwards, 1997. Internet Service Dyslexia Paper Archive: *http:// www.rmplc.co.uk/orgs/nellalex/adtvisuospatial.html.*

International Synaesthesia Association Index Web site: *http://nevis.sitr.ac.uk.*

Klutz products: *http://www.klutz.com.*

LEONARDO is the world's leading arts-sciences and arts-technology journal. Most of the ideas we discuss are explored here: *http://mitpress.mit.edu/e-journals/Leonardo/home.html.*

Montessori Foundation Bookstore: *http://www.montessori.org/bookstor.htm.*

Painting with atoms — the ultimate in dimensional art: *http://www.almaden.ibm.com/vis/stm/gallery.html.*

Paleomap Project. Geological pattern forming at: *http://www.scotese.com.*

Roger Penrose Web site: *http://rysy.msm.cam.ac.uk/~msms/penrose.html.*

Tensegrity Web site with information about Kenneth Snelson: *http://www.teleport.comb/~pdx4d/docs.*

Visible Human Project, National Library of Medicine: *http://www.npac.syr.edu/projects/vishuman/VisibleHuman.html.*

BOOKS FOR THE VERY YOUNG

Anno, Mitsumasa. 1969. *Topsy-Turvies.* New York: Weatherhill. Dimensional thinking.

———. 1971. *Upside-Downers: More Pictures to Stretch the Imagination.* New York: Weatherhill. More dimensional thinking.

Baum, Arline, and Joseph Baum. 1989. *Opt: An Illusionary Tale.* New York: Puffin Books (Viking). Excellent introduction to visual pattern recognition, dimensional thinking, and play.

Clement, Claude, and Frederic Clement. 1986. *The Painter and the Wild Swans.* New York: Dial. A painter empathizes with the swans he paints, becoming one.

Hepworth, Cathi. 1992. *Antics!* New York: G. P. Putnam's Sons. Pattern recognition based on finding the word "ant" in other words.

Johnson, Crockett. 1960. *Harold and the Purple Crayon; Harold's ABC;* and other titles. New York: Harper and Row. Pattern recognition, pattern forming, and analogizing.

Jonas, Ann. 1983. *Round Trip.* New York: Scholastic. Every picture in this unusual book can be seen in two ways. Pattern play.

Juster, Norton. 1963. *The Dot and the Line: A Romance in Lower Mathematics.* New York: Random House. Introduction to pattern forming in art and math.

Kunhardt, Dorothy. 1970. *Pat the Bunny.* New York: Golden Books. Kinesthetic thinking for the very, very young.

Moore, Frank J. 1978. *The Magic Moving Alphabet Book.* New York: Dover Publications. As the cover says, "26 Hidden Pictures Come to Life and Move with the Magical Moiré." A truly unique book that uses moiré patterns to hide and reveal images.

Shaw, Charles G. 1947. *It Looked Like Spilt Milk*. New York: Harper and Row. Classic in pattern recognition of forms in clouds.

READING FOR THE NOVICE LEARNER IN ALL OF US

Agee, Jon. 1999. *So Many Dynamos! And Other Palindromes*. Verbal pattern play.

Anno, Mitsumasa. 1985. *Anno's Sundial*. New York: Philomel Books. A pop-up book that covers a wide range of dimensional thinking issues, linking art and science in the process. All of Anno's books combine thinking skills that transcend disciplines.

Augarde, Tony. 1984. *The Oxford Guide to Word Games*. New York: Oxford University Press. Pattern forming, pattern recognition, playing.

Bang, Molly. 1991. *Picture This*. Boston: Bullfinch Press. An introduction to principles of visual design and visual thinking.

Berry, S. L. 1994. *E. E. Cummings*. Mankato, Minn.: Creative Education. Intriguing synthesis of biography, poetry, and resonant art by Stasys Eldrigevicius.

Byrom, Thomas. 1977. *Nonsense and Wonder: The Poems and Cartoons of Edward Lear*. New York: E. P. Dutton. Verbal and visual playing; synesthesia.

Cassidy, John, and the Exploratorium. 1996. *Explorabook: A Kids' Science Museum in a Book*. Palo Alto: Klutz Books. This book does it all.

Cassidy, John, Paul Doherty, and Pat Murphy. 1997. *Zap Science*. Palo Alto: Klutz Books. Observe, play, and imagine to your heart's content!

Cole, Allison. 1993. *Color: An Eyewitness Book*. London: Dorling Kindersley. Observing, imaging, and playing.

Elffers, Joost. 1997. *Play with Your Food*. New York: Stewart, Tabori and Chang. 3-D play.

Ennion, E. A. R., and N. Tinbergen. 1967. *Tracks*. Oxford: Clarendon Press. A masterpiece of transforming between 2-D and 3- and 4-D thinking, beginning with animal tracks.

Fleischman, Paul. 1988. *Joyful Noise: Poems for Two Voices*. New York: Harper and Row. Pattern forming resulting from syncopated readings of multiple voices.

Frayling, Christopher, Helen Frayling, and Ron Van der Meer. 1992. *The Art Pack*. New York: Alfred A. Knopf. A unique 3-D look at the processes by which artists invent and perceive.

Greenberg, Jan, and Sandra Jordan. 1991. *The Painter's Eye: Learning to Look at Contemporary American Art*. New York: Delacorte Press. Pattern forming, proprioceptive thinking, transformational thinking, and synosia.

———. 1993. *The Sculptor's Eye: Learning to Look at Contemporary American Art*. New York: Delacorte Press. Proprioceptive, 3-D, transformational thinking, and synosia.

Hall, Donald, ed. 1985. *The Oxford Book of Children's Verse in America*. New York: Oxford University Press. Full of playful experiments in verbal patterning, analogizing, imaging, and other skills.

Jackson, Brenda. 1972. *Model Making in Schools*. New York: Van Nostrand Reinhold. An excellent guide to multidisciplinary projects, from very simple to quite complex, from history and cultural models to engineering and science.

Joyce, Mary. 1973. *First Steps in Teaching Creative Dance to Children*. Integrates proprioceptive thinking with imaging, analogizing, patterning, abstracting, and more.

Judson, Horace Freeland. 1980. *The Search for Solutions*. New York: Holt, Rinehart and Winston. A well-illustrated book about scientific thinking that stresses pattern forming, modeling, and so on.

Juster, Norton. 1961. *The Phantom Tollbooth*. New York: Random House. An adventure about perception, wordplay, mathematics, patterns, synesthesia, and much more.

Koch, Kenneth, and Students of Public School 61 in New York City. 1970. *Wishes, Lies and Dreams: Teaching Children to Write Poetry*. New York: Harper and Row. Combines sensual thinking, metaphors and analogies, pattern recognition and pattern forming, and more.

Koch, Kenneth, and Kate Farrell, eds. 1985. *Talking to the Sun: An Illustrated Anthology of Poems for Young People*. New York: Metropolitan Museum of Art/Henry Holt. A wonderfully synthetic and synergistic interaction between the patterns of poetry and of art.

Lankford, Mary D. 1992. *Hopscotch Around the World*. New York: Morrow Junior Books. Combines pattern recognition and proprioceptive thinking.

Lear, Edward. 1975. *A Book of Bosh*. Chosen and edited by Brian Alderson. London: Puffin Books. Verbal playing.

Loyd, Sam. 1912. *Sam Loyd's Puzzles*. Philadelphia: David McKay. Reprint, 1975: New York: Dover Books. The best transformational thinking puzzles around.

Martin, Bill, Jr., and John Archambault. 1987. *Knots on a Counting Rope*. New York: Bantam Doubleday Dell. A blind boy is introduced to the concept of "seeing" with his other senses.

Marsalis, Wynton. 1995. *Marsalis on Music*. New York: W. W. Norton. An excellent introduction to musical patterns and the emotions they express.

Miller, Jonathan. 1978. *The Body in Question*. London: Jonathan Cape. An unexpectedly multitooled look at how the body functions, with sections on modeling, anamorphosis, and other tools.

Miller, Jonathan, and David Pelham. 1983. *The Human Body*. New York: Viking. One of the first and best pop-up books, combining science with art via dimensional thinking.

Morrison, Philip, Phylis Morrison, and the Office of Charles and Ray Eames. 1982. *Powers of Ten: A Book about the Relative Size of Things in the Universe and the Effect of Adding Another Zero*. San Francisco: Scientific American Library/ W. H. Freeman. Dimensional thinking at its best.

Munthe, Nellie. 1983. *Meet Matisse.* Boston: Little, Brown. A great introduction to abstracting.

Nash, Ogden. Anything by this prolific nonsense poet will amuse and teach pattern
play.

Pawson, Des. 1999. *The Handbook of Knots.* London: Dorling Kindersley. Kinesthetic
imaging that is useful.

Preiss, Bryon, and William R. Altschuler, eds. 1989. *The Microverse.* New York:
Bantam. A look at the infinitely small from scientific, literary, and artistic perspectives that explore dimensional thinking, empathizing, imaging, and other
tools.

Rudolph, James Smith. 1999. *Make Your Own Working Paper Clock.* Transformational
thinking, visual thinking, dimensional thinking.

Thurber, James. 1957. *The Wonderful O.* Reprint, 1985: New York: Dell. What would
happen if all the Os were eliminated from all the words in the world? A masterpiece of imaginative play.

White, T. H. 1958. *The Once and Future King.* New York: G. P. Putnam's Sons. The
young King Arthur's adventures with Merlin include many empathic explorations of animal behavior.

Winslow, Marjorie. 1999. *Mud Pies and Other Recipes.* Hands-on make-believe for
creating one's own universe with dolls.

ILLUSTRATION CREDITS

All images not otherwise credited are © Robert Root-Bernstein. Fig. 3-1: Photo by Evan Lewis, from G. H. Thayer, *Concealing-Coloration in the Animal Kingdom*, 1909. Fig. 3-2: © 1999 The Georgia O'Keeffe Foundation/Artists Rights Society (ARS), New York. Photograph © Board of Trustees, National Gallery of Art, Washington, D.C. Bequest of Georgia O'Keeffe. Fig. 3-3: Amsterdam, van Gogh Museum (Vincent van Gogh Foundation). Fig. 3-4: Portfolio. 4 on Plexiglas. Laminated vacuum-formed vinyl, screenprinted vinyl, felt, and Plexiglas; rayon cord. 39″ × 28″ × 3½″ (99.1 × 71.1 × 8.9 cm). Courtesy of Claes Oldenburg and Coosje van Bruggen. Fig. 4-2: Used by permission of A. P. Watt Ltd. on behalf of The Royal Library Fund. Courtesy of the Berg Collection of English and American Literature, The New York Public Library, Astor, Lenox and Tilden Foundations. Fig. 4-3: © Tom Thaves, 1999. Fig. 5-1: © 1999 Estate of Pablo Picasso/Artists Rights Society (ARS), New York. Fig. 5-2: CERN Photo, reprinted by permission of CERN Press and Publications. Fig. 5-3: From J. Maynard Smith, *Mathematical Ideas in Biology*, Cambridge University Press, 1968. Fig. 5-4: © 1999 Estate of Pablo Picasso/Artists Rights Society (ARS), New York. Fig. 5-6: *Left*, from Asa Gray, *How Plants Grow*, 1858. *Right*, from F. Church, "On the Interpretation of Phenomena of Phyllotaxis," *Botanical Memoirs* No. 6, 1920; reprinted by permission of Oxford University Press. Fig. 5-7: From F. M. Jaeger, *Lectures on the Principle of Symmetry and Its Applications in All Natural Sciences*, Elsevier, 1920. Fig. 5-8: From Eadweard Muybridge, *The Human Figure in Motion*, Dover, 1955; reprinted by permission of Dover Publications. Fig. 5-9: © J. Cl. Couval; courtesy of the Musée E. J. Marey, Beaune. Fig. 5-10: From Richer, *Physiologie artistique l'homme en mouvement*, 1895; reprinted by permission of the British Library, shelfmark 7857dd25. Fig. 5-11: © Artists Rights Society (ARS), New York/ADAGP, Paris/The Estate of Marcel Duchamp. Reproduced by permission of the Philadelphia Museum of Art: The Louise and Walter Arensberg Collection. Fig. 5-12: From Santiago Ramón y Cajal, *Recollections of My Life*, 1937; reprinted by permission of MIT Press. Fig. 6-1: Museo

Civico, Cremona, Italy; Scala/Art Resource, New York. Fig. 6-5: From Leonard Bernstein, *The Unanswered Question,* Harvard University Press, 1976. Fig. 6-6: From S. E. Parkinson and J. H. Edwards, "Innovative Visual-Spatial Powers in Dyslexics: A New Perspective?" Reprinted by permission of the Arts Dyslexia Trust, Internet Service Dyslexia Paper Archive, U.K.. Fig. 6-7: From Alfred Wegener, *The Origin of Continents and Oceans,* 1915; reprinted by permission of Dover Publications. Fig. 6-8: Department of Natural Sciences, Michigan State University. Fig. 6-9: Reprinted by permission of the Children's Museum of Boston. Fig. 6-10: *Left, Symmetry Drawing 45,* and *center, Circle Limit IV* by M. C. Escher © 1998 Cordon Art, B. V., Baarn, Holland. All rights reserved. *Right,* Kaleidocycle reproduced courtesy of Doris Schattschneider; photo by Robert Root-Bernstein. Fig. 6-13: Department of Natural Sciences, Michigan State University. Fig. 7-1: © Reuters/David Gray/Archive Photos. Figs. 7-2, 7-3, 7-4: From Simha Arom et al., *African Polyphony and Polyrhythm,* 1991; reprinted by permission of Cambridge University Press. Figs. 7-5, 7-6: From Joseph Schillinger, *The Mathematical Basis of the Arts,* 1948; reprinted by permission of the Philosophical Library, New York. Fig. 7-10: From Edward G. Mazur, *Graphic Representations of the Periodic System,* 1974. Fig. 8-4: *Top,* © Chris Wilkinson Architects. *Bottom,* Designed by Chris Wilkinson Architects and Gifford & Partners for Gateshead Council. Fig. 8-5: *Top,* photo by Michio Noguchi; courtesy of the Isamu Noguchi Foundation, Inc. *Bottom,* courtesy of the Isamu Noguchi Foundation, Inc. Fig. 8-6: Photo courtesy of Nathaniel A. Friedman; model reproduced by permission of the Henry Moore Foundation. Fig. 8-7: Photos by Paul Waldo Schwartz from Schwartz, *The Hand and Eye of the Sculptor,* 1969. Works by Chillida © 1999 Artists Rights Society (ARS), New York/VEGAP, Madrid. Fig. 8-8: *Top,* reproduced by permission of Kenneth Snelson. *Bottom,* reprinted by permission of Steven R. Heidemann, from "A New Twist on Integrins and the Cytoskeleton," *Science* 260: 1080–81. © American Association for the Advancement of Science. Fig. 8-10: *Left,* courtesy of The Royal Collection © Her Majesty Queen Elizabeth II; *right,* from the collection of the authors, reproduced courtesy of the artist. Fig. 8-11: Photo by Eeva-Inkeri. Courtesy Ronald Feldman Fine Arts, New York. Fig. 9-1: From Wolfgang Kohler, *The Mentality of Apes,* Routledge & Kegan Paul, 1925. Fig. 9-2: © Jerry van Amerongen. Fig. 9-3: © 1991 Hans Namuth Estate, Collection Center for Creative Photography, The University of Arizona. Fig. 9-4: Courtesy of Jacques Mandelbrojt. Fig. 9-5: Bauhaus Archive Inv. 8377; © 1999 Artists Rights Society (ARS), New York/ BEELDRECHT, Amsterdam. Fig. 9-6: Reproduced by permission of The Henry Moore Foundation. Fig. 9-7: © Musée Rodin; ph 1020, papier albuminé (albumin print). Figs. 9-8, 9-9, 9-10: © 1999 The Oskar Schlemmer Theatre Estate, 1-28824 Oggebbio, Italy; Photo Archive C Raman Schlemmer, 1-28824 Oggebbio, Italy. Fig. 10-1: Neg. no. 329853 (photo, Logan). Courtesy of the Department of Library Services, American Museum of Natural History. Fig. 10-2: Australian News and Information Bureau; courtesy of the Department of Foreign Affairs and Trade, Australia. Fig. 10-3: *Left,* courtesy of Vernon and Frankie Reynolds, Oxford, England. *Right,* © Robert Campbell/NGS Image Collection, NGM 1971/10 578. National Geographic Society.

Fig. 10-4: Courtesy of Desmond Morris. Collection of Dr. John Godfrey, London. Fig. 10-5: Photograph © Michio Noguchi. Courtesy of the Isamu Noguchi Foundation, Inc. Fig. 10-6: Photo from William Seabrook, *Doctor Wood, Modern Wizard of the Laboratory,* © 1941 by Harcourt Brace & Company and renewed 1969 by Constance Seabrook, reproduced by permission of the publisher. Fig. 11-2: From Variou, *Art and Artist,* University of California Press, Berkeley, 1956, reprinted by permission of the publisher. Fig. 11-3: © 1999 Artists Rights Society (ARS), New York/DACS, London. Fig. 11-4: MRIs of the author by Ronald Meyer. Fig. 11-5: From Walter Strauss, ed., *The Complete Engravings, Etchings and Drypoint of Albrecht Dürer,* Dover Publications, 1972. Fig. 11-6: Reproduced by permission of the Swedish National Art Museums. Fig. 11-7: From D'Arcy Thompson, *On Growth and Form,* 1942; reprinted by permission of Cambridge University Press. Fig. 11-8: From Colin Blakemore, *Mechanics of the Mind,* 1977; reprinted by permission of Cambridge University Press. Fig. 11-9: *Left,* photo by Markus Hawlik, © Bauhaus Archive Berlin. *Right,* © 1998 Cordon Art B.V., Baarn, Holland. All rights reserved. Fig. 11-10: Photo by Reinhard Friedrich, © Bauhaus Archive Berlin. Courtesy Arieh Sharon Archive, Tel Aviv. Fig. 11-11: *Left,* photo by Lucia Moholy 1/40 © Bauhaus Archive Berlin. *Right,* photo courtesy of Tree Blocks®. Fig. 12-1: From H. G. Wells, *Little Wars,* 1913, reprinted by permission of A. P. Watt, Ltd., and The Literary Executors of The Estate of H G Wells. Fig. 12-2: Photo by Gary McKinnis © 1983. Courtesy of the Fairmount Park Art Association. Fig. 12-3: Courtesy of the Peabody Essex Museum, Salem, Mass. Fig. 12-4: From Leonard Colebrook, *Almroth Wright,* William Heinnemann Ltd., 1954. Fig. 12-6: From C. S. Smith, *A Search for Structure,* MIT Press, 1981, reprinted by permission of MIT Press. Fig. 12-7: Photo by Gerd Fischer. From Gerd Fischer, *Mathematical Models,* Vieweg & Sohn, 1986; reprinted by permission of the author. Fig. 13-1: From André Maurois, *Alexander Fleming,* 1959; reprinted by permission of Robert Fleming. Fig. 13-2: Photo by André Kertesz. © Ministry of Culture — France (Association Française pour la Diffusion du Patrimonie Photographique). Fig. 13-3: Courtesy of Kenneth Snelson, © Kenneth Snelson. Fig. 13-4: Penrose images courtesy of Roger Penrose © Roger Penrose; M. C. Escher's *Relativity* © 1998 Cordon Art B.V., Baarn, Holland. All rights reserved. Fig. 13-5: From *Scientific American,* January 1977; reprinted by permission of Slim Films. Fig. 14-1: Courtesy of the Getty Conservation Institute, Los Angeles, California, USA, © 1995 the J. Paul Getty Trust. Fig. 14-2: Neg. no. 2A21119 (photo by ANMH Photo Studio). Courtesy Department of Library Services, American Museum of Natural History. Figs. 14-3, 14-4, 14-5, 14-6: © Harold & Esther Edgerton Foundation, 1999, courtesy of Palm Press, Inc. Fig. 14-7: From Francis Galton, *Inquiries into Human Faculty and Its Development,* 1883. Fig. 14-8: From Sherman K. Stein, *Mathematics: The Man-Made Universe* © 1963 by W. H. Freeman. Used with permission. Fig. 14-10: From the author's collection; reprinted by permission of Nathaniel A. Friedman. Fig. 14-11: Courtesy Charles Sweeley, Michigan State University, Department of Biochemistry; reprinted from the *Journal of Chromatography* 399 (1987): 179, by permission of Elsevier Science. Fig. 14-12: *Bildnerische Formenlehre* — Faltblatt, BF, S. 52 © 1999 Artists Rights Society (ARS), New York/VG

INDEX

Pattern recognition (*cont.*)
  by Escher, 94–95
  in games, 107–9
  in mathematics, 102–3, 109–10
  meta-patterns, 113
  nothingness in, 106–7
  in punning riddles, 92, 93
  in puzzles, 107, 111–12, 113
  by scientists, 103–7, 283–86
  in transforming, 271, 277–80, 283–86
Pauli, Wolfgang, 4, 18
Pauling, Linus, 238, 243–44, 288
Pavarotti, Luciano, 59–60
Pellegrino, Edmund, 46
Penfield, Wilder, 211
Penicillin, 237, 246, 248
Penrose, L. S., 241, 257, 258, 259
Penrose, Roger, 224, 241, 257–58, 259,
  260
Penseur, Le (Rodin sculpture), 168–69
Pepper, Beverly, 44
Perceptual fusion. *See* Synesthesia
Percy, Walker, 185
Periodic table of chemical elements,
  131, 135, 199
Periodic tables of compounds, 207
Perle, George, 278–79
Perspective, 207–8
Pestalozzi, Johann Heinrich, 16, 63,
  325
Petersen, James R., 218
Petroski, Henry, 52, 242, 266
Phantom limbs or senses, 176
Phantom Tollbooth, The (Juster), 14, 22–
  23, 29
Physicians. *See* Medicine
Piaget, Jean, 248
Piano, and microtones, 261, 268
Picasso, Pablo
  and abstracting, 71–72, 73, 74, 77, 78,
    79, 80, 81, 84, 90, 91
  on art, 24
  and body thinking, 179

  on interconnections, 7
  on modeling, 230
  and observing, 33, 48
  on process of painting, 2
  and transforming, 273
Pictonyms, 292
Piene, Otto, 312
Pilobolus (dance company), 266–67
Pinter, Harold, 299
Pioneering education, 319, 322
Piranhas and Lobsters (tessellation), 96
Pirsig, Robert M., 186
Plague, The (Camus), 185
Planck, Max, 10, 136, 137–38
Platt, John Rader, 319
Play with Your Food (Elffers), 266
Playacting. *See* Empathizing
Playing, 26, 248–49, 267–68
  with anagrams, 262–64
  by Calder, 252–53
  by Carroll, 256–57, 258
  development of, 266–67
  and discovery of Laetoli footprints,
    269
  by Escher, 257–58
  by Feynman, 248, 249–50, 265–66
  by Fleming, 246–48, 249
  by inventors, 250–52, 254, 274
  by Lear, 254–56
  and music, 260–62, 263–64
  and pattern recognition, 114
  practical applications of, 258, 260
  resources for, 365–67
  with symmetry, 264–65
  in synthesizing, 311
  in transforming, 269, 272, 274, 276
  usefulness of, 265–66
  See also Games; Puzzles; Toys
Plication, 213. *See also* Origami
Poetry
  and abstracting (cummings), 72
  and analogy, 145–49
  concrete, 291–92

© Mark Bell

Robert and Michèle Root-Bernstein have been studying and consulting on creativity for more than a decade. Robert, a professor in the Physiology Department of Michigan State University and the winner of a MacArthur Fellowship, has also written *Discovering: Inventing and Solving Problems at the Frontiers of Scientific Knowledge*. Michèle, an award-winning historian, has written about and taught history and creative writing. Together the Root-Bernsteins are the authors of *Honey, Mud, Maggots, and Other Medical Marvels*. They live in East Lansing, Michigan.